APPROACHING CHINA
ELEMENTARY CHINESE

走近中國 初級漢語教程

劉樂寧 朱永平 主編
劉樂寧 閻 玲 編著

圖書在版編目（CIP）數據

走近中國：初級漢語教程 / 劉樂寧，朱永平主編. —北京：北京大學出版社，2015.4
ISBN 978-7-301-25021-1

Ⅰ. ①走… Ⅱ. ①劉… ②朱… Ⅲ. ①漢語-對外漢語教學-教材 Ⅳ. ①H195.4

中國版本圖書館CIP數據核字（2014）第245509號

書　　　　名	走近中國——初級漢語教程
著作責任者	劉樂寧　朱永平　主編　劉樂寧　閻　玲　編著
責任編輯	孫　嫻
標準書號	ISBN 978-7-301-25021-1
出版發行	北京大學出版社
地　　　　址	北京市海淀區成府路205號　100871
網　　　　址	http://www.pup.cn　　新浪官方微博：@北京大學出版社
電子信箱	zpup@pup.cn
電　　　　話	郵購部 62752015　發行部 62750672　編輯部 62753027
印　刷　者	北京大學印刷廠
經　銷　者	新華書店
	889毫米×1194毫米　16開本　23.5印張　472千字
	2015年4月第1版　2016年9月第2次印刷
定　　　　價	480.00元（含1張MP3盤）

未經許可，不得以任何方式複製或抄襲本書之部分或全部內容。
版權所有，侵權必究
舉報電話：010-62752024　電子信箱：fd@pup.pku.edu.cn
圖書如有印裝質量問題，請與出版部聯繫，電話：010-62756370

編寫說明

適用對象

　　本書是哥倫比亞大學漢語系列教材的初級部分，是爲北美地區零起點漢語學習者而編，既適用於北美本土的大學漢語課程，又可供北美來華暑期班使用。學習者學完本書，可以掌握漢語拼音、基本的漢語語法結構、漢字書寫及認讀知識，並對日常生活中的交際漢語有一定的瞭解，爲以後的漢語學習打下基礎。

編寫原則

　　本書是以美國大學生的日常生活爲主綫編寫的，通過與學生日常生活密切相關的話題，讓學生掌握學了即可使用的漢語語法結構及詞彙，爲其提供相互交流溝通的必要場景，目的是爲學習者進一步提高漢語水平打下堅實的基礎。

本書特色

　　與其他初級階段的漢語教材相比，本書具有以下特點：

❶ 富於趣味性

　　常言道：興趣是最好的老師。一套教材若不能激發學習者的學習興趣則不能算是成功。本著加強趣味性的原則，我們在選材和編排順序方面都下了很大的工夫。我們安排了兩個學生——英國人"李家奇"和美國人"李家興"——爲主角，選擇了與美國大學生日常生活內容關係密切的話題，如《新學生》《上課第一天》《我的家》《請人吃飯》《語伴》《要考試了》《愛好》《失戀了》及《約會》等，同時也選入了美國的《感恩節》和中國的《春節》。在編排順序上，我們也充分考慮實際情況，如讓學生在過感恩節前後學習《感恩節》這一課，在中國新年前後學習《春節》。這樣一來，現學現用，課本上的句型、詞彙一旦與實際生活相結合，就不再顯得單調乏味了。此外，我們還根據課文內容拍出了一些視頻，使得課文內容有了具體情景再現，更有利於學生學習（http://www.columbia.edu/cu/ealac/chinese/audiolab_level1/videoclip.htm）。

❷ 注重實用性

　　漢語課是語言課，身爲漢語教師的我們不得不面臨很多具體情況，比如學時有限，美國學生學習漢語沒有漢語環境，而且在學習漢語的同時還要學習其他功課，等等。因此，教材是否實用，也是教學能否成功的關鍵因素之一。我們把每課所有的句型都清楚地羅列出來，並附上語法要點總結和句型歸納，學生在看書時一目了然。我們還爲每課製作了PPT，放在網上，一方面可以讓學生上課時把注意力集中在操練上而非記筆記上，另一方面也爲教師節省了大量時間，讓他們可以去思考如何提高教學品質，而不是如何爲教材補充材料。另外，我們還爲學生編寫了Flash Cards、漢字練習冊等。

❸ 其他特點

（1）在詞彙的處理上，我們也有別於其他教材。每課詞彙分爲：必須掌握的（讀寫）、只需認讀的（會認不必會寫）及補充詞彙。補充詞彙是爲中小學學過中文或學有餘力的學生而準備的。學生可以根據自己的能力因需而取，教師則根據學生的能力因材施教。很多補充詞彙在後面的課文中也會出現，那時或列爲必須掌握的，或編入只需認讀的。每課詞彙數量的安排是根據該課語法結構的難易程度而定的。語法難的課文生詞就少一些，較爲容易的課文生詞就相對多一點。

（2）在語法的處理上，我們有意識地將較難掌握的結構提前、分步介紹。比如，在第四課，我們就讓學生接觸了"Verb 了"的最基本用法，在後邊的課文中又進一步介紹此句式，使教師在課堂中有更多的時間幫助學生練習、掌握這些較爲複雜的句子，從而達到熟練運用的目的。同時，我們應學生的要求，給每個語法結構都舉出了不少例句，加上英文翻譯，亦適合學生在課下自學。此外，我們對每課的語法點及句型結構都進行了提煉性總結，使得學習重點一目了然。

（3）本書還有一個特點，就是我們直接從拼音跳到漢字課文上，課文內容不標注拼音。這樣做大大加速了學生對漢字音形義的整體掌握。如何才能做到讓學生看到漢字就可以直接認讀呢？我們的做法是在前一課課後練習中（第五個練習），將下一課的課文內容以語音練習的形式展現出來，那麼學生在練習語音的同時，就熟悉了將要學習的課文內容，可謂一石二鳥。

致謝

在本教材編寫的過程中，哥倫比亞大學使用該教材的學生，尤其是2006年的北京暑期班學生，以及使用過該教材的老師提供了寶貴的修改意見。北京大學出版社的孫嫻編輯做了大量認真細緻的工作，提出了很好的修改意見，使得本書以全新的面貌展現在讀者面前。在此一併致以衷心的感謝！

編者
2015.3

目　錄　CONTENTS

縮略語表	LIST OF ABBREVIATIONS	ii
漢語語音	CHINESE PRONUNCIATION	1
漢字書寫	CHINESE WRITING SYSTEM	23
LESSON 1	新學生	39
LESSON 2	上課第一天	53
LESSON 3	我的家	69
LESSON 4	請人吃飯	91
LESSON 5	中餐館兒	111
LESSON 6	語伴	130
LESSON 7	感恩節	150
LESSON 8	要考試了	177
LESSON 9	老朋友見面	198
LESSON 10	春節	218
LESSON 11	愛好	237
LESSON 12	失戀了	259
LESSON 13	約會	278
LESSON 14	中國城	299
LESSON 15	快樂的一年級	319
詞語索引	VOCABULARY LIST	335

縮略語表
LIST OF ABBREVIATIONS

Abbreviation	Terms	中文
Adj.	Adjective	形容詞（含stative verb）
Adv.	Adverb	副詞
Aux. V.	Auxiliary Verb	能願動詞
Conj.	Conjunction	連詞
IE	Idiom Expression	習慣用語
Int.	Interjection	嘆詞
MW	Measure Word	量詞
N.	Noun	名詞
NP	Noun Phrase	名詞短語
Num.	Numeral	數詞
Onom.	Onomatopoetic Word	擬聲詞
Pt.	Particle	助詞
PN	Proper Noun	專有名詞
Pref.	Prefix	詞頭
Prep.	Preposition	介詞
Pron.	Pronoun	代詞
PW	Place Word	處所詞
Q.	Quantifier	數量詞
Suf.	Suffix	詞尾
TW	Time Word	時間詞
V.	Verb	動詞
V.-C.	Verb plus Complement	動補複合詞
V.-O.	Verb plus Object	動賓複合詞
VP	Verb Phrase	動詞短語

漢語語音 CHINESE PRONUNCIATION

Chinese is not a phonetic language. As a result, its pronunciation is not entirely based on the written Chinese words (characters). In order to help non-native speakers to learn correct Chinese pronounciation, a system called "Pinyin" was developed by a government committee in the People's Republic of China (PRC) in 1958 to transcribe the sounds of Standard Chinese. Pinyin uses the letters of the familiar English alphabet to help students determine the pronunciation of the unfamiliar Chinese words. Most Mandarin sounds are easy for English speakers to pronounce although some require more practice than others.

Pinyin is also a useful tool for learning new vocabulary and for looking things up in a dictionary as well as for typing Chinese. Other than this, however, it has no practical usage since Chinese people do not read or write in pinyin. Therefore, it is critical that you learn to read and write in characters as soon as possible.

I. The four tones

Chinese is a tonal language. Tones are the variation of pitch levels in the pronunciation of a syllable. A syllable may be composed of three components: (a) initials; (b) finals; (c) tones. Except for nasal sound like "n" and "m", all Chinese syllables end with vowels. We call them "final sounds". The consonants at the beginning of a syllable are called "initial sounds".

There are altogether 21 initials (shown in Table 2). Initials only refer to the consonants that appear in the initial position of a syllable. Although it is possible to have a syllable without an initial, there must always be a final. A final may have one or more vowel sounds and sometimes a consonant ending like -n and -ng . In fact, other than -n and -ng, the consonants can't appear in a final at all. Altogether, there are 39 finals (listed in Table 3).

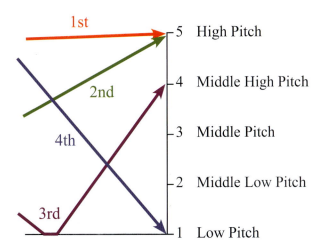

Figure 1: Mandarin Chinese Tone Contours (Yuen Ren Chao)

There are 4 tones in Mandarin Chinese (illustrated in Table 1). Every Chinese character carries a tone. Perhaps the most important thing to remember at this stage is that different tones of a certain syllable generally indicate completely different meanings. The features of the four tones are clearly illustrated in Figure 1.

The representation of tonal pitch contours as numbers was devised by Yuen Ren Chao to illustrate the tonal aspects of the Chinese language as well as other tonal languages. Unlike the music score, it consists of five arbitrary levels and each is labeled from the bottom upwards from 1 to 5. As with the music score, the lowest line represents the lowest pitch, and the highest line, the highest pitch. The variance of the pitch is captured using the reference pitch numbers by observing the starting, middle and end-points of the tone. The numbers are then enclosed in two forward slash marks. For example, /55/ is a high level tone, while /11/ is a low level tone. /51/ indicates a high falling tone, /35/ is a mid rising tone, while /31/ is a mid falling tone. /214/ is a tone that starts low, falls and then rises again. Short tones can also be represented as a single number. For instance a short mid level tone is represented by /3/.

Using this numbered system, tone one is /55/; tone two is /35/; tone three is /214/ and tone four is /51/. The lines in the above table indicate the pitch contours of the four tones. The four tones can also be represented with the following symbols (See Table 1):

Tone	Symbol	Example
First	‾	dī
Second	´	dí
Third	ˇ	dǐ
Fourth	`	dì

Table 1: Symbols of Tonal Accent

If we use musical notes to illustrate on the five scale, the four tones have the following patterns:

Figure 2: Mandarin Tones in Musical Notation

■ Tone One:

Tone One has the highest pitch level. It starts and ends high. It is near the top of your comfortable range. As a result, you should be able to sound the first tone syllable continuously without effort.

mā: mā a a a a a......

漢語語音
CHINESE PRONUNCIATION

■ Tone Two:

Tone Two starts in the middle of your voice range and rises straight toward the level of the first tone. It is similar to the English tone when you are questioning: What?

má: má?

■ Tone Three:

Tone Three is the lowest tone of all. It starts low and then rises towards the middle high pitch level and has longer duration. Your pitch level should drop until you feel out of breath and then release.

mǎ

■ Tone Four:

Tone Four begins at the top of your comfortable range and proceeds quickly to the bottom. It is short and sounds as if you are being stern.

mà: mà!

Tonal exercise:

1. Listen to the recording and read aloud:

mā↔mà	fā↔fà	tā↔tà	dā↔dà	pā↔pà
má↔mā	fá↔fā	tá↔tā	dá↔dā	pá↔pā
mà↔mǎ	fà↔fǎ	tà↔tǎ	dà↔dǎ	pà↔pǎ
mī↔mì	nī↔nì	tī↔tì	dī↔dì	pī↔pì
mí↔mī	ní↔nī	tí↔tī	dí↔dī	pí↔pī
mì↔mǐ	bì↔dǐ	tì↔dǐ	lì↔nǐ	nì↔mǐ
lì↔lǐ	ní↔lī	lí↔nī	nì↔lǐ	lì↔nǐ
lā↔mà	lá↔mā	mà↔lǎ	là↔mà	pà↔mǎ

> **2. Listen and indicate the tonal accent for the following syllables:**
>
> ta   da   ni   mi   fa   ma   pu   tu   hen   bo
>
> ting ding ning ming lin   ping hao   lao   dong nin

II. The initials

   As was introduced earlier, Mandarin Chinese has a total of 21 initials. Initials are similar to English consonants. However, the term "initial" only refers to consonants that appear in the initial position of a syllable. The 21 initials are listed below according to the positioning of one's mouth in producing the sounds. (See Table 2)

Table 2: Table of Initials

	Unaspirated	Aspirated	Nasal	Voiceless fricative	Voiced fricative	Continuants
Labial	b(o)	p(o)	m(o)	f(o)		
Alveolar	d(e)	t(e)	n(e)			l(e)
Guttural	g(e)	k(e)		h(e)		
Palatal	j(i)	q(i)		x(i)		
Retroflex	zh(i)	ch(i)		sh(i)	r(i)	
Dental sibilant	z(i)	c(i)		s(i)		

   Please note that the initials can not be pronounced without adding certain finals. Please practice with your teacher in class and listen to the audio sounds after class. The initials listed in row 1 are called labials because the lips must be used to pronounce them. The sounds in row 2 are dentals because the teeth are employed to produce these sounds. The initials listed in row 3 are called "gutturals", which means their pronunciation is controlled by the muscles in the back of the mouth. They are different from the English velar consonants *g*, *k*, *h* mainly because of the position of articulation. Actually, since the initials listed in rows 1-3 are very similar to English consonants, you should be able to achieve the sounds very easily.

   The "palatals" in row 4 require more practice. When pronouncing *j* and *q*, you must first raise the front of the tongue to the hard palate and press the tip of the tongue against the back of the lower teeth, and then loosen the tongue and let the air squeeze out through the channel. The two sounds differ only in that the *q* is an aspirated sound. To pronounce *x*, you should raise the front of the tongue towards (almost touching) the hard palate and then let the air squeeze out. In short, *j(i)* is like *j* in *jeep*. *q(i)* is like *ch* in *cheap* and *cheese*. *x(i)* like *sh* in *banshee*, between the *s* in *see* and the *sh* in *she*. Refer to Figure 3 for a better understanding.

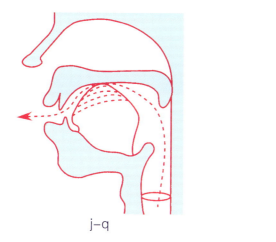
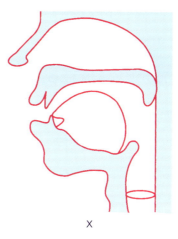

Figure 3: Palatals

The initials in row 5 are "retroflexes". To pronounce these sounds, the tongue is curled back (retroflexed) until the tip touches the front part of the roof of the mouth. The tongue is only a little farther toward the back of the mouth than when pronouncing the initial *r* in *run*. To pronounce **zh** and **ch**, the tip of the tongue begins by touching the roof of the mouth, then quickly moves away. The two sounds differ only in that a strong puff of air accompanies with *ch* sound. **Zh(i)** is similar to *dg* in *fudge*, and **ch(i)** is like *ch* in *church*, but curl the tongue up toward the roof of the mouth while pronouncing the *ch* sound. However, when producing the sound of **sh** and **r**, the tip of the tongue never touches the roof of the mouth but simply rests in a close-by position as illustrated in Figure 4 below. **sh(i)** sounds like sh in English, but you should curl the tongue up toward the roof of the mouth while pronouncing the *sh* sound. **r(i)** sounds *zhr* as in *pleasure*. Please note that *r* is the only initial that is voiced in a real sense. The two nasals *n* and *m* as well as the continuant *l* are only considered as semi-voiced.

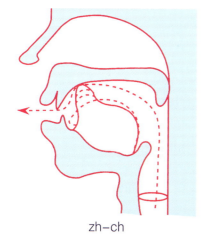
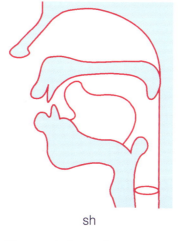
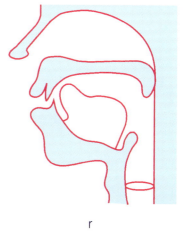

Figure 4: Retroflexes

Dental sibilants (buzzing or hissing sounds) are listed in the last row. They are called "dental sibilants" because their pronunciation involves the tip of the tongue placed behind the top of front teeth. The tongue must be farther towards the front than when pronouncing an English *s* and *z*, is not too far from *ds* in *reads*. **c** is similar to the *ts* in *carts* though more air should be blown out.

Exercises on Initials:

1. Listen and repeat:

b:	bābǐ	bàiběi	bāobì	bēnbō	búbì
p:	pǐpèi	páipào	pápō	pōpí	piānpáng
f:	fāfàng	fànfǎ	fāfú	fāngfǎ	fēnfù
h:	héhǎo	hēihǎi	hēhù	huīhuáng	huāhuì
d:	dàdāo	dédào	dìdiǎn	dàidòng	dōngdān
t:	tǐtán	tiáotíng	tāntú	tīngtáng	tōngtiān
l:	línlì	lúnluò	láilín	línglì	lánlǐng
r:	róuruǎn	réngrán	rènrén	róngrǔ	rùnrì
j:	jiājī	jīnjī	jìngjià	jìngjiè	jiājǐn
q:	qīqì	qīnqíng	qīngqì	qīngquán	qīnqiè
x:	xiàxiāng	xìxīn	xīxià	xìnxī	xiànxiàng
zh:	zhīzhōng	zhàizhǔ	zhāngzhōu	zhāzhēn	zhùzhái
ch:	chūchù	chéngchē	cháchāo	cháchǎng	chuánchū
sh:	shīshēng	shūshì	shénshèng	shānshuǐ	shàngshū
z:	zìzú	zǔzōng	zàizào	zìzūn	zàngzú
c:	céngcì	cáncún	cāicè	cùncǎo	cuīcù
s:	sīsuǒ	sùsòng	sānsī	sīsuì	sùsuàn

2. Listen and pronounce the following syllables. Please pay attention to the unaspirated initials and aspirated initials:

b–p:

piāobó	biānpái	píngpāo	píngbǐ	píbāo	pānbǐ
pāibǎn	bānpíng	pàobīng	pèngbì	pèibèi	piānpì

d–t:

tóngděng	détǐ	tīdù	diàntī	tídān	dìtú
dītóu	dàitì	tīdǎ	diàotóu	dāntián	dītáng

漢語語音
CHINESE PRONUNCIATION

z–c:

| zàicì | cízǔ | zìcè | càizǐ | zácǎo | cāzǎo |
| cāozuò | zàncí | cānzàn | zàicè | cèzì | zìcán |

g–k:

| gékāi | kāiguó | kèkǔ | kàngù | gùkè | kāigōng |
| gōngkāi | kōnggǎng | gūkǔ | kuàigǎn | guókù | kùguǎn |

3. Please pronounce the following retroflexes:

zhùchù	chíchěng	chīshuǐ	chūshǒu	zhīchí	cáishuǐ
shìzhǎng	shìchǎng	chángchù	zhēnzhèng	chuāngshāng	chóuchú
shíshī	shūshēng	chuánchàng	shēnzhí	chángchéng	chuánchǎng
zhīzhū	shǎoshù	zhènzhōng	chíshuǐ	shīcè	shāshí
chūshì	zhàshī	chūshù	zhèngshì	chūzhōng	shàngrèn
rèshuǐ	rìzhào	shīrén	zhīrǎn	rùshí	réngrán
ruòshì	ruìzhì	rènzhī	rénzhì	zhírù	rùchǎng

4. Please practice the following palatals with the recording:

pìjìng	qīxiàn	xīqì	chūqù	jiàqī	píngjìng
qījiān	jīngqì	jíjǐn	chāijiàn	píngxī	jiāoqì
qícái	xiàqí	qìxiàng	jiùjì	jiànqǐ	xíngjìn
xīqín	qíxí	jīnxīng	xīngqī	qīnxìn	jǐnqí
qǐjià	jiāxiào	xiàojìng	qīngjīn	qíngjǐng	jìqiǎo
qīnqiè	xiànxiàng	xiāngxìn	jīngjì	qiángquán	jiājié
jīqì	qínjiǎn	xiàjì	jīngxǐ	xiángjìn	qíngxíng

5. Read aloud and compare:

b–f:	bāfāng	fābiǎo	bīnfēn	fāngbiàn	bùfú
p–f:	pífū	fúpín	pīfā	fàngpíng	píngfán
d–l:	dàilǐ	lìdài	dàlián	lādà	dǎnliàng
t–l:	túliào	lǐtǐ	tíliàn	lántiān	tiānliàng
f–h:	fāhuī	huīfā	fǎnhuán	héfǎ	fánhuá
r–l:	lùrù	ránglì	rìlì	ránliào	lìrèn

zh–z:	zhìzào	zìzhù	zhùzú	zēngzhǎng	zhízé
ch–c:	cánchuǎn	chūcì	chàngcí	chēcì	chīcù
sh–s:	shísì	sìshí	shēnsī	shānsè	shīsàn
zh–j:	zhíjìng	jìzhě	zhījǐn	jiàzhí	zhījǐ
ch–q:	chàqì	qíchē	chāiqiǎn	qīnchāi	chángqīng
sh–x:	xīshōu	shānxī	xiāoshī	shíxí	xīshū

III. The finals

The simple finals:

There are altogether six basic vowels in Chinese as shown in Figure 5.

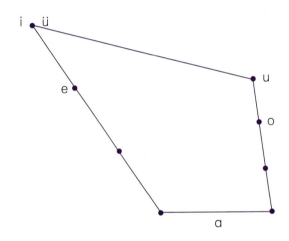

Figure 5: Basic Vowels

a is a central vowel. To pronounce it, the tongue remains in a natural, relaxed position, as *a* in *father*.

o is a rounded semi-high back vowel. It sounds like *o* as in *or*, or like the *wa* in *wall*. You should have your lips rounded to pronounce it.

e is an unrounded semi-high back vowel. To produce this vowel, first pronounce *o*, then change the shape of your mouth from rounded to unrounded. At the same time open the mouth wider. This vowel is different from *e* in English, which is pronounced with the tongue raised slightly forward. It needs special practice. Also *ê* can be regarded as its variant sound of *e* as in *ye*.

i is an unrounded high front vowel. The tongue is raised higher than when pronouncing its counterpart in English as in *tea*.

u is a rounded high back vowel. The tongue is raised higher than it would be to pronounce its counterpart in English. It slightly resembles the *o* as in English *oo*. To pronounce it:

(1) The tongue must be pulled toward the back of the mouth while the lips make a very small

opening in front.

(2) Imagine that you hold as much water as possible without either swallowing or spilling any of it out of the lips.

(3) Try to whistle the lowest note possible, then vocalize instead of actually whistling.

ü is a rounded high front vowel. It is a combination of *i* and *u*. To produce this vowel, (1) first pronounce *i*, then modify the shape of the mouth from unrounded to rounded; (2) try to whistle the highest note, but vocalize instead of actually whistling.

-i represents two additional special vowels: one is an alveolar front vowel, it goes with *z, c, s*; the other is an alveolar back vowel, it goes with *zh, ch, sh, r*.

■ The compound finals:

A final may have one or more vowel sounds and sometimes a consonant ending like *-n* and *-ng*. In fact, other than *-n* and *-ng*, the consonants don't appear in a final at all. 39 finals are listed in Table 3.

Table 3: The Compound Finals

Row		Ending				
		–i	–o/–u	–n	–ng	–r
–a	–i a o e (ê)	ai	ei ao ou	an en	ang eng ong	er
–i	i ia ie		iao iu/iou	ian in	iang ing iong	
–u	u ua	uai ui/uei	uo	uan un/uen	uang ueng	
–ü	ü	üe		üan ün/üen		

- ei sounds like *eigh* in *sleigh* and *eight*.
- ao sounds like *ow* like the *au* in *sauerkraut*.
- ou sounds like *oh*, as in *soul*.
- an sounds of *ahn*, between the *an* in *can* and the *on* in *con*.
- en sounds like *un* as in *run*, *en* as in *chicken*.
- ang sounds like *ahng*, *a* as in *father* and *ng* as in *sing*.
- eng has the sound of *ung* as in *hung* and *lung*.
- ong (ueng) is like the *ung* in German *jung* or, *u* as in *put* plus *ng* as in *sing*.
- er crosses between *ar* and *er*.
- ia sounds like *ee-ah* (quickly, as one syllable), like the *ya* in *yacht*.
- ie sounds like *ee-eh* (quickly), like the *ye* in *yet*.
- iao starts with *ee* in *see* and end with *ow* in *now*.
- iu (iou) sounds like *yo* as in *you* or *eo* as in *Leo*, close to *u* in *union*.
- ian sounds like *ee-en* (quickly)(an after *i* sounds between *man* and *men* in English)

走近中國——初級漢語教程
APPROACHING CHINA : ELEMENTARY CHINESE

in (ien) sounds like *een* as in *seen*, like the *ine* in *machine*.
iang sounds like *ee-ahng* (quickly).
ing (ieng) is similar to *ing* as in *ring*.
iong sounds like *ee-ong* (quickly), almost like German *jung*.
ua sounds like *wa* as in *wash* and the *wa* in *wander*.
uo sounds like *wo* as in *wore* and the *wa* in *waltz*.
uai sounds like *why* or like the *wi* in *wide*.
ui (uei) sounds like *way*, between *we* and *weigh*.
uan is similar to *wahn*, as in *wander*.
un (uen) is similar to *when* or the *wen* in *Owen*.
uang sounds like *wahng*.
ueng starts with *u* as in *put* then quickly goes to *eng*.
üe sounds like the German umlaut *u* in *uber* plus *e* in *ie*.
üan starts with *ü* and then goes on to *wan* as in *wander*.
ün (üen) starts with *ü* and then goes on to *en* quickly.

Please note that the vowel quality of some finals varies with different tones. For example, the final *iu* (you) with the first and the third tone will sound different. Therefore, our focus should be on the accuracy of the tones instead of on the distinctions.

Exercises on Finals:

1. Please read the following syllables aloud:

o:	pōmò	bōluó	fótuó	mòluò	mópò
e:	lèhé	kēkè	tèsè	hégé	jī'è
u:	bùfú	pùbù	zhùchù	túshū	fúwù
ü:	yùjù	xùqǔ	qūjū	qūyù	yùnǚ
er:	èrjiù	èrhú	érxì	jī'ér	ěrsāi
ei:	fēichē	xuéfèi	bèihòu	lèihén	wèisuō
ao:	pāomáo	gāozhāo	bàodào	láobǎo	bàochǎo
ou:	shòuhóu	ōuzhōu	dòu'ōu	shōugòu	gōushǒu
uo:	zuòcuò	nuòruò	guòcuò	tuōluò	cuòluò
üe:	xuéxiào	tóngxué	hūlüè	yuányuè	yuènán
ui:	huìcuì	zhuīsuí	huíguī	cuīhuǐ	hèsuì
an:	cànlàn	tánpàn	gānhàn	cānzàn	shànshì
en:	zhēnrén	rènzhēn	gēnběn	ménzhěn	shēnchén
in:	bīnlín	qīnxìn	pīnyīn	xìnxīn	xīnyīn
un:	chūnsǔn	hùndùn	kūnlún	shùncóng	zūnguì

漢語語音
CHINESE PRONUNCIATION

2. Contrasts:

ou–(u)o:	dōushuō	gòuduō	shòucuò	dǒuluò	guǒròu
u–ü:	lùshù	lùxù	jùzǔ	lǔtú	qūchú
ei–ui:	duìlěi	cuīféi	bēiwēi	lèituī	léizhuì
ao–ou:	bàochóu	lāoròu	chāoshōu	shòutáo	róudào
an–ang:	dàngrán	nánfāng	bàngwǎn	hángbān	kàngzhàn
en–eng:	zhēnzhèng	zhēnchéng	chéngrèn	zhèngshěn	lèngshén
in–ing:	xīnxīng	xīnqíng	jìnlìng	pìnqǐng	yíngxīn
ong–iong:	lóngxiōng	yònggōng	qiónglóng	xiōngyǒng	yōngzhǒng
üan–ün:	yuánquān	qúnxuǎn	yuánjūn	xuànyūn	quánjūn
uan–un:	luànlún	huánhún	lùnduàn	lúnchuán	cūnguān
ie–üe:	jiéyuē	xuéjiè	quēxiě	xiéyuē	juéliè
ü–iu:	jiùjū	qūjiù	lǜxiù	jiùqù	liúyù
en–an:	sānzhēn	chánshēn	shānshén	zhènchàn	nánfēn
ao–iao:	xiāoyáo	jiàohǎo	gāoqiāo	liàokào	dāoqiào

IV. Pinyin Romanization-spelling rules

Pinyin Romanization has been the official romanization system in the People's Republic of China since 1958. Some of the finals listed in Table 3 are spelled different shown below in Table 4.

Table 4: Finals in Pinyin Romanization

Row	Ending					
		–i	–o/–u	–n	–ng	–r
–a	–i a o e (ê)	ai	ei ao ou	an en	ang eng ong	er
–i	yi ya ye		yao you	yan yin	yang ying yong	
–u	wu wa	wai wei wo		wan wen	wang weng	
–ü	yu yue			yun yun		

The spelling rules are summarized as below:

Tone marks:

We know that the four tones are indicated by the diacritical marks: ¯, ´, ˇ, ` that appear above the vowels of spelled syllables. There are rules to follow about where to put the diacritical marks. First, if there is a single vowel in the syllable, put it over the vowel. Second, if there is more than one vowel, put it over the vowel in this order: *a, o, e, i, u, ü*. When two vowels *i* and *u* are together, you put it over the last vowel. Third, if the diacritical mark is over an *i*, omit the dot.

xīn - new (Adj.)	rén - person (N.)	lěng - cold (Adj.)	gāo - tall (Adj.)
rè - hot (Adj.)	duì - correct (Adj.)	liú - to stay (V.)	kǒu - mouth (N.)

Spelling rules:

1. When the final *ü* combines with the palatal initials *j, q,* or *x*, the umlaut drops out. This is because only the final *ü* can go with *j, q,* or *x*, but not the final *u*. Therefore, any time a *u* comes after *j, q,* or *x*, one knows it has to be the final *ü* even though the umlaut is not there.

jú (jǘ) - office or bureau (N.)	qù (qǜ) - to go (V.)	xǔ (xǚ) - to permit (V.)

The only other initials that *ü* combines with are *l* and *n*. In these cases, the umlaut stays:

nǚ - female (Adj.)	lǜ - green (Adj.)

2. When the final *uo* combines with the labial initials *b, p, m, f*, the *u* drops out.

bō - wave (N.)	pò - broken or worn out (Adj.)
mó - to rub (V.)	fó - Buddha (N.)

But the *u* stays when the following other initials such as *d, t, n, l, g, k, h, zh, ch, sh, r, z, c, s* are used.

duō - much or many (Adj.)	cuò - wrong (Adj.)

3. When the finals beginning with *i* occur without an initial, the *i* changes to *y*.

iě → yě - also (Adv.)	iào → yào - want (V.)

The three finals *i, in,* and *ing* are exceptions to rule three, in which case a *y* is added while the *i* remains:

ī → yī - one (Num.)	ìn → yìn - to print (V.)	ìng → yìng - hard (Adj.)

When the final *iu* (*iou*) goes without an initial, the *i* changes to a *y* by rule four and an *o* is added:

漢語語音
CHINESE PRONUNCIATION

> iǔ → yǒu - to have (V.)

4. When finals beginning with **u** occur without an initial, the **u** changes to **w**.

> uǒ → wǒ - I or me (Pron.)   uǎn → wǎn - bowl (N.)

The final **u** is an exception to rule four. When it occurs without an initial, the **w** is added:

> ǔ → wǔ - five (Num.)

When the finals **ui** (**uei**) and **un** (**uen**) occur without an initial, the **u** changes to a **w** by rule four and an **e** is added:

> uì → wèi - stomach (N.)   ùn → wèn - to ask (V.)

5. When the finals beginning with **ü** occur without an initial, the umlaut drops out and a **y** is added in front.

> ǘ → yú - fish (N.)   üǎn → yuǎn - distant (Adj.)

6. If the noun is a place name, then capitalize the first letter. If it is a Chinese name, capitalize the first letter of the surname and given name.

> běijīng → Běijīng (Peking)   niǔyuē → Niǔyuē (New York)
> wáng xiǎoxiǎo → Wáng Xiǎoxiǎo (*a name*)

Spelling exercises:

1. Please correct the spellings for the following syllables:

uàn →	üǎn →	dìu →	buǒ →
iàn →	wùn →	zò →	iě →
ǘen →	wuěi →	yiǔ →	jàn →
qóng →	chùen →	wùi →	yüǎn →

2. Spell the dictated syllables and add the diacritical marks:

_____   _____   _____   _____

_____   _____   _____   _____

_____   _____   _____   _____

13

V. Tone sandhi

Tone sandhi refers to the sound change in tones when different sounds come together. Sandhi in Sankrit means "putting together".

■ Third tone sandhi:

In Mandarin Chinese, the most common tone sandhi rule is that the leading syllable in a set of two third-tone syllables is raised to the second tone. For example, nǐ hǎo (你好), the most common Mandarin greeting, is pronounced ní hǎo. If there are more than two third tones, the same rule applies although other rules may apply.

Exercise:

Please read the following syllables:

hěnhǎo	mǎijiǔ	shuǐjiǎo	qǐzǎo	cǎozǐ	yǔnxǔ
chǎomǐ	mǐjiǔ	jiǔguǐ	suǒyǐ	zǎozǒu	liǎojiě
yǔfǎ	lǎolǐ	yuǎnzǔ	xiǎngzǒu	xiǎogǒu	xǐzǎo
shuǐguǒ	nǐhǎo	lǎohǔ	dǎgǔ	shǒubiǎo	fǔdǎo

■ Half third tone:

If a third tone is followed by the first, second or the fourth tone, the third tone will only keep the falling pitch and remains there instead of rising. Since it is half realized, it is called a half third tone. Actually, a full third tone is only possible when it is phrase final or when it is by itself. Figure 6 will indicate the change.

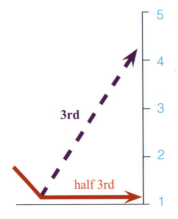

Figure 6: Half Third Tone

漢語語音
CHINESE PRONUNCIATION

Exercises:

Please read the following syllables:

Niǔyuē (New York)	kěshì (but)	qǐngwèn (May I ask?)
Běijīng (Beijing)	Měiguó (America)	Fǎguó (France)
lǎoshī (teacher)	hǎokàn (good-looking)	nǚhái (girl)
cǎihóng (rainbow)	fǎlǜ (law)	nǐ shuō (You speak)
wǒ lái (I will do it.)	qǐng zuò (Please sit.)	dǎ qiú (to play a game)
wǎngqiú (tennis)	qǐng shuō (Please speak.)	nǐ kàn (You see.)
zǒu lù (to walk)	hǎoshū (good book)	lǚyóu (to travel)

■ Fourth tone sandhi:

When a fourth tone is followed by another fourth tone, the first one becomes a variant of the regular fourth tone as illustrated below in Figure 7.

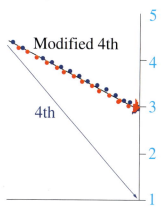

Figure 7: Fourth Tone Sandhi

As indicated in Figure 7, the modified fourth tone starts as a regular fourth tone does. But its pitch level only drops to scale 3, half as far as a full fourth.

Exercise:

Please read the following syllables:

duìhuà (dialogue)	guìxìng (honorable surname)	zàijiàn (goodbye)
shàng kè (to go to class)	Yìdàlì (Italy)	diànshì (TV)
zhàogù (to take care of)	jièshào (to introduce)	sùshè (dormitory)
kàn bào (to read newspaper)	jiàoshì (classroom)	shuì jiào (to sleep)

■ Tone Sandhi for yī and bù:

Yī (one; once) and bù (no; not) will also undergo tone sandhi under certain conditions. Preceding a syllable with the first, second or third tone, yī becomes yì, and bù keeps the fourth tone without any change.

yìqǐ (together)	yì jiā (a family)	yì nián (one year)
bù hǎo (not good)	bùtóng (not same)	bù tīng (not listen)

When preceding a syllable with a fourth tone, both yī and bù become a second tone.

yígòng (altogether)	yíxià (a little bit)	yíyàng (same)
búhuì (can not)	búguò (but)	búkàn (not to look)

When yī and bù are phrase final or used alone, they keep their original tones: yī and bù. Please note that the tone of yī and bù will change only when they mean yī (one; once) bù (no; not).

Exercise:

Please read the following syllables:

yìtiān (a day)	yì shí (in a short time)	yìzǔ (a group)
bù lěng (not cold)	bù zhīdào (I don't know.)	bù zǎo (not early)
yídìng (definitely)	yí gè (one + measure word)	bú rè (not hot)
bú tài hǎo (not that good)	bú duì (not correct)	bú shì (not to be)
bú dà (not big)	bú qù (not to go)	bú mài (not to sell)
bù lái (not to come)	dìyī (the first)	bù xíng (not okay)

■ Neutral tone:

In actual speech, all unstressed syllables are pronounced with a "neutral tone", which is sometimes considered as a lack of tone. In most varieties of Mandarin, the second syllable in two-syllable compounds is weaker in tonal prominence than the first one. A neutralized tone takes very little time to pronounce and does not hold or stick to its original tone. When actually pronouncing a neutral tone, one should not consider how a neutral tone sounds but focus on the tonal feature of the syllable that goes before it. Generally speaking, the pitch level of a neutral tone differs when following different tones as indicated in Figure 8.

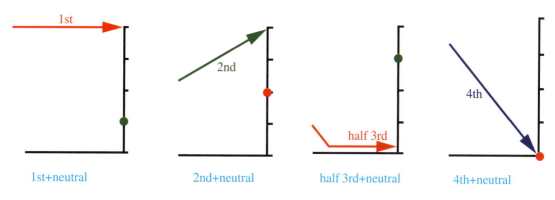

Figure 8: Pitch Level of Neutral Tones

From Figure 8, we know that when following the first tone, the pitch level of a neutralized syllable is around the middle low pitch, i.e. at scale 2. When it is after a second tone, the pitch level settles around middle pitch, i.e. scale 3. When it goes after a third tone (half third tone actually), the pitch level is around middle high pitch, i.e. scale 4. Its pitch level is the lowest, when a neutral tone is right after the fourth tone, i.e. scale 1.

Whether a syllable is neutralized or not, one can not tell from the Pinyin. We will either put a dot before a neutralized syllable or simply indicate it without a tone mark.

Exercise:

Please read the following syllables:

xuésheng (student)	tiān.qì (weather)	péngyou (friend)
xǐhuan (to like)	shūfu (comfortable)	shénme (what)
dìfang (place)	rènshi (to know sb.)	juéde (to feel)
héqi (gentle)	tāmen (they/them)	míngzi (name)
yīn.wèi (because)	wǒmen (we/us)	gēge (elder brother)
dìdi (younger brother)	xièxie (Thank you.)	fù.qīn (father)
mǔ.qīn (mother)	jiějie (elder sister)	māma (mom)
bàba (dad)	cōng.míng (smart)	yéye (grandfather)
nǎinai (grandmother)	érzi (son)	sūnzi (grandson)
míngbai (clear)	xìng.fú (happy)	shìqing (things)
kě.yǐ (may)	suǒ.yǐ (therefore)	ài.hào (hobby)
duìfu (to deal with)	ěrduo (ear)	gèzi (height)
gōngfu (Kongfu)	guàibude (no wonder)	kàn.qǐ.lái (it seems that)
shuō.chū.lái (to speak out)	xǐhuan.shàng (to begin to like)	shuō.bùde (can't be blamed)

The fickle *r* sound:

Northerners, especially Beijingese tend to add the fickle *r* to a word.

Exercise:

Please read the following syllables:

huār (flower)	báimiànr (drug, cocain)	qiúr (ball)	diànyǐngr (movie)
ménr (door)	nǎr (where)	yúcìr (fish bone)	dàhuǒr (everybody)
xiǎoniǎor (little bird)	xiǎoháir (little kid)	yíkuàir (together)	xiāngwèir (fragrance)
yìdiǎnr (a bit)	méizhǔnr (not sure)	méishìr (nothing)	huàhuàr (to draw)
liáotiānr (to chat)	xiàohuàr (joke)	chànggēr (to sing)	gēmenr (buddy)
fànguǎnr (restaurant)	guǎiwānr (to make a turn)	miàntiáor (noodles)	

More Pinyin Exercises:

1. Please read the following syllables:

tóngxué (classmate)	gāoxìng (happy)	Měiguó (America)
wàiguó (foreign country)	Zhōngguó (China)	péngyou (friend)
xiǎoxiǎo (*a Chinese name*)	liúxuéshēng (international student)	
Shànghǎi (Shanghai)	Yīngguó (Britain)	xǐhuan (to like)
Jiāzhōu (California)	Lúndūn (London)	zhīdào (to know)

2. Please read the following sentences:

① Jīntiān tiānqì hěn hǎo, bù lěng bú rè.
   (The weather is good today, neither cold nor hot.)
   今天天氣很好, 不冷不熱。

② Xīn tóngxué dōu hěn gāoxìng.
   (The new students are all very happy.)
   新同學都很高興。

③ Robert shì Měiguó xuésheng.
   (Robert is an American student.)
   Robert 是美國學生。

④ Tā yǒu hěn duō tóngxué, yǒu Měiguó tóngxué, hái yǒu wàiguó tóngxué.
   (He has many classmates, American classmates and also foreign classmates.)
   他有很多同學, 有美國同學, 還有外國同學。

⑤ Tā yǒu yí ge Zhōngguó tóngxué, xìng Zhāng, jiào Zhāng Yīzhōng.

(He has a Chinese classmate, whose surname is Zhang and is called Zhang Yizhong.)

他有一個中國同學,姓張,叫張一中。

⑥ Zhāng Yīzhōng shì Shànghǎirén.

(Zhang Yizhong is from Shanghai.)

張一中是上海人。

⑦ Robert hái yǒu yí ge Yīngguó tóngxué, jiào Alex, shì Lúndūnrén.

(Robert also has a British classmate, whose name is Alex, from London.)

Robert 還有一個英國同學,叫 Alex,是倫敦人。

⑧ Robert hé Alex dōu hěn xǐhuan Zhōngguó, yě dōu hěn xǐhuan Zhōngwén.

(Robert and Alex both like China. Also they both like Chinese.)

Robert 和 Alex 都很喜歡中國,也都很喜歡中文。

⑨ Robert hái yǒu yí ge Zhōngguó péngyou, xìng Wáng, jiào Wáng Xiǎoxiǎo.

(Robert also has a Chinese friend, whose surname is Wang, and is called Wang Xiaoxiao.)

Robert 還有一個中國朋友,姓王,叫王小小。

⑩ Wáng Xiǎoxiǎo bú shì Shànghǎirén, shì Běijīngrén.

(Wang Xiaoxiao is not from Shanghai but from Beijing.)

王小小不是上海人,是北京人。

⑪ Tā yě shì Zhōngguó liúxuéshēng.

(He is also an international student who is from China.)

他也是中國留學生。

3. Please read the following poems:

静夜思

Jìng Yè Sī

Lǐ Bái

李白

chuáng qián míng yuè guāng　　yí shì dì shàng shuāng

床 前 明 月 光 , 疑 是 地 上 霜 。

jǔ tóu wàng míng yuè　　dī tóu sī gù xiāng

舉 頭 望 明 月 , 低 頭 思 故 鄉 。

(So bright a gleam on the foot of my bed! Could there have been a frost already? Lifting myself to look, I found that it was moonlight. Sinking back again, I thought suddenly of home.)

春曉 Chūn Xiǎo

Mèng Hàorán
孟浩然

chūn mián bù jué xiǎo　　chù chù wén tí niǎo
春眠不覺曉，處處聞啼鳥。
yè lái fēng yǔ shēng　　huā luò zhī duō shǎo
夜來風雨聲，花落知多少。

(Awake light-hearted this morning of spring; Everywhere around me the singing of birds; But now I remember the night, the storm; And I wonder how many blossoms were broken.)

詠鵝 Yǒng É

Luò Bīnwáng
駱賓王

é é é　　qū xiàng xiàng tiān gē
鵝鵝鵝，曲項向天歌。
bái máo fú lǜ shuǐ　　hóng zhǎng bō qīng bō
白毛浮綠水，紅掌撥清波。

(Twisting its neck, the goose is singing to the sky. With its white feather on the green water, the red palms are striking on the clear water.)

回鄉偶書 Huí Xiāng Ǒu Shū

Hè Zhīzhāng
賀知章

shào xiǎo lí jiā lǎo dà huí　　xiāng yīn wú gǎi bìn máo cuī
少小離家老大回，鄉音無改鬢毛衰。
ér tóng xiāng jiàn bù xiāng shí　　xiào wèn kè cóng hé chù lái
兒童相見不相識，笑問客從何處來。

(I left home young, and I return old; Speaking as then, but with hair grown thin; And the children, meeting me, do not know me; They smile and say:"Stranger, where do you come from?")

4. Tongue twisters:

Sì shì sì.	四是四。	Four is four.
Shí shì shí.	十是十。	Ten is ten.
Shí sì shì shí sì.	十四是十四。	Fourteen is fourteen.
Sì shí shì sì shí.	四十是四十。	Forty is forty.
Sì shí sì shì sì shí sì.	四十四是四十四。	Forty four is forty four.

Chē shang yǒu ge pén,	車上有個盆，	There is a basin in the car,
Pén li yǒu ge píng,	盆裡有個瓶，	and a bottle in the basin.
pīng pīng pīng, pāng pāng pāng,	乒乓乒，乓乒乓，	Bin bin bin, bang bang bang,
bù zhī shì pén pèng píng,	不知是盆碰瓶，	Not knowing
hái shi píng pèng pén.	還是瓶碰盆。	which is hitting which.

Shù shang yǒu zhī xiǎo táo zi,	樹上有隻小桃子，	There is a peach on the tree,
Shù xià yǒu zhī xiǎo hóu zi.	樹下有隻小猴子。	There is a monkey under the tree.
Fēng chuī táo shù huā huā xiǎng,	風吹桃樹嘩嘩響，	The wind blows and the tree talks,
Shù shang diào xià xiǎo táo zi.	樹上掉下小桃子。	With the wind, the peach falls,
Táo zi dǎ zháo xiǎo hóu zi,	桃子打著小猴子，	Right onto the monkey.
Hóu zi chī diào xiǎo táo zi.	猴子吃掉小桃子。	And the monkey eats the peach.

走近中國──初級漢語教程
APPROACHING CHINA : ELEMENTARY CHINESE

Table of Relations Between Initials and Finals

Initials\Finals	a	o	e	ê	-i	er	ai	ei	ao	ou	an	en	ang	eng	ong	i	ia	iao	ie	iu	ian	in	iang	ing	iong	u	ua	uo	uai	ui	uan	un	uang	ueng	ü	üe	üan	ün
b	a	o	e	ê		er	ai	ei	ao	ou	an	en	ang	eng	ong	yi	ya	yao	ye	you	yan	yin	yang	ying	yong	wu	wa	wo	wai	wei	wan	wen	wang	weng	yu	yue	yuan	yun
b	ba	bo					bai	bei	bao		ban	ben	bang	beng		bi		biao	bie		bian	bin		bing		bu												
p	pa	po					pai	pei	pao	pou	pan	pen	pang	peng		pi		piao	pie		pian	pin		ping		pu												
m	ma	mo	me				mai	mei	mao	mou	man	men	mang	meng		mi		miao	mie	miu	mian	min		ming		mu												
f	fa	fo						fei		fou	fan	fen	fang	feng												fu												
d	da		de				dai	dei	dao	dou	dan	den	dang	deng	dong	di	dia	diao	die	diu	dian			ding		du		duo		dui	duan	dun						
t	ta		te				tai		tao	tou	tan		tang	teng	tong	ti		tiao	tie		tian			ting		tu		tuo		tui	tuan	tun						
n	na		ne				nai	nei	nao	nou	nan	nen	nang	neng	nong	ni		niao	nie	niu	nian	nin	niang	ning		nu		nuo			nuan				nü	nüe		
l	la		le				lai	lei	lao	lou	lan		lang	leng	long	li	lia	liao	lie	liu	lian	lin	liang	ling		lu		luo			luan	lun			lü	lüe		
z	za		ze		zi		zai	zei	zao	zou	zan	zen	zang	zeng	zong											zu		zuo		zui	zuan	zun						
c	ca		ce		ci		cai	cei	cao	cou	can	cen	cang	ceng	cong											cu		cuo		cui	cuan	cun						
s	sa		se		si		sai		sao	sou	san	sen	sang	seng	song											su		suo		sui	suan	sun						
zh	zha		zhe		zhi		zhai	zhei	zhao	zhou	zhan	zhen	zhang	zheng	zhong											zhu	zhua	zhuo	zhuai	zhui	zhuan	zhun	zhuang					
ch	cha		che		chi		chai		chao	chou	chan	chen	chang	cheng	chong											chu	chua	chuo	chuai	chui	chuan	chun	chuang					
sh	sha		she		shi		shai	shei	shao	shou	shan	shen	shang	sheng												shu	shua	shuo	shuai	shui	shuan	shun	shuang					
r			re		ri				rao	rou	ran	ren	rang	reng	rong											ru	rua	ruo		rui	ruan	run						
j																ji	jia	jiao	jie	jiu	jian	jin	jiang	jing	jiong										ju	jue	juan	jun
q																qi	qia	qiao	qie	qiu	qian	qin	qiang	qing	qiong										qu	que	quan	qun
x																xi	xia	xiao	xie	xiu	xian	xin	xiang	xing	xiong										xu	xue	xuan	xun
g	ga		ge				gai	gei	gao	gou	gan	gen	gang	geng	gong											gu	gua	guo	guai	gui	guan	gun	guang					
k	ka		ke				kai	kei	kao	kou	kan	ken	kang	keng	kong											ku	kua	kuo	kuai	kui	kuan	kun	kuang					
h	ha		he				hai	hei	hao	hou	han	hen	hang	heng	hong											hu	hua	huo	huai	hui	huan	hun	huang					

漢字書寫 CHINESE WRITING SYSTEM

I. Introduction

Chinese is written with characters called 漢字 (hànzì). Each character represents a syllable of spoken Chinese and also has a meaning. Therefore, problems caused by homonyms in spoken Chinese are not a question in written Chinese. The characters were originally pictures of people, animals or other things but over the centuries they have become increasingly stylized and no longer resemble the things they represent. Many of the characters are actually compounds of two or more characters. The written language is also a unifying factor culturally, for although the spoken languages and dialects may not be mutually comprehensible in many instances, the written form is universal.

Characters are made up of multiple parts. They are sometimes slightly distorted in order to maintain a uniform size and shapes. Because of this, beginners often practice on squared graph paper, and the term "Square-Block Characters" (方塊字, fāngkuàizì) is another name for Chinese characters.

Four percent of Chinese characters are derived directly from individual pictograms (象形字, xiàngxíngzì). The other 93.5% are logical aggregates (會意字, huìyìzì, 12.3%), which are characters combined from multiple parts indicative of meaning, and pictophonetics (形聲字, xíngshēngzì, 81.2%), characters containing two parts where one indicates a general category of meaning and the other the sound, though the sound is often only approximate to the modern pronunciation because of changes over time and differences between source. Other than these, there are also ideographic (指事字, zhǐshìzì, 1.3%), borrowing (假借字, jiǎjièzì, 1.2%) as well as explanatory (轉注字, zhuǎnzhùzì, 0.07%).

How many characters?

It is said that the Chinese writing system is an open-ended one, which means that there is no upper limit to the number of characters. The largest Chinese dictionaries include about 56,000 characters, but most of them are archaic, obscure or rare variant forms. Nowadays, only about 10,000 characters are used. Actually, a knowledge of about 3,000 characters enables you to read about 99% of the characters in Chinese newspapers and magazines. To read Chinese literature, technical writings or Classical Chinese though, you need to be familiar with about 6,000 characters.

There are numerous styles, or scripts, in which Chinese characters can be written, deriving from various calligraphic and historical models. Most of these originated in China and are now common, with minor variations, in all countries where Chinese characters are used. Table 1 is an illustration of the many scripts.

Table 1: Scripts

Oracle Bone Script	Seal Script	Clerical Script	Semi-Cursive Script	Cursive Script	Regular Script	Pinyin	Meaning
		日	日	日	日	rì	sun
		月	月	月	月	yuè	moon
		山	山	山	山	shān	mountain
		水	水	水	水	shuǐ	water
		雨	雨	雨	雨	yǔ	rain
		木	木	木	木	mù	wood
		禾	禾	禾	禾	hé	grain (rice)
		人	人	人	人	rén	human
		女	女	女	女	nǚ	woman
		母	母	母	母	mǔ	mother
		目	目	目	目	mù	eye
		牛	牛	牛	牛	niú	bull
		羊	羊	羊	羊	yáng	sheep
		馬	馬	馬	馬	mǎ	horse
		鳥	鳥	鳥	鳥	niǎo	bird

漢字書寫
CHINESE WRITING SYSTEM

■ Simplification in China

The use of traditional characters versus simplified characters varies greatly, and can depend on both the local customs and the medium. Since the 1950s, and especially with the publication of the 1964 list, the PRC has officially adopted a simplified script, while some districts like Hong Kong, Macau and Taiwan still use traditional characters.

II. How to write Chinese characters

■ Stroke types

A Chinese character is composed of basic strokes. The simplest ones have only one stroke while the more complex ones can have more than 20-30 strokes. The strokes are to be written in the right order and in the right way. It is important to follow those rules. Proportions are very important so you have to have it in mind when you write.

Table 2: Strokes

Stroke	Direction	Name	Example
丶	↘	diǎn	你 字
一	→	héng	大 三
丨	↓	shù	中 上
丿	↙	piě	你 千
丶	↘	nà	天 人
／	↗	tí	海 我
⁻	→ ↓	hénggōu	字 家
亅	↓	shùgōu	水 你
╲	↘	xiégōu	我 式
⁻	→↓	héngzhé	票 克
∟	↓→	shùzhé	忙 每

■ How to write a héng and a shù?

A héng must be kept level but may be raised slightly at the right end. The spaces between héng must be even. Héng must be of different lengths, usually the one on top is shorter than the one below. If there are three héng, the middle one is the shortest. E.g. 永 一 大 干 三

A shù must be perpendicular. If there are two or more shù in a character, they should be parallel with even spaces in between and differ in length, usually with the left one a bit shorter than the right one.

E.g. 永 中 木 十 川

Practice:

Please write the following characters:

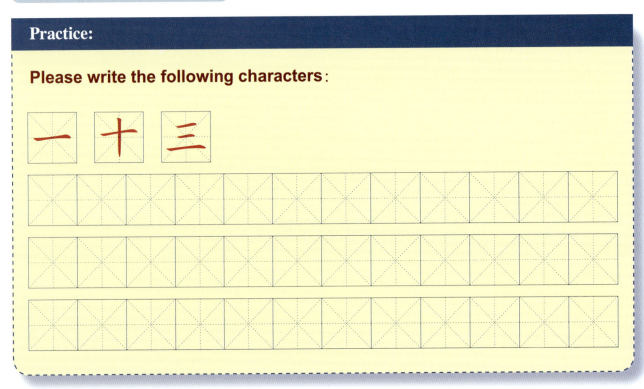

■ How to write a piě?

There are three kinds of piě: horizontal (⼀), slanting (丿) and vertical (丿)

The horizontal piě (⼀) is usually shorter and somewhat level. E.g. 千

A slanting piě (丿) is made slightly inclined to the left and is of medium length. E.g. 永

A vertical piě (丿) must be kept somewhat vertical and rather long. In characters which contain several piě, make sure they are different from one another in length. E.g. 人

In characters which contain two similar piě (彳), make sure the one above is shorter than the one below. E.g. 街

In Characters with three such piě (彡), make sure the one below starts from under the middle of the one above. E.g. 影

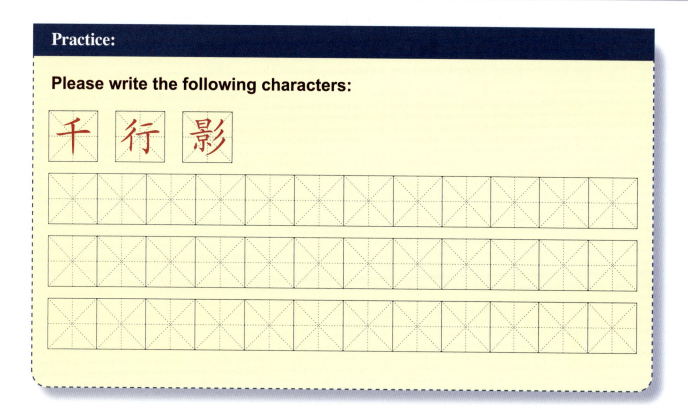

How to write a nà?

The length of a nà depends on its position in a character.

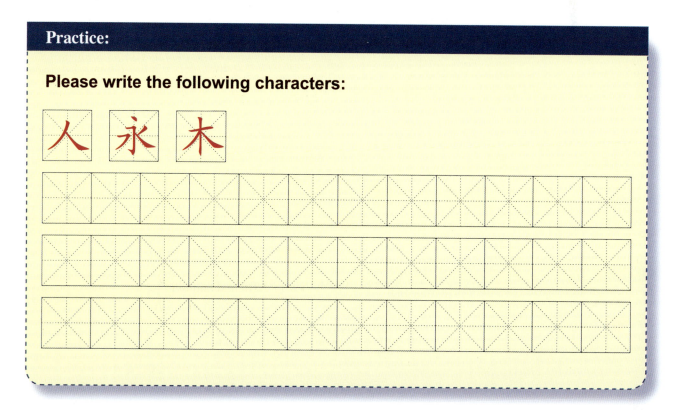

■ How to write a diǎn?

There are four kinds of diǎn: short, long, left-and-right and four parallel.

A short diǎn (丶) must be short and roundish at the lower end.   E.g. 字 方

A long diǎn (丶) must be somewhat longer and narrower.   E.g. 你

The left-and-right diǎn (丷) must be symmetrical.   E.g. 你

When writing the four parallel diǎn, the first diǎn must incline somewhat to the left while the fourth diǎn (灬) to the right. The two in between should be a bit smaller than the other two.   E.g. 照

Practice:

Please write the following characters:

小 黑

■ How to write a gōu, a tí and a zhé?

There are three kinds of gōu: horizontal (→), vertical (↓) and slanting (╲). All these gōu must be forceful and sturdy.   E.g. 字 家 水 你 我 式

A tí (╱) must be short and forceful.   E.g. 海 我

A horizontal zhé (┐) must look natural.   E.g. 票 克

A vertical zhé (ㄴ) must look forceful and sturdy.   E.g. 忙 每

A héngzhégōu (ㄱ) and a shùwānggōu (ㄴ) both look forceful and natural.

E.g. 力 也 北 高

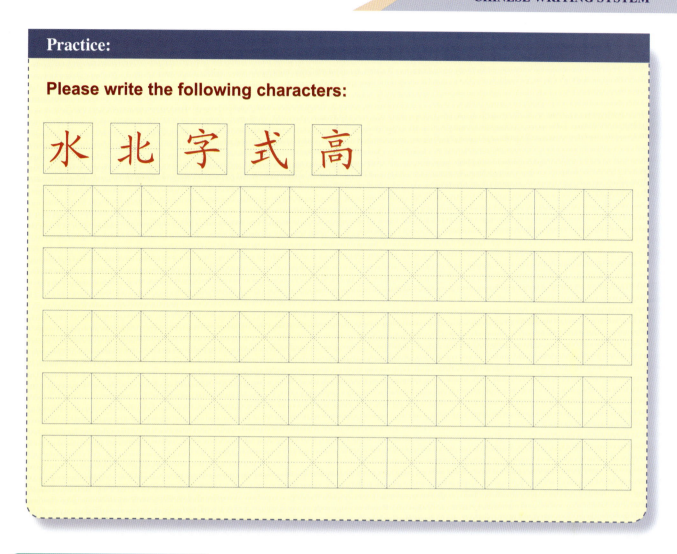

III. Stroke Order

Writing characters in the correct order is essential for the character to look correct. Two basic rules are:

1. Top before bottom: E.g. 三 三 三

2. Left before right: E.g. 八 八

These rules conflict whenever one stroke is to the bottom and left of another. There are several additional rules that resolve many of these conflicts.

3. Left vertical stroke (usually) before top horizontal stroke: E.g. 口 口 口

4. Bottom horizontal stroke last: E.g. 王 王 王 王

5. Center stroke before wings: E.g. 小 小 小

6. Horizontal strokes before intersecting vertical strokes: E.g. 十 十

7. Left-falling strokes before right-falling strokes: E.g. 文 文 文 文

A final rule (8) can contradict other rules:

8. Minor strokes (often) last: E.g. 玉 玉 玉 玉 玉

Despite these conflicts between rules, it won't take you long to figure out the proper stroke order.

Practice:

Please write the following characters, paying special attention to the stroke order:

小 人 口 文 玉

■ Component Order

Most Chinese characters are combinations of simpler, component characters. Usually the two parts are written at top and bottom like 古 古 or left and right such as 仁 仁 so that the main two stroke order rules readily apply. Occasionally these rules also conflict with respect to components. When one component is at the bottom-left, and the other at the top-right, the top-right component is sometimes written first. E.g. 迷 迷

When there are several components, top components are written first. E.g. 品 品

These rules usually imply each component is written before another component is written.

Exceptions may arise when one component divides another, E.g. 街 街 街 encompasses another, E.g. 囚 囚 囚 or the individual components are no longer discernible in modern writing.

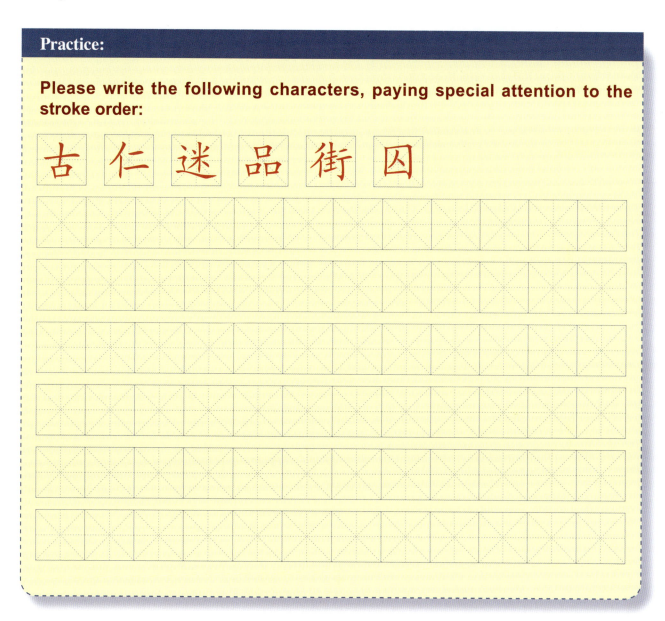

■ Tips for writing single component characters:

Quite a number of Chinese characters are composed of only a few strokes and have no other components. Since there are only a few basic strokes in characters of this kind, each stroke plays an important role. Therefore, in writing such a character, one must make sure that each stroke is placed at its proper position and the whole character is well-balanced, or else the character will look awkward.

• In a longish character, the héng must be shorter than the shù.

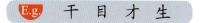

- In a shortish character, the héng must be longer than the shù.

  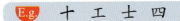 十 工 士 四

- A shù must be right in the middle of the character.

   中 半 走

- A piě and a nà, if they cross each other, cross at the centre of the character.

   人 义 天

Practice:

Please write the following characters, paying special attention to the stroke order and balance of components:

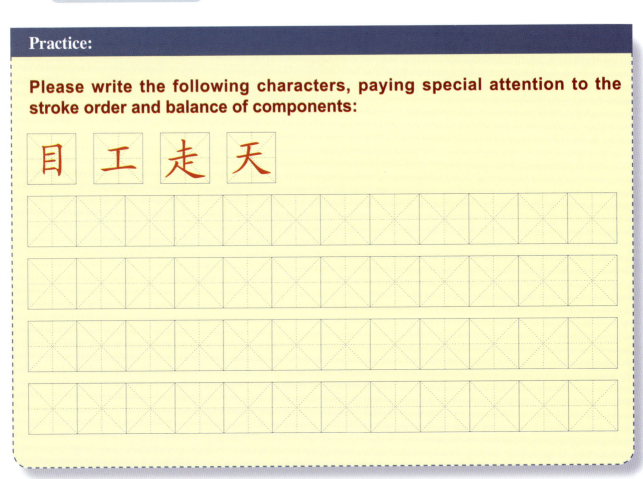

■ **Tips for writing characters with one component on top of the other:**

- If the upper component consists of fewer strokes than the lower one, it occupies a smaller space. E.g. 英 第

- If the upper component consists of more strokes than the lower one, it occupies a bigger place. E.g. 黑 照

- If the two components are identical, the upper should be smaller than the lower one. E.g. 多 哥

漢字書寫
CHINESE WRITING SYSTEM

Practice:

Please write the following characters, paying special attention to the stroke order and balance of components:

第 照 多

■ **Tips for writing two components side by side:**

• If the left-hand component consists of fewer strokes than the right-hand one, it occupies a smaller space. **E.g.** 操 校

• If the left-hand component consists of more strokes than the right-hand one, it occupies a bigger space. **E.g.** 影 歌

• In some characters, the two components must be of similar height and width. **E.g.** 能 解

• In some characters, if the two components are identical, the left-handed component is made smaller than the right-hand one. **E.g.** 朋 林

• If the left-hand component is short, then it should be placed a little above the middle of the character. **E.g.** 唱 明

• If the right-hand component is short, then it should be placed a little below the middle of the character. **E.g.** 知 和

• If a character has three components, they must be of similar height and width. **E.g** 街 假

走近中國──初級漢語教程
APPROACHING CHINA : ELEMENTARY CHINESE

Practice:

Please write the following characters, paying special attention to the stroke order and balance of components:

校 歌 能 朋 知

■ **Tips for writing characters with one component enclosed in the other:**

• If the enclosure comes from above, the enclosed component should be slightly closer to the top stroke of the enclosure. **E.g.** 同 勞

• If the enclosure comes from below, the enclosed component should be a bit near to the bottom stroke of the enclosure, which is of medium length. **E.g.** 山

• If the enclosure comes from the left, the enclosed component must be somewhat close to it. The bottom stroke of the component must be a little longer than its top stroke.
E.g. 屋 病

• If the enclosure comes from the right, the enclosed component must be somewhat close to the upper cover stroke on the right. **E.g.** 句 可

• If the enclosure is the component "口", it must be of rectangular shape, and the enclosed component stands in the middle and should be made well-balanced and plump. **E.g.** 四

漢字書寫
CHINESE WRITING SYSTEM

Practice:

Please write the following characters, paying special attention to the stroke order and balance of components:

同 句 四 山 屋

■ Other tips to note:

• If the component on the left starts with a dot stroke, the dot should not be placed too much to the left. **E.g.** 站

• If the character has a dot stroke above the right upper cover, it should not be placed too far away. **E.g.** 球

• The "阝" component on the left must be comparatively smaller. **E.g.** 院

• The "阝" component on the right must be comparatively larger. **E.g.** 那

• The character "口", whether standing by itself or forming part of a character, must not be in the shape of a square "口" but a trapezium "口" with the top always wider than the bottom. **E.g.** 和

• All the components, "宀", "穴", "人", "夂", "文", and "夫" must be big enough to cover the bottom component. **E.g.** 室 窗 舍 冬 齐 春

• All the bottom components "心", "女", and "皿" must be big enough to support the top component. **E.g.** 感 要 篮

35

- All the components of "辶", "廴", "走" and "是" must be big enough to hold all the strokes of the other component. E.g. 遍 建 起 匙

Practice:

Please write the following characters, paying special attention to the stroke order and balance of components:

站 球 院 那 和 舍 要 起

LESSON 1 新學生

　　今天天氣很好，不冷不熱，新同學都很高興。Robert 是美國學生。他有很多同學，有美國同學，還有外國同學。他有一個中國同學，姓張，叫張一中。張一中是上海人。Robert 還有一個英國同學，叫 Alex，是倫敦人。Robert 和 Alex 都很喜歡中國，也都很喜歡中文。Robert 還有一個中國朋友，姓王，叫王小小。王小小不是上海人，是北京人。他也是中國留學生。

1 (At registration, Robert met Yizhong and Alex.)

Robert：你好！我叫 Robert。請問，你叫什麼名字？

張一中：我姓張，叫張一中。我是外國留學生，你呢？

Robert：我不是外國留學生，我是美國人。你是中國人嗎？

張一中：對，我是中國人。

Robert：我有一個朋友，叫王小小，他也是中國人。

張一中：是嗎？他是中國什麼地方人？

Robert：他是北京人。你呢？你也是北京人嗎？

張一中： 不，我不是北京人。我是上海人。

Robert： 我很喜歡中國，也很喜歡中文。

Alex： 你好！我叫 Alex，我是英國人，我也很喜歡中國和中文。

Robert： 你好！我叫 Robert。

張一中： 我叫張一中。

2 (After registration, Robert, Yizhong and Alex went outside.)

張一中： 今天天氣真好！

Alex： 是啊，不冷不熱。

Robert： 真舒服。

張一中： Robert，你是美國什麼地方人？

Robert： 美國什麼地方不冷不熱？

Alex： 你是加州人吧？

Robert： 不對，我是紐約人。

Alex： 可是紐約天氣不太好吧？

Robert： 今天呢？

張一中／Alex： 不冷不熱。（Laughing）

3

張一中： Alex，你是英國什麼地方人？

Alex： 英國什麼地方不冷不熱？

張一中： 不知道！

Alex： 我是倫敦人。一中，上海天氣好不好？

Robert： 不冷不熱，對不對？

張一中： 上海天氣不太好，很熱！

……

Alex： 認識你們很高興，再見！

張一中／Robert： 再見！

……

Lesson 1 新學生

VOCABULARY

1	新	新	xīn	Adj.	new
2	*學生	学生	xuésheng	N.	student
3	*今天	今天	jīntiān	TW	today
4	天氣	天气	tiānqì	N.	weather
5	*很	很	hěn	Adv.	very
6	*好	好	hǎo	Adj.	good
7	*不	不	bù	Adv.	not
8	*冷	冷	lěng	Adj.	cold
9	熱	热	rè	Adj.	hot
10	同學	同学	tóngxué	N.	classmate
11	*都	都	dōu	Adv.	all
12	高興	高兴	gāoxìng	Adj.	happy
13	*是	是	shì	V.	to be
14	*美國	美国	Měiguó	PW	America
15	*他	他	tā	Pron.	he, him
16	*有	有	yǒu	V.	to have
17	*多	多	duō	Adj.	many
18	還	还	hái	Adv.	also
19	外國	外国	wàiguó	N.	foreign country
20	*一	一	yī	Num.	one
21	*個	个	gè	MW	used before nouns without a special classifier of their own
22	*中國	中国	Zhōngguó	PW	China
23	*姓	姓	xìng	V.	to be surnamed
24	張	张	Zhāng	PN	*surname*
25	*叫	叫	jiào	V.	to be named
26	上海	上海	Shànghǎi	PW	Shanghai
27	*人	人	rén	N.	person

注：標有*號的詞彙必须掌握讀寫。

28	英國	英国	Yīngguó	PW	Britain
29	倫敦	伦敦	Lúndūn	PW	London
30	*和	和	hé	Conj.	and
31	*喜歡	喜欢	xǐhuan	V.	to like
32	*中文	中文	Zhōngwén	N.	Chinese language
33	*朋友	朋友	péngyou	N.	friend
34	*王	王	Wáng	PN	*surname*
35	小小	小小	Xiǎoxiǎo	PN	*a name*
36	北京	北京	Běijīng	PW	Beijing
37	留學生	留学生	liúxuéshēng	N.	international student
38	你好	你好	nǐ hǎo	IE	hello
39	*我	我	wǒ	Pron.	I, me
40	請問	请问	qǐngwèn	V.	May I ask?
41	*你	你	nǐ	Pron.	you
42	*什麼	什么	shénme	Pron.	what, what kind of
43	名字	名字	míngzi	N.	name
44	*呢	呢	ne	Pt.	*particle used for inquiry*
45	*嗎	吗	ma	Pt.	*question particle*
46	對	对	duì	Adj.	correct
47	*地方	地方	dìfang	N.	place
48	*真	真	zhēn	Adv.	truly
49	啊	啊	a	Int.	*to indicate an agreement*
50	舒服	舒服	shūfu	Adj.	comfortable
51	加州	加州	Jiāzhōu	PW	California
52	紐約	纽约	Niǔyuē	PW	New York
53	*可是	可是	kěshì	Conj.	but
54	*太	太	tài	Adv.	too
55	*吧	吧	ba	Pt.	*particle showing uncertainty*
56	*知道	知道	zhīdào	V.	to know (a fact)
57	對不對	对不对	duì bu duì	IE	correct or not
58	*認識	认识	rènshi	V.	to know sb.
59	再見	再见	zàijiàn	V.	goodbye

Lesson 1 新學生

Supplementary Vocabulary:

1	的	的	de	Pt.	to indicate possessive
2	對話	对话	duìhuà	N.	dialogue
3	您	您	nín	Pron.	you (polite form of 你)
4	貴姓	贵姓	guìxìng	N.	honorable surname
5	春天	春天	chūntiān	N.	spring
6	夏天	夏天	xiàtiān	N.	summer
7	秋天	秋天	qiūtiān	N.	autumn, fall
8	冬天	冬天	dōngtiān	N.	winter
9	位	位	wèi	MW	used to show respect for people

GRAMMAR

1 Subject[1] + 很 + Adj.

Adjectives (好 "good", 冷 "cold", 熱 "hot", etc.) in Chinese can be used as *verbal expressions* (to be good, to be cold, to be hot, etc.). When used as predicates, they are also called state verbs. Since Adjectives can also be used to indicate comparison as shown in (a), usually an adverb is used to remove comparison as is shown in (b). The most commonly used adverb in this case is 很 (very), but 很 here is not necessarily a degree modifier like the English "very". The negative is formed by putting the adverb 不 before the Adjective as exemplified in (c).

漢語中的形容詞（"好""冷""熱"等）可以充當謂語。當形容詞充當謂語時又被稱爲狀態動詞。由於形容詞單獨使用時有比較義，如例（a），所以常在形容詞前使用副詞"很"以消除比較義，如例（b），但是這裡"很"不像英語中的"very"，並不一定表示程度深。否定形式則是將副詞"不"放在形容詞前，如（c）。

 a. 他好。(He is better.)

b. 他很好。(He is good/well.)

c. 他不好。(He is not good/well.)

---

[1] Subject will be abbreviated as S hereafter.

2 Topic-comment structure

A noun phrase, a verb phrase, or even a sentence can appear in a topic position. The comment, as the name indicates, is what the speaker thinks about the topic.

名詞短語、動詞短語，甚至一個句子都可出現在話題的位置，後邊的部分是説話者表達的關於話題的評論。

 a. 今天天氣很好。
(As for today's weather, it is good.)
b. 認識你們，很高興。
(As for knowing you, it is my pleasure./I am very happy to know you.)

3 S + (Adv.) + V + O

Structurally speaking, just like English, Chinese is also mainly of SVO[1] structure. However, unlike English, the position of a Chinese adverb is fixed. It can only go before the verb.

從結構來説，跟英語一樣，漢語也是以"主謂賓"結構爲主，但跟英語不同，漢語副詞的位置是固定的，副詞只能出現在動詞前邊。

 a. 我很喜歡中國。(I like China very much.)
b. 他的中國朋友都姓王。(His Chinese friends all have the surname Wang.)
c. 他不叫王小小。(His name is not Wang Xiaoxiao.)

4 A (Adv.) 是 B

是 with the meaning "to be" is by no means used in the same way as the English "to be". It only connects nouns or pronouns. Its usage is two-fold: equation and classification.

"是"雖翻譯爲"to be"，但用法與"to be"並不相同。"是"只連接名詞和代詞，表示等同或類別。

 a. 他是張一中。(He is Zhang Yizhong.)
b. 他是學生。(He is a student.)

In (a), A is exactly B, or A and B are the same; thus 是 can denote a precise "equation".

---

1 SVO=Subject+Verb+Object.

In (b), 是 suggests categorical identification, which tells us that A is a part of or a member of B. Please note that the negative form is formed by putting the adverb 不 before 是 as exemplified in (c).

例 (a) 中，A 就是 B，或者說 A 和 B 一樣，"是"表示等同。例 (b) 中"是"表示類別，A 是 B 的一部分或 A 是 B 的成員之一。請注意其否定形式是將副詞"不"放在"是"前，如例 (c)。

> **E.g.** c. 他不是留學生。(He is not an international student.)

5 A 和 B 都 (Adv.) V O

If the subjects are plural, the adverb 都, which means "both" or "all", is used.
如果主語爲複數，常會使用副詞"都"。"都"的意思是"both"或者"all"。

> **E.g.** 張一中和王小小都是中國人。
> (Zhang Yizhong and Wang Xiaoxiao are both Chinese.)

When it comes to negation, the position of 都 may indicate either total negation or partial negation:
否定時，"都"的位置將說明語義是全部否定還是部分否定：

S 都 不 VP. → Total Negation 全部否定 (None of S VP.)

> **E.g.** a. 我們都不認識他。(None of us know him.)
> b. 你們都不是新學生。(None of you are new students.)
> c. 張一中和王小小都不是英國人。
> (Neither Zhang Yizhong nor Wang Xiaoxiao is British.)

S 不 都 VP. → Partial Negation 部分否定 (Not all S VP.)

> **E.g.** a. 他們不都很高興。(Not all of them are happy.)
> b. 我們不都是新學生。(Not all of us are new students.)
> c. 新學生不都是留學生。(Not all of the new students are international students.)

6 N. / Pron. 的 NP

The particle 的 can be used to form possessive pronouns.
助詞"的"可以用於表示代詞的所屬格。

我 + 的 = my/mine   你 + 的 = your/yours   他 + 的 = his

> **E.g.** a. 你的是我的。他的也是我的。我的不是他的。我的也不是你的。
> (Yours is mine. His is mine too. Mine is not his. Mine is not yours either.)

的 is very frequently used to modify a noun to indicate possessiveness or distribution.
"的"還經常用來修飾名詞，表示領屬關係。

Pron. + 的 + N.

> **E.g.** 我的朋友 (my friend)

N. + 的 + N.

> **E.g.** 同學的朋友 (classmate's friend)

Pron. + 的 + N. + 的 + N.

> **E.g.** 我的同學的朋友 (my classmate's friend)

7 Num. + M W + N.

Another characteristic feature of the Chinese language is its use of quantifiers (hereafter referred to as measure words). In short, whenever a noun is quantified, there must be a measure word in between. While quantifiers do exist in English, e.g. "a *slice* of bread", "a *cup* of tea", "a *box* of apples", etc., they are not mandatory in a sentence.

漢語的另一個特徵就是量詞的使用。簡而言之，當名詞前有數詞修飾時，數詞與名詞間一定要有量詞。英語中也有量詞，如"a *slice* of bread""a *cup* of tea""a *box* of apples"等，但它們在句中並不都是必須的。

Numberal	Measure Word	Noun	Structure
一 a/one	個 MW	人 person	一個人 a/one person
一 a/one	個 MW	學生 student	一個學生 a/one student
一 a/one	本 běn MW	書 book	一本書 a/one book
一 a/one	杯 cup of	茶 tea	一杯茶 a/one cup of tea
一 a/one	瓶 píng bottle of	水 water	一瓶水 a/one bottle of water
一 a/one	枝 zhī MW	筆 pen	一枝筆 a/one pen

Lesson 1 新學生

8 不A不B

This pattern corresponds with the English structure "neither...nor". Quite often, A and B are monosyllabic words and antonyms.

這個句型對應於英語中的"neither...nor"。A 和 B 常常是單音節的詞, 并且是反義詞。

> **E.g.** a. 不冷不熱 (neither cold nor hot)
> b. 不大不小 (neither big nor small)

9 Question forms

There are several ways to turn a statement into a question. The most basic is to simply add the particle 嗎 to the end of a sentence.

漢語中將陳述句轉換成問句有幾種方法。最基本的方法就是在句末加助詞"嗎"。

Sentence + 嗎?

> **E.g.** 他是學生。→ 他是學生嗎?

However, our focus will be on the affirmative-negative structure.

但是，我們的重點是正反疑問句。

S V 不 V (O)?

——S V(O).
——S 不 V(O).

> **E.g.** a. 他是不是學生? (Is he a student?)
> ——是（的），他是學生。(Yes, he is a student.)
> ——不（是），他不是學生。(No, he is not a student.)
> b. 你喜(歡)不喜歡學中文? (Do you like learning Chinese?)
> ——喜歡，我喜歡學中文。(Yes, I like learning Chinese.)
> ——不(喜歡)，我不喜歡學中文。(No, I don't like learning Chinese.)
> c. 紐約天氣好不好? (Is the weather in New York good?)
> ——好，紐約天氣很好。(Yes, it is very good.)
> ——不好，紐約天氣不好。(No, it is not good.)

Also, we can have an interrogative sentence by using a wh-word like 什麼 (what). However, unlike English Wh-questions, the word order of a Chinese Wh-question will never change from that of a regular sentence. In this lesson, 什麼地方人 "Where are you from?" doesn't apply to nationality.

同時，漢語中還有一種是用疑問代詞的特殊疑問句。但不像英語中的 Wh-questions，漢語特殊疑問句的語序與一般句的相同。這課中的"什麼地方人"（where are you from?）不用於詢問國籍。

> **S 是 什麼地方人?**

> 他是 (中國) 什麼地方人?
> [Literally: he is (China) what place person?/Where is he from?]
> ——他是北京人。 (He is from Beijing.)

Sometimes, we can simply add other particles to make a question. For instance:
有時，加其他助詞也可構成問句。例如：

> **NP + 呢?**

> 王小小是中國人，張一中呢?
> (Wang Xiaoxiao is Chinese. How about Zhang Yizhong?)

The particle 呢 is mainly used to inquire more information about the item that precedes it. It is similar to the English "How about...?" question.
助詞"呢"主要表示詢問信息，與英語中的"How about...?"問句相似。

> **Sentence + 吧?**

> a. 你是中國人吧? (You are Chinese, right?)
> b. 你是留學生吧? (You are an international student, right?)

The question formed with particle 吧 denotes uncertainty.
帶助詞"吧"的疑問句表示不確定。

 Summary:

 Chinese adjectives can be used as verbs to indicate state.

 The position of adverbs is fixed: S Adv. VP

 Modifiers must precede the items that they modify.

 都 quantifies the NPs that precede it.

 There must be a measure word between the number and noun.

Time words can be put either at the beginning of a sentence or after the subject.

Lesson 1 新學生

- **Patterns:**

- Subject + 很 +Adj. ‖ 他很好。(He is good/well.)
- Topic-comment structure ‖ 今天天氣很好。(As for the weather of today, it is good.)
- S+(Adv.)+ V +O ‖ 我很喜歡中國。(I like China very much.)
- A 和 B 都 (Adv.) V O ‖ 張一中和王小小都是中國人。
  (Both Zhang Yizhong and Wang Xiaoxiao are Chinese.)
- S 都 不 VP ‖ 我們都不認識他。(None of us know him.)
- S 不 都 VP ‖ 他們不都很高興。(Not all of them are happy.)
- A (Adv.) 是 B ‖ 他不是張一中。(He is not Zhang Yizhong.)
- N. / Pron. 的 NP ‖ 你的是我的。(Yours is mine.)
- Num. + M W + N. ‖ 一個學生 (a student)
- 不 A 不 B ‖ 不冷不熱 (neither cold nor hot)
- Sentence + 嗎？ ‖ 他是學生嗎？ (Is he a student?)
- S V 不 V (O)? ‖ 你喜不喜歡我？ (Do you like me or not?)

  S V(O). ‖ 喜歡，我喜歡你。(Yes, I do.)

  S 不 V(O). ‖ 不喜歡，我不喜歡你。(No, I don't like you.)
- S 是什麼地方人？ ‖ 他是（中國）什麼地方人？ (Where is he from in China?)
- NP + 呢？ ‖ 王小小是中國人，張一中呢？
  (Wang Xiaoxiao is Chinese. How about Zhang Yizhong?)
- Sentence + 吧？ ‖ 你是中國人吧？ (You are Chinese, right?)

HOMEWORK

1 Change the following statements into questions:

① 今天天氣很好。 ➡ 今天天氣好不好？

② 我叫 Robert。 ➡

③ 我很喜歡中國。 ▸ ☐

④ 認識你們很高興。 ▸ ☐

⑤ 你不是加州人。(uncertainty) ▸ ☐

2 Please negate the following statements:

① 我很喜歡新朋友。 ▸ 我不喜歡新朋友。

② 我知道他是外國留學生。 ▸ ☐

③ 新同學都很高興。(total negation) ▸ ☐

④ 新同學都是朋友。(partial negation) ▸ ☐

⑤ 我也叫王小小。 ▸ ☐

3 Translate the following sentences into Chinese:

① What part of Britain are you from?

② His friends are my friends too.

③ My American friend has a new friend.

④ All of my classmates like the kind of weather that is neither too cold nor too hot.

Lesson 1 新學生

⑤ None of his friends are happy.

_____

⑥ Not all of my Chinese friends know your friends.

_____

4 Please organize the following groups of characters into grammatical sentences:

① 是　我　人　上海

我是上海人。

② 認識　我　也　他

_____

③ 什麼　你　地方　是　人

_____

④ 天氣　倫敦　不　好　今天

_____

⑤ 留學生　紐約　朋友　有　很多　都　也

_____

⑥ 不　喜歡　都　美國人　英國

_____

5 Please mark the pauses you hear in each of the following sentences and then read:

① Jīntiān shì shàng kè de dìyī tiān, Robert hěn xīngfèn.

② Tā de Zhōngwén lǎoshī hěn héqi, hěn piàoliang.

③ Zhōngwénbān de tóngxué hěn duō, yǒu Měiguórén、Fǎguórén、Yìdàlìrén、Yīngguórén、Déguórén、Hánguórén、Rìběnrén、Jiānádàrén、Tǔ'ěrqírén、Àodàlìyàrén, hái yǒu Zhōngguórén.

51

④ Nèi ge Yīngguórén jiù shì Alex.

⑤ Dàjiā dōu yǒu Zhōngwén míngzi le.

⑥ Robert jiào Lǐ Jiāxīng, Alex jiào Lǐ Jiāqí.

⑦ Jiāxīng hé Jiāqí yīnwèi bú huì shuō Zhōngwén, suǒyǐ xué Zhōngwén. Kěshì Zhōngguórén yě xué Zhōngwén, Jiāxīng juéde tài qíguài le!

Chinese Names

Unlike English names, Chinese surnames always come first, before the given name. Surnames are passed down from the father's side. Some people even believe that a person's given name may determine their luck in life. Usually, boys' names are suggestive of ambition, power, luck, etc., while among girls, poetic names are cherished. A typical Chinese girl's name contains characters that evoke an image of beauty and grace: flowers, clouds, leaves, etc.

In general, it is considered impolite for members of the younger generation to address their elders by name. It is also common practice to avoid naming children after their parents or ancestors. Most Chinese people prefer to have a name that is unique. Parents will spend a lot of time selecting a special and meaningful name for their new-born children.

Among some 440 family names, the 100 most common ones account for 90% of the total population. Brides in China do not adopt their husband's surnames. Among Chinese, a popular way to address each other, regardless of gender, is to add an age-related term of honor before the family name. These include: lǎo (honorable old one), xiǎo (honorable young one) or occasionally dà (honorable middle-aged one).

When people first meet, to show respect, they will usually start their conversation by asking the other party "貴姓", which means "honorable surname." The appropriate way to respond to this question is "我姓……, 名字叫……".

How do you like your Chinese name? May your Chinese name bring you good luck!

LESSON 2 上課第一天

今天是上課的第一天，Robert 很興奮。他的中文老師很和氣，很漂亮。中文班的同學很多，有美國人、法國人、意大利人、英國人、德國人、韓國人、日本人、加拿大人、土耳其人、澳大利亞人，還有中國人。那個英國人就是 Alex。大家都有中文名字了，Robert 叫李家興，Alex 叫李家奇。家興和家奇因爲不會説中文，所以學中文。可是中國人也學中文，家興覺得太奇怪了！

1

王老師： 大家好！我姓王，叫王文英。我是中國人，是你們的中文老師。請問，你貴姓？你是哪國人？

Robert： 我叫 Robert，我是美國人。老師，我想要一個中文名字。

王老師： 好，你姓李，叫李家興。

Alex： 我叫 Alex……我的中文名字也叫李家興，我是英國人。

王老師： 一樣的名字不太好。你叫李家奇，好不好？

Alex： 好吧。

……

李家興：	老師，太好了，我們有意大利朋友、法國朋友、德國朋友、韓國朋友、日本朋友、加拿大朋友、土耳其朋友、澳大利亞朋友、中國朋友……
李家奇：	家興，還有英國朋友。
李家興：	你不是我的朋友……
李家奇：	什麼？我不是你的朋友？
李家興：	對，你不是我的朋友，你是我的家人。
李家奇：	家人？我不叫家人，也不是你的。
李家興：	哈哈，家人就是一家人！
李家奇：	對，對，我是你哥哥，你是我弟弟。

2

李家興：	家奇，你喜歡不喜歡我們的中文老師？
李家奇：	很喜歡。我覺得她很好，很和氣，也很……
李家興：	也很漂亮，對不對？
李家奇：	對。我也很喜歡中文班的同學。
李家興：	家奇，我們因為不會說中文，所以學中文。可是中國人也學中文，我覺得太奇怪了！
李家奇：	他們不是中國人，他們是華裔美國人。
李家興：	他們也不會說中文？
李家奇：	不會，很多華裔美國人都不會說中文。

3

李家興：	一中，你好！
張一中：	Robert，Alex，是你們啊！你們好！
李家奇：	我不叫Alex了。
張一中：	你不叫Alex了？
李家奇：	我們有中文名字了，我叫李家奇，他叫李家興。
李家興：	你覺得我們的中文名字好不好？
張一中：	好，真好！
李家興：	中文班的同學都有中文名字了。
張一中：	中文班的同學都是哪國人？

Lesson 2　上課第一天

李家奇：　我是英國人，他是美國人……

李家興：　還有法國人、意大利人、日本人，還有……還有……

李家奇：　還有韓國人，還有華裔美國人。

張一中：　太好了，你們有新朋友了。

李家興：　你是我們的好朋友。

VOCABULARY

1	上	上	shàng	V.	to go to
2	課	课	kè	N.	course, class, lesson
3	*上課	上课	shàng kè	V.-O.	to go to class
4	*的	的	de	Pt.	*particle indicating possessive*
5	*第一	第一	dìyī	Num.	the first
6	天	天	tiān	MW	day
7	*興奮	兴奋	xīngfèn	Adj.	excited
8	*老師	老师	lǎoshī	N.	teacher
9	和氣	和气	héqi	Adj.	gentle
10	漂亮	漂亮	piàoliang	Adj.	beautiful
11	*班	班	bān	N.	class
12	法國	法国	Fǎguó	PW	France
13	意大利	意大利	Yìdàlì	PW	Italy
14	德國	德国	Déguó	PW	German
15	韓國	韩国	Hánguó	PW	Korea
16	日本	日本	Rìběn	PW	Japan
17	加拿大	加拿大	Jiānádà	PW	Canada
18	土耳其	土耳其	Tǔ'ěrqí	PW	Turkey
19	澳大利亞	澳大利亚	Àodàlìyà	PW	Australia
20	*那	那	nà/nèi	Pron.	that
21	*就	就	jiù	Adv.	just, then
22	*大家	大家	dàjiā	Pron.	everybody
23	李	李	Lǐ	PN	*surname*
24	家興	家兴	Jiāxīng	PN	*Chinese name*

走近中國——初級漢語教程
APPROACHING CHINA : ELEMENTARY CHINESE

25	家奇	家奇	Jiāqí	PN	*Chinese name*
26	*因爲	因为	yīnwèi	Conj.	because
27	*會	会	huì	V.	can
28	*所以	所以	suǒyǐ	Conj.	therefore
29	*覺得	觉得	juéde	V.	to feel, to think
30	*奇怪	奇怪	qíguài	Adj.	strange
31	*了	了	le	Pt.	*particle indicating a change of state*
32	文英	文英	Wényīng	PN	*Chinese name*
33	*你們	你们	nǐmen	Pron.	you (plural)
34	貴姓	贵姓	guìxìng	N.	honorable surname
35	*哪	哪	nǎ/něi	Pron.	which
36	*想	想	xiǎng	Aux. V.	would like to, to miss, to think
37	*要	要	yào	V.	need
38	*一樣	一样	yíyàng	Adj.	same
39	家人	家人	jiārén	N.	family
40	哈哈	哈哈	hāhā	Int.	*sound of laughter*
41	*哥哥	哥哥	gēge	N.	elder brother
42	*弟弟	弟弟	dìdi	N.	younger brother
43	我們	我们	wǒmen	Pron.	we, us
44	*她	她	tā	Pron.	she, her
45	華裔	华裔	huáyì	N.	overseas Chinese

■ Supplementary Vocabulary:

1	說話	说话	shuō huà	V.-O.	to speak, to talk
2	好看	好看	hǎokàn	Adj.	good-looking
3	菜	菜	cài	N.	dish (cooked), vegetable
4	書	书	shū	N.	book(s)
5	衣服	衣服	yīfu	N.	clothes, clothing
6	水	水	shuǐ	N.	water
7	筆	笔	bǐ	N.	pen, writing tools
8	本子	本子	běnzi	N.	notebook

Lesson 2 上課第一天

9	枝	枝	zhī	MW	*measure word for stick-like objects*
10	本	本	běn	MW	*measure word for books*
11	件	件	jiàn	MW	*measure word for clothes*
12	瓶	瓶	píng	MW	*bottle*

GRAMMAR

1 很 Adj. 的 N

的 is very often used as a non-modifier. It creates a link between an adjective and a noun. In English, this is done simply by putting the adjective before the noun: "hot food", "cold weather". In Chinese, the adjective and the noun usually need be linked by 的.

"的"常作爲助詞，用在定語後面，使定語和中心詞之間產生聯繫。英語將形容詞置於名詞前就能產生這種聯繫，如"hot water""cold water"。但在漢語中，定語和中心詞之間一般要有"的"聯接。

> **E.g.** 很熱的飯菜 (hot food)   很冷的天氣 (cold weather)

2 Pronouns

So far we have encountered most of the common Chinese pronouns, which are listed below in the following tables for your reference:

迄今爲止，漢語中的常見代詞我們都已經接觸過了。現在我們將這些代詞列表如下，以備參考：

Person	Characters	Pronunciation	Notes
First	我	wǒ	I; me
Second	你 / 您 [1]	nǐ/nín	you/ you (showing respect)
Third	他，她	tā, tā	he, she

---

[1] The pronoun 您 nín is used as a formal version of the second person pronoun, showing politeness. But it is not used in the plural.

The collective pronouns are formed by simply adding 們 [1] to the end of each pronoun; thus, 你們, 我們, 他/她們 would mean "you (plural)", "we" and "they" respectively.
集合代詞是在每個代詞後面加上"們",因此"我們""你們""他/她們"就分別表示"你""我""他/她"的複數。

Person	Characters	Pronunciation	Meaning
First	我們	wǒmen	we; us
Second	你們	nǐmen	you
Third	他們, 她們	tāmen, tāmen	they; them

To indicate possession, 的 is appended to the pronoun in Chinese.
漢語中在代詞後面加"的"表示所有格。

Person	Characters	Pronunciation	Notes
First	我的	wǒ de	my; mine
Second	你的 / 您的	nǐ de / nín de	your; yours
Third	他的, 她的	tā de, tā de	his, her/hers

3 Ordinal numbers: 第 + number

The ordinal prefix 第 makes a number become an ordinal one. For instance, 一 (one) will become 第一 (the first) with the prefix 第.
數詞加上前綴"第"構成序數詞。例如,"一"加上前綴"第",構成"第一"。

> **E.g.** a. 我的第一個朋友是美國人。(My first friend is an American.)
> b. 他的第一個中文老師很和氣。(His first Chinese teacher is very nice.)

4 S 覺得 + Sentence

覺得 is used a lot when expressing personal opinions.
"覺得"常被用來表達個人的觀點。

> **E.g.** 他覺得中文老師很和氣。
> (He thinks that the Chinese teacher is very gentle and nice.)

The negative form is:
其否定形式是:

---

[1] 們 men can also be used to plurize human nouns (學生們). Non-human nouns can't take 們. Once a noun is plurized by 們, it becomes definite in reference and is incompatible with the "Num. + MW + N." structure.

Lesson 2　上課第一天

S 不覺得 + Sentence

This form is often used to show contrast.
此句型被用來表達對比的不同觀點。

 a. 他覺得很冷，可是我不覺得冷。
(He thinks it is cold, but I don't think it is very cold.)
b. 我的朋友說中文很好學，可是我不覺得中文好學。
(My friend says that Chinese is easy to learn, but I don't think so.)

5 (S) 有 A, (有) B, (有) C, 還有 D

This structure means "somebody has A, B, C, and as well as D". The verb 有 before B, C is optional but the first and last one are obligatory.
這個結構表示某人有 A、B、C，還有 D。B、C 前面的動詞"有"可以選擇性使用，但是第一個事物（A）和最後一個事物（D）的前面必須要加動詞"有"。

 a. 中文班的同學很多，有美國人、法國人、意大利人、英國人、韓國人、日本人，還有中國人。
(There are a lot of students in Chinese class. There are Americans, French, Italians, British, Koreans, Japanese and also Chinese.)
b. 我們有意大利朋友、法國朋友、韓國朋友、日本朋友、中國朋友，還有英國朋友。
(We have Italian friends, French friends, Korean friends, Japanese friends, Chinese friends, and also British friends.)

6 A 就是 B

The adverb 就 here is used to emphasize the fact that A is exactly B.
這裡的副詞"就"用來強調 A 恰好正是 B 這一事實。

 a. 那個英國人就是 Alex。[That British person is Alex (the Alex you have heard of.)]
b. 我就是我，不是你。(I am just myself, not you.)
c. 你的就是我的。(What's yours is mine.)

7 因為 A，所以 B

In English, it is common to say "I want to learn Chinese, because I don't know how to speak it". In Chinese, it is far more common to turn it around and say "Because (因為) I don't know how to speak Chinese, therefore (所以) I want to learn it."

英語中常說"我想學漢語，因爲我不會說漢語"，但漢語中更常見的是把兩句話的順序顛倒過來，說"因爲我不會說漢語，所以我想學漢語"。

 a. 因爲我不會說中國話，所以我想學中文。
(Literally：Because I not can speak Chinese, so I want to learn Chinese. / I want to learn Chinese because I don't know how to speak it.)
b. 因爲 Robert 和 Alex 是好朋友，所以他們想要一樣的名字。
(Since Robert and Alex are good friends, they want to have the same name.)

8 S(不)會/想 VP

Both 會 and 想 can be used as auxiliary/modal verbs as well as main verbs. In this pattern, they belong to the first category.
"會"和"想"做助動詞/情態動詞的同時，也都可以做實義動詞。在這個句型中，它們的詞性屬於前者。

 a. 外國人不會說中國話。(Foreigners can't speak Chinese.)
b. 我們不想要一樣的名字。(We don't want to have the same name.)
c. 我想學中文。(I want to learn Chinese.)

When 想 and 要 are used together, namely, 想要, it means "would like to have sth.". Thus it usually takes a noun phrase as its object. When 想 means "want to do sth.", it is followed by a verb phrase.
當"想"和"要"同時使用，也就是用作"想要"時，它可以表示"希望擁有某物"，後面常接名詞短語做賓語。當"想"表示"要做某事"時，後面常接動詞短語。

S 想要 NP.

 我們想要一樣的名字。(We would like to have the same name.)

S 想 VP.

 我想學中文。(I want to learn Chinese.)

會 used as main verb only means that a person has acquired a specific language or skill by learning.
"會"用作實義動詞時只表示某人已經通過學習掌握了某種語言或技巧。

 a. 我會中文。(I know Chinese.)
b. 他會書法。(He can do calligraphy.)

想 used as a main verb means "to miss somebody" or "to think."
"想"用作實義動詞時，表示"想念某人"或者"思考、認爲"。

> E.g. a. 我想你。(I miss you.)
> b. 我想他會中文。(I think that he knows Chinese.)

Please note that when 想 means "to think", it can never be negated directly. If it is negated directly, this would mean that the action of thinking never happens. When saying "I don't think that...", the negator 不 can only appear in the embedded clause.
注意，當"想"意爲"思考、認爲"的時候，永遠不可以直接否定。如果直接否定，就表示這個動作從來沒有發生過。所以在表達"I don't think that..."時，否定詞"不"只能插入從句中。

> E.g. 我想他不會中文。(I don't think that he knows Chinese.)

 太 Adj. 了

This pattern indicates excessiveness. It can have either a positive or a negative connotation depending on the meaning of the adjective.
這個句型表示"格外、極度"。由於形容詞的意義不同，這個句型既可以表示積極意義，也可以表示消極意義。

> E.g. a. 太好了！(It is great!)
> b. 太對了！(You are so right!)
> c. 太奇怪了！(It is so strange!)
> d. 太熱了！(It is too hot!)
> e. 太貴了！(It is too expensive!)

When it is negated, 了 is dropped.
否定時，要去掉"了"。

> E.g. a. 不太好。(Not that good.)
> b. 不太對。(Not quite right.)

 S VP 了

The modal particle 了 has many functions. In this lesson, we are dealing with the particle 了 occurring at the end of a sentence, the function of which is to indicate a change of state.
情態助詞"了"有很多功能。本課，我們學習的是句末助詞"了"，它表示一種狀態的改變。

a. 我認識你了。[I know you now (but I did not know you earlier.)]
b. 我喜歡學中文了。[Now I like learning Chinese (but I didn't earlier.)]

When 了 appears at the end of the negative statement, it means "not... any more", or "no longer...".
當"了"出現在否定句的句末時，表示"不再"。

S 不 VP 了.

 a. 我不喜歡學中文了。(I don't like studying Chinese anymore.)
b. 我不是美國人了。(I am not an American anymore.)
c. 我不叫 Alex 了。(My name is not Alex anymore.)
d. 我沒有朋友了。(I don't have any friends anymore.)
e. 我沒 (méi) 有錢了。(As of now, I have no money.)

NOTE: Although the last two sentences do not contain 不, they are still the negative patterns, because of the special case of the verb 有 which is always negated by 沒.
注意：儘管最後兩個句子不含否定詞"不"，但它們仍是否定結構，因為動詞"有"是用"沒"來否定的。

11 Question forms

您貴姓？(What is your honorable surname?)

To answer this question, you may just tell the person your surname or your full name. You are never expected to answer the question by saying: 我貴姓王.
回答這一問題，只告訴對方你的姓或者全名，永遠都不要回答對方"我貴姓王"。

 ——您貴姓？(What is your honorable surname?)
——我姓王，我叫王小小。(My surname is Wang. My full name is Wang Xiaoxiao.)

您是哪國人？(Which country are you from? / What's your nationality?)

 ——您是哪國人？(Which country are you from? / What's your nationality?)
——我是法國人。(I am from France. / I am French.)
——我是韓國人。(I am from Korea.)
——我是意大利人。(I am Italian.)
——我是日本人。(I am Japanese.)

NOTE: Don't say 我是意大利國人。
注意：不要說"我是意大利國人"。

Lesson 2　上課第一天

Summary:

▶ The ordinal prefix 第 makes a number become an ordinal.

▶ 因爲 precedes 所以.

▶ 了 indicates a change of state.

▶ When 想 means "to think", it can never be negated directly.

▶ 太 goes with 了 unless it is negated.

Patterns:

- S（不）覺得 + Sentence ‖ 他覺得中文老師很和氣。
  (He thinks that the Chinese teacher is very gentle.)

- S 有 A，（有）B，（有）C，還有 D ‖ 中文班的同學很多：有美國人、法國人、意大利人、英國人、韓國人、日本人，還有中國人。
  (There are a lot of students in Chinese class. There are Americans, French, Italians, Koreans, Japanese and also Chinese.)

- A 就是 B ‖ 我就是我，不是你。(I am just myself, not you.)

- 因爲 A，所以 B ‖ 因爲我不會說中國話，所以我想學中文。
  (I want to learn Chinese because I can't speak it.)

- S (不) 會/想 VP ‖ 外國人不會說中國話。(Foreigners can't speak Chinese.)
  　　　　　　　　我們不想要一樣的名字。(We don't want to have the same name.)

- S 想要 NP ‖ 他們想要一樣的名字。(They would like to have the same name.)

- S 想 VP ‖ 我想學中文。(I want to learn Chinese.)

- 太 Adj. 了 ‖ 太好了！(Great!)

- S VP 了 ‖ 我喜歡學中文了。(Now I like learning Chinese.)

- S 不 VP 了 ‖ 我不是美國人了。(I am not an American any more.)

- 您貴姓？ ‖ ——您貴姓？ (What is your honorable surname?)
  　　　　　　——我姓王，我叫王小小。
  　　　　　　(My surname is Wang. My full name is Wang Xiaoxiao.)

- 您是哪國人？ ‖ ——您是哪國人？ (What is your nationality?)
  　　　　　　　——我是中國人。 (I am Chinese.)

走近中國──初級漢語教程
APPROACHING CHINA : ELEMENTARY CHINESE

IN CLASS ACTIVITIES

1 Complete the following sentences according to the information given in the text:

① 今天是上課的第一天，Robert _____

② 中文老師 _____

③ 大家都有 _____

④ 家興和家奇因爲不會説中文，所以 _____

⑤ 李家興覺得中國人也學中文，就 _____

⑥ 很多華裔美國人都不會 _____

2 Please do role play according to the dialogues given below:

A: 你好！我姓_____，叫_____。請問，您貴姓？您是哪國人？
B: 我姓_____。我叫_____。我是_____人。請問，您是哪國人？
A: 我是_____。你是_____什麼地方人？
B: 我是紐約人。你呢？你是_____國什麼地方人？
A: 我是_____人。對了，你的中文老師是哪國人？
B: 我的中文老師是中國人。
A: 她是中國什麼地方人？
B: 她説她是北京人。

Lesson 2 上課第一天

A 你們中文班的同學都是哪國人？
B 我們中文班的同學有法國人、英國人、意大利人、韓國人、日本人，還有華裔美國人。

A 請問，你的中文名字是什麼？
B 我的中文名字是_____。你的呢？
A 我的中文名字是_____。你喜不喜歡你的中文名字？
B 我很喜歡我的中文名字。你喜不喜歡你的中文名字？
A 我也很喜歡。
B 認識你很高興。再見！
A 認識你我也很高興。再見！

HOMEWORK

1 Rewrite the following statements by adding 了：

① 今天天氣很好。 ➡ 今天天氣好了。

② 我叫 Robert。 ➡

③ 我很喜歡中國。 ➡

④ 我沒有中文名字。 ➡

⑤ 中文老師很和氣。 ➡

2 Please negate the following statements indicating not anymore:

① 我很喜歡新朋友。 ➡ 我不喜歡新朋友了。

走近中國——初級漢語教程
APPROACHING CHINA : ELEMENTARY CHINESE

❷ 我是你的老師。 ➡ _____

❸ 他會說中國話。 ➡ _____

❹ 你是我的朋友。 ➡ _____

❺ 他們想要一樣的名字。 ➡ _____

3 Translate the following sentences into Chinese:

❶ What is your nationality?

_____

❷ It is so strange! My Chinese teacher can't speak Chinese anymore.

_____

❸ My Italian friend wants to learn Chinese.

_____

❹ I know he knows Chinese.

_____

❺ I don't think his Chinese name is good.

_____

❻ I can speak Chinese because I have many Chinese friends.

_____

4 Please organize the following groups of characters into grammatical sentences:

❶ 是 我 人 上海

我是上海人。

Lesson 2 上課第一天

② 天　的　上課　今天　第一　是

③ 哪　你　國　老師　的　是　人

④ 很　的　同學　班　多　中文

⑤ 有　我們　名字　了　中文

⑥ 我　也　好看　覺得　她　很

5 Please mark the pauses you hear in each of the following sentences and then read:

① Lǐ Jiāxīng jiā yǒu wǔ kǒu rén: fùqīn、mǔqīn、gēge、jiějie hé tā.

② Tā fùqīn shì yīshēng, mǔqīn shì lǎoshī, gēge shì yánjiūshēng, jiějie shì dàxuéshēng.

③ Tā fùqīn yīnwèi gōngzuò máng, hěn xīnkǔ, suǒyǐ měi tiān wǎnshang dōu juéde hěn lèi, bù xiǎng shuō huà, bù xiǎng kàn bào, yě bù xiǎng kàn diànshì.

④ Tā mǔqīn suīrán yě hěn máng, kěshì cónglái bù juéde lèi.

⑤ Měi tiān tā mǔqīn dōu zuò hěn duō hǎochī de fàn cài. Zhōngguócài、Fǎguócài、Yìdàlìcài, tā dōu huì zuò.

⑥ Yīnwèi Jiāxīng shì lǎoxiǎo, rén yòu cōngmíng, suǒyǐ tā mǔqīn tèbié xǐhuan tā.

⑦ Lǐ Jiāqí jiā yǒu liù kǒu rén: bàba、māma、liǎng ge dìdi、yí ge mèimei, hái yǒu tā.

⑧ Jiāqí shì lǎodà. Tā bàba shì zuò shēngyi de, yě hěn máng, hěn xīnkǔ, jiā lǐ rén dōu jiào tā dà máng rén.

⑨ Yīnwèi dìdimèimei hěn xiǎo, suǒyǐ tā māma bù gōngzuò, zài jiā zhàogù dìdi mèimei.

⑩ Tóngxué shuō, yīnwèi tā bàba hěn yǒuqián, suǒyǐ tā māma bù gōngzuò.

⑪ Jiāqí shuō bú duì, shì yīnwèi tāmen jiā qián bú gòu, suǒyǐ bù néng qǐng rén zhàogù tā de dìdimèimei.

Overseas Chinese

華僑 huáqiáo, or 華裔 huáyì are ethnic Chinese people who live outside of China. Regardless of where they originally came from, mainland China, Taiwan, Hong Kong or Macau, they are all referred to as "overseas Chinese."

Strictly speaking, these two words in Mandarin for overseas Chinese have subtle differences in meaning. 華僑 refers to overseas Chinese who were born in China, while 華裔 refers to any overseas Chinese with a Chinese ancestry.

There are approximately 34 million overseas Chinese mostly living in Southeast Asia where they constitute a majority of the population in Singapore and significant minority populations in Malaysia, Indonesia, Thailand, Vietnam and the Philippines. The Chinese populations in these areas arrived between the 16th and the 19th centuries, mostly from the maritime provinces of Guangdong, Fujian, and, later on, Hainan.

More recent emigration from the mid-19th century onward has been directed primarily to western countries such as the United States, Canada, Australia and New Zealand, as well as South America.

LESSON 3　我的家

　　李家興家有五口人：父親、母親、哥哥、姐姐和他。他父親是醫生，母親是老師，哥哥是研究生，姐姐是大學生。他父親因為工作忙，很辛苦，所以每天晚上都覺得很累，不想說話，不想看報，也不想看電視。他母親雖然也很忙，可是從來不覺得累。每天他母親都做很多好吃的飯菜。中國菜、法國菜、意大利菜，她都會做。因為家興是老小，人又聰明，所以他母親特別喜歡他。

　　李家奇家有六口人：爸爸、媽媽、兩個弟弟、一個妹妹，還有他。家奇是老大。他爸爸是做生意的，也很忙，很辛苦，家裡人都叫他大忙人。因為弟弟妹妹很小，所以他媽媽不工作，在家照顧弟弟妹妹。同學說，因為他爸爸很有錢，所以他媽媽不工作。家奇說不對，是因為他們家錢不夠，所以不能請人照顧他的弟弟妹妹。

1

王老師：今天我們要介紹一下自己的家庭，誰先說？
李家興：王老師，我先說吧！

王老師： 好，家興，請你先說。(To the class) 你們可以問問題。

李家興： 大家好！

同學： 你好！

李家興： 我家一共有六口人：父親、母親、哥哥、姐姐、我和我的狗弟弟。

李家奇： 狗也是人嗎？

李家興： 狗雖然不是人，可是它跟我們的親人一樣。

同學： 請問，你父親是做什麼的？

李家興： 我父親是醫生。

同學： 你母親呢？

李家興： 我母親是老師。

同學： 請問，你母親是教什麼的？

李家興： 她是教音樂的。

同學： 你哥哥和姐姐是做什麼的？

李家興： 我哥哥和姐姐都是學生，哥哥是研究生，姐姐和我一樣，也是大學生。

同學： 你父親工作忙不忙？

李家興： 我父親工作很忙，很辛苦。每天晚上他都覺得很累，不想說話，不想看報，也不想看電視。

同學： 請問，你母親的工作也很累，很辛苦嗎？

李家興： 是的。雖然母親的工作也很忙，可是她從來不覺得累。每天她都做很多好吃的飯菜。中國菜、法國菜、意大利菜，她都會做。我覺得母親特別喜歡我。她常說："家興是老小，人又聰明，又可愛……"

同學： 你是很可愛。

李家興： 謝謝大家，謝謝！

2

李家奇： 我叫李家奇，我是英國人。

李家興： 請問，你家有幾口人？

李家奇： 我家也有六口人：爸爸、媽媽、一個妹妹、兩個弟弟，還有我。

同學： 請問，你爸爸是做什麼的？

李家奇： 他是做生意的。

Lesson 3　我的家

同學：　他的工作忙不忙？

李家奇：　他的工作很忙，我們都叫他大忙人。

同學：　那你媽媽是做什麼的？

李家奇：　我媽媽不工作。

同學：　為什麼？

李家奇：　因為弟弟妹妹還很小，我媽媽在家照顧他們，所以她不工作。

李家興：　因為你爸爸很有錢，所以你媽媽不工作，對吧？

李家奇：　不對，不對，是因為我們家錢不夠，所以不能請人照顧弟弟妹妹。

3

李家興：　一中，給我們介紹一下你的家庭，好不好？

張一中：　好的。

李家奇：　你家有幾口人？

張一中：　我家有七口人：爺爺、奶奶、父親、母親、兩個姐姐，還有我。

李家興：　不對，不對，你的爺爺奶奶是一家，所以你家只有五口人。

張一中：　中國人的家庭是大家庭。爺爺奶奶只有一個兒子，就是我爸爸。所以爺爺奶奶和我們是一家人。

李家興：　我明白了。

李家奇：　和爺爺奶奶在一起，一定很幸福吧？

張一中：　是啊，爺爺奶奶特別愛我。

李家興：　他們叫你小可愛，對不對？

張一中：　呵呵，他們叫我小寶寶。

李家奇：　你有兩個姐姐，你是你們家的寶貝。

張一中：　我爸爸媽媽覺得兒子女兒都一樣，可是我爺爺奶奶只有我這一個孫子。

李家興：　我的爺爺奶奶也很愛我，可是他們有自己的事情，太忙了。

李家奇：　家興、一中，你們都是老小。我是老大，我跟你們不太一樣。我很會照顧我自己和我的弟弟妹妹，所以他們都叫我"小大人"。

張一中：　那我們就叫你老大吧！

李家興：　家奇，你弟弟妹妹有你這樣的哥哥一定很幸福。

VOCABULARY

1	*五	五	wǔ	Num.	five
2	*口	口	kǒu	MW	*measure word for population*
3	*父親	父亲	fùqīn	N.	father (formal)
4	*母親	母亲	mǔqīn	N.	mother (formal)
5	*姐姐	姐姐	jiějie	N.	elder sister
6	醫生	医生	yīshēng	N.	doctor
7	研究生	研究生	yánjiūshēng	N.	graduate student
8	大學生	大学生	dàxuéshēng	N.	college student
9	*工作	工作	gōngzuò	N.	work
10	*忙	忙	máng	Adj.	busy
11	辛苦	辛苦	xīnkǔ	Adj.	laborious
12	*每	每	měi	Pron.	each
13	晚上	晚上	wǎnshang	TW	evening
14	*累	累	lèi	Adj.	tired
15	*說話	说话	shuō huà	V.-O.	to speak, to talk
16	*看	看	kàn	V.	to read
17	報	报	bào	N.	newspaper
18	電視	电视	diànshì	N.	T.V.
19	*雖然	虽然	suīrán	Conj.	although
20	從來	从来	cónglái	Adv.	never
21	*做	做	zuò	V.	to make, to do
22	*好吃	好吃	hǎochī	Adj.	delicious
23	*飯	饭	fàn	N.	food
24	*菜	菜	cài	N.	dish (of food)
25	老小	老小	lǎoxiǎo	N.	the youngest child
26	*又	又	yòu	Adv.	furthermore
27	聰明	聪明	cōngmíng	Adj.	smart
28	特別	特别	tèbié	Adv.	especially
29	*六	六	liù	Num.	six
30	*爸爸	爸爸	bàba	N.	dad
31	*媽媽	妈妈	māma	N.	mom

Lesson 3 我的家

32	*兩	两	liǎng	Num.	two (when followed by a measure word)
33	妹妹	妹妹	mèimei	N.	young sister
34	老大	老大	lǎodà	N.	the first child
35	生意	生意	shēngyi	N.	business
36	裡	里	lǐ	N.	in, inside
37	小	小	xiǎo	Adj.	young
38	*在	在	zài	Prep.	to be at
39	照顧	照顾	zhàogù	V.	to take care of
40	有錢	有钱	yǒu qián	VP	to be rich
41	錢	钱	qián	N.	money
42	*夠	够	gòu	V.	enough
43	*能	能	néng	Aux.V.	can
44	請人	请人	qǐng rén	VP	to hire sb.
45	要	要	yào	Aux.V	will
46	介紹	介绍	jièshào	V.	to introduce
47	*一下	一下	yíxià	Q.	a little bit
48	*自己	自己	zìjǐ	Pron.	self
49	家庭	家庭	jiātíng	N.	family
50	*誰	谁	shéi/shuí	Pron.	who
51	*先	先	xiān	Adv.	first
52	說	说	shuō	V.	to speak, to say
53	可以	可以	kěyǐ	Aux.V.	may
54	問	问	wèn	V.	to ask
55	*問題	问题	wèntí	N.	question
56	*一共	一共	yígòng	Adv.	altogether
57	狗	狗	gǒu	N.	dog
58	*跟	跟	gēn	Prep.	with, from
59	親人	亲人	qīnrén	N.	close relative
60	*教	教	jiāo	V.	to teach
61	*音樂	音乐	yīnyuè	N.	music
62	常（常）	常（常）	cháng(cháng)	Adv.	often
63	可愛	可爱	kě'ài	Adj.	being adorable
64	謝謝	谢谢	xièxie	V.	Thank you.

65	* 幾	几	jǐ	Pron.	how many
66	爲什麽	为什么	wèi shénme	IE	why
67	* 爺爺	爷爷	yéye	N.	grandfather
68	* 奶奶	奶奶	nǎinai	N.	grandmother
69	* 只	只	zhǐ	Adv.	only
70	* 兒子	儿子	érzi	N.	son
71	* 明白	明白	míngbai	V.	to be clear
72	一起	一起	yìqǐ	N.	together
73	一定	一定	yídìng	Adv.	definitely
74	幸福	幸福	xìngfú	Adj.	happy
75	愛	爱	ài	V.	to love
76	呵呵	呵呵	hēhē	Int.	*a sound made in imitation of laughter*
77	寶寶	宝宝	bǎobao	N.	baby
78	寶貝	宝贝	bǎobèi	N.	sweet heart
79	* 女兒	女儿	nǚ'ér	N.	daughter
80	* 這	这	zhè; zhèi	Pron.	this
81	孫子	孙子	sūnzi	N.	grandson
82	事情	事情	shìqing	N.	things
83	這樣	这样	zhèyàng	Pron.	this kind of

■ Supplementary Vocabulary:

1	分鐘	分钟	fēnzhōng	TW	minute
2	鐘頭	钟头	zhōngtóu	TW	hour (colloquial)
3	小時	小时	xiǎoshí	TW	hour (formal)
4	星期	星期	xīngqī	TW	week
5	月	月	yuè	TW	month
6	年	年	nián	TW	year
7	西班牙文	西班牙文	Xībānyáwén	N.	Spanish (language)
8	俄文	俄文	Éwén	N.	Russian (language)
9	談	谈	tán	V.	to talk
10	等	等	děng	V.	to wait

Lesson 3 我的家

11	住	住	zhù	V.	to live (at a place)
12	休息	休息	xiūxi	V.	to rest
13	游泳	游泳	yóu yǒng	V.-O.	to swim
14	走路	走路	zǒu lù	V.-O.	to walk
15	喝酒	喝酒	hē jiǔ	V.-O.	to drink
16	睡覺	睡觉	shuì jiào	V.-O.	to sleep
17	跳舞	跳舞	tiào wǔ	V.-O.	to dance
18	唱歌	唱歌	chàng gē	V.-O.	to sing
19	看電影	看电影	kàn diànyǐng	VP	to see a movie
20	聽音樂	听音乐	tīng yīnyuè	VP	to listen to music
21	踢足球	踢足球	tī zúqiú	VP	to play football
22	打籃球	打篮球	dǎ lánqiú	VP	to play basketball
23	打網球	打网球	dǎ wǎngqiú	VP	to play tennis

GRAMMAR

1 Numbers

The Chinese numeration system has characters that correspond to the numbers zero to nine. Unlike the number system you are used to in English, the Chinese system also has special characters to represent ten, a hundred, a thousand, ten thousand, as well as other multiples.

漢語中的計數系統由與 0 到 9 相對應的漢字組合而成。與英語的數字系統不同，漢語的計數系統中有單獨的漢字表示 10、100、1000、10000，以及其他倍數。

Arabic	Chinese	Pronunciation	English
1	一	yī	one
2	二	èr	two
3	三	sān	three
4	四	sì	four
5	五	wǔ	five
6	六	liù	six

（續表）

Arabic	Chinese	Pronunciation	English
7	七	qī	seven
8	八	bā	eight
9	九	jiǔ	nine
10	十	shí	ten
11	十一	shíyī	eleven
20	二十	èrshí	twenty
21	二十一	èrshíyī	twenty one
99	九十九	jiǔshíjiǔ	ninety nine
100	一百	yìbǎi	one hundred
1,000	一千	yìqiān	one thousand

The number 35 is written in Chinese using the characters 三, 十, and 五 together as 三十五. In Chinese you need to say that you have "3 tens" first. "3 tens" is how 30 is represented. Once you have the tens in place, you can finish writing the number with the character for 5. Chinese has no character for ones, but a character is used for the other place values. These characters are strictly necessary; you cannot write 35 as 三五. Likewise, 896 is written in Chinese as 8 hundreds, 9 tens, and 6: 八百九十六.

漢語使用"三""十"和"五"組成"三十五"來表示數字35。在漢語中需要先表達出"三個十"，即"三十（30）"的意思。一旦十位數放在了合適的位置，就可以寫上"五（5）"來完成這個數字了。漢語沒有表示個位的字，但是表示其他位數的字卻很重要。這些表示位數的字是必須寫的，不能把35僅僅寫成"三五"。同理，896在漢語中寫爲"八百九十六"。

There is one more rule to writing numbers in Chinese. If a number ends in zeros, you do not need to include the zero character. However, if a zero digit does not end a number, you need to include the zero character. If a zero digit is followed by one or more zero digits, only one zero character is used, for instance, 1004.

漢語中數字的書寫還有一個規則。如果一個數字是以0結尾的，寫的時候不需要寫"零"。但是，如果0不是該數字的個位數，就必須要寫"零"。如果0後面還有一個或更多個0，只用一個"零"就可以了，如1004。

 690 = 六百九十
609 = 六百零九
1004 = 一千零四

Lesson 3 我的家

2 Demonstrative + Num.+ MW + NP

This structure is not something new at all. As introduced in the Grammar of Lesson One, whenever a noun is quantified, there must be a measure word between the number and the noun: 五口人，一家人，一個兒子. Sometimes, demonstrative 這 (this) or 那 (that) may also appear in this structure, in which case, it is usually put before the number: 爺爺奶奶只有我這一個孫子. 這，那 can be translated into either this or these, that or those, depending the number that follows them. For instance:

這不是一個新結構。第一課的語法中已經介紹過了，當一個名詞有數量的限定，那麼在數詞和名詞之間必須要有一個量詞，如"五口人""一家人""一個兒子"。有時，指示詞"這"或"那"可能在這一結構中出現，出現時常常置於數量詞前，如"爺爺奶奶只有我這一個孫子"。"這""那"可以根據它們自身後面的數字表達爲"這/這些"和"那/那些"。例如：

Demonstrative	Numberal	Measure word	NP	Meaning
這	（一）	個	學生	this student
那	兩	家	人	those two families

There is one special case, involving the number two (2).When followed by a measure word，"two" in Chinese is not 二，but 兩. For instance，*two brothers* becomes 兩個弟弟.This rule only applies to the number two. Therefore *22 people* and *12 students* are written as 二十二個人，十二個學生.

有一個涉及數字"二（2）"的特殊例子。當處於量詞前時，數字2在漢語中寫作"兩"。例如，two brothers 是"兩個弟弟"。這一個規律只適用於數字2，因此"22 people"和"12 students"只能寫作"二十二個人""十二個學生"。

There are some measure words (of volume, weight, space, time, etc.) that do not require a noun following them. This is because they are also nouns themselves.

有一些容量、重量、空間、時間等的度量不需要接名詞。這是因爲它們本身也是名詞。

> **E.g.** 兩天　　　　(two days)
> 兩年　　　　(two years)
> 兩歲　　　　(two years old)

There are also cases when either number or noun can be left out of the sentence. For instance, when 一 (yī) means "a" or "an", rather than "one", it can often be omitted.

還有一些情況，句中可以省略數詞或者名詞。例如，當"一"表示"任何一個"或"每一"，而不是"數量一"時，就可以將其省略。

> **E.g.** 我想要個兒子。 (I want to have a son.)

If, in a conversation, at some point it becomes obvious what noun you are talking about, it can be left out of the sentence.
若在對話中所談論的名詞清楚明確，那麼就可以將該名詞省略。

> **E.g.** ——你有外國朋友嗎？ (Do you have foreign friends?)
> ——有。我有三個。 (Yes. I have three of them.)

When inquiring about the quantity of a noun, we can use the Wh-word 幾. When 幾 is used, it always implies that the number is smaller than 10.
當詢問名詞的數量時，可以使用疑問詞"幾"；而使用"幾"的時候，通常意味著數字不超過十。

> **E.g.** ——你有幾個外國朋友？ (How many foreign friends do you have?)
> ——我有三個。 (I have three of them.)

 雖然 S VP₁，可是 VP₂: although VP₁, S VP₂
S 雖然 VP₁，可是 VP₂: although VP₁, S VP₂

Structurally speaking, "雖然 S VP₁，可是 VP₂" is pretty easy to learn. Like "因爲 A，所以 B", 雖然 and 可是 complete one another. Although in English "although" and "but" do not co-occur, it is just the opposite in Chinese. Actually, it is better to have both 雖然 and 可是 together. 雖然 can also go after the subject: S 雖然 VP₁，可是 VP₂.

從結構上來講，"雖然 S VP₁，可是 VP₂"這個結構很容易掌握。像"因爲 A，所以 B"一樣，"雖然……可是"也使得彼此變得完整。儘管在英語中"雖然"和"可是"不能同時出現，而在漢語中正好相反。實際上，最好將"雖然"和"可是"兩個一起使用。"雖然"也可以用在主語後：S 雖然 VP₁，可是 VP₂。

> **E.g.** a. 雖然母親的工作也很忙，可是她從來不覺得累。
> (Although my mother is also busy with work, she never feels tired.)
> b. 狗雖然不是人，可是它跟我們的親人一樣。
> (Although dog is not a human being, he is still a member of my family.)

 S 每天都 VP: sb. does sth. everyday

The demonstrative 每 with the literal meaning of "each" or "every" modifies a quantifier or a noun. Like 這 and 那, its default position is the same as where they appear.
指示代詞"每"的字面意義是"每一個"，修飾限定數量詞或名詞。它的位置也

Lesson 3 我的家

跟"這"和"那"一樣。

Demonstrative	Numeral	Measure word	NP	Meaning
這(那)		個	學生	this / that student
每	(一)	個	人	each person
每	(一)		天	each day / everyday

Whenever you see 每 in the sentence, the adverb 都 is always used behind as exemplified below:
如果前面有了"每",後面一般要使用"都"。例如:

> E.g. a. 每天她都做很好吃的飯菜。(She cooks very delicious food every day.)
> b. 她每天都學中文。(She studies Chinese everyday.)
> c. 每個學生都喜歡學中文。(All of the students like learning Chinese.)

5 Object₁、Object₂,S 都 Verb

都 quantifies the NP(s) that go(es) before it but not the ones after it.
"都"限制它之前的名詞短語而不是它之後的。

> E.g. 中文、英文、法文,他都會說。
> (As for Chinese, English and French, he can speak them all.)

If the proposed object is singular, we don't use 都.
當賓語只有一項事物時,不用"都"。

> E.g. 中國菜,他喜歡吃。(As for Chinese food, he likes eating it.)

However, if more than one object has been proposed, then the use of 都 is obligatory:
但當賓語是多項事物時,一般要用"都"。

> E.g. 中國菜、法國菜、意大利菜,她都會做。
> (As for Chinese food, French food and Italian food, she can cook all of them.)

If the subject is also plural, then 都 may quantify both.
當主語也是複數時,"都"限定兩者。

> E.g. 中國菜、法國菜、意大利菜,她們都會做。
> (As for Chinese food, French food and Italian food, they can cook all of them.)

6 S 是 VP 的

This is a structure that is used colloquially to express what career/major the person is engaged in or doing.

這個表達方式用於口語，可回答一個人所從事的職業或學習的專業。

> E.g. a. 他的爸爸是做生意的。 (His father is a business man.)
> b. 她是教音樂的。 (She teaches music.)
> c. 李家奇是學中文的。 (Li Jiaqi's major is Chinese.)
> d. 我哥哥是做飯的。 (My elder brother is a cook.)

7 S 叫 sb. sth. : sb. calls sb. else sth.
S 叫 sb. VP : sb. asks/tells sb. else to do sth.

Just like the English structure "S call A B," the first structure is the Chinese equivalent. 叫 here doesn't mean to "be named", but "to call". 叫 can also mean "to ask/tell somebody to do something". See the second structure.

第一個結構是英語結構 "S call A B" 在漢語中的對應表達。"叫" 在這裡並不表示 "被命名爲"，而是 "稱呼"。"叫" 還可以表示 "讓某人做某事" 的意思，見第二個結構。

S 叫 sb. sth.

> E.g. a. 他們叫他大忙人。(They refer to him as "Mr. Busy".)
> b. 他們叫我小可愛。(They call me "little cutie".)
> c. 我叫他老北京，他叫我小上海。
>   (I call him "old Beijing" and he calls me "little Shanghai".)
> d. 中國人叫外國人老外。
>   (Chinese people refer to foreigners as "Laowai".)

S 叫 sb. VP

> E.g. a. 我媽媽叫我學中文，我爸爸叫我學醫。
>   (My mother told me to learn Chinese. My father told me to go to Medical School.)
> b. ——他爸爸想叫他學什麼呢？ (What does his father want him to learn?)
>   ——他爸爸叫他學做生意。
>   (His fathers wants him to learn how to do business.)

8 S 在 PW (VP) : sb. does sth. at some place

The function of 在 here is to indicate location. Thus, the word following 在 is always a place word. Geographic names and names of institutions are natural place words that can go after 在.

這個結構中 "在" 表示所處的地點。因此，"在" 後面的詞一般是一個地點詞語。地點名稱和機構名稱都是放在"在"後面的處所詞。

 a. 我在美國。(I am in the United Sates.)
b. 你在中國。(You are in China.)
c. 他在意大利。(He is in Italy.)
d. 我們都在紐約。(We are all in New York.)
e. 他們都在倫敦。(They are all in London.)
f. 我的朋友在家。(My friend is at home.)
g. 你的朋友在北京。(Your friend is in Beijing.)

在 in the sentence 媽媽在家照顧他們 is a preposition telling at what place the action takes place. This structure is very productive.

"媽媽在家照顧他們"這個句子中的"在"作爲介詞,告知動作發生的地點是哪裡。用這一結構可以生成很多句子。

 a. 我在美國學中文。(I am learning Chinese in the United States.)
b. 他在大學學音樂。(He is learning music in the university.)
c. 你在大學教中文。(You teach Chinese at a college.)
d. 我在紐約做生意。(I am doing business in New York.)
e. 他在上海學醫。(He goes to Medical School in Shanghai.)
f. 我哥哥在北京工作。(My older brother is working in Beijing.)
g. 我媽媽在家照顧我奶奶。
(My mother is taking care of my grandmother at home.)
h. 我在中文課上介紹我的家庭。(I am introducing my family in Chinese class.)

9 (S) 請 sb. VP

請 : used in polite request

 請你說。(You go ahead, please.)

請 : to treat sb.

 我請你吃飯。(I will treat you to a meal.)

請 : to ask sb. to do sth.

 我請他照顧我的妹妹。(I asked him to take care of my younger sister.)

請 : to hire sb. to do sth.

 不能請人照顧我的弟弟妹妹。
(I can't hire somebody to take care of my younger brother and sister.)

Here are some other examples:
還有一些其他的例子：

 a. 你想請誰就請誰。(Invite whomever you want to.)
b. 我想請你看電影。(I would like to invite you to see a movie.)
c. 他想請人看他的狗。(He would like to hire somebody to look after his dog.)
d. 我們想請老師唱歌。(We would like to invite our teacher to sing a song.)

10 S（不）能 VP ⟷ S（不）會 VP

Structurally, these two patterns don't differ. Their difference comes from the semantic difference between the two auxiliary verbs 能 and 會. 會 always refers to the skill acquired through learning and practice while 能 focuses on the performance ability that is either physically possible or environmentally allowed.

這兩個句型在結構上沒有區別，它們的區別體現在"能"和"會"兩個助動詞的語義差別上。"會"通常指通過學習和練習獲得的能力，而"能"更側重體現身體或客觀條件允許而展現出來的能力。

 a. 我會說中國話。(I can speak Chinese.)
b. 他會做飯。(He can cook.)
c. 在美國，我能說中國話。(I can speak Chinese in America.)
d. 因為我不會中文，所以（我）不能看中文電視。
(I don't know Chinese, so I can't watch TV in Chinese.)

11 S 要 VP

When 要 is used as an auxiliary verb, it indicates that an action will happen as has been scheduled.

當"要"用作助動詞時，它表示已計劃好的動作將要發生。

 a. 我要學中文。(I will learn Chinese, as I have planned.)
b. 今天我要工作，不能跟你說話。(I am going to work and I can't talk with you.)

12 A 跟 B（不）一樣：A is (not) the same as B.

 a. 姐姐跟我一樣，也是研究生。(My sister is also a graduate student like me.)

Lesson 3 我的家

b. 弟弟跟我一樣，也愛學中文。
　　(My younger brother is the same as I am. He also likes learning Chinese.)
c. 你是你，我是我，你跟我不一樣。
　　(You are you. I am me. You are and I are different.)

A 跟 B 一樣 Adj. : A is as Adj. as B

 a. 中國跟美國一樣漂亮。(China is as beautiful as the United States.)
b. 你弟弟跟我弟弟一樣可愛。(Your brother is as cute as my brother.)
c. 紐約跟北京一樣冷。(New York is as cold as Beijing.)
d. 你的朋友跟我的朋友一樣多。(You have as many friends as I do.)

13 S 跟 sb. VP：sb. does sth. with/to/from sb. else

跟 in this structure is not a conjunction which means "and". Just like 在 in "S 在 PW VP", 跟 in this case is also a preposition. 跟 as a preposition can mean "to" "with" or "from". As was the case with place words, prepositions have two aspects: a *vocabulary* aspect (when do I use which preposition?) and a *grammatical* aspect (what is the correct word order?). The semantic meanings of prepositions have to be learned individually. As for word order, just remember: prepositions always come before the verb.

在這一結構中，"跟"不是表示"和"的連詞。正如"S 在 PW VP"中的"在"，"跟"在本結構中同樣也是介詞。介詞"跟"可以表示"對""向""從"的意思。如同與處所詞連用，介詞要注意兩個層面：詞彙方面（什麼時候使用哪個介詞）以及語法方面（正確的詞序是怎樣的）。每個介詞的語義都需要單獨學習。詞序方面，只要記住：介詞永遠都在動詞前。

 a. 我跟你學中文。(I study Chinese from/with you.)
b. 你跟我說。(Say it to me. / You tell it to me.)
c. 他跟我在一起。(He stays with me. / He was/is together with me.)

14 S 是 Adj./VP，可是/但是……

是 here is used to for assertion and it is stressed when reading it. 是 is often translated as "It is true that...", which often indicates concession. It is usually followed by 可是 or 但是.
這裡"是"表示判斷，讀出來時要讀重音。"是"通常譯為"It is true that..."，表示承認，後面常常接"可是"或"但是"。

 a. 他是很可愛，可是我不喜歡他。
　　(It is true that he is very adorable, but I don't like him.)

b. 我是很累，可是你也很累。(It is true that I am very tired but you are too.)
c. 我是很高興，但是我的女朋友不高興。
(It is true that I am very happy, but my girlfriend is not.)
d. 我是想學中文，可是中文太難了。
(It is true that I want to learn Chinese, but Chinese is too difficult.)
e. 我的狗是很聰明，但是它不喜歡學中文。
(It is true that my dog is very smart, but he doesn't like learning Chinese.)
f. 我的老師是很和氣，可是他的朋友不多。
(It is true that my teacher is very gentle, but he doesn't have a lot of friends.)

15) S V 一下

This structure indicates that the action won't last long.
這一結構表示動作不會持續很長時間。

a. 請你介紹一下你自己。(Please introduce a little bit about yourself.)
b. 請你說一下你的狗。(Please say a little bit about your dog.)
c. 請你看一下。(Please take a look.)
d. 請你照顧一下我的狗。(Please look after my dog for a little while.)

16) S 是誰？↔ 誰是 NP？

Unlike English, Chinese Wh-questions do not incur the change of word order. For instance, in the sentence 我喜歡中國菜, if we want to question the subject, then we just replace the subject with the relevant Wh-word: 誰喜歡吃中國菜？In the same manner, if we choose to question the object, then we have: 你喜歡吃什麼（菜）？Thus, if we have the Chinese sentence: 他是我的老師, then the possible Wh-question forms may either be 他是誰？or 誰是你的老師？

與英語不同，漢語中的特殊疑問句不需要改變詞的順序。例如，在"我喜歡中國菜"這個句子中，如果我們想對主語進行提問，那麼我們只需把主語部分用相應的疑問詞代替即可："誰喜歡吃中國菜？"同樣，如果我們選擇對賓語進行提問，那麼我們就說："你喜歡吃什麼（菜）？"因此，"他是我的老師"這句漢語，可能的疑問句形式將是："他是誰？"或者："誰是你的老師？"

Summary:

▶ When followed by a measure word, 二 becomes 兩.

▶ 每 and 都 go together.

▶ When more than one object is preposed, 都 is used.

Lesson 3 我的家

> 在 is always followed by a place word when indicating location.
>
> Prepositions always come before the verb.
>
> Chinese Wh-questions does not incur the change of word order.

Patterns:

- Demonstrative + Num.+ MW + NP ‖ 這（一）個學生 (this student)

- 雖然 S VP_1，可是 VP_2 ‖ 雖然母親的工作也很忙，可是她從來不覺得累。
  (Although my mother is also busy with work, she never feels tired.)

- S 雖然 VP_1，可是 VP_2 ‖ 狗雖然不是人，可是它跟我們的親人一樣。
  (Although the dog is not a human being, he is still a member of my family.)

- S 每天 都 VP ‖ 她每天都做很好吃的飯菜。(She cooks very delicious food everyday.)

- $Object_1$、$Object_2$，S 都 Verb ‖ 中國菜、法國菜、意大利菜，她都會做。
  (As for Chinese food, French food and Italian food, she can cook all of them.)

- S 是 VP 的 ‖ 他的爸爸是做生意的。(His father is a businessman.)

- S 叫 sb. sth. ‖ 中國人叫外國人老外。(Chinese refer to foreigners as "Laowai".)

- S 叫 sb. VP ‖ 我媽媽叫我學中文，我爸爸叫我學醫。
  (My mother told me to learn Chinese. My father told me to go to Medical School.)

- S 在 PW（VP）‖ 我在美國，你在中國。(I am in the United States. You are in China.)

- (S) 請 sb. VP ‖ 我請你吃飯。(I will treat you to a meal.)

- S（不）能 VP ⟷ S（不）會 VP ‖ 因為我不會中文，所以（我）不能看中文電視。
  (I don't know Chinese, so I can't watch TV in Chinese.)

- S 要 VP ‖ 我要學中文。(I will learn Chinese, as I have planned.)

- A 跟 B（不）一樣 ‖ 弟弟跟我一樣，也愛學中文。
  (My younger brother is the same as I am. He also likes learning Chinese.)

- A 跟 B 一樣 Adj. ‖ 中國跟美國一樣漂亮。(China is as beautiful as the United States.)

- S 跟 sb. VP ‖ 我跟你學中文。(I study Chinese from/with you.)

- S 是 Adj. / VP, 可是 / 但是…… ‖ 他是很可愛，可是我不喜歡他。
  (It is true that he is very adorable, but I don't like him.)

85

走近中國——初級漢語教程
APPROACHING CHINA : ELEMENTARY CHINESE

- S V 一下 ‖ 請你介紹一下你自己。(Please introduce a little bit about yourself.)
- S 是 誰？ ⟷ 誰是 NP？ ‖ 他是誰？ (Who is he?)
   誰是你的老師？ (Who is your teacher?)

IN CLASS ACTIVITIES

1 Answer the following questions according to the information given in the text:

① 李家興家有幾口人？他們是誰？

② 他父親是做什麽的？他母親呢？

③ 爲什麽李家興的父親每天晚上都覺得累？

④ 他母親的工作忙不忙？她覺得累不累？

⑤ 他母親會做什麽飯菜？

⑥ 爲什麽他的母親特別喜歡他？

⑦ 李家奇家有幾口人？他們是誰？

⑧ 他的爸爸是做什麽的？家裡人叫他什麽？

⑨ 他媽媽爲什麽不工作？

Lesson 3 我的家

⑩ 同學們說什麼？ _____

⑪ 家奇說什麼？ _____

2 Please ask your classmate about his/her family and write down the relevant information:

Ⓐ 請你給我介紹一下你的家庭，好不好？
Ⓑ 好的，我家有_____。他們是_____。

Ⓐ 請問，他們是做什麼的？
Ⓑ _____

Ⓐ 他／她的工作忙不忙？
Ⓑ _____

Ⓐ 你是老幾？
Ⓑ _____

Ⓐ 你家人叫你什麼？
Ⓑ _____

HOMEWORK

1 Change the following statements into questions, replacing the underlined part with a Wh-word.

① 我姓<u>李</u>。 ⟹ 你姓什麼？

② 李家興家有<u>五口</u>人。 ⟹ _____

③ <u>他的</u>父親是醫生。 ⟹ _____

④ 我母親是教<u>音樂</u>的。 ⟹ _____

⑤ 家興是老小。 ▸ ☐

⑥ 他們都叫我"小大人"。 ▸ ☐

2 Please insert 的 where necessary:

① 我 _的_ 新朋友是美國 _/_ 人。

② 他＿＿母親＿＿工作也很忙。

③ 每天她都做很好吃＿＿菜。

④ 新＿＿同學都是很好＿＿朋友。

⑤ 請介紹一下你＿＿家庭。

⑥ 你＿＿弟弟妹妹有你這樣＿＿哥哥一定很幸福。

3 Translate the following sentences into Chinese:

① Who only has two British friends?

② I don't think your dog is the same as mine.

③ Although I only have one job, I work everyday.

④ My mom stays at home taking care of my younger sister and brother.

⑤ His major is music.

Lesson 3 我的家

⑥ I want to introduce myself a little bit to you first.

_____

⑦ As for Chinese, French and Japanese food, I like all of them.

_____

⑧ It is true that I don't know English, but I will learn it.

_____

⑨ I don't have enough money. So I can't (afford to) eat French food everyday.

_____

4 Please write the following numbers in Chinese characters:

① 33 三十三

② 41 _____   29 _____   78 _____

③ 105 _____   250 _____   519 _____

④ 1,005 _____   2,356 _____

⑤ 30,369 _____   35,079 _____

⑥ 11,626 _____   65,728 _____

5 Please mark the pauses you hear in each of the following sentences and then read:

① Jiāxīng qǐng Yīzhōng hé Jiāqí dào zìjǐ de sùshè chī wǔfàn.

② Jiāqí hé Yīzhōng hěn gāoxìng. Tāmen zhōngwǔ zhǔnshí dàole Jiāxīng de sùshè.

③ Jiāxīng wèn tāmen xiǎng xiān hēdiǎnr shénme.

④ Yīzhōng shuō hē shénme dōu xíng.

⑤ Jiāqí xiǎng hēdiǎnr kāfēi, kěshì Jiāxīng de sùshè lǐ méiyǒu kāfēi, zhǐ yǒu chá.

⑥ Jiāxīng yòng Zhōngguó fǎzi gěi Jiāqí hé Yīzhōng pàole chá.

⑦ Hēle chá, Jiāqí wèn Jiāxīng qǐng tāmen lái chī shénme hǎo dōngxi.

⑧ Jiāxīng shuō zhēn bù hǎoyìsi, běnlái xiǎng qǐng tāmen lái chī Zhōngguócài, kěshì tā de Zhōngguó péngyou jīntiān yǒu shì bù néng lái, tā zìjǐ yòu bú huì zuò, suǒyǐ xiànzài zhǐ néng qǐng tāmen hē chá le.

⑨ Jiāqí shuō bú huì zuò bú yàojǐn, Yīzhōng kěyǐ jiāo tā.

⑩ Dàjiā dōu juéde zhè shì yí ge hǎo zhǔyi.

Chinese Family

In China, family plays a key role not only in individuals' social lives, but also Chinese culture at large. Chinese people value close family relationships and prefer to live with or near their families.

Confucius (551BCE – 479 BCE), the great Chinese teacher and philosopher, advised his people not to study or work far away from home while their parents were still alive. This concept has become one of the main traditions of Chinese culture. Even in today's society, many people working far from home feel a certain kind of guilt simply because they are not able to live close to their aged parents or grandparents. Those aged persons would feel proud to have four generations living in the same house, and would consider their children's presence as the greatest of joys. Because of this emphasis on close family ties, Chinese families are usually very large. Since the one-child policy (計劃生育) was implemented in 1979, large families have become increasingly rare in China. However, the Chinese concept of family seems not to have changed very much.

In today's China, for instance, it is still the general rule that the younger generation must respect the older generation. Kinship terms such as grandfather, father, or even elder brother still represent authority and superiority, while terms such as grandchildren, children, or even younger brother suggest inferiority and obedience. Even today, the younger generation is not permitted to call their superiors by name, for that would be considered to go against the moral and social order.

The Chinese kinship system uses a set of terms unique to the Chinese language, forming a lexicon with deep cultural roots. This system is the combined product of an agricultural society, a family-centered economy, and a hierarchical family structure. Although Chinese society has experienced drastic changes over the past several centuries, the kinship system managed to survive intact.

LESSON 4　請人吃飯

　　家興請一中和家奇到自己的宿舍吃午飯。家奇和一中很高興。他們中午準時到了家興的宿舍。家興問他們想先喝點兒什麼。一中說喝什麼都行。家奇想喝點兒咖啡，可是家興的宿舍裡沒有咖啡，只有茶。家興用中國法子給家奇和一中泡了茶。喝了茶，家奇問家興請他們來吃什麼好東西。家興說真不好意思，本來想請他們來吃中國菜，可是他的中國朋友今天有事不能來，他自己又不會做，所以現在只能請他們喝茶了。家奇說不會做不要緊，一中可以教他。大家都覺得這是一個好主意。

1　(Knocking...)

家興：　誰呀？

一中:
家奇：　是我們！

家興：　呵，真準時。請進，請進！

一中：　謝謝！你的宿舍真大！

家奇：　真漂亮！

家興：　謝謝，請坐，請坐！請問，你們想先喝點兒什麼？

91

一中： 我喝什麼都行。

家奇： 我想喝點兒咖啡。

家興： 對不起，我沒有咖啡，只有茶。

一中： 你有什麼茶？

家興： 紅茶、綠茶，我都有。你要紅茶還是綠茶？

一中： 那我就喝綠茶吧。家奇，你呢？你們英國人是不是都愛喝紅茶？

家奇： 是的，那就給我杯紅茶吧。

家興： 好。我今天用中國法子給你們泡茶，馬上就好，請稍等。

一中： 家奇，你看！家興的這套中國茶具真漂亮。

家奇： 嗯，是不錯。一會兒，我要問問他是在哪兒買的。

(After a while...)

家興： 茶來了！二位，請慢用。

家奇： 多謝了，家興。對了，你這套茶具是在哪兒買的？真好看，我也想買一套。

家興： 我在中國城買的，下次，我和你一起去。

家奇： 謝謝。

家興： 不客氣。一中，茶怎麼樣？

一中： 好茶，好茶，真不錯！謝謝。

2 (After a while...)

家奇： 我餓了，一中，你呢？

一中： 我也餓了。家興，你打算請我們吃什麼好東西啊？

家興： 我本來想請你們來吃中國菜，可是我的中國朋友今天有事不能來，我自己又不會做，所以現在只能請你們喝茶了。

家奇： 啊？

家興： 真不好意思。

家奇： 家興，不會做不要緊，一中可以教你。

家興： 好，這是一個好主意。一中，你覺得呢？

Lesson 4 請人吃飯

一中： 教外國人做中國菜，沒問題。

家奇： 太好了，那你的拿手菜是什麼呢？

一中： 西紅柿炒雞蛋，怎麼樣？

家興： 你做什麼我們就吃什麼。

一中： 你有西紅柿嗎？

家興： 沒有。

一中： 雞蛋呢？

家興： 沒有。我只有一點兒米，不知道夠不夠。

家奇： 樓下的超市什麼都有，你要什麼我們就買什麼。

一中： 米夠了。好，你們去買東西，我先做米飯。

3

家奇： 家興，什麼東西？這麼香！

家興： 是米飯。一中還真有兩下子。

家奇： 一中，這是你要的雞蛋，這是西紅柿，這是蔥。

一中： 好極了！五分鐘後開飯。家興，你有菜油嗎？

家興： 對不起，我只有橄欖油，不知道行不行。

一中： 行，橄欖油更好。

家奇： 家興，你有筷子嗎？

家興： 有，可是我只有兩雙，還差一雙。

一中： 你們用筷子，我用叉子吃就行了。

家奇： 那怎麼行？中國人不是習慣用筷子吃飯嗎？

一中： 可是，我也會用叉子。對了，我還不知道你們會不會用筷子呢。

家奇： 我沒問題，家興，你呢？

家興： 小看我了，是不是？呵呵，我不會用，可以學啊！

一中： 開飯了！

家奇： 真香！

走近中國——初級漢語教程
APPROACHING CHINA : ELEMENTARY CHINESE

VOCABULARY

#					
1	*到	到	dào	V.	to go to, to arrive
2	宿舍	宿舍	sùshè	N.	dormitory
3	*吃	吃	chī	V.	to eat
4	*午飯	午饭	wǔfàn	N.	lunch
5	中午	中午	zhōngwǔ	TW	noon
6	*準時	准时	zhǔnshí	Adv.	on time
7	*喝	喝	hē	V.	to drink
8	（一）點兒	（一）点儿	(yì)diǎnr	Q.	a little bit of, some
9	*行	行	xíng	V.	(to indicate agreement) ok, fine
10	*咖啡	咖啡	kāfēi	N.	coffee
11	*沒	没	méi	Adv.	not (to negate 有)
12	*茶	茶	chá	N.	tea
13	*用	用	yòng	V.	to use
14	*法子	法子	fǎzi	N.	way
15	*給	给	gěi	Prep.	for
16	*泡茶	泡茶	pào chá	V.-O.	to steep tea
17	*東西	东西	dōngxi	N.	thing
18	不好意思	不好意思	bù hǎoyìsi	IE	to feel embarrassed
19	*本來	本来	běnlái	Adv.	originally
20	*事	事	shì	N.	matter, thing
21	*現在	现在	xiànzài	TW	now
22	不要緊	不要紧	bú yàojǐn	IE	It doesn't matter.
23	*主意	主意	zhǔyi	N.	idea
24	呵	呵	hē	Int.	*to indicate a nice surprise*
25	*進	进	jìn	V.	to enter
26	*坐	坐	zuò	V.	to sit
27	對不起	对不起	duìbuqǐ	IE	I am sorry.
28	紅茶	红茶	hóngchá	N.	black tea (red tea in Chinese)
29	綠茶	绿茶	lǜchá	N.	green tea
30	*還是	还是	háishi	Conj.	or
31	*那	那	nà	Conj.	in that case

Lesson 4 請人吃飯

#	繁	简	Pinyin	POS	English
32	*馬上	马上	mǎshàng	Adv.	right away
33	請稍等	请稍等	qǐng shāo děng	IE	Please wait a minute!
34	套	套	tào	MW	a set of
35	茶具	茶具	chájù	N.	china, porcelain ware
36	嗯	嗯	ǹg	Int.	*to show agreement*
37	*不錯	不错	búcuò	Adj.	not bad
38	一會兒	一会儿	yíhuìr	Q.	in a while
39	哪兒	哪儿	nǎr	Pron.	where
40	茶來了	茶来了	chá lái le	IE	Here comes the tea!
41	請慢用	请慢用	qǐng màn yòng	IE	Please enjoy.
42	多謝了	多谢了	duō xiè le	IE	Thanks a lot!
43	對了	对了	duìle	IE	by the way, in other news
44	中國城	中国城	Zhōngguóchéng	N.	China town
45	*下次	下次	xiàcì	TW	next time
46	次	次	cì	MW	time(s)
47	*去	去	qù	V.	to go
48	不客氣	不客气	bú kèqi	IE	You are welcome.
49	怎麼樣	怎么样	zěnmeyàng	Pron.	how about...
50	*餓	饿	è	Adj.	hungry
51	*打算	打算	dǎsuàn	V.	to plan
52	啊	啊	ǎ	Int.	*to indicate a surprise*
53	拿手菜	拿手菜	náshǒucài	N.	(sb.'s) specialty
54	西紅柿	西红柿	xīhóngshì	N.	tomato
55	炒	炒	chǎo	V.	to stir fry
56	雞蛋	鸡蛋	jīdàn	N.	chicken egg
57	米	米	mǐ	N.	rice
58	樓下	楼下	lóuxià	PW	downstairs
59	超市	超市	chāoshì	N.	supermarket
60	*買	买	mǎi	V.	to buy
61	*米飯	米饭	mǐfàn	N.	cooked rice
62	這麼	这么	zhème	Pron.	so
63	香	香	xiāng	Adj.	delicious
64	有兩下子	有两下子	yǒu liǎng xiàzi	IE	to be really sth.

走近中國──初級漢語教程
APPROACHING CHINA : ELEMENTARY CHINESE

65	蔥	葱	cōng	N.	scallion
66	…極了	…极了	…jí le		extremely…
67	分鐘	分钟	fēnzhōng	N.	minutes
68	*（以）後	（以）后	(yǐ)hòu	TW	later
69	開飯	开饭	kāi fàn	V.-O.	start eating
70	菜油	菜油	càiyóu	N.	veggie oil
71	橄欖油	橄榄油	gǎnlǎnyóu	N.	olive oil
72	*更	更	gèng	Adv.	even
73	筷子	筷子	kuàizi	N.	chopsticks
74	雙	双	shuāng	MW	pair
75	差	差	chà	V.	to lack
76	叉子	叉子	chāzi	N.	fork
77	習慣	习惯	xíguàn	V.	to be used to doing sth.
78	小看我了	小看我了	xiǎokàn wǒ le	IE	I am not that silly.

▪ Supplementary Vocabulary:

1	點	点	diǎn	MW	o' clock
2	油	油	yóu	N.	oil
3	旁邊	旁边	pángbiān	PW	side
4	中間	中间	zhōngjiān	PW	middle
5	張	张	zhāng	MW	*measure word for things those are flat*
6	頓	顿	dùn	MW	*measure word for meals*
7	把	把	bǎ	MW	*measure word for things with handles*
8	台	台	tái	MW	*measure word for equipment*
9	四	四	sì	Num.	four
10	快	快	kuài	Adv.	quickly
11	做好	做好	zuòhǎo	V.-C.	to finish cooking
12	決定	决定	juédìng	V.	to decide
13	寫信	写信	xiě xìn	V.-O.	to write a letter
14	商店	商店	shāngdiàn	N.	store
15	椅子	椅子	yǐzi	N.	chair
16	屋子	屋子	wūzi	N.	room

Lesson 4 請人吃飯

17	電影院	电影院	diànyǐngyuàn	N.	movie theater
18	圖書館	图书馆	túshūguǎn	N.	library
19	北京烤鴨	北京烤鸭	Běijīng kǎoyā	NP	Peking Roast Duck
20	歷史	历史	lìshǐ	N.	history
21	經濟	经济	jīngjì	N.	economy, economics
22	哲學	哲学	zhéxué	N.	philosophy
23	時間	时间	shíjiān	N.	time
24	天安門	天安门	Tiān'ānmén	PN	Tian'anmen (Square)
25	故宮	故宫	Gùgōng	PN	Forbidden City
26	長城	长城	Chángchéng	PN	Great Wall
27	貓	猫	māo	N.	cat
28	計算機	计算机	jìsuànjī	N.	computer (formal)
29	電腦	电脑	diànnǎo	N.	computer (colloquial)
30	電話	电话	diànhuà	N.	telephone
31	牛奶	牛奶	niúnǎi	N.	milk
32	果汁	果汁	guǒzhī	N.	fruit juice
33	毛筆	毛笔	máobǐ	N.	brush (pen)
34	生日	生日	shēngrì	N.	birthday
35	哈佛大學	哈佛大学	Hāfó Dàxué	PN	Harvard University
36	哥倫比亞大學	哥伦比亚大学	Gēlúnbǐyà Dàxué	PN	Columbia University
37	清華大學	清华大学	Qīnghuá Dàxué	PN	Tsinghua University
38	北京大學	北京大学	Běijīng Dàxué	PN	Peking University

GRAMMAR

1 S 到 PW（來/去）VP

Just like 在，到 also requires a place word as its complement. Unlike 在, which indicates the state of being *in* a specific location，到 emphasizes the action of going *to* a place. 來／去 indicate the relevant direction of an action that is going to happen with respect to the speaker's present location – coming or going, respectively. The structure "S 到 PW（來／去）VP" indicates the action of going to some place to do something.

跟"在"一樣，"到"的後面同樣要搭配一個處所詞；而跟"在"不一樣的是，"在"後面是人或事物的具體位置，"到"強調去某地的動作。"來/去"表示與説話人相關的動作方向，向著説話者的方向則爲"來"，反之則爲"去"。"S 到 PW（來/去）VP"這個結構表示去某地做某事。

> **E.g.** 家興請一中跟家奇中午到自己的宿舍吃飯。
> (Jiaxing invites Yizhong and Jiaqi to come to his dorm to eat at noon.)

NOTE: 來/去 can be optional, as in this particular example.
注意："來/去"是可選的，如上面的這個例句。

2 Time expressions

Unlike in English, if the date, time of day, hour, etc. are expressed at once, then the largest unit always comes first. There are two positions for time words: either before the subject or between the subject and the verb.

在漢語中，如果同時説日期、時間等，那麽應該從最大的單位説起，這一點和英語是不一樣的。時間名詞有兩種位置：主語之前或者主謂之間。

> **E.g.** 我明天請客。/明天我請客。(I will treat somebody to a meal tomorrow.)

NOTE: Time words always precede adverbs after the subject.
注意：時間名詞通常在主語之後，副詞之前。

> **E.g.** 我明天晚上六點（準時）看電視。
> [I will watch TV at six o'clock tomorrow evening (on time)./I will watch TV tomorrow evening at six o'clock (on time).]

3 這/那是 NP：this / that is...

這 and 那 here are both pronouns. This structure is mainly used to identify objects or to introduce people.
"這"和"那"在這裡都是代詞。此結構常用於辨別物體或介紹人物。

> **E.g.** a. 這是我朋友的屋子。那是你朋友的桌子。
> (This is my friend's room. That is your friend's table.)
> b. 這是北京，那是上海。(This is Beijing and that is Shanghai.)
> c. 這位是我的老師，那位是你的老師。
> (This is my teacher and that is your teacher.)
> d. 這是我弟弟。(This is my younger brother.)

> e. ——那是什麼？ (What is that？)
> ——那是西紅柿炒雞蛋。 (That is fried eggs with tomatoes.)

4 Particle 了

> Question form: S V (Object) 了沒有？ /S V 了 (Object) 沒有？
> Positive: S V 了。
> Negative: S 沒(有) V。

When 了 follows a verb, it acts as a particle, indicating the completion of an action. No particle 了 in the negative form.
動詞之後的"了"是一個助詞，表示動作的完成。否定形式中不用助詞"了"。

> E.g. ——你昨天去那兒了沒有？ (Did you go there yesterday?)
> ——我昨天去了。你呢？ (I went there yesterday. How about you?)
> ——我昨天沒有去。 (I didn't go there yesterday.)

The object in this structure is very often quantified.
這個結構中的賓語常常是限定的。

> S V 了 time duration（的）N

> E.g. ——你學了幾年的中文？ (How long have you studied Chinese?)
> ——我學了兩年的中文。 (I have studied Chinese for two years.)

> S V 了 frequency word N

> E.g. a. 我今天喝了三次酒。(I have drunk three times today.)
> b. 我昨天做了兩次飯。 (I cooked twice yesterday.)

5 NP + Localizer

We have known that 在 and 到 must be followed by a place word, such as the name of a country or a geographic term. To describe something's/someone's location in greater detail requires the use of localizers such as 裡，旁邊，中間，下，etc.
我們已經知道了"在"和"到"的後面必須有處所詞，比如國家名或地方名。如果想非常具體地描述某樣東西或某個人的位置，我們需要使用一些地點詞，如"裡""旁邊""中間""下"等。

NP/ Pron. + Localizer → PW

 a. 宿舍裡 (in the dormitory)
b. 老師旁邊兒 (by the teacher)
c. 你(的)旁邊 (beside you)
d. 桌子跟椅子的中間 (in between the table and the chair)
e. 樓下 (downstairs)

Those newly formed place words together with other are required after 在 and 到. In addition, 這兒，那兒 can also be used to follow 在 and 到 as place words.

這些處所詞要放在"在"和"到"的後面。此外，"這兒、那兒"也要放在"在"和"到"的後面表示處所。

 a. 我在這兒。(I am here.)
b. 他到那兒去了。(He went there.)

6 S 問 sb. + Question form
S 不知道 + Question form

In Chinese, there are few verbs /verb phrases that require the clause that follows to take the question form. 問 (to ask) and 不知道 (to wonder) are among the few.

在漢語裡，很少有動詞或動詞短語後面可以跟疑問句，而"問"和"不知道"就是其中兩個。

 a. 家興問他們想不想先喝點什麼。
(Jiaxing asked them whether or not they would like something to drink.)
b. 家奇問家興請他們來吃什麼好東西。
(Jiaqi asked Jiaxing what kind of snack he is going to treat them.)
c. 我不知道他在不在北京。(I wonder if he is in Beijing or not.)

In the structure "S 不知道 + Question form", the subject very often can be dropped. But the implied subject is always the first person singular form 我 (I).

在"S 不知道 + Question form"這一句型中，主語常常可以省略掉。但是隱含的主語總是第一人稱"我"。

7 Prepositions：用，給

用 and 給 are two other verbs that can be used as prepositions to indicate "means" and "beneficiaries" respectively. As prepositions, the preposition and its object precede the main verb phrase.

"用"和"給"是兩個動詞，也可以用來作介詞，分別表示方式和受益者。介詞和它的賓語應在動詞短語之前。

> S 用 NP VP　　　　S 給 sb. VP

> E.g. 他想用中國法子給他們泡茶。
> (He would like to make tea for them in the Chinese way.)

This sentence actually involves two preposition phrases:
這個句子實際上涉及兩個介詞短語：

> ① 用中國法子 (in the Chinese way)
> ② 給他們 (for them)

 S V A 還是 B?

還是 in this structure is a choice type conjunction word which is similar to the English word "or". But unlike the English "or", 還是 mostly is used in an interrogative sentence.
這個結構中的"還是"是一個表示選擇的連詞，跟英語中的"or"類似。但是不同於"or"，"還是"多數情況下用於疑問句中。

> E.g. a. 你想要紅茶還是綠茶？(Would you like black tea or green tea?)
> b. 紅茶或者 (huòzhě) 綠茶都行。(Either black tea or green tea will do.)

 S 教 sb. VP

This structure is pretty straightforward. 教 as a transitive verb can either take an NP as its object or an extra verb phrase to indicate to teach somebody how to do something.
這個結構非常簡單。"教"作爲一個及物動詞，賓語可以是名詞短語，也可以是動詞短語，表示教某人做某事。

> E.g. a. 你可以叫一中教你。
> (You could ask Yizhong to teach you.)
> b. 一中決定教家興做西紅柿炒雞蛋。
> (Yizhong decided to teach Jiaxing how to fix fried eggs with tomatoes.)

10 Num. + MW + NP

Numberal	Measure word	NP	Meaning
一	杯	茶	a cup of tea
一	套	茶具	a set of china

（續表）

Numberal	Measure word	NP	Meaning
一	張	桌子	a table
四	把	椅子	four chairs
一	把	叉子	a fork
一	雙	筷子	a pair of chopsticks

11 S Wh-word 都 V

——你想買什麼？（What do you want to buy?）
——我什麼都想買。（I want to buy everything.）

都 in this sentence modifies the question word that precedes it. In this pattern, the emphasis is on "inclusiveness". Therefore, the so-called Wh-words in this structure have lost their original function and semantic meaning: 什麼都 (anything), 哪兒都 (anywhere), 誰都 (anybody, everybody); when the structure is negative, they mean 什麼都不 / 沒 (nothing), 哪兒都不 / 沒 (nowhere), 誰都不 / 沒 (nobody) respectively.
這個句子裡的"都"修飾它之前的疑問詞。這個句型中，重點是強調"所有的"。因此，這個結構中所謂的特殊疑問詞已經失去了它們本來的功能和語義，如"什麼（任何東西）都""哪兒（任何地方）都""誰（任何人）都"。當這個結構是否定形式時，它們分別意味著"什麼都不 / 沒（沒有東西）""哪兒都不 / 沒（沒有地方）""誰都不 / 沒（沒有人）"。

E.g. 樓下的超市什麼都有，你要什麼我們就買什麼。
 (There is everything in the supermarket downstairs. We will buy you anything you want.)

In the negative example, the character 都 may be replaced by 也.
在否定形式中，"都"字可以換成"也"。

S Wh-word 都 / 也不 / 沒 V

 a. 我哪兒都不喜歡。（I don't like anyplace./I like nowhere.）
b. 我什麼也沒有。（I don't have anything./I have nothing.）

NOTE: There is a change in the normal word order involved in these sentences: the object is brought forward and put between the subject and the verb.
注意：有些句子中正常的詞語次序會變化，賓語會被提前，放到主謂之間。

E.g. ——你吃了什麼？（What did you eat?）
——我什麼也沒吃。（I did not eat anything.）

However, the construction works just as well if the question word is in the subject position of the sentence, in which case the word order remains normal.
然而，如果疑問詞在主語位置上，則詞序維持正常不變。

> **Wh-word 都 / 也不 / 沒 VP**
>
> **Wh-word 都 VP**

> E.g.
> ——誰喜歡你？ (Who likes you?)
> ——誰都(不)喜歡我。 [Everybody (Nobody) likes me.]

12) Question forms：NP/VP 怎麼樣？ (How about...?)

This pattern is very useful when asking for one's opinion about certain things.
這個句型適用於問某人對某事的意見。

> E.g.
> a. 北大怎麼樣？ (How about Peking University?)
> b. 學中文怎麼樣？ (How about learning Chinese?)
> c. 做中國菜怎麼樣？ (How about cooking Chinese food?)

Summary:

▶ Just like 在，到 also requires a place word as its complement.

▶ Time words always precede adverbs after the subject.

▶ There are two positions for time words: either before the subject or between the subject and the verb.

▶ If there is more than one time indication, unlike English, the largest unit always comes first.

▶ When 了 follows a verb. it acts as a particle, indicating the completion of an action. No particle 了 in the negative form.

▶ The object in this structure is very often quantified.

▶ The 了 after adjectives always indicates change of a state.

▶ The embedded clause after 問 (to ask) and 不知道 (to wonder) must take the question form.

▶ 還是 mostly is used in an interrogative sentence.

Patterns:

- S 到 PW VP ‖ 家興請一中跟家奇中午到自己的宿舍吃飯。
  (Jiaxing invites Yizhong and Jiaqi to come to his dorm to eat at noon.)

- S V (Object) 了沒有？/ S V 了 (Object) 沒有？ ‖ 你昨天去那兒了沒有？
  (Did you go there yesterday?)

- S V 了 ‖ 我昨天去了。(I went there yesterday.)

- S 沒(有) V ‖ 我昨天沒有去。(I didn't go there yesterday.)

- S V 了 time duration （的）N ‖ 我學了兩年的中文。
  (I have studied Chinese for two years.)

- S V 了 frequency word N ‖ 我昨天做了兩次飯。(I cooked twice yesterday.)

- NP + Localizer ‖ 桌子這兒 (here close to the table)

- 這/那是 NP ‖ 這是我朋友的屋子。那是你朋友的桌子。
  (This is my friend's room. That is your friend's table.)

- S 問 sb. + Question form ‖ 家興問他們想不想先喝點什麼。
  (Jiaxing asked them whether or not they would like something to drink.)

- S 不知道 + Question form ‖ 我不知道他在不在北京。
  (I wonder if he is in Beijing or not.)

- S 用 NP VP；S 給 sb. VP ‖ 他想用中國法子給他們泡茶。
  (He would like to make tea for them in the Chinese way.)

- S V A 還是 B? ‖ 你要紅茶還是綠茶？(Would you like black tea or green tea?)

- S 教 sb. VP ‖ 一中決定教家興做西紅柿炒雞蛋。
  (Yizhong decided to teach Jiaxing how to fix fried eggs with tomatoes.)

- S Wh-word 都 V ‖ ——你想買什麼？ (What do you want to buy?)
  ——我什麼都想買。(I want to buy everything.)

- S Wh-word 都/也不/沒 V ‖ 我哪兒都不喜歡。(I don't like anyplace./I like nowhere.)

- Wh-word 都 VP ‖ ——誰喜歡你？ (Who likes you?)
  ——誰都喜歡我。(Everybody likes me.)

- NP/VP 怎麼樣? ‖ 學中文怎麼樣？ (How about learning Chinese?)

Lesson 4 請人吃飯

IN CLASS ACTIVITIES

1 Answer the following questions according to the information given in the text:

① 家興請一中跟家奇到自己的宿舍做什麼?

② 家興想用什麼法子給他們泡茶?

③ 家興本來想請他們吃什麼?

現在呢?

爲什麼?

2 Please do role play according to the dialogues given below:

- A 誰呀?
- B 是_____!
- A 請進,請進!
- B 謝謝! 這屋子真漂亮!
- A 謝謝! 請坐,請坐! 請問,你想先喝點兒什麼?
- B 給我來一杯綠茶吧。
- A 好的,茶馬上就好,請稍等。茶來了! 請慢用。
- B 嗯,這茶真不錯。這是什麼茶?
- A 龍井 (Lóngjǐng: *a kind of green tea*)。
- B ……

105

走近中國——初級漢語教程
APPROACHING CHINA : ELEMENTARY CHINESE

A 你會不會做飯?

B 會做。怎麼,你想學做中國菜?

A 你能不能教教我?

B 沒問題。你想學什麼,我就教你什麼。

A 太好了!我想學做西紅柿炒雞蛋。

B 這是我的拿手菜。

A 我得 (děi: must, have to) 買什麼?

B 西紅柿、雞蛋、菜油、蔥……

A 樓下的超市什麼都有,我馬上就買。

……

B 你看,很容易吧!

A 真香!你還真有兩下子!

B 謝了。你用筷子還是叉子?

A 吃中國菜當然 (dāngrán: of course) 得用筷子了。

B 開飯了!

HOMEWORK

1 Please identify the underlined 了 in the following structures:

	change of a state	completion of an action
① 今天天氣不好了。	✓	
② 我會做中國菜了。		
③ 我今天做了三頓飯。		
④ 你看了沒有?		
（我）看了。		

Lesson 4 請人吃飯

2 Please rewrite the following statements by using the words given:

① 我喜歡中文。 ➡ 他問我 [喜歡什麼]。

② 你喜歡學中文嗎? ➡ 她問我 [____]。

③ 他會說中國話嗎? ➡ 不知道 [____]。

④ 你們想吃中國菜嗎? ➡ 他不知道 [____]。

⑤ 你打算在中國城買一套中國茶具嗎?
　➡ 她問我 [____]。

3 Translate the following sentences into Chinese:

① I will treat you to a meal at my dorm.

② My teacher taught me Chinese for two years.

③ He asked me whether I knew Chinese or not.

④ Would you like Chinese food or American food?

⑤ The supermarket in Chinatown has everything. (Wh-word 都)

⑥ Did you watch TV last night (昨天晚上: zuótiān wǎnshang)? No, I didn't.

107

走近中國——初級漢語教程
APPROACHING CHINA : ELEMENTARY CHINESE

4 Please write the appropriate measure words for the following phrases when necessary:

一__套__ 茶具   兩_____ (family member) 人

三_____ 飯   四_____ 椅子

五_____ 桌子   六_____ 歲 (suì: age)

七_____ 年 (nián: year)   八_____ 茶

九_____ 叉子   十_____ 筷子

一_____ 好主意   兩_____ 天

5 Without referring back to the vocabulary, please fill in the missing entries for the following idiomatic expressions:

	Chinese	Pinyin	English
1		bù hǎoyìsi	to feel embarrassed
2	不要緊		
3		duìbuqǐ	I am sorry.
4	請稍等		
5		chá lái le	Here comes the tea!
6	請慢用		
7		duō xiè le	Thanks a lot!
8	不客氣		
9	有兩下子		

Lesson 4 請人吃飯

⑩   kāi fàn le   Time to eat!

⑪ 小看我了

6 Please mark the pauses you hear in each of the following sentences and then read:

① Jiāxīng hé Jiāqí yuè xué Zhōngwén yuè xǐhuan chī Zhōngguócài.

② Tāmen tīngshuō xuéxiào fùjìn de Zhōngguó fànguǎnr "Lǎo Sìchuān" hěn yǒumíng, jiù juédìng qù chīchi kàn.

③ Yí dào Lǎo Sìchuān, Jiāxīng jiù juéde è le.

④ Tāmen gēn fúwùyuán shuō, xiǎng chī yòu má yòu là de Sìchuāncài.

⑤ Fúwùyuán hé tāmen shuō Zhōngwén, kěshì tāmen juéde fúwùyuán shuō de tài kuài le, qǐng tā shuō de màn yìdiǎnr.

⑥ Zuìhòu tāmen diǎnle mápó dòufu、suāncàiyú, hái yàole yí ge suānlàtāng.

⑦ Chīwán hòu, fúwùyuán wèn tāmen wèidào zěnmeyàng. Tāmen zhǐ diǎn tóu, bù shuō huà.

⑧ Yuánlái, tāmen xíguàn chī là de, kěshì bù xíguàn chī yòu má yòu là de.

Chopsticks

Chopsticks were developed about 5,000 years ago in China. It is said that people cooked their food in large pots which retained heat well, and hasty eaters then broke twigs off trees to retrieve the food. It is also thought that Confucius, a vegetarian, advised people not to use knives at the table because knives would remind them of the slaughterhouse. Chinese chopsticks, called 筷子 (kuàizi) are usually 9 to 10 inches long and rectangular with a blunt end.

Traditionally, chopsticks have been made from a variety of materials. Bamboo has been the most popular because it is inexpensive, readily available, easy to split, resistant to heat, and has no

CULTURAL NOTES

perceptible odor or taste. Cedar, sandalwood, teak, pine, and bone have also been used. The wealthy, however, often had chopsticks made from jade, gold, bronze, brass, agate, coral, ivory, and silver. In fact, during dynastic times it was thought that silver chopsticks would turn black if they came into contact with poisoned food.

Some of the most important chopstick rules are:

- Hold your chopsticks towards their end, and not in the middle or the front third.
- When you are not using your chopsticks and when you finish eating, lay them down in front of you with the tip to the left.
- Do not stick chopsticks into your food, especially not into rice. Only at funerals are chopsticks stuck into the rice that is put onto the altar.
- Do not pass food with your chopsticks directly to somebody else's chopsticks. Only at funerals are the bones of the cremated body given in that way from person to person.
- Do not spear food with your chopsticks.
- Do not point with your chopsticks to something or somebody.

LESSON 5 中餐館兒

　　家興和家奇越學中文越喜歡吃中國菜。他們聽說學校附近的中國飯館兒"老四川"很有名，就決定去吃吃看。一到老四川，家興就覺得餓了。他們跟服務員說，想吃又麻又辣的四川菜。服務員和他們說中文，可是他們覺得服務員說得太快了，請她說得慢一點兒。最後他們點了麻婆豆腐、酸菜魚，還要了一個酸辣湯。吃完後，服務員問他們味道怎麼樣。他們只點頭，不說話。原來，他們習慣吃辣的，可是不習慣吃又麻又辣的。

1

家奇：家興，真奇怪，我越學中文越想吃中國菜。
家興：一點兒也不奇怪。我也是。
家奇：我聽說學校附近有一家中國飯館兒很有名。
家興：是嗎？哪一家啊？
家奇：就是那家老四川！可是聽說四川菜很辣。
家興：越辣越好吃。
家奇：那我們去吃吃看。今天晚上行不行？

家興： 不行，今天我要和我的女朋友一起吃晚飯。再說，她不能吃辣的。
家奇： 那明天中午，行嗎？
家興： 行，下了中文課就去。
家奇： 一言爲定。

2

服務員： 請問，幾位？
家興： 就我們兩個。
服務員： 好，請跟我來。
家奇： 謝謝你。
服務員： 不客氣，請這邊坐。
家興： 謝謝。
服務員： 這是菜單，二位先生，先來杯茶，好不好？
家奇： 好。聽説你們四川菜很辣，對不對？
服務員： 對。你們會説中文啊？
家興： 我們只會説一點兒中文，可是我們能吃很多的中國菜。
家奇： 特別是又麻又辣的四川菜。
服務員： 太好了！你們的中文説得真好。
家興： 請你説得慢一點兒，好不好？
服務員： 好。我説你們的中文説得真好！
家奇： 謝謝。我們老師也常常這麼説。
服務員： 請問，二位想吃點兒什麼？
家奇： 我聽説麻婆豆腐不錯，來一個。
服務員： 好，麻婆豆腐一個。您呢？
家興： 我想嚐一嚐你們的酸菜魚。
服務員： 好，一個麻婆豆腐，一個酸菜魚。請問，二位想喝點兒什麼呢？
家奇： 我最喜歡喝酸辣湯了。你們有嗎？
服務員： 有。還要什麼？
家奇：
家興： 不要了，謝謝。

Lesson 5 中餐館兒

3

服務員： 先生，這是你們點的麻婆豆腐，這是你們要的酸菜魚，這是酸辣湯。請慢用。

家奇:
家興： 謝謝！

家奇： 我先吃一口我要的麻婆豆腐。

家興： 我先嚐一嚐我點的酸菜魚。

家奇： 呵，真香！

家興： 嗯，不錯，不錯。

服務員： 先生，味道怎麼樣？

(Jiaxing and Jiaqi only nodded without saying anything.)

服務員： 四川菜太辣了，不知道你們習慣不習慣？ (Mumbling)

家奇： 我們習慣吃辣的……

家興： 可是不習慣吃又麻又辣的。

VOCABULARY

1	*中餐	中餐	zhōngcān	N.	Chinese food (formal expression)
2	中餐館兒	中餐馆儿	zhōngcānguǎnr	N.	Chinese restaurant
3	*越	越	yuè	Adv.	more
4	越⋯越⋯	越⋯越⋯	yuè⋯yuè⋯		the more…, the more…
5	*聽說	听说	tīngshuō	V.	to hear sth. from others
6	*學校	学校	xuéxiào	N.	school
7	*附近	附近	fùjìn	N.	vicinity, in the vicinity of
8	*飯館兒	饭馆儿	fànguǎnr	N.	restaurant (informal way)
9	*老四川	老四川	Lǎo Sìchuān	PN	old Sichuan (name of a restaurant)
10	有名	有名	yǒumíng	Adj.	famous
11	決定	决定	juédìng	V.	to decide
12	一⋯就⋯	一⋯就⋯	yī⋯jiù⋯		as soon as…, then…
13	*服務員	服务员	fúwùyuán	N.	waiter, waitress
14	又⋯又⋯	又⋯又⋯	yòu⋯yòu⋯		both… and…

113

走近中國——初級漢語教程
APPROACHING CHINA : ELEMENTARY CHINESE

15	* 麻	麻	má	Adj.	spicy (numb)
16	辣	辣	là	Adj.	spicy
17	四川菜	四川菜	Sìchuāncài	N.	Sichuan dish / food
18	* 得	得	de	Pt.	*resultative marker*
19	快	快	kuài	Adj.	quick
20	* 慢	慢	màn	Adj.	slow
21	最後	最后	zuìhòu	N.	finally
22	點	点	diǎn	V.	to order
23	麻婆豆腐	麻婆豆腐	mápó dòufu	NP	*name of a Sichuan dish*
24	* 酸菜魚	酸菜鱼	suāncàiyú	N.	*fish with pickled vegetable*
25	* 酸辣湯	酸辣汤	suānlàtāng	N.	*hot and sour soup*
26	完	完	wán	V.	(finish) up
27	* 味道	味道	wèidào	N.	taste
28	* 點頭	点头	diǎn tóu	V.-O.	to nod
29	原來	原来	yuánlái	Adv.	originally
30	* 家	家	jiā	MW	*measure word for restaurant*
31	女朋友	女朋友	nǚpéngyou	N.	girlfriend
32	* 再說	再说	zàishuō	Conj.	besides
33	* 一言爲定	一言为定	yì yán wéi dìng	IE	*Okay. / It is a deal. / set in stone*
34	* 位	位	wèi	MW	*measure word for people (polite form)*
35	請跟我來	请跟我来	qǐng gēn wǒ lái	IE	Please follow me.
36	* 請這邊坐	请这边坐	qǐng zhèbiān zuò	IE	Please be seated here.
37	菜單	菜单	càidān	N.	menu
38	* 嚐	尝	cháng	V.	to taste
39	嚐一嚐	尝一尝	cháng yi cháng	VP	*try (by tasting)*

■ Supplementary Vocabulary:

1	聽	听	tīng	V.	to listen to
2	最	最	zuì	Adv.	the most
3	豆腐	豆腐	dòufu	N.	tofu
4	酸	酸	suān	Adj.	sour

Lesson 5 中餐館兒

5	蛋糕	蛋糕	dàngāo	N.	cake
6	包子	包子	bāozi	N.	steam bread with fillings
7	饅頭	馒头	mántou	N.	steam bread
8	麵條兒	面条儿	miàntiáor	N.	noodles
9	餃子	饺子	jiǎozi	N.	dumplings
10	火鍋	火锅	huǒguō	N.	hot pot
11	可口可樂	可口可乐	kěkǒu-kělè	N.	coca-cola
12	水果	水果	shuǐguǒ	N.	fruit
13	蘋果	苹果	píngguǒ	N.	apple
14	西瓜	西瓜	xīguā	N.	watermelon
15	草莓	草莓	cǎoméi	N.	strawberry
16	葡萄	葡萄	pútao	N.	grape
17	橘子	橘子	júzi	N.	tangerine
18	香蕉	香蕉	xiāngjiāo	N.	banana
19	雜技	杂技	zájì	N.	acrobatics
20	西安	西安	Xī'ān	PW	Xi'an city
21	廣州	广州	Guǎngzhōu	PW	Guangzhou
22	特色菜	特色菜	tèsècài	N.	specialty in a restaurant
23	買單	买单	mǎi dān	V.-O.	Check, please.
24	結賬	结账	jié zhàng	V.-O.	Check, please.
25	時候	时候	shíhou	N.	time
26	什麽時候	什么时候	shénme shíhou	NP	when, at what time

GRAMMAR

1 S 越 A 越 B: the more..., the more....

This structure describes the progression in one process that is related to another one.
這個結構表示 B 隨 A 的變化而發生變化。

  a. 家興跟家奇越吃中國菜越喜歡學中文。
(The more Jiaqi and Jiaxing eat Chinese food, the more they like learning Chinese.)

115

b. 你越不喜歡我，我越喜歡你。(The more you dislike me, the more I like you.)
c. 天氣越好，我越高興。(The better the weather is, the happier I am.)

If we are only talking about one thing that is steadily augmenting or diminishing, then we have the following structure:
若我們只是討論某一項穩定增長或減少的事物，則用下面的結構：

S 越來越 Adj. 了 : sth. is becoming more and more

a. 我的中文越來越好了。(My Chinese is getting better and better.)
b. 他越來越有名了。(He is getting more and more famous.)
c. 哥大的學生越來越多了。(There are more and more students at CU.)
d. 我越來越喜歡紐約了。(I like New York more and more.)
e. 我的朋友越來越多了。(I have more and more friends.)
f. 我越來越喜歡中國跟中文了。(I like China and Chinese more and more.)
g. 她越來越漂亮了。(She is getting more and more beautiful.)

2 (S) V (一) V : 嚐一嚐

The verb phrase in this structure indicates that the action won't last long or it will be completed shortly. It is very often used especially when one is suggesting another one to do something, asking for a favor, or trying to do something.
這個結構中的動詞短語表示動作完成或持續的時間較短，常用於建議別人做某事、請求幫助，或者嘗試做某事。

a. 嚐一嚐 (Try it! / Taste it.)
b. 說一說 (Say something.)
c. 看一看 (Take a look!)
d. 聽一聽 (Listen to it.)
e. 喝一喝 (Sip it.)
f. 問一問 (Ask about it.)
g. 想一想 (Think about it.)
h. 用一用 (Use it for a while.)

The "一" can be dropped, and the meaning will not be changed.
"一"可以省略，意思不變。

3 V V 看 : do sth. first and see

This construction is very useful. It is used to indicate that somebody should try to do something first and then decide what they will think about it. The internal structure is

actually "V 一 V + 看". But this does not apply to the verb 看.
這個結構非常實用，表示某人應先嘗試某一行爲再作出決定或得出結論。其內部結構實際爲"V 一 V + 看"。但是動詞"看"並不適用於這個結構。

 a. 他們聽説那家飯館兒的飯菜不錯，就決定去吃吃看。
(They have heard that the food in that restaurant is pretty good and they decide to go there and try it.)
b. ——聽説中文很好學。(I have heard that Chinese is very easy to learn.)
——那你學學看。(Learn it and see.)
c. 綠茶很好喝，你喝喝看。(Green tea is very tasty. Try it and see if it is so.)
d. 我聽説中國菜很好吃，咱們吃吃看。
(I heard that Chinese dishes are tasty. Let's try it and see how it tastes or what it tastes like.)
e. ——我的中文很好。(My Chinese is very good.)
——説説看。(Say something and let's see.)

4 S 一 VP₁, (S) 就 VP₂: as soon as...; whenever..., then...

一 here appears right before the verb in the first clause; 就 appears, as usual, right before the verb in the second clause, and often remains untranslated. Please also remember that 就 is an adverb that can never go before a subject.
"一"用在第一個分句的動詞之前，"就"用於第二個分句的動詞之前。注意，"就"是副詞，不能用於主語前。

 他們一到老四川，家興就覺得餓極了。
(As soon as they arrived in Old Sichuan, Jiaxing felt extremely hungry.)

NOTE: If the subject is the same in both clauses, then the second one can be dropped.
注意：如果兩個分句的主語相同，那麼第二個主語可以省略。

 a. 他一學中文，(他)就覺得很餓。
(Whenever he studies Chinese, he feels hungry.)
b. 我一到紐約就想吃 Pizza.
(Whenever I come to New York, I want to have Pizza.)
c. 我一吃 Pizza 就很高興。(I feel happy whenver I eat Pizza.)
d. 我一高興就想學中文。
(Whenever I am happy, I would like to learn Chinese.)
e. 我一學中文就想喝酒。(I want to drink whenever I learn Chinese.)
f. 我一喝酒就想唱歌。(Whenever I drink, I want to sing.)

g. 我一唱歌，就想爸爸媽媽。(As soon as I sing, I will miss my dad and mom.)

h. 我一想父母，就想給他們打電話。
(When I miss my parents, I want to call them.)

5 最 Adj. / VP 的 NP；最 Adj. / VP

最 is an adverb. The translation always takes the superlative superior form of English adjectives.

"最"是副詞，意思相當於英語中的形容詞最高級。

最 Adj. / VP 的 NP

 a. 這是最辣的四川菜。(This is the spiciest Sichuan dish.)

b. 他是最有錢的人。(He is the richest person.)

c. 這是我最愛的女人。(This is the woman I love the most.)

d. 她是最好看的女人。(She is the most beautiful woman.)

e. 我弟弟是最可愛的孩子。(My younger brother is the cutest kid.)

最 Adj. / VP

 a. 我最喜歡點菜。(The thing that I like to do the most is to order dishes.)

b. 誰的中文最好？(Whose Chinese is the best?)

c. 他的中文最好。(His Chinese is the best.)

d. 他的宿舍最舒服。(His dorm is the most comfortable.)

e. 我最喜歡春天。(I like Spring the most.)

When 最好 modifies a verb phrase, it means "had better".
當"最好"修飾動詞短語時，它的意思為 had better。

 a. 你最好先喝一點兒茶。(You had better drink some tea first.)

b. 你最好先學中文。(You had better learn Chinese first.)

c. 你最好早點睡覺。(You had better go to bed early.)

d. 你最好先做功課再玩兒。(You had better do the homework first and then play.)

6 Predicative complement：S V 得 + Complement

Predicative complements refer to the words or phrases selected by the verb to provide more information about the verb (action) or to indicate how well an action (i.e. the verb) is performed. In Chinese, as in English, such comments appear in the sentence after the verb. The verb and the comment are connected by the particle *de*, in this case written as 得.

Lesson 5 中餐館兒

程度補語可以提供更多關於動詞（動作）的信息，或者表明動作完成的程度。和英語相似，漢語裡有關動詞的評價出現在句中的動詞之後。動詞和評價之間用助詞"得"連接。

> E.g. a. 可是他們覺得他説得太快了。(But they think that he speaks too fast.)
> b. 請服務員説得慢一點兒。(They ask the waitress to speak a little bit slowly.)

If the verb is transitive, the structure is:
如果動詞是及物動詞，那麼結構爲：

> **S V O V 得 + Complement**

> E.g. 他説中文説得很好。(He speaks Chinese very well.)

There are several ways to question "S V O V 得 + Complement" structure:
對"S V O V 得 + complement"結構提問有以下幾種方式：

> **S V O V 得 怎麼樣？**

> E.g. 他説中文説得怎麼樣？ (How well does he speak Chinese?)

> **S V O V 得 Adj. 嗎？**

> E.g. 他説中文説得好嗎？ (Does he speak Chinese well?)

> **S V O V 得 Adj. 不 Adj. ?**

> E.g. 他説中文説得好不好？ (Does he speak Chinese well or not?)

> **Positive answer: S V O V 得 Adv. Adj.**

> E.g. 他説中文説得很好。(He speaks Chinese very well.)

> **Negative answer: S V O V 得不（Adv.）Adj.**

> E.g. 他説中文説得不好。(He does not speak Chinese very well.)
> 他説中文説得不怎麼好。(He does not speak Chinese that well.)

The position of the object in this pattern may vary. The key point is that it should be in correspondence to the position of the object in the interrogative.
這一結構中賓語的位置可以發生變化，關鍵的一點是它必須與問句中賓語的位置一致。

> E.g. Q1: 他説中文説得怎麼樣？
> A1: 他説中文説得很好。

Q2: 中文他說得怎麼樣？
A2: 中文他說得很好。
Q3: 他中文說得怎麼樣？
A3: 他中文說得很好。

Here are some other examples:
下面還有一些其他的例句：

a. 他們跳舞跳得怎麼樣？／他們跳舞跳得好嗎？／他們跳舞跳得好不好？
   (How well do they dance?)
b. 他們跳舞跳得很好。／他們跳舞跳得不好。
   (They dance very well./They don't dance very well.)
c. 他們睡覺睡得很舒服。(They sleep very comfortably.)
d. 他們睡覺睡得不太舒服。／他們睡覺睡得不怎麼舒服。
   (They don't sleep very comfortably.)
e. 外面的雨 (yǔ) 下得很大。(It is raining heavily outside.)
f. 上個星期你玩兒得怎麼樣？ (Did you have fun last week?)
g. 你在哥大吃得好不好？ (Do you eat well at CU?)

7 S 又 A 又 B：both A and B

When using this structure, please note that the subject must be the same.
使用這一結構時要注意主語必須相同。

S 又 ADj.₁ 又 ADj.₂

a. 我的弟弟又聰明又可愛。(My younger brother is both smart and cute.)
b. 他的女朋友又漂亮又有錢。(His girlfriend is beautiful and rich.)
c. 我的大學老師又機智又有名。
   (My college teacher is both resourceful and famous.)
d. 我又累又餓。(I am both tired and hungry.)
e. 這張床 (chuáng) 又大又舒服。(This bed is both big and comfortable.)

S 又 VP₁ 又 VP₂

a. 兩件衣服都很好看，我又想買這件，又想買那件。
   (Both clothes are pretty. I want to buy this one and also that one.)
b. 她找了一個又高又帥的男朋友，高興得又唱又跳。
   (She found a boyfriend who is both tall and handsome. She is so happy that she dances and sings.)

Lesson 5 中餐館兒

8 Relative clause：S V 的 NP；V O 的 NP

A relative clause or an attributive clause has the attribute function for a noun or pronoun in the main clause. In other words, a relative clause is a sentence that is used to modify a noun (subject or object). Thus the noun that is being modified will be specific or definite. In English, the relative clause goes after the noun that it modifies, e.g. *I like the teacher [who teaches French]*. The Chinese relative clause like other modifiers in Chinese must go before the noun that it modifies. Unlike English, there is no relative pronouns in Chinese relative clause. Instead, the noun modifier marker 的 is inserted in between the noun and the attributive clause.

定語從句的作用主要是修飾主句裡的名詞或代詞。換言之，定語從句是用於修飾名詞（主語或賓語）的句子。但這個被修飾的名詞必須是特定的或限定性的。在英語中，定語從句位於它所修飾的名詞之後，如"I like the teacher [who teaches French]"。在漢語中，定語從句必須用在它所修飾的名詞之前，而且與英語不同，漢語的定語從句沒有關聯代詞，而是在名詞和定語從句之間插入名詞修飾語標誌"的"。

a. 我先吃一口 [我要的] 定語 麻婆豆腐。
   (I will try the Mapo Tofu [that I ordered] relative clause.)
b. 我先嚐一嚐 [我點的] 定語 酸菜魚。
   (I will taste the fish with pickles [that I ordered] relative clause first.)
c. 這是 [你們點的] 麻婆豆腐。
   (This is the MapoTofu that you have ordered.)
d. 這是 [你們要的] 酸菜魚。
   (This is the fish with pickles that you wanted.)

If the noun that is being modified is an object in sentence, then the attributive clause structure is:

如果被修飾的名詞是句子的賓語，那麼定語從句的結構是：

S V 的 NP

我喜歡吃菜。→ [我喜歡吃的] 菜是中國菜。
(The food that I like to eat is Chinese food.)
中國菜是 [我喜歡吃的] 菜。
(Chinese food is the thing that I like to eat.)

121

If the noun that is being modified is the subject in the sentence, the pattern is:
如果被修飾的名詞是句子的主語,那麼定語從句的結構是:

V O 的 NP

 張老師喜歡我。→ [喜歡我的老師] 是張老師。
(The teacher that likes me is Teacher Zhang.)
張老師是 [喜歡我的老師]。
(Teacher Zhang is the one who likes me.)

Here are some other examples:
下面還有一些其他的例句:

 a. 最愛我的人是我的父母。(The ones who love me the most are my parents.)
b. 我父母是最愛我的人。(My parents are the ones who love me the most.)
c. 這是我媽媽最愛吃的豆腐。(This is the Tofu that my mother likes the most.)
d. 我給你泡你最愛喝的紅茶。(I will steep the black tea that you like the most.)
e. 這是我昨天買的那套茶具。(This is the tea set that I bought yesterday.)

to emphasize

We have mentioned in earlier sections that 就 has the function to emphasize.
在前面我們已經講過"就"可以表示強調。

 就是那家老四川。 (It is just that Lao Sichuan.)

only

就 means "only" when a number goes after it.
當"就"後面有數詞時,它表示"僅僅"。

 a. 就我們兩個。(Only us two.)
b.——昨天你去韓國飯館兒吃了幾個菜?
(How many dishes did you have at the Korean restaurant yesterday?)
——不多,就三個菜。(Not many. Only three.)
c. 我們家很小,就三個人。
(Our family is very small. There are only three people.)

Lesson 5 中餐館兒

10) Num. + MW + NP

Numeral	Measure word	NP	Meaning
一	家	中國飯館兒	a Chinese restaurant
一	口	飯/菜	a mouthful or a little bit of food

11) Question forms

E.g
a. 今天晚上,行不行? (How about tonight?)
b. 來點茶, 好不好? (Have some tea, okay?)
c. 那明天中午, 行嗎? (Then tomorrow noon, will that be okay?)
e. 什麼時候去? (When are you going?)
f. 還想要什麼? (What else do you want?)

Summary:

▶ 就 appears, as usual, right before the verb in the second clause.

▶ 就 is an adverb that can never go before a subject.

▶ When 最好 modifies a verb phrase, it means "had better."

▶ The Chinese relative clause like other modifiers in Chinese must go before the noun that it modifies.

▶ Unlike English, there is no relative pronoun in Chinese relative clause.

▶ Instead, the noun modifier marker 的 is inserted in between the noun and the attributive clause.

Patterns:

● S 越 A 越 B ∥ 我越學中文越愛吃中國菜。
　　　　　　(The more I learn Chinese, the more I like eating Chinese food.)

● S 越來越 Adj. 了 ∥ 我的中文越來越好了。(My Chinese is getting better and better.)

● V (一) V ∥ 嚐一嚐! (Try it! / Taste it.)

● V V 看 ∥ 他們決定去吃吃看。(They decide to go there and try it.)

- S 一 VP₁, (S) 就 VP₂ ‖ 他們一到老四川，家興就覺得餓極了。
  (As soon as they arrived in Old Sichuan, Jiaxing felt extremely hungry.)

- 最 Adj. / VP 的 NP ‖ 最辣的四川菜 (the most spicy Sichuan dish)

- 最 Adj. / VP ‖ 我最喜歡點菜。(I like ordering dishes the most.)

- S V 得 + Complement ‖ 可是他們覺得他說得太快了。
  (But they think that he speaks too fast.)

- S V O V 得 + Complement ‖ 他說中文說得很好。(He speaks Chinese very well.)

- S V O V 得 怎麼樣？‖ 他說中文說得怎麼樣？ (How well does he speak Chinese?)

- S V O V 得 Adj. 嗎？‖ 他說中文說得好嗎？ (Does he speak Chinese well?)

- S V O V 得 Adj. 不 Adj.？‖ 他說中文說得好不好？
  (Does he speak Chinese well or not?)

- S V O V 得 Adv. Adj. ‖ 他說中文說得很好。(He speaks Chinese very well.)

- S 又 Adj.₁ 又 Adj.₂ ‖ 我的弟弟又聰明又可愛。
  (My younger brother is both smart and cute.)

- S 又 VP₁ 又 VP₂ ‖ 兩件衣服都很好看，我又想買這件，又想買那件。
  (Both clothes are pretty. I want to buy this one and also that one.)

- S V 的 NP ‖ 我喜歡吃的菜是中國菜。(The food that I like to eat is Chinese food.)

- V O 的 NP ‖ 喜歡我的老師是張老師。 (The teacher that likes me is Teacher Zhang.)

IN CLASS ACTIVITIES

1 Answer the following questions according to the text:

① 家興跟家奇越學中文越喜歡吃什麼菜？

② 他們聽說什麼？

③ 一到老四川，家興就覺得怎麼了？

Lesson 5　中餐館兒

④ 他跟服務員說什麼？

⑤ 他們覺得服務員說中文說得怎麼樣？

⑥ 他們點了什麼菜？

⑦ 服務員問他們什麼？

⑧ 他們習慣吃很辣的菜嗎？

2 Please do role play according to the dialogues given below:

- A 明天我想請你吃飯，行不行？
- B 行啊！什麼時候？
- A 明天中午，行嗎？
- B 真不好意思，明天中午我有點兒事。
- A 那明天晚上，好嗎？
- B 好。

- A 歡迎光臨 (huānyíng guānglín: welcome)。請問，幾位？
- B 兩位。
- A 請這邊來！
- B/C 謝謝！
  ……
- A 這是菜單。請問，二位想先喝點兒什麼？
- B 給我來一瓶綠茶。
- C 我要一瓶啤酒。
- A 好的，請稍等。
  ……

走近中國──初級漢語教程
APPROACHING CHINA : ELEMENTARY CHINESE

A 請問可以點菜了嗎？

B 你們的特色菜 (tèsècài: specialty) 是什麼？

A 辣子雞 (làzijī: spicy chicken)。

B 好，我們嚐嚐。

……

A 請慢用。

……

C 服務員，請結賬 (jié zhàng: to pay for a bill)。

A 這是你們的賬單 (zhàngdān: bill)。

C 謝謝！

……

A 請慢走！歡迎再來。

HOMEWORK

1 Please rewrite the following sentences with relative clause:

① 他是老師。我喜歡他。 ➜ 他是我喜歡的老師。

② 我的奶奶喜歡吃豆腐。這是豆腐。
➜

③ 我點了三個菜。這是菜。
➜

④ 這就是那套茶具。我昨天買了一套茶具。
➜

⑤ 我愛喝綠茶。我給你泡綠茶。
➜

Lesson 5 中餐館兒

2 Please rewrite or complete the following statements by using the structures given:

① 酸菜魚很好吃。(V 一 V)

➡ 請嚐一嚐。

② 我學中文。我想去中國。(越 A 越 B)

➡

③ 妹妹很漂亮。(越來越)

➡

④ 她請客 (qǐng kè: to treat sb. to a meal)。她說她沒有錢。(一 V, 就 V)

➡

⑤ 北京大學很漂亮，也很有名。(又 A 又 B)

➡

⑥ 中國音樂很好聽。(VV 看)

➡

3 Translate the following sentences into Chinese:

① Whenever I go to the French class, I want to drink wine.

② I like the girl who knows how to cook Chinese food.

③ The person who does business is an Italian.

④ He speaks Korean very well.

⑤ How does he use chopsticks? Very well.

_____

⑥ He is the best person that I know.

_____

⑦ You'd better work first.

_____

4 Please fill in the blanks with appropriate words without referring to the text (Some of them may be used more than once):

> 的　又　了　樣　辣　和　越　很　去　原來　得　就

家興 __和__ 家奇越學中文_____喜歡吃中國飯。他們聽說學校附近_____中國飯館兒"老四川"_____有名，就決定_____吃吃看。一到老四川，家興_____覺得餓_____。他跟服務員說他想吃又麻_____ _____的四川菜。他們覺得服務員說中文說_____太快了，請服務員說得慢一點兒。最後他們點_____麻婆豆腐、酸菜魚，還要了一個酸辣湯。吃完後，服務員問他們味道怎麼_____。他們只點頭，不說話。_____，他們習慣吃辣_____，可是不習慣吃_____麻又辣的。

5 Please read the following paragraph in Pinyin:

Jiāqí juéde shuō Zhōngwén de jīhuì tài shǎo le. Wáng lǎoshī shuō, kěyǐ bāng tóngxuémen zhǎo cóng Zhōngguó lái de liúxuéshēng zuò yǔbàn, Jiāqí hěn gāoxìng. Jiāxīng zhènghǎo yě xiǎng zhǎo ge yǔbàn liànxí Zhōngwén. Yúshì, liǎng ge rén dōu bàole míng. Yí ge xīngqī yǐhòu, Jiāqí shōudàole yǔbàn de yóujiàn. Tāmen yuēhǎo xiàwǔ sì diǎn zài túshūguǎn ménqián jiàn miàn. Jiāqí zhǐ zhīdào yǔbàn shì ge nǚ de, bù zhīdào tā de xìnggé zěnmeyàng, yě bù zhīdào tāmen néng bu néng hédelái, suǒyǐ tā yǒudiǎnr jǐnzhāng. Sān diǎn wǔshíwǔ, Jiāqí jiù dàole túshūguǎn ménqián. Liǎng fēnzhōng hòu, tā kànjiànle tā de yǔbàn, yí ge Zhōngguó nǚ xuésheng. Tāmen xiān shuōle bàn ge xiǎoshí de Yīngyǔ, ránhòu yòu shuōle bàn ge xiǎoshí de Hànyǔ. Tāmen dōu juéde zhè zhǒng yǔyán jiāohuàn duì tāmen bāngzhù hěn dà, juédìng yǐhòu měi ge lǐbài dōu jiàn yí cì miàn.

Chinese Food

Chinese food can be roughly divided into Northern and Southern styles of cooking. According to the Southerners, Northern dishes are relatively oily and the use of vinegar and garlic tends to be quite popular. Northern cooking has a lot of food that is made of wheat: noodles, ravioli like dumplings, steamed stuffed buns, fried meat dumplings, and steamed bread . The best known regional variations of Northern Chinese cuisine include those of Beijing, Tianjin, and Shandong.

Sichuan and Hunan cuisine belong to the Southern cooking styles, which are famous for their liberal use of chili peppers. The Jiangsu and Zhejiang regions emphasize freshness and tenderness, while Guangdong cuisine tends to be somewhat sweet and always full of variety. The typical foundation for Southern dishes includes rice and its byproducts such as noodles, cakes, and congee.

Chinese cooking focuses on color, aroma and flavor for every dish. Normally, any one entree is a combination of three to five colors, selected from ingredients that are light green, dark green, red, yellow, white, black, or caramel colored. Usually, a meat and vegetable dish is prepared from one main ingredient and two to three secondary ingredients of contrasting colors. They are then cooked appropriately, incorporating the proper seasonings and sauce to create an aesthetically attractive dish.

Not only does Chinese cooking focus on the color, aroma, and flavor but on nutrition as well. As a matter of fact, many of the plants used in Chinese cooking, such as scallions, fresh ginger root, garlic, dried lily buds, tree fungus, etc. have properties of preventing and alleviating various illnesses.

Chinese people believe in the medicinal value of food and that food and medicine share the same origin. This view could be considered a forerunner of nutritional science in China. The concept of the correct proportion of meat to vegetable ingredients maintained is very notable. It is believed that one third of meat based dishes should be vegetable ingredients and one third of vegetable dishes should be meat. When preparing soups, the quantity of water used should total seven-tenths the volume of the serving bowl. In short, the correct ingredient proportions must be adhered to in the preparation of each dish or soup in order to ensure full nutritional value.

Chinese people have several rules and customs that are associated with eating. For example, it is better to eat while seated; there is a set order of who may be seated first among men, women, old and young; and the main courses must be served with chopsticks, and soup with a spoon. Chinese banquets are arranged on a per table basis with each table usually seating ten to twelve people.

A typical banquet consists of four appetizer dishes, such as cold cut platters or hot hors d'oeuvres; six to eight main courses; then one savory snack type dish and a dessert. The methods of preparation include stir frying, stewing, steaming, deep frying, flash frying, pan frying etc. The main colors of a dish may include red, yellow, green, white and caramel color. A dish may be savory, sweet, tart or piquant. Food garnishes, such as cut or sculptured carrots, Chinese white radishes, cucumbers may be used to add to the visual appeal of a dish. All of these elements contribute to making Chinese food a true feast.

LESSON 6　語伴

　　家奇覺得說中文的機會太少了。王老師說，可以幫同學們找從中國來的留學生做語伴，家奇很高興。家興正好也想找個語伴練習中文。於是，兩個人都報了名。一個星期以後，家奇收到了語伴的郵件。他們約好下午四點在圖書館門前見面。家奇只知道語伴是個女的，不知道她的性格怎麼樣，也不知道他們能不能合得來，所以他有點兒緊張。三點五十五，家奇就到了圖書館門前。兩分鐘後，他看見了他的語伴，一個中國女學生。他們先說了半個小時的英語，然後又說了半個小時的漢語。他們都覺得這種語言交換對他們幫助很大，決定以後每個禮拜都見一次面。

1

老師：　大家好！你們的中文學得很不錯。

家奇：　可是說中文的機會太少了。

老師：　要是你們願意，我可以幫你們找個從中國來的留學生做語伴。

家興：　王老師，什麼是語伴呢？

老師：　語伴就是語言夥伴，你們互相幫助。中國留學生幫你們提高漢語水平，你們幫他們提高英語水平。

Lesson 6 語伴

家奇: 太好了。
老師: 有興趣的同學請在我這兒報名。
家興: 老師，我正好想找個語伴練習說中文呢。算我一個。
家奇: 也算我一個。
老師: 下課後請給我留下你們的郵件地址。

2 (A week later, Jiaqi told Jiaxing excitedly that he had received his language partner's email.)

家興: 家奇，這麼高興，有什麼好事？
家奇: 家興，我收到了我語伴的來信。我們約好下午四點在圖書館門前見面。
家興: 真為你高興！唉，我的語伴還不知道在哪兒呢。
家奇: 你不是有很多中國朋友嗎？
家興: 有是有，可是他們的英文那麼好，又都那麼忙，我不好意思總是麻煩他們。
家奇: 說的也是。我今天下午要跟我的語伴見面，可是我有點兒緊張。
家興: 又不是約會，緊張什麼？
家奇: 我只知道她是個女的，不知道她的性格怎麼樣，也不知道我們能不能合得來。
家興: 沒問題，你長得這麼帥，人見人愛。
家奇: 呵呵，我可不是"小可愛"！

3 (Li Jiaqi said to himself.)

家奇: 三點五十了，我得趕快去圖書館找我的語伴了。去晚了，不禮貌。我得走快點兒。總算到了。三點五十五分。那個中國女學生可能就是我的語伴吧？我去問問她。
家奇: 你好！你是不是趙可語？
可語: 你好！我就是。你是李家奇吧？
家奇: 對，是我。
可語: 你的中文說得真好！
家奇: 哪裡哪裡，差遠了。我的四聲還是有問題。你的英文也很好啊！

可語： 謝謝，其實也不行。

家奇： 你的要求太高了！我們先說半小時英文，好不好？

可語： 好，謝謝。

(30 minutes later...)

可語： 現在，我們該說中文了。

家奇： 請你幫我糾正我的聲調。

……

可語： 時間過得真快，五點了。

家奇： 是呀，我覺得這樣練習很有幫助。要是你願意，以後每個禮拜我們都可以見一次面。

可語： 好。下星期五見！

家奇： 再見！

VOCABULARY

1	*語伴	语伴	yǔbàn	N.	language exchange partner
2	*機會	机会	jīhuì	N.	opportunity
3	*少	少	shǎo	Adj.	few, less
4	幫	帮	bāng	V.	to help
5	*找	找	zhǎo	V.	to look for
6	從	从	cóng	Prep.	from
7	正好	正好	zhènghǎo	Adv.	to be about
8	練習	练习	liànxí	V.	to practice
9	於是	于是	yúshì	Conj.	herefore
10	報名	报名	bào míng	V.-O.	to register
11	*星期	星期	xīngqī	N.	week
12	收到	收到	shōudào	V.-C.	to receive
13	郵件	邮件	yóujiàn	N.	e-mail
14	約好	约好	yuēhǎo	V.-C.	to make an appointment
15	*點	点	diǎn	MW	o'clock

Lesson 6 語伴

16	圖書館	图书馆	túshūguǎn	N.	library
17	門	门	mén	N.	gate, door
18	*前	前	qián	TW	front, in front of
19	*見面	见面	jiàn miàn	V.-O.	to meet
20	女的	女的	nǚ de	NP	female
21	*性格	性格	xìnggé	N.	personality
22	*合得來	合得来	hédelái	Adj.	to get along well with
23	有點兒	有点儿	yǒudiǎnr	Adv.	a little bit
24	*緊張	紧张	jǐnzhāng	Adj.	nervous
25	看見	看见	kànjiàn	V.	to see
26	女	女	nǚ	Adj.	female
27	半	半	bàn	Num.	half
28	小時	小时	xiǎoshí	N.	hour
29	*英語	英语	Yīngyǔ	N.	English
30	*然後	然后	ránhòu	Conj.	afterwards
31	*漢語	汉语	Hànyǔ	N.	Chinese
32	*種	种	zhǒng	MW	kind
33	語言	语言	yǔyán	N.	language
34	交換	交换	jiāohuàn	V.	exchange
35	*幫助	帮助	bāngzhù	V.	to help
36	禮拜	礼拜	lǐbài	N.	week
37	要是	要是	yàoshi	Conj.	if
38	*願意	愿意	yuànyì	Aux. V.	to be willing
39	夥伴	伙伴	huǒbàn	N.	partner
40	*互相	互相	hùxiāng	Adv.	mutually
41	提高	提高	tígāo	V.	to improve
42	水平	水平	shuǐpíng	N.	level
43	*興趣	兴趣	xìngqù	N.	interest
44	算	算	suàn	V.	to count
45	留下	留下	liúxià	V.-C.	to leave
46	地址	地址	dìzhǐ	N.	address
47	*信	信	xìn	N.	letter
48	爲	为	wèi	Prep.	for
49	唉	唉	ài	Int.	to sigh

50	總是	总是	zǒngshì	Adv.	always
51	*麻煩	麻烦	máfan	V.	to bother, to trouble
52	說的也是	说的也是	shuō de yě shì	IE	I agree.
53	*約會	约会	yuēhuì	N./V.	dating; to date
54	*長	长	zhǎng	V.	to grow (appearance)
55	*帥	帅	shuài	Adj.	cool, handsome
56	人見人愛	人见人爱	rén jiàn rén ài	IE	to be loved by everybody
57	可	可	kě	Adv.	*used to emphasize*
58	得	得	děi	Aux. V.	have to
59	趕快	赶快	gǎnkuài	Adv.	hurry up
60	*晚	晚	wǎn	Adj.	late
61	禮貌	礼貌	lǐmào	Adj.	polite
62	*總算	总算	zǒngsuàn	Adv.	finally
63	可能	可能	kěnéng	Aux. V.	maybe, perhaps
64	哪裡哪裡	哪里哪里	nǎli nǎli	IE	No, no.
65	差遠了	差远了	chà yuǎn le	IE	Not good at all.
66	四聲	四声	sìshēng	N.	four tones
67	*其實	其实	qíshí	Adv.	actually
68	*要求	要求	yāoqiú	N.	requirement
69	*高	高	gāo	Adj.	high, tall
70	*該	该	gāi	Aux. V.	should
71	糾正	纠正	jiūzhèng	V.	to correct
72	聲調	声调	shēngdiào	N.	tones
73	*時間	时间	shíjiān	N.	time
74	*過	过	guò	V.	to pass
75	星期五	星期五	xīngqīwǔ	TW	Friday

Supplementary Vocabulary:

1	檸檬	柠檬	níngméng	N.	lemon
2	動作電影	动作电影	dòngzuò diànyǐng	NP	action movie
3	科幻電影	科幻电影	kēhuàn diànyǐng	NP	science fiction movie

Lesson 6 語伴

4 恐怖電影	恐怖电影	kǒngbù diànyǐng	NP	horror movie
5 愛情電影	爱情电影	àiqíng diànyǐng	NP	romance movie
6 廣場	广场	guǎngchǎng	N.	square
7 工人	工人	gōngrén	N.	worker
8 白領	白领	báilǐng	N.	white collar
9 農民	农民	nóngmín	N.	peasant
10 出租車	出租车	chūzūchē	N.	taxi
11 公司	公司	gōngsī	N.	company
12 甜	甜	tián	Adj.	sweet
13 告訴	告诉	gàosù	V.	to tell
14 逛街	逛街	guàng jiē	V.-O.	to stroll along the street, to go window shopping
15 賣報	卖报	mài bào	V.-O.	to sell newspaper
16 坐飛機	坐飞机	zuò fēijī	VP	to take an airplane
17 上網	上网	shàng wǎng	V.-O.	to surf on the internet
18 畢業	毕业	bì yè	V.-O.	to graduate
19 地	地	de	Pt.	to indicate the way that an action is carried out
20 自言自語	自言自语	zìyán-zìyǔ	IE	to talk to oneself

GRAMMAR

1 從 + PW V 的 NP：the NP (coming) from PW

從中國來的留學生想找人做語言交換。
(The foreign student who comes from China wants to find somebody to do language exchange.)

This is another case of relative clause. The structure "S 從 PW 來" is used a lot.
這是關係從句的另一個例子。"S 從 PW 來"結構使用頻繁。

 a. ——你從哪兒來？ (Where are you from?)
——我從美國來。 (I am from the United States.)
b. ——你是不是從意大利來的？ (Is it the case that you are from Italy?)
——是的，我是從意大利來的。 (Yes, I am from Italy.)
c. 從意大利來的朋友不喜歡吃意大利麵條兒。
(The friend who is from Italy doesn't like eating Italian noodles.)

d. 從紐約來的學生的聲調很好。
(The tones of the students who are from New York are very good.)

2 S 正好也想／要 VP：sb. is just about to do sth. (too)

E.g. a. 他正好也想找個語伴練習中文。
(He was about to find a language partner to practice Chinese.)
b. 你不是正好也要去中國學中文嗎？
(Isn't it the case that you are about to go to China to learn Chinese too?)
c. 我正好也想去老四川，我們一起走吧。
(I was just about to go to Old Sichuan too. Let's go together.)
d. 我正好也要去那兒，咱們一起走吧。
(I was just about to go there too. Let's go together.)

3 S 想找 sb. VP：S would like to find / hire sb. to do sth.

E.g. a. 我想找人幫我照顧我的狗。
(I would like to find somebody to take care of the dog.)
b. 我想找人一起做中國菜。
(I would like to find somebody to cook Chinese food together.)
c. 我喜歡的女孩子想找人跟她一起去超市買米。
(The girl whom I like would like to find somebody to go to the supermarket to buy rice with her.)
d. 你想不想找人幫你買書？
(Are you interested in finding somebody to help you buy books?)
e. 你不想找人教你做西紅柿炒雞蛋了？
(Don't you want to find somebody to teach you how to make fried eggs with tomato anymore?)

4 ……（以）後；……（以）前

E.g. 一個星期（以）後 (a week later)   兩分鐘後 (two minutes later)
下課後 (after class)   三天（以）前 (three days ago)
a. 去中國前，他買了很多吃的東西。
(Before he went to China, he bought a lot of food.)
b. 兩年前，我不會說中文。現在我說得很好了。
(Two years ago, I couldn't speak Chinese. Now I speak pretty well.)

以前，以後 can also be used as time words individually, in which case they mean "formerly, in the past" and "in the future" respectively. We also have learned the word 後來 "later". 後來, however, can not be used to describe an action that will happen in the future as the English word does. In the time line, we can put them in the sequence of:

"以前,以後"也可以單獨作爲時間詞使用,分別意爲"以前、過去"和"將來"。我們還學過"後來",然而,"後來"不能像在英語中那樣用來描述將會發生在將來的動作。在時間綫上,這幾個詞的順序是:

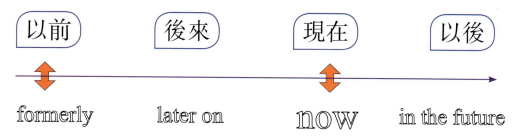

　a. Formerly, I couldn't speak Chinese.(以前我不會說中文。)
　b. Later on, I learned Chinese.(後來我學了中文。)
　c. I can speak some Chinese now.(現在我會說一點兒中文了。)
　d. I want to speak Chinese more in the future.(以後我要多說中文。)

5 S 有(一)點兒 Adj.: S a little bit (too) Adj.

有(一)點兒 means "a little bit". It has a negative connotation. Usually, the verb phrase that it modifies also has the negative denotation.
"有(一)點兒"意爲"a little bit",暗含否定的語義。通常,它修飾的動詞短語也有否定的語義。

　a. 考試的時候他有一點兒緊張。(He was a little bit nervous during the exam.)
　b. 我有一點兒累。(I am a little bit too tired.)
　c. 這家飯館兒有一點兒遠。(The restaurant is a little bit too far.)
　d. 漢字有一點兒難學。(Chinese characters are kind of too difficult to learn.)
　e. 我有一點兒不太喜歡他。(I have a bit of dislike towards him.)
　f. 她有點兒想家。(She is a little bit homesick.)
　g. 他喝得有點兒多。(He drank a little too more.)

6 S TW 就 V (了)

就 in this structure means that an action takes place sooner or earlier than expected. If the event has taken place, then 了 at the end of the sentence is a must.
在這個結構中,"就"表示一個動作比預想的發生得快或早。如果事件已經發生,那麽必須在句末用"了"。

a. 五分鐘就到那兒了。(It only takes five minutes to get there.)
b. 他昨天就來了。(He came yesterday. He was not expected to come so early.)
c. 我早就開始學中文了。(I started learning Chinese much earlier.)
d. 電影八點開始，我七點就到了。
(The movie would start at eight. But I was there at seven.)

S TW 才 V

This structure is the opposite of the previous one. It means that an action didn't take place until .... The implication is that the action took place later than expected.
這個結構和上面的相反，表示動作直到……才發生，暗示動作比預想的發生得晚。

 a. 你怎麼現在才來？
(How could you come so late? Or Literal: How come you didn't come until NOW?)
b. 我明年才去北京。(I won't go to Beijing until next year.)

7 More about particle 了

S (V O) V 了 duration ; S V 了 duration (的) Object

This structure is an other case of the particle 了. As introduced in the Grammar Note 4 of Lesson Four, the object in this structure is very often quantified especially when talking about the length or frequency of the action.
這個結構是助詞"了"的另一個用法。和第四課語法注釋4中介紹的一樣，這個結構的賓語常常會量化，尤其是在談論動作的進行時間和頻率時。

 a. 他們在一起說了一個小時的話。(They talked for an hour together.)
b. 先說了半個小時的英語，然後又說了半個小時的中文。
(They spoke English for half an hour first and then they spoke Chinese for another half an hour.)
c. 我學中文學了五年。(I learned Chinese for five years.)
d. 我學中文學了五年了。(I have been learning Chinese for five years.)

S (V O) V 了 frequency ; S V 了 frequency Object

 a. 我學中文學了三次。(I learned Chinese three times.)
b. 上個星期，我吃過三次中國菜。(I had Chinese food three times last week.)

When the object after the particle 了 is not quantified, the structure often indicates sequence, in which case there must be another sentence to follow to indicate a later action.

若助詞"了"後的賓語沒有被量化,這一結構則常用來指明順序。這時,在這一結構之後通常會有另一個句子來指明之後發生的動作。

 喝了茶,家奇問家興請他們來吃什麼好東西。
(After finishing the tea, Jiaqi asked Jiaxing what he has to offer them.)

S VP₁ 了 Object, 就 VP₂(了);S VP₁ 了 Object, 才(cái)VP₂

The sentences in this speech pattern describe a series of events. The verb followed by 了 describes the first event in the series. In sentences like this, you will often find either 就 or 才(cái)in the second part of the sentence. 就 simply means "then" and can often remain untranslated. 才 means "only then" and can indicate that what happens in the second part of the sentence happens later than expected, or that what happens in the first part of the sentence is a condition. For better illustration, let's look at some more examples:

這個結構用於表述一系列動作。"了"前的動詞表述諸多動作中的第一個。在這樣的句子中,第二部分一般會出現"就"或者"才(cái)"。"就"意爲"然後",通常不需要翻譯;而"才"意爲"只有這樣",表明句子第二部分發生的動作行爲比預期的要晚,或者句子第一部分發生的動作是後面動作進行的先決條件。下面的例子可以更好地說明這一點:

 a. 他吃了飯,就去上課了。
(After he finished eating, he went to class right away.)
b. 他吃了飯,才來上課。
(He did not come until he finished eating.)

NOTE: When 就 is used, 了 at the end of sentence indicates change of a state or completion of an action.
注意:使用"就"的時候,句尾的"了"表示狀態改變或動作完成。

8 S 對 sth. 很有興趣

 a. 我對學中文很有興趣。(I am very interested in learning Chinese.)
b. 我的好朋友對做飯很有興趣。(My good friend is very interested in cooking.)

有興趣的 NP

 有興趣的同學請在我這兒報名。
(Those who are interested please register here with me.)

走近中國──初級漢語教程
APPROACHING CHINA : ELEMENTARY CHINESE

9 Time expression

幾點了？	現在幾點（鐘）了？	What time is it?
x 點（了）。	六點（了）。	It is six now.
x 點鐘。	六點鐘。	Six o'clock.
x 點零 x（分）[1]。	六點零六（分）。	Six o'clock and six minutes.
x 點 x 分。	六點十分。	Ten past six.
x 點 xx（分）。	六點十六分。	Six o'clock and sixteen minutes.
x 點一刻。	六點一刻。	A quarter past six.
x 點半。	六點半。	Half past six.
差 x 分 x 點。	差五分六點。	Five to six./Five fifty five.

The rough time division of each day is as below:
一天的時間劃分大致如下：

1 a.m.-3 a.m.	4 a.m.-9 a.m.	9 a.m.-12 p.m.	12 p.m.-1 p.m.	1 p.m.-6 p.m.	6 p.m.-7 p.m.	8 p.m.-
凌晨 língchén	早上 zǎoshang	上午 shàngwǔ	中午 zhōngwǔ	下午 xiàwǔ	傍晚 bàngwǎn	晚上 wǎnshang

Day

大前天	前天	昨天	今天	明天	後天	大後天
3 days ago	the day before yesterday	yesterday	today	tomorrow	the day after tomorrow	3 days later

Year

大前年	前年	去年	今年	明年	後年	大後年
3 years ago	the year before last year	last year	this year	next year	the year after next	3 years later

The expressions of days and years are very much alike except for "last year 去年". Please note that "this afternoon", "this morning", "this year" can only be translated into "今天下午", "今天早上" and "今年". Please don't do the literal translation using "這個".

---

1 x點零x(分)： When the minute number is less than ten, we have to use 零 due to some prosodic reasons.

Lesson 6 語伴

除了"last year 去年","天"和"年"的表達都很相似。注意"this afternoon""this morning""this year"只可以翻譯爲"今天下午""今天早上"和"今年",不要按字面翻譯成"這個下午""這個早上""這個年"。

Week: 週 (zhōu : formal expression); 禮拜 (colloquial); 星期

週一 禮拜一 星期一	週二 禮拜二 星期二	週三 禮拜三 星期三	週四 禮拜四 星期四	週五 禮拜五 星期五	週六 禮拜六 星期六	週日 禮拜天 星期天
Monday	Tuesday	Wednesday	Thursday	Friday	Saturday	Sunday

上上週 / 上上個禮拜 / 上上個星期	上週 / 上個禮拜 / 上個星期	本週 / 這個禮拜 / 這個星期	下週 / 下個禮拜 / 下個星期	下下週 / 下下個禮拜 / 下下個星期
Monday	Tuesday	Wednesday	Thursday	Friday

Month

上上個月	上個月	本月 / 這個月	下個月	下下個月
2 months ago	last month	this month	next month	in 2 months

Unlike 天 and 年, 星期、禮拜 and 月 must take the measure word "個":"一個月""兩個星期". The expression of each month is very easy to learn as presented below:
跟"天"和"年"不同,"星期""禮拜"和"月"必須加量詞"個":"一個月""兩個星期"。每個月的表達很容易學習,具體如下:

一月	二月	三月	四月	五月	六月	七月	八月	九月	十月	十一月	十二月
Jan.	Feb.	March	April	May	June	July	Aug.	Sept.	Oct.	Nov.	Dec.

The useful expressions about at what time an action will take place or took place are listed below:
要表達在某個時間將要或已經發生的動作,常見的方式如下所列:

> a. 你什麼時候上課? (When will you go to class?)
> b. 我今天下午三點來。(I will come at three O'clock this afternoon.)
> c. 你是什麼時候來中國的? (When did you come to China?)

d. 我學中文學了兩個半小時了。
(I have been learning Chinese for two hours and a half.)

Also we should be aware of the fact that larger time and place units must precede the smaller ones.
同時，我們應該注意大的時間和地點單位必須放在小的時間和地點單位之前。

 a. 我是今天上午九點十五分到的。(I arrived at a quarter past nine this morning.)
b. 你是什麼時候生的？ (When were you born?)
c. 我是一九九九年三月三號/日生的。(I was born on March 3rd, 1999.)

10) V.-O. compound：S 跟 B 見面 (A meet B)

V.-O. compound is a special group of verbs that consist of a verb and its object. Words we have learnt that follow this group are:
動賓複合詞是一組特殊的動詞，由動詞和它的賓語組成。我們已經學過的這種詞有：

Verb	Object	Meaning
吃	飯	to eat
説	話	to speak
寫	字	to write
見	面	to meet
跑	步	to run, to jog
睡	覺	to go to bed, to sleep
約	會	to date

One characteristic of the V.-O. compound is that there can't be another object because the position has already been filled.
動賓複合詞的一個特徵是不可以另帶賓語，因為賓語位置已經被佔用了。

 a. 我喜歡吃飯。　⊙我喜歡吃飯牛肉。
b. 我要跟他見面。　⊙我要見面他。

Also, we can separate them by inserting modifiers.
我們還可以插入修飾語將動賓複合詞的兩個部分分開。

 a. 我昨天晚上只睡了兩個小時的覺。(I only slept for two hours last night.)
b. 我每天都跑兩個小時的步。(I run for two hours everyday.)

Lesson 6 語伴

> c. 他每天跟他哥哥跑半個小時的步。
> (He runs with his older brother for half an hour everyday.)
> d. 你喜歡跟什麼樣的人說話？ (What kind of people do you like to talk with?)

11 （S）爲 sb. Adj. / VP

爲 is also a preposition. The literal translation is "for (the sake of)".
"爲"也是一個介詞，字面意思是"for (the sake of)"。

> E.g.
> a. 真爲你高興！ (I am truly happy for you!)
> b. 我一學習媽媽就高興，所以我爲媽媽學習。
> (Whenever I study, my mother is happy. So I study for my mother.)
> c. 你爲媽媽學習還是爲自己學習？
> (Are you studying for yourself or your mother?)
> d. 我爲你擔心 (dānxīn)。(I was worried about you.)

12 S 該 VP 了：It is time to do sth.

> E.g.
> a. 我們該說中文了。(It is time for us to speak Chinese.)
> b. 我們該下課了。(It is time for us to finish our class.)
> c. 我該吃飯去了。(It is time for me to eat.)
> d. 我該睡覺了。(It is time to go to bed.)

Summary:

▶ 後來 "later" can not be used to describe an action that will happen in the future.

▶ 有（一）點兒 has a negative connotation.

▶ 就 simply means "then" and can often remain untranslated. 就 can also indicate an action that takes place sooner or earlier than expected. If the event has taken place, then 了 at the end of the sentence is a must which indicates change of a state or completion of an action.

▶ 才 means "only then" and can indicate that what happens in the second part of the sentence happens later than expected, or that what happens in the first part of the sentence is a condition.

▶ The object in this structure is very often quantified especially when talking about the length or frequency of the action.

▶ Please note that "this afternoon" "this morning" "this year" can only be translated into "今天下午""今天早上" and "今年".

▶ Larger time and place units must precede the smaller ones.

▶ One characteristic of the V.-O. compound is that there can't be another object because the position has already been filled.

🔸 Patterns:

- 從 + PW V 的 NP ‖ 從中國來的留學生想找人做語言交換。
  (The foreign student who comes from China wants to find somebody to do language exchange.)

- S 正好也想/要 VP ‖ 他正好也想找個語伴練習中文。
  (He was about to find a language partner to practice Chinese.)

- S 想 找 sb. VP ‖ 我想找人幫我照顧我的狗。
  (I would like to find somebody to tak care of the dog.)

- ……(以)後；……(以)前 ‖ 一個星期(以)後 (a week later)
  　　　　　　　　　　　　三天(以)前 (three days ago)

- S 有(一)點兒 Adj. ‖ 他有一點兒緊張。(He was a little bit nervous.)

- S TW 就 V 了 ‖ 五分鐘就到那兒了。(It only takes five minutes to get there.)

- S TW 才 V ‖ 我明年才去北京。(I won't go to Beijing until next year.)

- S VP$_1$ 了 Object，就 VP$_2$ 了 ‖ 他吃了飯，就上課去了。
  (After he finished eating, he went to class right away.)

- S VP$_1$ 了 Object，才 VP$_2$ ‖ 他吃了飯，才來上課。
  (He did not come to class until he finished eating.)

- 有興趣的 NP ‖ 有興趣的同學請在我這兒報名。
  (Those who are interested please register here with me.)

- S 對 sth. 很有興趣 ‖ 我對學中文很有興趣。(I am very intersted in learning Chinese.)

- Time expression ‖ 幾點了？(What time is it now?)

- S 跟 B 見面 ‖ 我要跟他見面。(I want to meet him.)

- (S)爲 sb. Adj./VP ‖ 真爲你高興！ (I am truly happy for you!)

- S 該 VP 了 ‖ 我們該說中文了。(It is time for us to speak Chinese.)

Lesson 6 語伴

IN CLASS ACTIVITIES

1 Answer the following questions according to the information given in the text:

① 李家奇覺做什麼的機會太少了？

② 家興正好也想做什麼？

③ 一個星期以後，家奇跟他的語伴約好做什麼？

④ 為什麼他有一點兒緊張？

⑤ 他幾點就到了圖書館門前？

⑥ 他們在一起說了多長時間的話？

⑦ 他們都覺得語言交換怎麼樣？

2 Please do role play and complete the dialogue with your idea or experience about language change:

> A 我覺得我們說中國話的機會不夠多。
> B 是呀，說中文的機會太少了。
> A 老師說可以幫我們找個從中國來的留學生做語伴。
> B 什麼是語伴呢？
> A 語伴就是語言夥伴，中國留學生幫我們提高漢語水平，我們幫他們提高英語水平。
> B 太好了！我想報名。

HOMEWORK

1 Please make sentences with the time given:

① 1:00 p.m. ➡ 我明天下午一點去圖書館。

② 2:03 a.m. ➡

③ 3:10 p.m. ➡

④ 4:15 a.m. ➡

⑤ 6:30 p.m. ➡

⑥ 9:40 p.m. ➡

⑦ 12:00 p.m. ➡

2 Translate the following sentences into Chinese:

① I will meet my best friend in front of the supermarket.

② He likes the female student who is from France.

③ I was just about to watch TV too.

④ I would like to find somebody to cook for me.

Lesson 6 語伴

⑤ Before I went to class, I got an email from my language partner.

_____

⑥ My younger brother knew that it was time for school.

_____

⑦ I want to have more opportunities to practice Chinese.

_____

3 Please write a short paragraph about your (would-be) language partner by using at least eight of the following structures:

從 + PW V 的 NP； S 正好也想 / 要 VP； S 想 找 sb. VP；

……（以）後，……（以）前； S 有一點兒 Adj.

S V 了 duration（的）Object；

S V 了 frequency Object； S 對 sth. 很有興趣；

S 跟 B 見面；（S）為 sb. Adj. /VP；

4 Please read the following paragraph in Pinyin:

Gǎn'ēn Jié kuài dào le. Jiāxīng dǎsuàn zuò fēijī qù Jiāzhōu kàn tā de nǚpéngyou. Niǔyuē lí Jiāzhōu hěn yuǎn. Cóng Niǔyuē zuò fēijī dào Jiāzhōu děi wǔ ge duō xiǎoshí. Tā juéde zuò fēijī de shíjiān tài cháng le, méi yìsi. Jiāqí jiànyì tā ná běn shū zài fēijī shàng kàn, huòzhě yòng iPod tīng yīnyuè, yàoshi kùn le, jiù shuìshuì jiào. Jiāxīng wèn Jiāqí Gǎn'ēn Jié shì bu shì dǎsuàn huí jiā gēn zìjǐ de jiārén yìqǐ chī huǒjī. Jiāqí shuō Yīngguórén bú guò Gǎn'ēn Jié, tā zhǔnbèi zài Niǔyuē hǎohāor wánwánr, kànkàn Gǎn'ēn Jié yóuxíng, gēn tóngwū liáoliáo tiānr, dào bówùguǎn cānguān cānguān, dào diànyǐngyuàn kànkàn diànyǐng, shuōbudìng hái néng zhǎo ge piàoliang de nǚpéngyou.

Chinese Lunar Calendar

The Chinese Lunar Calendar is based on the cycles of the moon, and is constructed in a different fashion compared with the Western solar calendar. In the Chinese calendar, the beginning of the year falls somewhere between late January and early February. Chinese people have adopted the Western calendar since 1911, but the lunar calendar is still used for festive occasions such as the Chinese New Year. Actually, many Chinese calendars will have both the solar dates and the Chinese lunar dates.

The Twelve Animal Signs

In Chinese tradition, dating methods were cyclical. For instance, a popular folk method which reflected this cyclical method of recording years are the Twelve Animal Signs. Every year is assigned an animal name or "sign" according to a repeating cycle: Rat, Ox, Tiger, Rabbit, Dragon, Snake, Horse, Sheep, Monkey, Rooster, Dog, and Boar. Therefore, every twelve years the same animal name or "sign" would reappear.

A cultural sidelight of the animal signs in Chinese folklore is that horoscopes have developed around the animal signs, much like monthly horoscopes in the West have been developed for the different moon signs, Pisces, Aries, etc. For instance, a Chinese horoscope may predict that a person born in the Year of the Horse would be, "cheerful, popular, and loves to compliment others". Of course, these are not regarded seriously by the Chinese people.

The animal signs also serve a useful social function for finding out people's ages. Instead of asking directly how old a person is, people often ask what is his or her animal sign. This would place that person's age within a cycle of 12 years, and with a bit of common sense, we can deduce the exact age. More often, though, people ask for animal signs not to compute a person's exact numerical age, but to

Lesson 6 語伴

simply know who is older among friends and acquaintances.

According to Chinese legend, the twelve animals quarreled one day as to who was to head the cycle of years. The gods were asked to decide and they held a contest: whoever was to reach the opposite bank of the river would be first, and the rest of the animals would receive their years according to their finish.

All the twelve animals gathered at the river bank and jumped in. Unknown to the ox, the rat had jumped upon his back. As the ox was about to jump ashore, the rat jumped off the ox's back, and won the race. The pig, who was very lazy, ended up last. That is why the rat is the first year of the animal cycle, the ox second, and the pig last.

Zodiac Chart

The rotating cycle of twelve animal signs was a folk method for naming the years in Chinese tradition. The animal signs for one another in an established order, and are repeated every twelve years. 2012 was the Year of the Dragon, and 2013 was the year of the Snake.

鼠	牛	虎	兔	龍	蛇	馬	羊	猴	雞	狗	豬
1900	1901	1902	1903	1904	1905	1906	1907	1908	1909	1910	1911
1912	1913	1914	1915	1916	1917	1918	1919	1920	1921	1922	1923
1924	1925	1926	1927	1928	1929	1930	1931	1932	1933	1934	1935
1936	1937	1938	1939	1940	1941	1942	1943	1944	1945	1946	1947
1948	1949	1950	1951	1952	1953	1954	1955	1956	1957	1958	1959
1960	1961	1962	1963	1964	1965	1966	1967	1968	1969	1970	1971
1972	1973	1974	1975	1976	1977	1978	1979	1980	1981	1982	1983
1984	1985	1986	1987	1988	1989	1990	1991	1992	1993	1994	1995
1996	1997	1998	1999	2000	2001	2002	2003	2004	2005	2006	2007
2008	2009	2010	2011	2012	2013	2014	2015	2016	2017	2018	2019
2020	2021	2022	2023	2024	2025	2026	2027	2028	2029	2030	2031

LESSON 7　感恩節

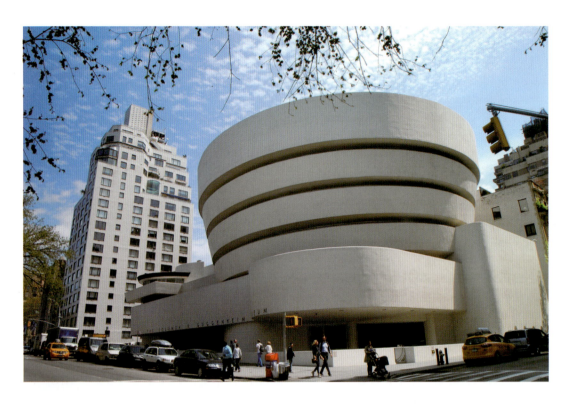

感恩節快到了。家興打算坐飛機去加州看他的女朋友。紐約離加州很遠。從紐約坐飛機到加州得五個多小時。他覺得坐飛機的時間太長了，沒意思。家奇建議他拿本書在飛機上看，或者用 iPod 聽聽音樂，要是睏了，就睡睡覺。家興問家奇感恩節是不是打算回家跟自己的家人一起吃火雞。家奇說英國人不過感恩節，他準備在紐約好好兒玩玩兒，看看感恩節遊行，跟同屋聊聊天兒，到博物館參觀參觀，到電影院看看電影，說不定還能找個漂亮的女朋友。

1

家奇：　家興，感恩節你打算做什麼？

家興：　我打算去加州看我的女朋友。

家奇：　你一定很激動吧？

家興：　我一想到很快就要跟女朋友見面了，當然很高興。可是……

家奇：　可是什麼？

家興：　可是從紐約坐飛機到加州得五個多小時。我覺得坐飛機的時間太長了，沒意思。

Lesson 7 感恩節

家奇： 你可以拿本書在飛機上看看，也可以用 iPod 聽聽音樂。要是睏了，還可以睡睡覺。

家興： 我知道，可是在飛機上睡不好。出了機場也很麻煩。我得先坐地鐵，再坐公共汽車。

家奇： 你可以坐出租車啊？

家興： 我去年是坐出租車去的。坐出租車也很麻煩，要是塞車，還沒有坐地鐵快。再說，出租車費也很貴。

家奇： 那你還是坐地鐵好了。

2

家興： 家奇，感恩節你打算去哪兒？

家奇： 我哪兒也不去，就在紐約。

家興： 我以為你打算回家跟自己的家人一起吃 Turkey 呢？

家奇： Turkey 用中文怎麼說？

家興： 你有字典嗎？我要英漢字典。

家奇： 有，漢英字典、英漢字典我都有。

家興： 我怎麼找不到呢？……找到了！是土——耳——其——

家奇： 土耳其，不對吧？土耳其是一個國家的名字。

家興： 應該是火雞，呵呵！吃土耳其，哈哈哈！

家奇： 幸虧我們又多看了一下，要不然，哈哈……

家興： 你是不是想跟家人一起吃火雞呢？

家奇： 英國人不過感恩節。

家興： 跟你開個玩笑，嘿嘿。那你打算做什麼呢？

家奇： 我準備在紐約好好兒玩玩兒，看看 Macy's 感恩節遊行，跟同屋聊聊天兒。

家興： 感恩節遊行挺不錯的。

家奇： 我還打算到博物館參觀參觀，到電影院看看電影。

家興： 一個人到博物館參觀，到電影院看看電影，有點兒寂寞吧？

家奇： 當然不會是我一個人了。

家興： 呵呵，有女朋友了？

家奇： 說不定我還真能找個漂亮的女朋友呢。

家興： 祝你好運！

3

家奇： 你現在就去機場嗎？

家興： 嗐，要不是我已經買好了飛機票，我就不去了。

家奇： 怎麼這麼說呢？你去加州看女朋友多好啊！

家興： 看女朋友當然很好，可是看女朋友的家人就不自在了。

家奇： 他們對你不好？

家興： 他們對我很客氣。可是他們越客氣我就越不自在。

家奇： 哦？

家興： 不過那兒的風景倒不錯。

家奇： 那你就多看風景，少看他們好了。

家興： 呵呵，我女朋友的父親特別奇怪。

家奇： 為什麼？

家興： 我也不知道。

家奇： 我覺得你有問題。

家興： 也許吧！

家奇： 可能你太緊張了，別亂想了。

家興： 呵呵。

家奇： 祝你一路平安！玩兒得開心！

家興： 謝謝！

VOCABULARY

1	感恩節	感恩节	Gǎn'ēn Jié	PN	Thanksgiving Day
2	飛機	飞机	fēijī	N.	airplane
3	*離	离	lí	V.	to be… away from
4	遠	远	yuǎn	Adj.	far
5	*長	长	cháng	Adj.	long

Lesson 7 感恩節

6	沒意思	没意思	méi yìsi	IE	boring
7	建議	建议	jiànyì	V.	to suggest
8	*拿	拿	ná	V.	to bring
9	書	书	shū	N.	book
10	*或者	或者	huòzhě	Conj.	or
11	聽	听	tīng	V.	to listen to
12	*睏	困	kùn	Adj.	sleepy
13	*睡覺	睡觉	shuì jiào	V.-O.	to sleep
14	*回家	回家	huí jiā	V.-O.	to return home
15	*火雞	火鸡	huǒjī	N.	turkey
16	過	过	guò	V.	to celebrate
17	*準備	准备	zhǔnbèi	V.	to plan
18	玩玩兒	玩玩儿	wánwanr	VP	to have some fun
19	遊行	游行	yóuxíng	V.	parade
20	*同屋	同屋	tóngwū	N.	room mate
21	聊天兒	聊天儿	liáo tiānr	V.-O.	to chat
22	博物館	博物馆	bówùguǎn	N.	museum
23	參觀	参观	cānguān	V.	to visit
24	*電影院	电影院	diànyǐngyuàn	N.	cinema
25	說不定	说不定	shuōbudìng	Adv.	perhaps
26	激動	激动	jīdòng	Adj.	excited
27	*當然	当然	dāngrán	Adv.	of course
28	出	出	chū	V.	to go out
29	*（飛）機場	（飞）机场	(fēi)jīchǎng	N.	airport
30	*地鐵	地铁	dìtiě	N.	subway
31	*公共汽車	公共汽车	gōnggòng qìchē	NP	bus
32	*出租車	出租车	chūzūchē	N.	taxi
33	塞車	塞车	sāi chē	V.-O.	traffic jam
34	費	费	fèi	N.	fee, expense
35	以為	以为	yǐwéi	V.	to think wrongly
36	*字典	字典	zìdiǎn	N.	dictionary
37	英漢	英汉	Yīng–Hàn	NP	English-Chinese
38	國家	国家	guójiā	N.	country

走近中國——初級漢語教程
APPROACHING CHINA : ELEMENTARY CHINESE

39	* 應該	应该	yīnggāi	Aux. V.	should
40	* 幸虧	幸亏	xìngkuī	Adv.	luckily
41	要不然	要不然	yàobùrán	Conj.	otherwise
42	開個玩笑	开个玩笑	kāi ge wánxiào	IE	Just kidding
43	嘿嘿	嘿嘿	hēihēi	Int.	laugh (something funny)
44	* 挺	挺	tǐng	Adv.	quite
45	寂寞	寂寞	jìmò	Adj.	lonely
46	祝你好運	祝你好运	zhù nǐ hǎo yùn	IE	Good luck!
47	嗐	嗐	hài	Int.	sigh
48	要不是	要不是	yàobúshì	Conj.	if it were not for
49	* 已經	已经	yǐjīng	Adv.	already
50	* 買好	买好	mǎihǎo	V.-C.	to have bought
51	* 飛機票	飞机票	fēijīpiào	N.	plane ticket
52	怎麼	怎么	zěnme	Pron.	how come
53	* 自在	自在	zìzài	Adj.	comfortable, at ease
54	* 客氣	客气	kèqi	Adj.	polite
55	哦	哦	ó	Int.	oh
56	不過	不过	búguò	Conj.	but
57	* 風景	风景	fēngjǐng	N.	scenery
58	倒	倒	dào	Adv.	surprisingly
59	* 也許	也许	yěxǔ	Adv.	perhaps
60	別亂想了	别乱想了	bié luàn xiǎng le	IE	Don't think too much!
61	一路平安	一路平安	yí lù píng'ān	IE	Have a safe trip!
62	玩兒得開心	玩儿得开心	wánr de kāixīn	IE	Have a good time!

▶ Supplementary Vocabulary:

1	聖誕節	圣诞节	Shèngdàn Jié	PN	Christmas Day
2	聖誕老人	圣诞老人	Shèngdàn Lǎorén	NP	Santa Claus
3	聖誕樹	圣诞树	shèngdànshù	N.	Christmas tree
4	中秋節	中秋节	Zhōngqiū Jié	PN	Mid-autumn Festival

Lesson 7 感恩節

5	月餅	月饼	yuèbing	N.	moon cake
6	國慶節	国庆节	Guóqìng Jié	PN	National Day
7	雞翅	鸡翅	jīchì	N.	chicken wings
8	司機	司机	sījī	N.	driver
9	身體	身体	shēntǐ	N.	health
10	時代廣場	时代广场	Shídài Guǎngchǎng	NP	Times Square
11	山	山	shān	N.	mountain
12	咖啡廳	咖啡厅	kāfēitīng	N.	cafe

GRAMMAR

1 Imminent action：NP 快／快要／就要 V 了

Together with adverbs such as 快 (soon) or 就，了 is also frequently used with expressions of imminent action, intention or change.

"了"常跟副詞"快"或"就"連用，表示馬上要發生的動作、意圖或變化。

E.g.
a. 就要下雨了。(It is going to rain soon.)
b. 快過來！馬上就要上課了！
(Come here quickly! The class is going to start soon.)
c. 感恩節快到了！(Thanksgiving Day is coming!)
d. 我的生日快到了。(My birthday is coming.)
e. 我們快要到北京了。 (We will arrive in Beijing soon.)

When you use 快, the verb (if understood) can be left out. But 快要 and 就要 can not be used in this way.

用"快"時，如果不影響理解，可以省略動詞，但"快要"和"就要"不能這麼用。

E.g.
——什麼時候下課？ (When are we going to finish class?)
——快了。(Very soon.)
☹快要了。　　☹就要了。

2 從 A（坐……）到 B 得 time duration

This pattern tells us how long it takes to get to B from A (by transportation).

這個句型用於表達從 A 地方到 B 地方（使用交通工具）需要多長時間。

> **E.g.** 從紐約坐飛機到加州得五個多小時。
> (It takes at least five hours from New York to California by air.)

從 A（坐……）到 B 得 多久/多長時間？

> **E.g.** a.——從北京坐飛機到紐約得多長時間？
> (How long does it take from Beijing to New York by air?)
> ——從北京坐飛機到紐約得十三個小時。
> (It will take at least thirteen hours from Beijing to New York by air.)
> b.——從哥大坐地鐵到時代廣場 (Shídài Guǎngchǎng) 得多久？
> (How long does it take from CU to Times Square by subway?)
> ——從哥大坐地鐵到時代廣場二十分鐘就到了。
> (It only takes twenty minutes to get to Times Square from CU by subway.)

3 A 離 B Adj.：A is (how far) away from B

> **E.g.** a. 紐約離加州太遠了。(New York is too far away from California.)
> b. 紐約離波士頓不太遠。(New York is not that far from Boston.)

A 離 B 遠不遠？

> **E.g.** ——紐約離費城遠不遠？ (How far is it from New York to Philadelphia?)
> ——紐約離費城不遠，很近。
> (New York is not far from Philadelphia. They are very close.)

4 A 或者 B：A or B

Like 還是，或者 also means "or". They are different in that 還是 is used in an interrogative while 或者 is used in a statement.

"或者"和"還是"的意思相近，都表示"or"，但是兩個用法不同："還是"用於疑問句，而"或者"用於陳述句。

> **E.g.** a. 你還可以用 iPod 或者 MP3 聽音樂。
> (You may also listen to music with iPod or MP3 player.)
> b.——你想參觀博物館還是看感恩節遊行？
> (Do you want to visit the museum or watch the Thanksgiving Day Parade?)
> ——我覺得參觀博物館或者看感恩節遊行都不錯。
> (I think either visiting the museum or watching the parade will be fine with me.)
> c.——你想跟同屋聊天兒還是去電影院看電影？
> (Do you want to chat with your roommate or go to a movie theater?)

——跟同屋聊天兒或者去看電影都行。(Either will do.)

d. ——你想找個聰明的女朋友還是漂亮的女朋友？

(Do you want to find a smart girlfriend or a beautiful one?)

——聰明的或者漂亮的都行。(Either she is smart or beautiful.)

e. 吃西紅柿炒雞蛋或者吃又麻又辣的麻婆豆腐都不錯。

(It is fine with me either to have fried eggs with tomato or Mapo Tofu.)

f. 天氣太冷或者太熱都不好。

(It is not good when the weather is either too cold or too hot.)

5 S 過……節：to celebrate a holiday or a special occasion

when used as a verb, 過 has the meanings of "to celebrate", "to pass", "to cross", "to live (a... life)", etc.

"過"用作動詞時有很多意思，如"to celebrate（慶祝）""to pass（經過）""to cross（穿過）""to live (a... life)（生活、過日子）"等。

to celebrate

 a. 家奇說英國人不過感恩節。

(Jiaqi said that British people don't celebrate Thanksgiving Day.)

b. 今天你過生日，你想怎麼過？

(It is your birthday today. How are you going to celebrate it?)

c. 過中秋節 (Zhōngqiū Jié) 的時候，應該吃月餅 (yuèbing)。

(People should have mooncakes when celebrating the Mid-autumn Festival.)

to pass

 a. 時間過得真快！ (Time flies!)

b. 週末你打算怎麼過？ (What do you plan to do for the weekend?)

c. 過一會兒我要去超市買東西。

(I will go to the supermarket to buy things after a while.)

d. 過兩個月就是感恩節了。

(It will be Thanksgiving Day in two months.)

to cross

 a. 在中國過馬路 (mǎlù) 真難。

(It is really difficult to cross the street in China.)

b. 請你過來！ (Come here, please.)

to live a ... life

> **E.g.** 他在山裡過著平靜(píngjìng)、幸福的生活。
> (He lives a peaceful and happy life in the mountains.)

過 can also be used as an aspect marker, meaning "to have had the experience of". "過"還可以用在動詞後，表示"有……經歷"，讀輕聲。

S V 過……

> **E.g.** a. 我二十年前去過中國。(I have been to China twenty years ago.)
> b. 我在美國朋友家吃過火雞。
> (I have had turkey at my American friend's.)
> c. 你以前用中國法子泡過綠茶沒有？
> (Have you ever steeped green tea in a Chinese way before?)
> d. 你聽過什麼中國歌兒？ (What kind of Chinese songs have you listened to?)
> e. 你吃過北京烤鴨沒有？ (Have you ever had Peking Roast Duck?)
> f. 你喝過中國白酒嗎？ (Have you had Chinese liquor?)
> g. ——你去沒去過中國的博物館？ (Have you been to a Chinese museum?)
> ——我去過。(Yes, I have.) / 沒去過。(No, I haven't.)

6 V V (Object)

V V structure can also take object as in: 看看 Macy's 遊行 / 跟同屋聊聊天兒。This structure is pretty useful.
"V V"這個句型後面還可以帶賓語，如"看看 Macy's 遊行""跟同屋聊聊天兒"。這個結構很常用。

> **E.g.** 我今天晚上想看看小說，聽聽音樂，寫(xiě)寫字，跟朋友聊聊天兒、唱唱歌兒，好好兒地休息一下。
> (Tonight, I would like to totally relax: read a novel for a while, then listen to some music, write the calligraphy for a while, and then chat and sing with my friend for some time.)

7 要是 A，S 就 B：If A, then B
要不是 A，S 就 B：If it were not A, then B

"要是 (if) A，S 就 B" is equivalent to the English conditional clause. Unlike the "要是 A，S 就 B" English one, 要是 very often can be dropped.
"要是 (if) A，S 就 B"這個句型等同於英語的條件從句，不同的是，漢語裡"要是"常常可以省略。

> **E.g.** (要是)你喜歡這枝筆，(你)就拿走吧。
> (If you like this pen, then you can take it away.)

Lesson 7 感恩節

要不是, however, is often translated into English with the subjunctive mood. The sentence that follows 要不是 usually suggests fact, while the second part of the structure indicates a hypothetical situation. The adverbs of 就, 才 and 真 are often used to show tones of speech. 會 is used to indicate the action has been completed.
"要不是"常被譯爲英語的虛擬語氣。"要不是"後邊的句子陳述一個事實,而第二個小句表述一個假設的情況,常用副詞"就""才""真"來表達説話的語氣,用"會"表示動作已經完成。

> **E.g.**
> a. 要不是你喜歡這枝筆,我就不會買了。
>   (If it were not the case that you liked the pen, I would not have bought it.)
> b. 要不是他來晚了,我們早就到(那兒)了。
>   (If it were not the case that he came late, we would have already arrived.)
> c. 要不是我們是好朋友,我才不會幫你呢。
>   (If we were not good friends, I wouldn't help you at all.)
> d. 要不是我喜歡你,我真不想跟你再説話了。
>   (If it were not for the fact that I like you, I really didn't want to talk to you again.)
> e. 要不是太興奮,他就不會摔倒(shuāidǎo)了。
>   (If he had not been too excited, he would not have fallen.)

Unlike the conditional sentence, 要不是 can't be dropped.
不像條件句,"要不是"不可以省略。

> **E.g.** 家興説要不是他已經買好了去加州的飛機票,他就不去了。
> (Jiaxing said that if it were not for the fact that he has bought the tickets, he would not go at all.)

8 S 已經……了

This pattern indicates that an action has been completed.
這個句型表示動作已經完成。

> **E.g.**
> a. 我已經買好飛機票了。(I have already bought the air ticket.)
> b. 我已經會説一點兒中國話了。(I have been able to speak a little Chinese.)
> c. 他已經給我做好了飯,所以今天晚上我得回家吃飯。
>   (He has cooked for me already. So I have to go back to eat tonight.)
> d. 我已經不願意説英文了。(I am not willing to speak English already.)
> e. 天氣已經熱了。(It has been very hot already.)
> f. 我的中文水平已經很高了。(My Chinese level has already gotten pretty high.)
> g. 今天已經是星期五了。(Today is already Friday.)

9 Resultative compound verbs

Resultative compound refers to the group of verbs that indicates the result of the action together with their resultative complements. Usually, a resultative compound consists of a verb and an adjective (or sometimes a verb).

動結複合詞是指由動詞與其結果補語組合來表示動作結果的一組動詞，通常由一個動詞和一個形容詞（或個別動詞）構成。

Verb	Adjective	Meaning
買	好	to purchase
學	好 / 會	to master
約	好	to have agreed to do sth. with sb.
說	好	to have agreed to do sth. with sb.
做	好	to have done sth. to one's satisfaction
看	懂	to understand by reading
說	對 / 錯	to speak correctly/wrongly
做	對 / 錯	to do correctly/wrongly
找	到 / 見	to find
看	到 / 見	to see
聽	到 / 見	to hear
喝 / 吃	慣	to be used to drinking/eating

 a. 我給你買好地鐵票了。(I have bought the subway ticket for you.)

b. 我跟他說好明天下午在圖書館門前見面。

(He and I have agreed that we will meet each other in front of the library tomorrow afternoon.)

c. 你看！你看見了沒有？ (Look! Did you see it?)

d. 我找了很長時間，可是還沒找到。

(I have been looking for it for quite a while, but I still have not found it yet.)

e. 我約好明天跟語伴見面。(My language partner and I decide to meet tomorrow.)

f. 我做好了晚飯。(I have fixed dinner.)

g. 我能看懂中文電影了。(I can understand Chinese movies now.)

h. 老師說我的作業做對了。

(My teacher said that my homework was done correctly.)

i. 我找到了一個語伴幫我練習中文。

(I have found a language partner to help me practice Chinese.)

j. 在五道口，我看到了小張。(I saw Xiao Zhang at Wudaokou.)

k. 在中國，我聽到了美國音樂。(I heard American music in China.)

Since a resultative compound always indicates an completed action, it often takes the particle 了.
動結複合詞總是表示已經完成的動作，所以常和助詞"了"連用。

 中文，你學好了沒有？我已經學好了。
(Have you mastered Chinese? I have mastered it.)

10) Potential complement

Potential complement is a kind of complement. Verb complements are words that are added to the end of a verb to give it a specific meaning or a specific nuance. There are various types of verbal complements: Resultative, Directional, Predicative, Potential, etc. Potential complements refer to the fact that if somebody has the potential to perform a task or not.
可能補語是補語的一種。補語是加在動詞後補充說明的部分。漢語中有結果補語、趨向補語、程度補語、可能補語等多種類型的補語。可能補語反映的是某人有沒有潛力做某事。

Some common potential complements are listed below:
一些常見的可能補語如下：

Affirmative	Negative	Meaning
吃得慣	吃不慣	to be / be not used to eating
學得好	學不好	can / cannot master
看得懂	看不懂	can / cannot understand

S + V 得 Adj. + V 不 Adj. + (O)？

 你吃得慣吃不慣又麻又辣的菜？
(Can you accustom yourself to eating the dish that is both spicy and hot?)

S + V 得 Adj. + (O) + 嗎？

 你吃得慣又麻又辣的菜嗎？
(Can you accustom yourself to eating the dish that is both spicy and hot?)

S + V 得 Adj. + (O)

 我吃得慣又麻又辣的菜。
(Yes, I can accustom myself to the dish that is both spicy and hot.)

S + V 不 Adj. + (O)

E.g. 我吃不慣又麻又辣的菜。
(No, I can't accustom myself to the dish that is both spicy and hot.)

Here are some other examples:
還有一些其他的例子：

E.g. 我不知道你們吃得慣吃不慣？
(I wonder if you can accustom yourself to eating it or not?)
我們吃得慣辣的，可是吃不慣又麻又辣的。
(We are used to spicy food but we are not used to the food that is so spicy.)

Contrasts between potential complement and predicative complement:
可能補語與程度補語的對比：

Predicative complement	Potential complement
你吃得好不好？ (Do you eat well?) 我吃得很好。(Yes, I eat very well.) 我吃得不好。(No, I don't eat well.)	你吃得好吃不好？ (Can you eat well?) 我吃得好。(Yes, I can eat well.) 我吃不好。(No, I can't eat well.)
你學中文學得好不好？ (Do you learn Chinese well?) 我學得很好。(Yes, I learn it very well.) 我學得不好。(No, I don't.)	你學中文學得好學不好？ (Can you learn Chinese well?) 我學得好。(Yes, I can.) 我學不好。(No, I can't.)
中國菜，你做得好不好？ (As for Chinese food, do you cook it well?) 我做得很好。(Yes, I do it very well.) 我做得不好。(No, I don't.)	中國菜，你做得好做不好？ (As for Chinese food, can you cook it well?) 我做得好。(Yes, I can.) 我做不好。(No, I can't.)

11 S 先 A，再 B，(最後 C)：S A first, then B, (finally C)

E.g. a. 我得先坐地鐵，再坐公共汽車。
(I have to take the subway first, then take the bus.)
b. 學中文，你得先學好拼音 (pīnyīn)，再學漢字。
(As for learning Chinese, you have to master *Pinyin* first, and then learn the characters.)
c. 做西紅柿炒雞蛋，得先炒雞蛋，再炒西紅柿，最後兩個一起炒。
(To make fried eggs with tomato, we have to stir-fry the eggs first, then tomatoes and finally stir-fry the two together.)

Lesson 7 感恩節

12. S 以爲 + sentence, 其實……: I thought..., but actually...

以爲 means "to think wrongly". It is very often used with 其實.
"以爲"意思是"錯誤地認爲",常與"其實"連用。

E.g.
a. 我以爲你打算回家跟自己的家人一起吃 Turkey 呢。
(I thought it wrongly that you planned to go back home to eat turkey together with your family.)
b. 我以爲他是坐飛機來的,其實他是坐火車來的。
(I thought he came here by plane. Actually he came here by train.)
c. 我以爲他是先參觀了博物館,再去看感恩節遊行的,其實剛好 (gānghǎo) 相反 (xiāngfǎn)。
(I thought that he visited the museum first, and then went to watch the parade. Actually, it was just the opposite.)
d. 我以爲他是女生,其實他是男生。
(I thought he was a female student but actually he is a male student.)

13. "再 VP" and "又 VP"

再 and 又 can be translated into "again". Both words refer to action repeated or resumed. But they are different. 再 applies to actions not yet completed, and is used to indicate the repetition or continuation of a certain presupposition, which can never imply the completion of a thing. For instance, 我還想再吃一點兒飯. By the time of speaking, the speaker hasn't finished eating yet.

"再"和"又"都可譯爲"again",兩者都表示動作的重複或繼續,但兩者是不同的。"再"用於尚未完成的動作,表示某一預想動作的重複或繼續,從不用於表示完成的動作。如"我還想再吃一點兒飯",截至說話的時間,說話人都還沒有吃完飯。

E.g. 要是再學,我就太累了。(I will be too tired if I study any longer.)

又 indicates the repetition of the same thing. For instance, 我又喝了一杯茶. By the time of speaking, the speaker has finished another cup of tea.

"又"表示同一事件的重複。如"我又喝了一杯茶",截至說話的時間,說話人已經喝完了另一杯茶。

又 also indicates branching out into further activity of a related but not identical kind.
"又"還可表示擴展到相關卻不相同的活動。

E.g.
a. 他以前學過法語,現在又開始學漢語了。
(He studied French, and now he goes on to learn Chinese.)

163

> b. 天氣冷了又熱，熱了又冷。
> (It gets cold and then gets warm. Then it gets cold again.)

In a word, 再 can never be used to indicate an action that has happened. It can only be used to indicate the repetition of an action to come. While 又 very often indicates a certain action happened again.

總之，"再"一定不能用於表示已經發生的動作，只能用來修飾將要發生的動作；"又"常表示某個特定的動作再次發生。

> a. 他今天來了，明天會再來。
> (He came today and will come again tomorrow.)
> b. 要是你今天再不來，老師會生氣的。
> (If you won't show up again today, the teacher will be angry.)
> c. 你怎麼今天又沒來。(How come you didn't show up once again?)
> d. 他昨天來了，今天又來了。(He came yesterday and today again.)
> e. 他昨天沒來，今天又沒來。
> (He didn't come yesterday and today he did not come again.)

14 S 倒 VP：S did sth. unexpectedly

The adverb 倒 indicates an action that is not expected, or contrary to one's expectation.
副詞"倒"表示沒有預料到，或與期待的相反。

> a. 風景倒不錯。(The scenery is unexpectedly good.)
> b. 這個四川人不愛吃四川菜，倒愛吃上海菜。
>   (The Sichuan person doesn't like eating Sichuan dish, on the contrary he loves eating Shanghai dish.)
> c. 大人一個也沒來，小孩子倒來了很多。
>   (None of the adults came. Unexpectedly, a lot of children came.)
> d. 有的中國人說不好普通話，有的美國人倒說得很好。
>   (Some Chinese people can't speak Mandarin well. Unexpectedly, some Americans speak it very well.)
> e. 你不幫自己的女朋友，倒幫別人。
>   (You didn't help your girlfriend, but on the contrary helped other people.)
> f. 夏天來了，天氣倒不熱。
>   (It is already summer but surprisingly it is not very hot.)

15 S 多 VP₁，少 VP₂：do... more; do... less

This pattern is used to express suggestions or wishes.
這個句型用於表達建議或希望。

Lesson 7 感恩節

> E.g.
> a. 那你就多看風景，少看他們好了。
>   (Then you enjoy the scenery instead of looking at them.)
> b. 他們以後決定多聚（jù）幾次。
>   (They decided to gather more often later on.)
> c. 中國人覺得應該少說話，多做事。
>   (Chinese people think that we should speak less and do more.)
> d. 多吃菜，少喝酒對身體（shēntǐ）好。
>   (Eating more vegetables and drinking less will be good for one's health.)

16 S 是 VP 的

> E.g. 我去年是坐出租車去的。(I went there by taxi last year.)

The "是……的" structure is often used to emphasize the time, place, manner, purpose, etc. of an action that has taken place.
"是……的"結構用於強調事情發生的時間、地點、方式、目的等。

> E.g.
> a. 我是一個星期前到中國來的。   Focus: **time**
>   (It is a week ago that I came to China.)
> b. 他是一年前生的。   Focus: **time**
>   (He was born a year ago.)
> c. 我是在中國學的中文。   Focus: **place**
>   (It was in China that I learned Chinese.)
> d. 我的語伴是走路來學校的。   Focus: **means**
>   (My language partner came to school on foot.)
> e. 他是急急忙忙去的飯館兒。   Focus: **manner**
>   (It is in a hurry that he went to the restaurant.)
> f. 我是來學中文的,不是來學英文的。   Focus: **purpose**
>   (I came to study Chinese not to learn English.)

The question form will be in response to the part that is being focused.
其疑問形式主要是對強調部分進行提問。

> E.g.
> a.——你是在哪兒認識你的女朋友的？
>   (Where did you get to know your girlfriend?)
>   ——我是在紐約認識我的女朋友的。
>   (It was in New York that I got to know my girlfriend.)
> b.——你的語伴是怎麼來的？ (How did your language partner get here?)
>   ——我的語伴是走路來的。(My language partner got here on foot.)

165

c.——你是什麼時候到美國來的？ (When did you come to America?)
——我是一個星期前到美國來的。 (I came to America a week ago.)

There are other ways to ask questions too:
還有一些其他的提問方式：

Question form: S 是不是……的 (……)？／S 是……的 (……) 嗎？

Negative form: S 不是……的 (……)。

Positive form: S 是……的 (……)。

E.g. a.——你是不是在中國生的？／你是在中國生的嗎？
(Were you born in China?)
——我是在中國生的。／我不是在中國生的。
(I was born in China. / I was not born in China.)
b.——昨天他是不是在圖書館學的中文？
(Did he study Chinese in the library yesterday?)
——不是，他不是在圖書館學的中文，他是在家學的中文。
(No, he didn't. He did it at home.)
c. 你是不是跟他一起去的中國？
(Did you go to China together with him?)
d. 你是不是在哥大書店 (shūdiàn) 買的這本書？
(Is it at the bookstore at CU that you bought this book?)

Sometimes 是 can be omitted.
有時候，"是"可以省略。

E.g. 我 (是) 在中國生的。(It was in China that I was born.)

Although the object can never be the focus of the structure, the subject can.
儘管這個結構裡賓語不能成爲被強調的部分，但主語可以。

是 S VP 的

E.g. 是他教的我中文。(It was he who taught me Chinese.)
是他給我買的酒。(It was he who bought me wine.)
他給我買是酒的。(It was wine that he bought me.)

If we take the "是……的" structure as the focus range, then anything that is not between 是 and 的 can be considered not focused.
在"是……的"結構中，"是"和"的"中間的那部分是被強調的，其他部分不是。

Lesson 7 感恩節

Summary:

> Together with adverbs such as 快 (soon) or 就, 了 is also frequently used with expressions of imminent action, intention or change.

> When you use 快, the verb (if understood) can be left out. But 快要 and 就要 can not be used in this way.

> Like 還是, 或者 also means "or". They are different in that 還是 is used in an interrogative while 或者 is used in a statement.

> 過 when used as a verb, it has the meanings of "to celebrate","to pass","to cross", "to live a... life".

> 過 can also be used as an aspect marker, meaning "to have had the experience of".

> "要是 (if) A, 就 B" is equivalent to the English conditional clause. Unlike the English one, 要是 very often can be dropped.

> 要不是, however, is often translated into English with the subjunctive mood. The sentence that follows 要不是 usually suggests fact, while the second part of the structure indicates a hypothetical situation. The adverbs of 就, 才 and 真 are often used to show tones of speech. 會 is used to indicate the action has been completed. Unlike the conditional sentence, 要不是 can't be dropped.

> Since the resultative compound always indicates an completed action, it often takes the particle 了.

> 以爲 means "to think wrongly". It is very often used with 其實.

> 再 and 又 can be translated into "again". Both words refer to action repeated or resumed. But they are different.

> 再 applies to actions not yet completed, and is used to indicate the repetition or continuation of a certain presupposition, which can never imply the completion of a thing.

> 又 indicates the repetition of the same thing, and can also indicate branching out into further activity of a related but not identical kind.

> In a word, 再 can never be used to indicate an action that has happened. It can only be used to indicate the repetition of an action to come. While 又 very often indicates a certain action happened again.

走近中國——初級漢語教程
APPROACHING CHINA : ELEMENTARY CHINESE

> The adverb 倒 indicates an action that is not expected, or contrary to one's expectation.

> The object can never be the focus of the "是……的" structure.

Patterns:

- **Imminent action：NP 快 / 快要 / 就要 V 了** ‖ 就要下雨了。(It is going to rain soon.)

- **從 A（坐……）到 B 得 time duration** ‖ 從紐約坐飛機到加州得五個多小時。
  (It takes at least five hours from New York to California by air.)

- **從 A（坐……）到 B 得 多久 / 多長時間?** ‖ 從哥大坐地鐵到時代廣場得多久?
  (How long does it take from CU to Times Square by subway?)

- **A 離 B Adj.** ‖ 紐約離加州太遠了。
  (New York is too far away from California.)

- **A 離 B 遠不遠?** ‖ 紐約離費城遠不遠? (How far is it from New York to Philadelphia?)

- **A 或者 B** ‖ 也可以用 iPod 或者 MP3 聽音樂。
  (You may also listen to music with iPod or MP3 player.)

- **S 過……節** ‖ 家奇說英國人不過感恩節。
  (Jiaqi said that British people don't celebrate Thanksgiving Day.)

- **V V (Object)** ‖ 我今天晚上想看看小說，聽聽音樂，寫寫字，跟朋友聊聊天兒、唱唱歌兒，好好地休息一下。
  (Tonight, I would like to totally relax: read a novel for a while, then listen to some music, write the calligraphy for a while, and then to chat and sing with my friend for some time.)

- **要是 A, S 就 B。** ‖ 要是你喜歡這枝筆，你就拿走吧。
  (If you like this pen, then you can take it away.)

- **要不是 A, S 就 B。** ‖ 要不是你喜歡這枝筆，我就不會買了。
  (If it were not the case that you liked the pen, I would not have bought it.)

- **S 已經……了** ‖ 我已經買好飛機票了。(I have already bought the air ticket.)

- **Resultative compound verbs** ‖ 我給你買好地鐵票了。
  (I have bought the subway ticket for you.)

Lesson 7 感恩節

- S + V 得 Adj. + V 不 Adj. + (O) ？ ‖ 你吃得慣吃不慣又麻又辣的菜？
  (Can you accustom yourself to eating the dish that is both spicy and hot?)

- S + V 得 Adj. + (O) + 嗎？ ‖ 你吃得慣又麻又辣的菜嗎？
  (Can you accustom yourself to eating the dish that is both spicy and hot?)

- S + V 得 Adj. + (O) ‖ 我吃得慣又麻又辣的菜。
  (Yes, I can accustom myself to the dish that is both spicy and hot.)

- S + V 不 Adj. + (O) ‖ 我吃不慣又麻又辣的菜。
  (No, I can't accustom myself to the dish that is both spicy and hot.)

- S 先 A, 再 B, (最後 C) ‖ 我得先坐地鐵，再坐公共汽車。
  (I have to take the subway first, then take the bus.)

- S 以爲 + sentence, 其實…… ‖ 我以爲英國人也過感恩節，其實並不是這麼回事。
  (I thought that British people also celebrate Thanksgiving Day, but actually not.)

- S 是 VP 的 ‖ 我是一個星期前到中國來的。(It is a week ago that I came to China.)

- S 是不是……的 (……) ‖ 你是不是跟他一起去的中國？
  (Did you go to China together with him?)

- S 是……的 (……) 嗎? ‖ 你是在中國生的嗎？(Were you born in China?)

- S 不是……的 (……)。‖ 我不是在中國生的。(I was not born in China.)

- S 是……的 (……)。‖ 我是在中國生的。(I was born in China.)

- 是 S VP 的 ‖ 是他教的我中文。(It was he who taught me Chinese.)

- "再 VP" and "又 VP" ‖ 我還想再吃一點兒飯。(I want more rice.)
  我又喝了一杯茶。(I had another cup of tea.)

- S 倒 VP ‖ 風景倒不錯。(The scenery is unexpectedly good.)

- S 多 VP$_1$ 少 VP$_2$ ‖ 那你就多看風景，少看他們好了。
  (Then you enjoy the scenery instead of looking at them.)

走近中國——初級漢語教程
APPROACHING CHINA : ELEMENTARY CHINESE

IN CLASS ACTIVITIES

1 Answer the following questions according to the information given in the text:

① 感恩節快到了，李家興打算做什麽？

② 從紐約坐飛機到加州得多久？

③ 爲什麽他覺得紐約離加州太遠了？

④ 家奇跟他説什麽？

⑤ 爲什麽李家奇不回家跟家人一起吃火雞？

⑥ 李家奇打算在紐約做什麽？

2 Please do role play according to the dialogues given below:

A: 你過節打算做什麽呢？
B: 我準備去_____。我兩個月前就買好了飛機票。你呢？
A: 我也要去_____。可是我買飛機票買得太晚了，票可貴了。
B: 就是，就是！這就是我爲什麽兩個月前就買票了。
A: 我現在打算在那兒多住 (zhù: to stay) 幾天。
B: 你訂 (dìng: to reserve) 旅館 (lǚguǎn: hotel) 了嗎？
A: 沒有，我的女朋友住在那兒。我住女朋友家。
B: 去看女朋友，你一定很激動吧。
A: 那當然了。我女朋友做飯做得可好吃了。對了，歡迎你來做客。
B: 謝謝，我一定去。

Lesson 7 感恩節

- A 你知道怎麼到我女朋友家去嗎?
- B 你給我地址，我租 (zū: to rent) 輛車，開車去。
- A 好，給你地址。到了那兒給我打電話 (dǎ diànhuà: to call)。
- B 謝謝！祝你一路平安！
- A 一路平安！

買火車票

- A 請給我買一張到北京的火車票。
- B 哪天的？
- A 六月十四號。
- B 要臥鋪 (wòpù: sleeper) 嗎？軟臥 (ruǎnwò: hard sleeper) 還是硬臥 (yìngwò: hard sleeper)？
- A 請給我一張硬臥。
- B 你要上鋪 (shàngpù: upper level)、下鋪，還是中鋪？
- A 請給我一張下鋪。
- B 一共二百四。
- A 好，這是二百五十塊。
- B 找您十塊。(zhǎo nín shí kuài: Here is your ten dollar change.)
- A 謝謝。

HOMEWORK

1 Please rewrite or complete the following sentences with the given structures:

① 感恩節是下個禮拜。（快 V 了）

➡ 感恩節快到了。

② 從紐約坐飛機到加州得五個多小時。(Question form)

➡

③ 紐約離波士頓不太遠。(Question form)

➡

④ 你想參觀博物館還是看感恩節遊行？（A 或者 B 都行）

　　⇒ _____

⑤ 你過生日做什麼？（V V）

　　⇒ _____

⑥ 我昨天買了一張票。（S 已經……了）

　　⇒ _____

2 Please fill in the following blanks with appropriate resultative compound verbs given:

> 約好　　學好　　看到　　做好　　買好　　寫對　　看懂

① 我已經___學好___中文了。

② 我已經_____飛機票了。

③ 你_____晚飯了沒有？

④ 這個字，我_____了沒有？

⑤ 我已經_____課文了。

⑥ 我們已經_____明天下午兩點在圖書館門前見。

⑦ 今天下午在超市_____我的老師了。

3 Please rewrite or complete the following sentences with 是……的：

① 我明天要去北京。

　　⇒ 我是昨天去的北京。

② 我在紐約學中文。

　　⇒ _____

③ 是誰教的你中文？

　　⇒ _____

Lesson 7 感恩節

④ 你什麼時候來的？

➡

⑤ 昨天我在中國城買了一套茶具。

➡

4 Translate the following sentences into Chinese:

① We are approaching New York soon.

② Watching TV or visiting a museum will both be fine.

③ We will celebrate your birthday this Friday.

④ If it were not for my parents, I would not come to London University.

⑤ To go to the museum, you have to go to the West Gate first, then take the bus, and finally take the subway.

⑥ I thought my girlfriend cooked dinner for me, actually she bought it for me.

⑦ My best friend did not eat with me, but on the contrary he had dinner with my parents.

⑧ If we want to master Chinese, we should watch less TV and read more books.

⑨ My roommate came back again after 11:00 p.m. I told him if he came back again at that time, I would not let him in.

⑩ Are you used to drinking tea?

⑪ I was born in 1985 in New York.

5 Please complete the following sentences:

① 中國茶，你喝得慣喝不慣？

Positive:

Negative:

② 中文，你學得好不好？

Positive:

Negative:

③ 你說得太快了，請你

④ 我聽說他泡茶泡得很好。(Please turn the underlined part into a question.)

⑤ 我聽說他學不好中文。(Please turn the underlined part into a question.)

Lesson 7 感恩節

6 Please write something about your plan for Thanksgiving Day by using the following patterns:

NP 快/就要 V 了； S 打算 VP； S 已經……了； A 離 B Adj.

從 A（坐……）到 B 得 time duration； S 先 A，再 B，（最後 C）；

A 或者 B； S 過……節； V V (Object)； 要不是 A，就 B；

S 以爲 + sentence, 其實……；

7 Please read the following paragraph in Pinyin:

  Yào kǎoshì le, dàjiā dōu máng de bùdéliǎo. Jiāxīng měi tiān shuì jiào shuì de hěn wǎn, qǐ chuáng qǐ de hěn zǎo, yì tiān dào wǎn dōu zài niàn shū, fùxí gōngkè. Tā měi tiān dōu juéde lèi jí le, chī fàn fàn bù xiāng, shuì jiào jiào bú gòu, méijīng-dǎcǎi de. Xiànzài fùxí gōngkè de shíhou, ta juéde měi ge hànzì dōu yíyàng, lián zìjǐ de míngzi yě bú huì xiě le. Tā yǐwéi duō hē yìdiǎnr kāfēi jiù huì hǎo de, kěshì hēle kāfēi yě méiyǒu yòng. Tā gěi jiā lǐ dǎle ge diànhuà. Māma shuō tā tài lèi le, yīnggāi hǎohāor shuì yí jiào cái xíng. Tā juéde Jiāqí zhēn qíguài: měi tiān dōu hěn jīngshen, hǎoxiàng yǒu yòngbùwán de jìnr shìde. Yí wèn cái zhīdào, Jiāqí xiànglái zǎo shuì zǎo qǐ, měi tiān dōu yào pǎo bù duànliàn. Jiāxīng zhè tiān wǎnshang zǎozǎo de jiù shuì le. Tā shuì de hěn xiāng, hái zuòle yí ge hǎo mèng. Dì'èr tiān qǐlái de shíhou, tā juéde shūfu duō le.

How to Approach Chinese: Dos and Don'ts

Unlike the Japanese, Chinese people nowadays do not bow as a form of greeting. Instead, a brief handshake is the commom practice. While meeting elders or senior officials, one's handshake should be even more gentle and accompanied by a slight nod. Sometimes, as an expression of warmth, a Chinese person will cover the nomal handshake with his/her left hand. As a sign of respect, Chinese people usually lower their eyes slightly when they meet others.

Moreover, embracing or kissing when greeting or saying good-bye is highly unusual. Generally, Chinese do not show their emotions and feelings in public. Consequently, it is better not to behave in too carefree a manner in public.

There is an unwritten code that one should not accept a gift, invitation or favor when it is first presented. Politely refusing two or three times is thought to show modesty and humility. Accepting something in haste makes a person look aggressive and greedy, as does opening it in front of the giver. Traditionally the monetary value of a gift indicated the importance of a relationship, but with the increasing contact with foreigners in recent years, the symbolic nature of gifts has become more popular.

When giving gifts, one should present them with both hands. And when wrapping, be aware that different colors indicate very different things. For instance, red stands for luck, pink and yellow represent happiness and prosperity; white, grey and black are funeral colors. The popular items that make a good gift include: cigarette lighters, stamps (stamp collecting is a popular hobby), T-shirt, the exotic coins…. And the following gifts should be avoided:

- White or yellow flowers (especially chrysanthemums). These are used for funerals.
- Pears. The word 梨 for *pear* in Chinese sounds the same as 離 " to separate" and pear is therefore considered bad luck.
- Cards or letters written in red ink. They symbolize the end of a relationship.
- Clocks of any kind. The word 鍾 for *clock* in Chinese sounds the same as the expression 終 "the end of life".

In China, tipping is not practiced and almost no one asks for tips. The same thing goes even in the regions like Hong Kong and Macao, except in some luxurious hotels.

LESSON 8　要考試了

　　要考試了，大家都忙得不得了。家興每天睡覺睡得很晚，起床起得很早，一天到晚都在唸書，復習功課。他每天都覺得累極了，吃飯飯不香，睡覺覺不夠，沒精打采的。現在復習功課的時候，他覺得每個漢字都一樣，連自己的名字也不會寫了。他以為多喝一點兒咖啡就會好的，可是喝了咖啡也沒有用。他給家裡打了個電話，媽媽說他太累了，應該好好兒睡一覺才行。他覺得家奇真奇怪：每天都很精神，好像有用不完的勁兒似的。一問才知道，家奇向來早睡早起，每天都要跑步鍛煉。家興這天晚上早早地就睡了。他睡得很香，還做了一個好夢。第二天起來的時候，他覺得舒服多了。

1

家奇：　家興，最近怎麼樣？

家興：　別提了，忙死了。

家奇：　是呀，要考試了，大家都忙得不得了。

家興：　真要命！我每天都睡覺睡得很晚，起床起得很早，一天到晚都在唸書，復習功課。

家奇： 的確很辛苦。

家興： 不知道怎麼搞的，最近我每天都覺得很累。

家奇： 是嗎？

家興： 咳，吃飯飯不香，睡覺覺不夠。

家奇： 你沒精打采的，是不是生病了？

家興： 你說奇怪不奇怪，我現在覺得每個漢字都一樣，一個比一個難記。

家奇： 中國字是很難記。

家興： 我連自己的名字也不會寫了。

家奇： 哦？

家興： 我以為多喝一點兒咖啡就會好的，可是今天喝了三大杯咖啡也沒有用。

家奇： 你爸爸不是醫生嗎？你給他打個電話問一問。

家興： 我是應該給家裡打個電話了。

2

家興： 喂？

媽媽： 喂？家興？你好嗎？

家興： 還行，就是覺得累。

媽媽： 你是不是生病了？你爸爸現在不在家，怎麼回事？

家興： 一天到晚都沒精神，睡覺睡不夠。

媽媽： 你昨天晚上幾點睡的？

家興： 昨天晚上四點才睡，今天早上八點就起來了。

媽媽： 你睡得太少了，得早點兒睡才行，還要吃好。

家興： 可是，我得復習功課，準備考試。

媽媽： 你睡不好，怎麼能復習好呢？

家興： 媽媽，您說得對。

媽媽： 家興，聽媽媽的話，今天晚上早點兒睡。要是還覺得不舒服，就去看醫生。

家興： 好的，媽媽。

媽媽： 別總是去快餐店吃快餐，多喝一點兒橙汁，多吃水果、蔬菜。

Lesson 8　要考試了

家興：　知道了，媽媽。
媽媽：　還有，要少喝可樂。
家興：　媽媽，我最近很少喝可樂。
媽媽：　記住了，一定要早早休息。
家興：　記住了，媽媽，再見！
媽媽：　再見。

3

家興：　家奇，我覺得你真奇怪。
家奇：　我怎麼了？
家興：　你怎麼每天都很有精神，好像有用不完的勁兒似的？
家奇：　我向來早睡早起。每天都要鍛煉——跑半個小時的步。
家興：　可是我不習慣早睡早起，也沒有時間跑步。
家奇：　那你怎麼能有精神呢？我睡覺睡得比你多多了！你也應該早睡早起才行。
家興：　今天晚上我不去圖書館學習了，我想回宿舍睡覺。
家奇：　這就對了。祝你做個好夢！
家興：　謝謝，明天見！

(On the next day)

家奇：　呵！真精神！今天怎麼樣？
家興：　比昨天強多了。我昨天晚上睡得好極了！還夢見了我們學過的漢字。
家奇：　哦？
家興：　一個跟一個不一樣，呵呵。
家奇：　呵呵。
家興：　不一樣就是不一樣，今天覺得舒服多了！

VOCABULARY

1	*考試	考试	kǎo shì	V.-O.	to take an exam
2	不得了	不得了	bùdéliǎo	Adj.	extremely
3	*起床	起床	qǐ chuáng	V.-O.	to get up
4	一天到晚	一天到晚	yì tiān dào wǎn	IE	from morning till night
5	唸	念	niàn	V.	to attend school
6	*唸書	念书	niàn shū	V.-O.	to study
7	*復習	复习	fùxí	V.	to review
8	*功課	功课	gōngkè	N.	homework
9	沒精打采	没精打采	méijīng-dǎcǎi	IE	to look tired and unhappy
10	*連	连	lián	Prep.	even
11	*寫	写	xiě	V.	to write
12	*打電話	打电话	dǎ diànhuà	VP	to call
13	*才	才	cái	Adv.	not …until
14	*精神	精神	jīngshen	Adj.	vigorous
15	*好像	好像	hǎoxiàng	V.	it seems
16	完	完	wán	V.	to run out
17	勁兒	劲儿	jìnr	N.	strength
18	*似的	似的	shìde	Pt.	It seems that...
19	*向來	向来	xiànglái	Adv.	all along
20	*跑	跑	pǎo	V.	to run
21	*步	步	bù	N.	step
22	跑步	跑步	pǎo bù	V.-O.	to jog
23	*鍛煉	锻炼	duànliàn	V.	to exercise
24	夢	梦	mèng	N.	dream
25	起來	起来	qǐlái	V.-C.	to get up
26	*最近	最近	zuìjìn	N.	recently
27	別提了	别提了	bié tí le	IE	Don't bring it up.
28	*死	死	sǐ	Adj.	extremely
29	真要命	真要命	zhēn yào mìng	IE	It is killing me.
30	*的確	的确	díquè	Adv.	indeed
31	怎麼搞的	怎么搞的	zěnme gǎo de	IE	What's wrong?

Lesson 8 要考試了

32	咳	咳	hāi	Int.	*a sigh*
33	生病	生病	shēng bìng	V.-O.	to get sick
34	*比	比	bǐ	Prep.	compared with
35	難	难	nán	Adj.	hard, difficult
36	記	记	jì	V.	to remember
37	*難記	难记	nán jì	VP	difficult to remember
38	怎麼回事	怎么回事	zěnme huí shì	IE	What has happened?
39	快餐	快餐	kuàicān	N.	fast food
40	橙汁	橙汁	chéngzhī	N.	orange juice
41	*水果	水果	shuǐguǒ	N.	fruits
42	*蔬菜	蔬菜	shūcài	N.	vegetables
43	可樂	可乐	kělè	N.	coke
44	記住	记住	jìzhù	V.-C.	to remember
45	*休息	休息	xiūxi	V.	to rest
46	*祝	祝	zhù	V.	to wish
47	*強	强	qiáng	Adj.	strong, good
48	夢見	梦见	mèngjiàn	V.-C.	to dream of

Supplementary Vocabulary:

1	風	风	fēng	N.	wind
2	雪	雪	xuě	N.	snow
3	啤酒	啤酒	píjiǔ	N.	beer
4	老虎	老虎	lǎohǔ	N.	tiger
5	超人	超人	chāorén	N.	superman
6	黑	黑	hēi	Adj.	black
7	白	白	bái	Adj.	white
8	矮	矮	ǎi	Adj.	short (in height)
9	胖	胖	pàng	Adj.	over-weight
10	瘦	瘦	shòu	Adj.	skinny
11	重	重	zhòng	Adj.	heavy
12	遲到	迟到	chídào	V.	be late
13	抽菸	抽烟	chōu yān	V.-O.	to smoke

14	結婚	结婚	jié hūn	V.-O.	to get married
15	刷牙	刷牙	shuā yá	V.-O.	to brush teeth
16	照相	照相	zhào xiàng	V.-O.	to take pictures
17	哭	哭	kū	V.	to cry
18	轉告	转告	zhuǎngào	V.	to pass a message to sb.
19	公斤	公斤	gōngjīn	MW	kilogram

GRAMMAR

1. Intensifying complements

In Chinese, there are many different ways to indicate the degree of adjectives. Here are some structures that are used a lot in colloquial Chinese.

漢語中表達形容詞程度的方式有很多，下面是漢語口語中常用的一些結構。

- Adj. 極了
- Adj. 得很
- Adj. 得不得了
- Adj. 得 + clause

 E.g.
a. 要考試了，大家都忙極了。
   (The exam is coming. Everybody is extremely busy.)
b. 要考試了，大家都忙得很。
   (As the exam approaches, everybody is very busy.)
c. 要考試了，大家都忙得不得了。
   (As the exam is approaching, everybody is terribly busy.)
d. 要考試了，大家都忙得吃飯飯不香，睡覺睡不著。
   (With the arrival of the tests, everybody is so busy that they can't eat and sleep well.)
e. 天氣冷極了。(The weather is extremely cold.)
f. 天氣冷得很。(The weather is very cold.)
g. 天氣冷得不得了。(The weather is terribly cold.)
h. 天氣冷得誰都不想出去。(The weather is so cold that nobody wants to go out.)

2. S 在 VP：S is doing sth.

在 can also be used as a progressive marker indicating a progressive action.

"在"還可以用作進行式的標記，表示動作正在進行。

 a. 我一天到晚都在唸書，復習功課。
(I have been reading all day long, reviewing the lessons.)
b. ——你在做什麼？ (What are you doing there?)
——我在鍛煉。 (I am exercising.)

The adverb 正 and the particle 呢 very often goes in this pattern，in which case either 在 or 正，or both of them can be dropped.
副詞"正"和助詞"呢"常常出現在這一結構中，這時"在"或"正"可以省略，二者也可以同時省略。

S 正在 VP 呢

——你在做什麼呢？ (What are you doing？)
——我正在看書呢。/ 我在看書呢。/ 我正看書呢。/ 我看書呢。
(I am reading.)

3 應該 VP，才行

This is a the topic-comment structure, which is very useful.
這是一個非常實用的主題評論句。

 a. 應該早睡早起，才行。
(It won't work unless we go to bed early and get up early.)
b. 學中文，應該天天練才行。
(As for learning Chinese, we should practice everyday. Only this will do.)

We can also express the same idea with the following pattern.
我們也可以用下面的句型表達同樣的意義。

不 / 沒 VP, 不行

 a. 要想有精神，不早睡早起不行。
(If you want to feel energetic, you have to go to bed and get up early.)
b. 學中文，沒有英漢詞典不行。
(As for learning Chinese, it won't work without an English-Chinese dictionary.)
c. 做西紅柿炒雞蛋，沒有雞蛋不行。
(As for making fried eggs with tomato, it won't work without eggs.)

183

④ S 好像 VP（似的）: It seems that ...

  a. 他好像有用不完的勁兒似的。(It seems that he is always energetic.)
b. 她好像很喜歡參觀博物館。(It seems that she likes visiting museums a lot.)
c. 你沒精打采的，好像生病了。(You look tired. It seems that you are sick.)
d. 好像快要下雨了。(It seems that it is going to rain.)
e. 好像快到哥大了，我們該下車了。
(It seems that we are approaching CU. We are supposed to get off.)

⑤ S 向來(不)VP；S 從來不 VP/沒 V 過 Object

"向來不 VP" means that somebody doesn't do something all along. While "從來不 VP" indicates that an action never takes place and perhaps never will it happen.
"向來不 VP" 表示某人從來沒做過某事，而"從來不 VP" 表示某一動作行爲從未發生或永遠不會發生。

  a. 我向來不喜歡看電視。(I don't like watching TV all along.)
b. 我從來不喝酒。(I don't drink.)
c. 他向來喜歡聊天兒。(He likes chatting all along.)
d. 英國人從來不過感恩節。(British people don't celebrate Thanksgiving Day.)

We can say "向來 VP", but can only say "從來不 VP/沒 V 過 Object".
我們可以説"向來 VP"，卻只能説"從來不 VP/沒 V 過 Object"。

  a. 我向來喜歡聽中國音樂。(I like listening to Chinese music all along.)
b. ——你是不是去過意大利？(Have you been to Italy?)
——我從來沒去過那兒。(I have never been there.)

⑥ S VP 的時候: at the time of doing...; when/while doing sth. ...

  a. 早上起來的時候，我很累。(I felt very tired when I got up in the morning.)
b. 吃飯的時候，最好不要説話。(Please don't talk while you are eating.)
c. 小的時候，我非常喜歡看感恩節遊行。
(I like watching Thanksgiving Day Parade a lot when I was little.)
d. 我在中國住的時候，天天吃四川菜。
(When I was staying in China, I ate Sichuan dishes every day.)
e. 你開玩笑的時候，跟真的一樣。
(When you were joking, nobody realized that it was only a joke.)

Lesson 8 要考試了

7 連 -construction

S 連 Object 也/都（不）V

This is another pattern to show focus. It is very often translated with the English word "even". And the focused element goes between 連 and 都. If the sentence is negative, then 也 and 都 will be interchangeable. However, this pattern is only used to show extreme case. The context should be introduced when using this structure.

這是另一個表示強調的結構，常被譯為"even"。被強調的部分常處於"連"和"都"中間。如果句子是否定意義的，那麼"也"和"都"可以互換。然而，這個結構只用於表示極端的情況，使用時需要說出語境。

a. 我什麼都忘了，連我的名字也不會寫了。
   (I have forgotten everything. I don't even know how to write my name.)
b. 他是我的男朋友，可是他現在連我都不認識了。
   (He is my boyfriend. But now he doesn't even know who I am.)
c. 他太忙了，連飯都沒有時間吃。
   (He is too busy. He doesn't even have time to eat.)
d. 他們玩兒得太高興了，連考試都忘了。
   (They had so much fun that they even forgot the test.)
e. 他連這件事都知道。(He even knows about this matter.)
f. 那個人很窮 (qióng)，連一分錢都沒有。
   (That person is very poor. He doesn't even have a single penny.)

The focused element may also be a verb phrase or a sentence.
被強調的部分也可以是動詞短語或句子。

a. 你是學生，可是你怎麼連圖書館在哪兒都不知道呢？
   (You are a student. But how come you don't even know where the library is?)
b. 你是紐約人，可是你怎麼連怎麼去大都 (dū) 會博物館都不知道呢?
   (You are a New Yorker. But how come you don't even know how to go to the Metropolitan Museum?)

連 S 也/都（不）VP

If 連 is before the subject, then the subject will be the focus.
如果"連"在主語的前面，那麼強調的是主語。

a. 姚明 (Yáo Míng) 很有名，連很多美國人都知道他。
   (Yao Ming is very famous. Even a lot of Americans know him.)

b. 這個問題太難了，連老師都不會。
   (This problem is too difficult. Even the teacher can't solve it.)
c. 買東西一點兒也不難，連三歲的孩子都會。
   (It is not difficult to buy things at all. Even a three year old knows how to do it.)

8 S 回 + PW (VP)：to go back to a place；to return

 a. 我想回宿舍睡覺。(I want to go back to my dorm to sleep.)
b. 我的同屋打算下下個禮拜回國。
   (My roommate plans to go back to his country the week after next.)
c. 你準備什麼時候回家？(When do you plan to go back home?)

Combined with other characters,"回"has different meanings.
與其他漢字使用時，"回"的語義解釋會不同。

 a. 你什麼時候才給我回話呢？(When will you give me a reply？)
b. 我常常回想起我們在一起的幸福日子。
   (I often recall the happy days when we were together.)

9 S（不）會 VP 的：it is likely / unlikely that...

 a. 我以爲我多喝一點兒咖啡就會好的。
   (I thought that I would get better if I drank a little bit more of coffee.)
b. 要是你今天晚上好好兒睡一覺，明天你就會覺得好多了。
   (If you could have a good sleep tonight, you would feel much better tomorrow.)
c. 要是你早一點兒告訴我，我不會不幫你的。
   (If you can tell me earlier, it is unlikely that I would not help you.)
d. 要考試了，我會好好兒復習的。/ 我不會不復習的。
   (The test is coming. I will review thoroughly.)

10 The comparative structure

A 比 B + Adj.

Question form：A 是不是比 B + Adj.？；A Adj. 還是 B Adj.？；A 比 B + Adj. + 嗎？

Positive answer：是的，A 比 B + Adj.

Negative answer：不，A 沒有 B + Adj.

Other：A 跟 B 差不多（一樣 Adj.）。

E.g. a.——中文比英文難嗎？/ 中文是不是比英文難？
   (Is Chinese more difficult than English?)

Lesson 8 要考試了

——是的，中文比英文難。 (Yes, it is more difficult than English.)

——不，中文沒有英文難。 (No, Chinese is not as difficult as English is.)

——中文跟英文差不多一樣難。 (Chinese is almost as difficult as English is.)

b. ——坐飛機比坐火車快嗎？ (Is it faster to take an airplane than a train?)

——是的，坐飛機比坐火車快。 (Yes, it is faster to take an airplane than a train.)

c. ——哥大的學生比紐約大學的學生聰明嗎？

(Are students at CU smarter than those at NYU?)

——哥大的學生跟紐約大學的學生一樣聰明。

(Students at CU are as smart as students at NYU.)

NOTE: No adverb can go before the adjective word in this structure.

注意：這個結構中形容詞前不能放副詞。

 我比你很高。

If the object is involved, then we will use the following structure:

如果涉及賓語，那麼需要用下面的結構：

A V O V 得比 B + Adj.

 a. ——哥哥吃飯多還是弟弟吃飯多？

(Who eats more, the elder brother or the younger one?)

——哥哥吃飯吃得比弟弟多。 (The elder brother eats more than the younger one.)

b. ——誰吃飯吃得多，你還是他？ (Who eats more, you or he?)

——他吃飯吃得比我多。 (He eats more than I do.)

We can also use the following pattern to express the same idea:

我們還可以用下面的句型表達同樣的意思：

A V O 比 B + Adj.

 a. 哥哥吃飯比弟弟多。 (The elder brother eats more than the younger one.)

b. 他吃飯比我多。 (He eats more than I do.)

c. ——你跟同屋比，誰說中文說得好？

(Who speaks Chinese better, you or your roommate?)

——我的同屋說中文比我好。 (My roommate speaks better than I do.)

However, when both speakers know what the object is or when the verb is intransitive, we can use the following pattern:

然而，當談話雙方都知道談論的是什麼，或者動詞是不及物動詞的時候，我們可以使用下面的結構：

187

A 比 B V 得 + Adj.

  a. 我的同屋比我說得好。(My roommate speaks better than I do.)
b. 哥哥比弟弟吃得多。(The elder brother eats more than the younger one.)
c. 汽車比自行車走得快。(Cars move faster than bicycles.)

To sum up, the four patterns are listed below:
以上四個句型總結如下:

A 比 B + Adj.
A V O V 得比 B + Adj.
A V O 比 B + Adj.
A 比 B V 得 + Adj.

If we want to indicate to what degree A is better or worse than B. The following patterns are to go with:
如果我們要表達 A 比 B 好或者不好的程度，則需要使用下面的句型：

A V O V 得比 B + Adj. + 一點兒 (A is a little...than B)
A V O 比 B + Adj. + 得多 (A is much...than B)
A 比 B V 得 + Adj. + 多了 (A is much...than B)

  a. 哥哥比弟弟高一點兒。
　　(The elder brother is a little taller than the younger one.)
b. 哥哥說中文說得比弟弟好得多 / 多了。
　　(The elder brother speaks Chinese much better than the younger one.)
c. 你比我跑得快得多 / 多了。(You run much faster than I do.)
d. 你只比我跑得快一點兒。(You only run a little bit faster than I do.)

We can use the pattern below to be more specific when comparing:
我們還可以使用下面的句型使比較更加具體：

A 比 B Adj. ____

  a. 他比他弟弟大一歲。(He is one year older than his younger brother.)
b. 這枝筆比那枝筆貴一塊錢。(This pen is one dollar more expensive than that one.)

⑪ 祝 sb. VP：(I/We) wish sb. sth.

  a. 祝你做個好夢！　　　　(Have a nice dream!)
b. 祝你一路平安 (píng'ān)！　(Have a safe trip!)

Lesson 8 要考試了

c. 祝你生日快樂！　　　　　　(Happy birthday to you!)
d. 祝你玩兒得開心 (kāixīn)！　　(Have a good time!)
e. 祝你健康 (jiànkāng)！　　　　(Wish you good health!)
f. 祝你天天快樂！　　　　　　(I hope you will be happy each day!)
g. 祝你好運！　　　　　　　　(Good luck to you!)
h. 祝你幸福！　　　　　　　　(I wish you happiness!)
i. 祝福你！　　　　　　　　　(May you be blessed!)

12 Some useful expressions for making a phone call

E.g.
a. 喂？ (Hello?)
b. 請問，××在嗎？ (May I ask：is ×× there or not?)
c. 我就是。(This is He / She.)
d. ××不在。(×× is not here.)
e. 請問有什麼事，我可以轉告 (zhuǎngào) 嗎？ (May I take a message?)
f. 請告訴他……(Please tell him...)
g. 謝謝，不用了，我過一會兒再打。(No thanks. I will call back later.)

Summary:

> In Chinese, there are many different ways to indicate the degree of adjectives. Intensifying complements are one of them.

> 在 can also be used as a progressive marker indicating a progressive action.

> "向來不 VP" means that somebody doesn't do something all along.

> "從來不 VP" indicates that an action never takes place and perhaps never will it happen.

> We can say "向來 VP"，but can only say "從來不 VP / 沒 V 過 Object"。

> 連-construction is another pattern to show focus. It is very often translated with the English word "even". It is only used to show extreme case or situation.

> The focused element goes between 連 and 都．If the object is focused, it moves up to the preverb positional. If the sentence is negative, then 也 and 都 will be interchangeable.

> The focused element may also be a verb phrase or a sentence.

> If 連 is before the subject, then the subject will be the focus.

Patterns:

- **Adj. 極了** ‖ 要考試了，大家都忙極了。
  (The exam is coming. Everybody is extremely busy.)

- **Adj. 得很** ‖ 要考試了，大家都忙得很。
  (As the exam approaches, everybody is very busy.)

- **Adj. 得不得了** ‖ 要考試了，大家都忙得不得了。
  (The exam is approaching and everybody is terribly busy.)

- **Adj. 得 + clause** ‖ 要考試了，大家都忙得吃飯飯不香，睡覺睡不著。
  (With the arrival of the tests, everybody is so busy that they can't eat and sleep well.)

- **S 在 VP** ‖ 我一天到晚都在唸書，復習功課。
  (I have been reading all day long, reviewing the lessons.)

- **應該 VP, 才行** ‖ 應該好好兒睡一覺，才行。(Only a good rest will do.)

- **不 / 沒有 VP, 不行** ‖ 要想有精神，不早睡早起不行。
  (If you want to feel energetic, you have to go to bed and get up early.)
  學中文，沒有英漢詞典不行。
  (As for learning Chinese, it won't work without an English-Chinese dictionary.)

- **S 好像 VP（似的）** ‖ 他好像有用不完的勁兒似的。
  (It seems that he is always energetic.)

- **S 向來 (不) VP** ‖ 我向來喜歡聽中國音樂。(I like listening to Chinese music all along.)
  我向來不喜歡看電視。(I don't like watching TV all along.)

- **S 從來不 VP** ‖ 英國人從來不過感恩節。
  (British people don't celebrate Thanksgiving Day.)

- **S 從來沒 V 過 Object** ‖ 我從來沒去過那兒。(I have never been there.)

- **S VP 的時候** ‖ 早上起來的時候，我很累。(I felt very tired when I got up in the morning.)

- **S 連 Object 也 / 都（不）V** ‖ 他連這件事都知道。(He even knows this matter.)
  我什麼都忘了，連我的名字也不會寫了。
  (I have forgotten everything. I don't even know how to write my name.)

- **連 S 也 / 都（不）VP** ‖ 這個問題太難了，連老師都不會。
  (This problem is too difficult. Even the teacher can't solve it.)

Lesson 8 要考試了

- S 回 + PW (VP) ‖ 我想回宿舍睡覺。(I want to go back to my dorm to sleep.)
- S (不) 會 VP 的 ‖ 我以為我多喝一點兒咖啡就會好的。
  (I thought that I would get better if I drank a little bit more of coffee.)
  要是你早一點兒告訴我，我不會不幫你的。
  (If you could tell me earlier, it is unlikely that I would not help you.)
- A 是不是比 B + Adj.？；A 比 B + Adj. + 嗎？ ‖ 中文是不是比英文難？／中文比英文難嗎？
  (Is Chinese more difficult than English?)
- 是的，A 比 B + Adj. ‖ 是的，中文比英文難。(Yes, it is more difficult than English.)
- 不，A 沒有 B + Adj. ‖ 不，中文沒有英文難。(No, Chinese is not as difficult as English is.)
- A 跟 B 差不多 (一樣 Adj.) ‖ 中文跟英文差不多一樣難。
  (Chinese is almost as difficult as English is.)
- A V O V 得比 B + Adj. ‖ 哥哥吃飯吃得比弟弟多。
  (The elder brother eats more than the younger one.)
- A V O 比 B + Adj. ‖ 哥哥吃飯比弟弟多。
  (The elder brother eats more than the younger one.)
- A V O V 得比 B + Adj. + 一點兒 ‖ 哥哥比弟弟高一點兒。
  (The elder brother is a little taller than the younger one.)
- A V O 比 B + Adj. + 得多 ‖ 哥哥說中文說得比弟弟好得多。
  (The elder brother speaks Chinese much better than the younger one.)
- A 比 B V 得 + Adj. + 多了 ‖ 你比我跑得快多了。(You run much faster than I do.)
- A 比 B V 得 + Adj. ‖ 我的同屋比我說得好。(My roommate speaks better than I do.)
- 祝 sb. VP ‖ 祝你做個好夢！ (Have a nice dream!)

IN CLASS ACTIVITIES

1 Answer the following questions according to the information given in the text:

① 要考試了，大家都怎麼樣？

❷ 家興爲什麽每天睡覺睡得很晚，起床起得很早？

❸ 爲什麽他吃飯飯不香，睡覺覺不夠，沒精打采的？

❹ 家興爲什麽要喝咖啡？

❺ 家興爲什麽給家裡打電話？

❻ 媽媽説什麽？

❼ 爲什麽家奇每天都很精神，好像有用不完的勁兒似的？

2 Please do role play according to the dialogue given below:

打電話

A 喂！你好！請問你找誰？
B 喂，我找＿＿＿＿＿＿。請問他在不在？
A 我就是，請問你是哪位？
B 我是＿＿＿＿＿＿＿＿。
A ＿＿＿＿＿＿＿＿，是你呀！很久 (jiǔ: for a while) 沒有聽到你的消息 (xiāoxi: news about a person) 了，都好嗎？
B 都很好，謝謝，你呢？你在忙什麽？
A 別提了，快要考試了，一天到晚都在復習考試。
B 越是忙的時候，越要注意 (zhùyì: to pay attention to) 休息。
A 説的也是。可是，我最近不知怎麽搞的，吃飯飯不香，睡覺覺不夠。
B 我看你今天晚上最好早一點兒休息。

Lesson 8 要考試了

- A 好。你也很忙吧？
- B 也許 (yěxǔ: perhaps) 你不信 (xìn: to believe)，我越忙越精神。
- A 爲什麽？
- B 早睡早起，身體 (shēntǐ: health) 好。
- A 噢 (ō: oh)……
- B 你太忙了！等你考完試後，我們再聊吧。
- A 好，再見！
- B 再見！

HOMEWORK

1 Please rewrite or complete the following sentences with the given structures:

① 感恩節是下個禮拜。（快 V 了）

➡ 感恩節快到了。

② 紐約的冬天 (dōngtiān: winter) 冷不冷？
(Intensifying Complements：4 expressions)

➡

➡

➡

➡

③ 學中文得有語伴。(沒有……不行)

➡

④ 學中文，得天天練 。(應該 VP, 才行)

➡

⑤ 他沒精打采的，不知道是不是生病了。(好像……似的)
　➡

⑥ 英國人不過感恩節。(S 向來不 VP)
　➡

⑦ 我沒有喝過酒。(S 從來不 VP)
　➡

⑧ 誰都知道這件事。小王也知道了。(連 S 也/都 VP)
　➡

⑨ 這個字難寫還是那個字難寫？(A 比 B + Adj.)
　➡

2 Please fill in the blanks with the words given, one for each blank:

| 給　得　在　了　還　不　向來　的　祝　也　過 |

① 要考試了，大家都忙__得__不得了。

② 一天到晚都_____唸書，復習功課。

③ 我覺得累極_____。

④ 我已經看_____課文了。

⑤ 吃飯飯_____香，睡覺睡不夠，沒精打采_____。

⑥ 連自己的名字_____不會寫了。

⑦ 你_____他打個電話問一問。

⑧ 要是_____覺得不舒服，就去看醫生。

⑨ 我_____早起早睡，每天都要鍛煉：跑半個小時的步。

⑩ _____你做個好夢！

Lesson 8 要考試了

3 Translate the following sentences into Chinese:

① Xiao Wang is very tall, but I think Xiao Zhang even taller than he is.

② He runs a little faster than I do. But the way he drives (開車: kāi chē) is a little bit slower.

③ I don't have enough money. Can you give me some (一點兒: yìdiǎnr) money?

④ Yao Ming is much taller than I am. He is so tall that he can't even find a comfortable bed.

⑤ I am pretty sure that you will do a good job in the test.

⑥ It is unlikely that my roommate will come back by midnight (半夜: bànyè).

⑦ He is so busy that he doesn't even have time for lunch.

⑧ It seems that he never calls his girlfriend.

⑨ If you want to feel energetic, you have to exercise everyday. (應該 VP，才行)

⑩ What are you doing there? I am running.

4 Please write the English meaning for the following expressions:

① 祝你做個好夢！
→

② 祝你一路平安 (píng'ān: safe)！
→

③ 祝你生日快樂！
→

④ 祝你玩兒得開心 (kāixīn: happy)。
→

⑤ 祝你健康 (jiànkāng: healthy)！
→

⑥ 祝你天天快樂！
→

⑦ 祝你好運！
→

⑧ 祝你幸福！
→

⑨ 祝福你！
→

5 Please read the following paragraph in Pinyin:

Kǎowán shì hòu, dàjiā dōu jíjí-mángmáng de huí jiā guò Shèngdàn Jié hé xīnnián qù le. Sān ge xīngqī de jiàqī hěn kuài jiù guòqù le. Jīntiān shì chūnjì xuéqī kāi xué de dìyī tiān. Zhōngwénbān yǒule hěn duō xīn tóngxué. Jiāqí hé Jiāxīng

Lesson 8 要考試了

yòu zài Zhōngwénkè shàng jiàn miàn le. Liǎng ge lǎo péngyou jiàn miàn géwài gāoxìng, nǐ yì yán wǒ yì yǔ de shuōqǐle jiàqī lǐ fāshēng de shìqing. Jiāxīng shuō tā de gǒu dìdi Zhōngwén Yīngwén dōu tīngdedǒng, yídìng shì shìjiè shàng zuì cōngmíng de gǒu le. Jiāqí shuō tāmen jiā shōuyǎngle yì zhī māo, báisè de máo, lǜsè de yǎnjing, zhǎng de tèbié kě'ài. Tāmen yuè shuō yuè gāoxìng, lián lǎoshī shì shénme shíhou jìnlái de dōu méiyǒu zhùyìdào.

Chinese Concepts of the Body

It is believed that Chinese medicine is closely linked to Daoist philosophy, which holds that the universe exists because of two great opposing yet interdependent creative forces, known as *Yin* and *Yang*.

The body is often regarded as a microcosmic universe and the inner organs and their functions are classified according to their *Yin* and *Yang* properties. The relationship between the organs, and all natural phenomena, is described in terms of the five phases or elements (五行): wood, fire, earth, metal and water.

Thus the inner organs are paired off according to their *Yin* and *Yang* characteristics and ascribed an element. The kidney and urinary bladder, for example, make a pair and are related to the water element. The diagnosis and treatment are based on these relationships. For instance, water quells fire. Therefore, if there's a heart (fire) problem, underlying kidney deficiency may be diagnosed and treated.

Another key concept is that of "氣" or vital energy. This is said to flow through a network of channels, known as meridians, to vitalize the inner organs. 氣 also influences 精 (essence) and 神 (spirit) and is seen as the link between the physical body, the mind and higher consciousness.

When 氣 flows freely, there's a good balance between *Yin* and *Yang* in the body and good health. If it becomes blocked or deficient, due to dietary, lifestyle or other factors, disease will ensue.

Traditional diagnosis is based on four types of examination (四診 sìzhěn):

• Observation (望診 wàngzhěn) - includes tongue analysis and observation of facial characteristics, skin and gait.
• Listening (聞診 wénzhěn) - relates to the patient's voice and respiration.
• Questioning (問診 wènzhěn) - asks about diet, sleep, excretion and symptoms.
• Palpation (切診 qièzhěn) - involves taking six pulses on each wrist, one for each inner organ, and interpreting the depth, speed, strength and quality of each.

The best treatment is believed to be prevention. Ancient Chinese physicians were expected to keep their patients in good health and to lead, for example, by living in harmony with the seasons, eating a balanced diet and exercising regularly. Preventive treatments therefore include dietary and lifestyle advice and energetic exercises such as 氣功 qìgōng and 太極 tàijí. In actual treatment, therapies such as acupuncture, acupressure, moxibustion and herbal medicine are often used.

LESSON 9 老朋友見面

考完試後，大家都急急忙忙地回家過聖誕節和新年去了。三個星期的假期很快就過去了。今天是春季學期開學的第一天。中文班有了很多新同學。家奇和家興又在中文課上見面了。兩個老朋友見面格外高興，你一言我一語地說起了假期裡發生的事情。家興說他的狗弟弟中文英文都聽得懂，一定是世界上最聰明的狗了。家奇說他們家收養了一隻貓，白色的毛，綠色的眼睛，長得特別可愛。他們越說越高興，連老師是什麼時候進來的都沒有注意到。

1 (This is the first day of Spring Semester. Jiaqi and Jiaxing are chatting in the classroom.)

家興： 哥們兒，你什麼時候回來的？

家奇： 昨天下午。你呢？

家興： 我也是。

家奇： 現在很多同學我都不認識。

家興： 嗯，中文班來了很多新同學。去年你什麼時候回英國的？

家奇： 我一考完試就急急忙忙地回家去了。

Lesson 9　老朋友見面

家興：　怎麼樣，假期過得好嗎？

家奇：　好極了！就是太短了。

家興：　三個禮拜一下子就過去了，真希望天天都是假期。

家奇：　是啊。

家興：　對了，你還記得我的狗弟弟吧？

家奇：　怎麼能忘了呢？你一天到晚狗弟弟長狗弟弟短的。[1]

家興：　你知道它的中文名字嗎？

家奇：　哦？它有中文名字了？叫什麼？

家興：　叫家奇。哈哈。

家奇：　什麼，你說什麼？

家興：　別急，別急，跟你開玩笑呢。

老師：　你們好！很高興再次見到大家……

2　(After class...)

家興：　我們剛才說到哪兒了？

家奇：　你的狗有中文名字了。

家興：　我叫它老大。

家奇：　什麼意思？

家興：　別誤會，我叫它老大，是因為我不說"請"，它就不聽我的話。

家奇：　對你這種人，是應該用這樣的法子。

家興：　嘿嘿，老大聽得懂中文，現在中文英文它都聽得懂。我想它一定是世界上最聰明的狗了。

家奇：　哦？

家興：　你記得我們學"你跑得快跑不快"和"你跑得快不快"，這兩個句子嗎？

家奇：　是啊，我總是出錯。

家興：　我們家老大呀，可清楚呢。我一說"你跑得快不快"，它就跑得很快。

家奇：　嗯？

家興：　我一說你"跑得快跑不快"，它就跑不快了。

---

[1] 你一天到晚狗弟弟長狗弟弟短的。You talk about your dog all day long.

家奇： 廢話，它累了，還能跑得快嗎？

家興： 還有，我説"把飯吃了"，它馬上就把飯吃了。我説"把電視打開"，它就不幹了。你説它聰明不聰明？

家奇： 它肯定比你聰明，哈哈。

3

家興： 聽説你們收養了一隻貓。它叫什麽名字？

家奇： 它叫覓覓，今天正好是它的生日。

家興： 這麽巧。它幾歲了？

家奇： 一歲了。它長得特别可愛——白色的毛，緑色的眼睛。

家興： 可是我覺得貓没有狗可愛，也没有狗忠實、聰明。

家奇： 我家的貓比你家的狗聰明多了。

家興： 你怎麽知道？

家奇： 我問它："桌子旁邊有什麽？"它就跳到桌子旁邊的電視上。還有，我高興的時候它也高興，我不高興的時候它也不高興，是我的知心朋友。

家興： 貓也挺可愛的。你的貓跑得快不快？

家奇： 它跑得快，爬得高，跳得也高。

家興： 它聽得懂聽不懂你説的話？

家奇： 當然聽得懂。我説"把酒喝了"，它就説"妙——妙——妙"！

家興： 你的貓聲調有問題，是"喵喵喵"，不是"妙妙妙"。

家奇／家興： 哈哈。

Lesson 9 老朋友見面

VOCABULARY

#					
1	急急忙忙	急急忙忙	jíjí-mángmáng	IE	in a hurry
2	聖誕節	圣诞节	Shèngdàn Jié	PN	Christmas
3	*假期	假期	jiàqī	N.	vacation
4	*春季	春季	chūnjì	N.	Spring
5	*學期	学期	xuéqī	N.	semester
6	開學	开学	kāi xué	V.-O.	school starts
7	*格外	格外	géwài	Adv.	especially (formal expression)
8	你一言我一語	你一言我一语	nǐ yì yán wǒ yì yǔ	IE	eagerly to tell each other
9	*發生	发生	fāshēng	V.	to happen
10	聽懂	听懂	tīngdǒng	V.-C.	to understand
11	*世界	世界	shìjiè	N.	world
12	*上	上	shàng	N.	on, on the top of…
13	*收養	收养	shōuyǎng	V.	to adopt (a pet)
14	*隻	只	zhī	MW	*measure word for animals*
15	*貓	猫	māo	N.	cat
16	白色	白色	báisè	N.	white color
17	*毛	毛	máo	N.	fur
18	*綠色	绿色	lǜsè	N.	green color
19	*眼睛	眼睛	yǎnjing	N.	eyes
20	*注意到	注意到	zhùyìdào	V.-C.	to notice
21	哥們兒	哥们儿	gēmenr	N.	buddy
22	*短	短	duǎn	Adj.	short (in length)
23	*希望	希望	xīwàng	V./N.	to hope; hope
24	天天	天天	tiān tiān	NP	everyday
25	記得	记得	jìde	V.	to recall, to remember
26	*忘了	忘了	wàng le	VP	to forget
27	它	它	tā	Pron.	it
28	*別急	别急	bié jí	IE	Don't worry.
29	*剛才	刚才	gāngcái	TW	just now
30	說到	说到	shuōdào	V.-C.	to talk about
31	*意思	意思	yìsi	N.	meaning

32	*誤會	误会	wùhuì	V.	to misunderstand
33	*句子	句子	jùzi	N.	sentence
34	出錯	出错	chū cuò	V.-O.	to make mistakes
35	*清楚	清楚	qīngchu	Adj.	clear
36	*廢話	废话	fèihuà	N.	Nonsense.
37	*幹	干	gàn	V.	to do
38	*肯定	肯定	kěndìng	Adv.	definitely, I am positive that...
39	覓覓	觅觅	Mìmì	PN	name of the cat
40	這麼巧	这么巧	zhème qiǎo	IE	What a coincidence!
41	歲	岁	suì	N.	age
42	*忠實	忠实	zhōngshí	Adj.	loyal
43	*跳	跳	tiào	V.	to jump
44	知心	知心	zhīxīn	Adj.	to know what one is thinking about
45	知心朋友	知心朋友	zhīxīn péngyou	NP	one's best friend
46	*爬	爬	pá	V.	to climb
47	*酒	酒	jiǔ	N.	drink (alcohol)
48	*妙	妙	miào	Adj.	Great!
49	喵	喵	miāo	Onom.	cry of a cat

■ Supplementary Vocabulary:

1	養	养	yǎng	V.	to raise, to bring up
2	寵物	宠物	chǒngwù	N.	pet
3	嘴	嘴	zuǐ	N.	mouth
4	臉	脸	liǎn	N.	face
5	北	北	běi	N.	north
6	東	东	dōng	N.	east
7	西	西	xī	N.	west
8	南	南	nán	N.	south
9	一雙鞋	一双鞋	yì shuāng xié	NP	a pair of shoes
10	一條蛇	一条蛇	yì tiáo shé	NP	a snake
11	月亮	月亮	yuèliang	N.	the moon

| 12 | 星星 | 星星 | xīngxing | N. | star |
| 13 | 上樓 | 上楼 | shànglóu | V.-O. | to go upstairs |

GRAMMAR

1 Resumption

Sometimes, numbers are very often used to resume elements common to several words listed in succession. In other words, when a noun or pronoun is followed by a number, we have more information about the noun or pronoun. This is the so-called resumption. 當幾個詞被連續列出時，它們後面經常用數字來總結其數量。換言之，名詞或代詞後的數字爲我們提供了更多的信息，也就是所謂的同位語複指概念。

a. 我們兩個 (we two)
b. 我們兩個都喜歡學中文。(Both of us like learning Chinese.)
c. 你們三個 (you three)
d. 他們三個都是美國人。(All three of them are Americans.)
e. 我們兩個好朋友 (we two good friends)
f. 我們兩個好朋友喜歡相互幫助。
   (We two friends both like helping each other.)
g. 他們兩個，你一言我一語地說起了假期裡發生的事情。
   (They two started talking about what happened during the vacation.)
h. 英美法三國都有很多美麗的地方。
   (Britain, America and France, these three countries, all have many beautiful places.)
i. 紐約、倫敦、北京這三個地方我都去過。
   (As for New York, London and Beijing, I have been to all these three places.)

2 Reduplication

The reduplication of the adverbs/adjectives makes the description very vivid. For example, 他急忙回家過節去了, is not as vivid as 他急急忙忙地回家過節去了。 And the reduplicated words can be used to modify either nouns or verbs. When it modifies a noun, then 的 is used after the reduplicated words. When it modifies a verb, 地 is used. If the reduplicated word is monosyllabic, it takes the form of: A → A+A. 副詞/形容詞的重疊形式會使描述非常生動。例如"他急忙回家過節去了"就不

如"他急急忙忙地回家過節去了"生動。重疊詞可以用來修飾名詞或動詞，當它修飾名詞時，後面跟"的"；當它修飾動詞時，後面跟"地"。如果是單音節的詞重疊，用"A → A+A"的格式。

Adv. Adv.+ 地 +VP

 a. 快快兒地跑 (run quickly)
b. 慢慢兒地說 (speak slowly)
c. 他快快兒地跑了過來。(He ran over quickly.)
d. 請你慢慢兒地說。(Please speak slowly.)

Adj. Adj.+ 的 +N

 a. 紅紅的花 (red flower)
b. 藍藍的天空 (blue sky)
c. 白白的雲 (white cloud)
d. 大大的眼睛 (big eyes)
e. 紅紅的花真好看。(The red flowers are so beautiful.)
f. 藍藍的天空中飄著白白的雲。(There are white clouds in the blue sky.)
g. 他有一雙大大的眼睛。(He has big eyes.)

If the reduplicated words are dissyllabic, then it follows the pattern of: AB → A+A+B+B. 如果是雙音節的詞重疊，用"AB → A+A+B+B"的格式。

 a. 漂亮→漂漂亮亮的
b. 急忙→急急忙忙地
c. 他的女朋友漂漂亮亮的，客客氣氣的，大大方方的，真不錯。
(His girlfriend is beautiful, polite and open. She is really nice.)
d. 他急急忙忙地走了。(He left in a hurry.)

3 The usage of 的，地 and 得

The function of the three "de"s（的，地 and 得）is quite distinct as listed next page. 的，generally speaking, modifies a noun (phrase)，while 地 modifies a verb (phrase). 得 often follows a verb to introduce the result or degree of a certain action.

三個"de"的功能（的、地、得）截然不同，見下頁的表格。一般情況下，"的"修飾名詞（短語），"地"修飾動詞（短語），"得"常跟在動詞後面，引出動作的結果或程度。

Lesson 9 老朋友見面

Position of *De*	Usage	Examples
的 (+Noun)	a. Used to modify a noun: to provide more information or a typical feature about / of a specific noun; b. It is also used as a Possessive marker.	a. 很和氣的老師 喜歡我的女孩 愛教中文的老師 b. 你的朋友 朋友的家 我的老師的書
地 (+Verb)	Used to modify verbs to indicate the manner that an action is carried out.	慢慢地吃 高高興興地學習 快快樂樂地工作
(Verb+) 得	Used to indicate the result or the degree of an action: to provide more information about an action.	跑得很快 吃得很多 寫得完 學得好

4 Directional words

Directional words together with localizers can be used as place words.
方位詞和地點詞一起使用構成處所詞，表示一個地方。

Directional words

上　　下　　前　　後　　左 (zuǒ: left)　　右 (yòu: right)
東 (dōng: east)　　西 (xī: west)　　南 (nán: south)　　北　　中

On the map, they are described as：上北、下南、左西、右東、正中. Starting in the middle, looking to the right, and turn clockwise and then we get:
在地圖上，它們常被描述爲"上北、下南、左西、右東、正中"。從中間起，先看右邊，然後順時針旋轉，我們會得到：

東南 (Southeast)　　西北 (Northwest)　　東北 (Northeast)　　西南 (Southwest)

In colloquial Chinese, localizers are usually followed by 頭 (tou), 邊 or 面 . The meaning remains the same.
在漢語口語中，地點詞後面經常有"頭""邊"或"面"，但意思不變。

Localizers

頭：裡 ~(inside), 後 ~ (behind), 上 ~ (upward), 下 ~ (downward), 前 ~ (in front of)

205

> 邊/面：上～，下～，裡～，外～
> 部 (bù: region)：北～，西～，南～，東～，西北～，東北～，西南～，東南～
> 底下 (dǐxia: under; beneath)
> 中間 (in the middle of...; between)
> 旁邊 (by/beside...)
> 裡 (inside)、外 (outside)

Directional words + localizers

Not all directional words can take the same localizers. For instance:
不是所有的方位詞都能帶同樣的地點詞。例如：

> [東南西北] 邊/部；[中] 間；[左右] 邊/面
> [東南，西北，西南，東北] 方/部；
> [上下前後] 頭/面/邊；
> [裡外] 頭/面/邊；
> [底下]，[這，那，哪] 裡/邊

5 PW 有 NP

This structure means that there is something somewhere. The NP must be indefinite.
這個結構表示某地有某物。名詞短語必須是不確定的。

> E.g.
> a. 桌子上有兩本書，地上有一塊錢。
>   (There are two books on the table and a dollar on the ground.)
> b. 床底下的書包裡有一本字典。
>   (There is a dictionary in the backpack under the bed.)
> c. 宿舍的後邊有一家法國餐館兒。
>   (There is a French restaurant behind the dormitory.)

6 Directional complement：V 來/去

Directional complements are added to the verb to indicate that the action moves in a particular direction. The direction (away from or towards the speaker) can be further emphasised by adding 來 or 去 as a second complement. There are two types of complements: Simple directional words [A (Directional verbs) + B（來/去）] and Compound directional words (Verb + A + B).

趨向補語用在動詞後面表示動作的特定方向。加了"來"或"去"後，動作的方向（遠離說話者或靠近說話者）更加確定。趨向補語的類型有兩種：简單形式 [A（趨向動詞）+ B（來/去）] 和複合形式（Verb + A + B）。

Lesson 9 老朋友見面

Directional verbs

- 上 (to ascend): 上樓 (lóu: stairs)
- 下 (to descend): 下樓
- 進 (to enter): 進教室 (jiàoshì: classroom)
- 出 (to exit): 出教室
- 回 (to return): 回家
- 過 (to pass; to cross): 過馬路 (lù: road) / 過河 (hé: river)
- 起 (to rise): 起床
- 到 (to arrive): 到哥大
- 來 (to come): 來中國
- 去 (to go): 去圖書館

Simple directional words：A + B

A (Directional verbs)	B (來 / 去)
上、下、進、出、回、過	來 / 去
起	來

Compound directional words: Verb + A + B

Verb	A (Directional verbs)	B (來 / 去)
跑、走、打、跳 (tiào: to jump)、開 (kāi: to drive; to open)、拿 (ná: to take; to bring)、飛 (fēi: to fly)	上、下、進、出、回、過	來 / 去
	起	來

NOTE: "V 起來" may mean to act in a way that is away from the ground. It may also indicate that somebody starts doing something.

注意："V 起來" 可以表示一個從下往上的動作，也可以表示某人開始做某事。

V 來 – motion towards speaker

- 回來　　Come back
- 進來　　Come in
- 出來　　Come out
- 過來　　Come over here
- 上來　　Come up
- 下來　　Come down

V 去 – motion away from speaker

- 回去　Go back
- 進去　Go in
- 出去　Go out
- 過去　Go there
- 上去　Go up
- 下去　Go down

When 來 and 去 appear as additional complements, the object of the sentence may appear between the first and second complement.
當"來"和"去"作爲附加補語出現時，句子的賓語可以出現在複合趨向補語中間。

S + V + A + Object + B;　S + V + A + B + Object

E.g. 他拿出一套茶具來，請大家看。／他拿出來一套茶具，請大家看。
(He took out a set of china and let everybody look at it.)

Some directional complements have taken on conventional meanings that appear to have little to do with direction.
某些趨向補語所含的常用意義與方向的關係並不大。

E.g.
a. 想起來 (to come to think of something)
b. 說起來 (to bring something up)
d. 考上（大學）[to pass the entrance examination (for university)]
d. 你來中國以後吃的第一頓飯是什麼，你想得起來嗎？
　 (Do you still remember the first meal you had after you came to China?)
e. 家興和家奇見面以後，你一言我一語地說起什麼來了？
　 (What did Jiaxing and Jiaqi talk about after they met?)
f. 他們說起假期裡發生的事情來了。
　 (They start to talk about what has happened during the break.)
g. 他是去年考上哥大的。(He went to CU last year.)

Directional complements are used a lot in the structure of potential complements.
趨向補語也可用於可能補語的結構中。

S V 得 A + B V 不 A + B?

E.g.
——你跑得上來跑不上來？(Can you run up to me or not?)
——我跑得上來。(Yes, I can.)
——我跑不上來。(No, I can't.)

208

Lesson 9 老朋友見面

Usually, we put the object in the topic position.
通常，我們把賓語放在話題位置。

Object, S V 得 A+B V 不 A+B?

E.g.
a. 父母的話，你聽得進去聽不進去？
(Will you be able to take your parents' advice?)
b. 這個字，你寫得出來寫不出來？
(Can you write this character or not?)
c. 他做的飯，你吃得下去吃不下去？
(Can you swallow the food he cooked?)

7 S VP₁ 是因爲 S VP₂: the reason why S VP₁ is because S VP₂

E.g.
a. 我叫它老大是因爲我不説"請"，它就不聽我的話。
(The reason why I call him Laoda is that if I don't say "please", then he won't listen to me.)
b. 我覺得我的狗最聰明是因爲它聽得懂中文，也聽得懂英文。
(The reason why I think my dog is the smartest is that he understands both Chinese and English.)

8 The Ba-construction

The character 把 is used in two ways: a. As a measure word (for chairs and knives, among other things); b. In the Ba-construction, preceding an object.
"把"字有兩種用法：a. 用作量詞，修飾椅子、刀等；b. 用於把字結構的賓語前。

E.g. 我説把飯吃了，它馬上就把飯吃了。
(When I say "Eat the food", then he eats it right away.)

The normal Chinese structure is Subject – Verb – Object. In the Ba-construction, the object goes before the verb.
正常的漢語結構是主—謂—賓，而把字結構中賓語放在謂語動詞的前面。

Subject – 把 – Object – Verb (Complement) 了

E.g. 你看書了嗎？(Did you read?)
你把書看完了嗎？(Did you finish reading the book?)

Ba-construction is different from the normal structure because: a. 把 makes the object definite ("the wine" rather than just any "wine"); b. 把 needs to be followed by a verb with some sort of complement or particle indicating completion.

把字結構不同於正常的結構：一是"把"使賓語變得確定（是"這瓶酒"而不是泛指的任何酒）；二是"把"需要後面的動詞帶有補語或者表示完成的助詞。

 a. 我的狗把飯吃了。(My dog ate the food.)
b. 他把我的筆拿走了。(He took away my pen.)
c. 我說把電視打開，他就不幹了。
   (When I say "Turn on the TV", then he won't do it.)
d. 我說把酒喝了，她就說："妙，妙，妙！"
   (When I say finish the wine, she will say "Great!")

Usually, only action verbs (verbs that indicate Completion or have a natural ending point) are used in the Ba-construction, but not modal verbs. The following sentences are wrong:

通常，只有動作動詞（表示完成或者有自然結點的動詞）才能用於把字結構，情態動詞就不能。下面的這些句子都是錯的：

 ☹ 我把他愛了。(我愛他。)
☹ 我把中文會說了。（我會說中文了。）
☹ 我把他看見了。（我看見他了。）

Here are some other right examples in Ba-constructure:
這裡還有其他一些正確的把字結構例句：

 a. 他把今天的報紙給我了。(He has given me today's paper.)
b. 你怎麼把名字寫錯了？(How come you wrote the name wrongly?)
c. 我本來想把那杯茶給我的狗喝。
   (I originally wanted to give my dog the cup of tea to drink.)
d. 請把書給我。(Please give me the book.)

⑨ 真希望……：I wish that…

This structure is also translated into English with the subjunctive mood. It is different from "祝 sb. sth." in that 祝 is very formal and is used to express nice wishes for somebody else.

這個結構也可翻譯成英語的虛擬語氣，但不同於"祝 sb. sth."，後者中"祝"非常正式，而且用於表達對別人的美好祝願。

 a. 真希望天天都是假期。(I wish it was vacation everyday.)
b. 真希望你天天都來。(I wish you could come everyday.)
c. 真希望我一天就能學好中文。(I wish I could master Chinese in a single day!)

Lesson 9 老朋友見面

10 是 A 不是 B: it is A not B

> E.g.
> a. 是"喵喵喵"不是"妙妙妙"。(It is meow, not wonderful.)
> b. 是他不是我。(It is him not me.)
> c. 是他的狗不是我的貓。(It is his dog not my cat.)
> d. 是他喜歡你不是我。(It is he who likes you not me.)

Summary:

▶ Numbers are very often used to resume elements common to several words listed in succession.

▶ The reduplication of the adverbs /adjectives makes the description very vivid.

▶ The reduplicated words can be used to modify either nouns or verbs. When it modifies a noun, then 的 is used after the reduplicated words. When it modifies a verb, 地 is used.

▶ If the reduplicated word is monosyllabic, it takes the form of: A → A + A.

▶ If the reduplicated words are dissyllabic, then it follows the pattern of: AB → A + A + B + B.

▶ Directional words together with localizers can be used as place words.

▶ Not all directional words can take the same localizers.

▶ Directional complements are added to the verb to indicate that the action moves in a particular direction.

▶ The direction (away from or towards the speaker) can be further emphasised by adding 來 or 去 as a second complement.

▶ There are two types of complements: Simple directional words [A (Directional verbs) + B（來／去）] and Compound directional words (Verb + A + B).

▶ When 來 and 去 appear as additional complements, the object of the sentence may appear between the first and second complement.

▶ Some directional complements have taken on conventional meanings that appear to have little to do with direction.

▶ Directional complements are used a lot in the structure of potential complements.

▶ The character 把 is used in two ways: a. As a measure word (for chairs and knives, among other things) ; b. In the Ba-construction, preceding an object.

> In the Ba-construction, the object goes before the verb:
> Subject – 把 – Object – Verb (Complement) 了

> 把 makes the object definite.

> 把 needs to be followed by a verb with some sort of complement or particle indicating completion.

Patterns:

- **Resumption** ‖ 我們兩個都喜歡學中文。(Both of us like learning Chinese.)
  紐約、倫敦、北京這三個地方我都去過。
  (As for New York, London and Beijing, I have been to all these three places.)

- **Reduplication** ‖ 請你慢慢兒地説。(Please speak slowly.)
  紅紅的花真好看。(The red flowers are so beautiful.)
  他的女朋友漂漂亮亮的，客客氣氣的，大大方方的，真不錯。
  (His girlfriend is beautiful, polite and open. She is really nice.)
  他急急忙忙地走了。(He left in a hurry.)

- **PW 有 NP** ‖ 宿舍的後邊有一家法國餐館兒。
  (There is a French restaurant behind the dormintory)

- **S + V+ A+ Object +B; S + V+ A+ B + Object** ‖ 他拿出一套茶具來，請大家看。/
  他拿出來一套茶具，請大家看。
  (He took out a set of china and let everybody look at it.)

- **S V 得 A+B V 不 A+B?** ‖ ——你跑得上來跑不上來？(Can you run up to me or not?)
  ——我跑得上來。(Yes, I can.)
  ——我跑不上來。(No, I can't.)

- **Object, S V 得 A + B V 不 A + B?** ‖ 父母的話，你聽得進去聽不進去？
  (Will you be able to take your parents' advice?)

- **S VP₁ 是因爲 S VP₂** ‖ 我叫它老大是因爲我不説"請"，它就不聽我的話。
  (The reason why I call him Laoda is that if I don't say "please", then he won't listen to me.)

- **Subject – 把 – Object – Verb（Complement）了** ‖ 他把我的筆拿走了。
  (He took away my pen.)

- **真希望……** ‖ 真希望天天都是假期。(I wish it was vacation everyday.)

- **是 A 不是 B** ‖ 是他喜歡你不是我。(It is he who like you not I.)

Lesson 9 老朋友見面

IN CLASS ACTIVITIES

1 Answer the following questions according to the information given in the text:

① 考完試後，大家就做什麽去了？

② 爲什麽李家奇跟李家興見面的時候格外高興？

③ 他們兩個，你一言我一語地說起了什麽？

④ 李家興說他的狗怎麽樣？

⑤ 李家奇說他們家收養的貓怎麽樣？

⑥ 他們越說越高興，連什麽也沒有注意到？

2 Please do role play according to the dialogues given below:

- A 你的狗真可愛，幾歲了？
- B 昨天才過了兩歲的生日。
- A 我也很喜歡狗。有句話說得好：狗是人們忠實的朋友。
- B 狗也很聰明，愛鍛煉。每天都跑過來跑過去，很可愛。
- A 是啊！我的狗還能把東西從這兒放到那兒，從那兒拿到這兒。
- B 可是，養狗的人出門就不那麽容易了。
- A 嗯，每次跟狗說再見時，心裡都很難過 (nánguò: sad)！
- B 你每次出門是請人照顧狗呢，還是把狗送 (sòng: to send) 到別人家？
- A 我請過人，也把狗送到過朋友家。

213

B 下次，要是你出去沒有人幫你看狗的時候，你可以把狗送到我這兒來。
A 謝謝，太感謝你了。我們互相幫助，你出門的時候，也可以把狗送到我家來。
B 太好了！

看 病

A 你怎麼了？
B 醫生，我難受 (nánshòu: uncomfortable) 極了。
A 哪兒不舒服？
B 我哪兒都不舒服。頭疼 (tóuténg: to have a headache)、發燒 (fāshāo: to have a fever)、惡心 (ěxīn: to feel sick)、嗓子痛 (sǎngzi tòng: a sore throat)，一點兒力氣也沒有。
A 感冒 (gǎnmào: to catch a cold) 了。給你開一些感冒藥 (yào: medicine)。多喝點兒水，注意休息，過幾天就會好的。
B 謝謝！再見！
A 再見！

HOMEWORK

1 Please rewrite or complete the following phrases or sentences with the given structures:

① 感恩節是下個禮拜。（快 V 了）

➡ 感恩節快到了。

② 走進來 (Potential complement)

➡ Question：

➡ Positive：

➡ Negative：

Lesson 9 老朋友見面

③ 他們開心 (kāixīn: happily; happy) 地生活著。(Reduplication)

④ 你喜歡這隻狗。我也喜歡這隻狗。(Resumption)

⑤ 因為他喜歡幫助別人，所以我們都很喜歡他。(S VP₁ 是因為 S VP₂)

⑥ 他已經做好飯了。(The Ba-construction)

⑦ 要是天天都能上中文課，該多好啊！（真希望……）

⑧ 他以為我把他的飯吃了，其實是我的妹妹吃的。（是 A 不是 B）

2 Please fill in the following blanks with the words given, one for each blank:

去　懂　短　得　起　比　是　長　到　又

① 三個星期很快就過___去___了。

② 李家奇跟李家興_____在中文課上見面了。

③ 他們兩個，你一言我一語地說_____了假期裡發生的事情。

④ 他的狗很聰明，能聽_____他說的中文。

⑤ 他們家收養了一隻貓，白色的毛，綠色的眼睛，長_____特別可愛。

⑥ 他們越說越高興，連老師_____什麼時候進來的都沒有注意_____。

⑦ 你一天到晚狗弟弟_____，狗弟弟_____的。

⑧ 我家的貓_____你家的狗聰明多了。

3 Translate the following sentences into Chinese:

① I can speak English, Chinese and Italian, these three languages. (Resumption)

② My cat's eyes are greenish, with white fur, very pretty. (Reduplication)

③ Will you be able to cross the river (河：hé) or not? (Potential complement)

④ What were we talking about just now? (V 到)

⑤ As for the names of the two dogs, I always get confused (記錯：jìcuò).

⑥ I wish I could celebrate my birthday everyday.

⑦ There are many books on the table to the right side of me.

4 Please fill in the boxes with relevant directional words:

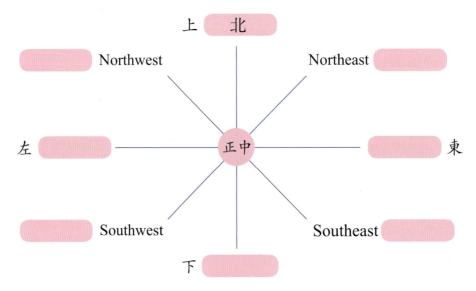

Lesson 9 老朋友見面

5 Please read the following paragraph in Pinyin:

Chūnjié shì Zhōngguó de chuántǒng jiérì, shì rénmen xǐyíng xīnnián qìnghè xīnchūn de rìzi. Zhōngguórén hěn zhòngshì zhè yī chuántǒng jiérì. Rénmen búlùn shì zài Zhōngguó háishi zài wàiguó dōu huì qìnghè zhè ge tèbié de rìzi. Wáng lǎoshī shuō Dōng Yà xì de Zhōngwén lǎoshī zhǔnbèi kāi yí ge Chūnjié wǎnhuì, yāoqǐng suǒyǒu xué Zhōngwén de xuésheng cānjiā. Dàjiā yìqǐ bāobāo jiǎozi, chī yi chī, hē yi hē, chàngchàng gē, tiàotiào wǔ, kuàikuàilèlè、rèrènàonào de guò yí ge xīnnián. Jiāxīng gēn Jiāqí tīngle yǐhòu xīngfèn jí le. Tāmen zhēn xīwàng míngtiān jiù shì Zhōngguó de Chūnjié. Kěshì, yì xiǎngdào hái yào biǎoyǎn jiémù, tāmen jiù fàn chóu le: jìrán zhè shì Zhōngwén wǎnhuì, dāngrán děi yòng Zhōngwén biǎoyǎn le. Tāmen zuǒsī–yòuxiǎng, zhōngyú xiǎngchūláile yí ge hǎo zhǔyi.

Chinese Philosophy

Whenever the terms Buddhism and Taoism are mentioned, one tends to relate it to temples, idol worships, incense sticks, fortune telling etc.. As a matter of fact, Buddhism and Taoism started not as a religion, but instead, as a philosophy.

Contrary to the superstitious versions of Buddhism and Taoism that come with a multitudes of gods, the concept of god in the original Buddhist and Taoist philosophy is irrelevant.

The ultimate goal in Buddhism is to reach a state that is free from earthly pains and sorrows. It is believed that this state could be attainable by following certain ways of getting rid of earthly attachments and desires. For instance, Buddhist believes in that anxiety is a result of desire. Thus, a person can release himself from all anxieties by getting rid of his desires. "Buddha" actually is not a god but a "state of being" to strive for.

The central theme in Taoism is the harmony of nature and the need for man to be part of that harmony. Everything we know is encompassed in nature. The universe, and all things in it, run according to the "Tao（道）". The concept of a rewarding and punishing god is considered to be ludicrous. This is evident in the sayings of Lao-Tzu（老子）: "Nature holds no prejudice and cares for all things the same. It views everything as so many stray dogs, neither loving nor hating them."

LESSON 10 春節

　　春節是中國的傳統節日，是人們喜迎新年慶賀新春的日子。中國人很重視這一傳統節日。人們不論是在中國還是在外國，都會慶賀這個特別的日子。王老師說東亞系的中文老師準備開一個春節晚會，邀請所有學中文的學生參加。大家一起包包餃子，吃一吃，喝一喝，唱唱歌，跳跳舞，快快樂樂、熱熱鬧鬧地過一個新年。家興跟家奇聽了以後興奮極了。他們真希望明天就是中國的春節。可是，一想到還要表演節目，他們就犯愁了：既然這是中文晚會，當然得用中文表演了。他們左思右想，終於想出來了一個好主意。

1

老師：　再過幾天，就是春節了。

家興：　老師，春節是一個什麼樣的節日？

老師：　春節是中國的傳統節日，是人們喜迎新年、慶賀新春的日子。

家奇：　可是，新年已經過去了。

老師：　中國人的傳統節日都是根據陰曆計算的。陰曆也叫農曆。

家興：　陰曆的新年是不是比陽曆的新年晚得多？

Lesson 10　春節

老師：　晚大約一個月左右。

家奇：　這個節日很重要嗎?

老師：　對中國人來說，這是一個非常重要的日子。人們不論是在中國還是在外國，都會慶賀這個特別的日子。

家興：　老師，您現在在國外，會怎麼慶賀呢?

老師：　東亞系的中文老師準備開一個春節晚會，邀請所有學中文的學生參加。

家奇：　我們做什麼呢?

老師：　大家一起包包餃子，吃一吃，喝一喝，唱唱歌，跳跳舞，快快樂樂、熱熱鬧鬧地過一個新年。

家奇:
家興：　太好了!

2

家興：　老大，你打算參加這個晚會嗎?

家奇：　我又不是你的狗……

家興：　瞧你，想到哪兒去了? 老大哥，行了吧?

家奇：　怎麼能不參加呢? 真希望明天就是中國的新年。

家興：　我也是這麼想的。可是……

家奇：　可是什麼?

家興：　王老師說我們還得表演節目。

家奇：　你給大家唱首歌不就行了?

家興：　可是得用中文唱啊? 再說，咱們再怎麼唱也是洋腔洋調的。

家奇：　對，一聽就是一個老外。

家興：　你有什麼好主意嗎?

家奇：　中國人除夕晚上喜歡做什麼?

家興：　吃年夜飯唄。

家奇：　年夜飯有什麼傳統食品?

家興：　餃子。

家奇：　對，一邊吃餃子一邊看什麼?

家興：　春節晚會唄。中國人不論在什麼地方，都喜歡看春節晚會。

219

家奇： 春節晚會人們最喜歡看的是什麼？

家興： 小品？

家奇： 對了，咱們就來個小品《包餃子》！

家興： 你會包嗎？

家奇： 那就加一個"學"字唄。

家興： 《學包餃子》。呵呵，妙！妙！妙！

家奇： 你怎麼成了我家的貓了？

3

同學： 下一個節目：小品《學包餃子》。表演者：李家奇、李家興。有請！

(Jiaqi and Jiaxing sing while walking to the stage.)

家奇： (Singing)"樹上的鳥兒，成雙對——"

家興： (Singing)"我跟我老公，是一對兒——"

家奇： 老婆，今天晚上給你親愛的老公做什麼好吃的？

家興： 想想看！咱們中國人過春節還能吃什麼？

家奇： 吃餃子唄！可是你想吃什麼啊？

家興： 還用問，你還能不知道嗎？

家奇： 不知道！

家興： 真不知道？還說是我的知心愛人呢？

家奇： 餃子唄！

家興： 那你為什麼說不知道呢，親愛的？

家奇： 我怕你累壞了，你知道我不會包餃子。

家興： 不會包餃子，沒關係，我教你。

家奇： 好。(Singing again)"你和麵來，我擀皮兒——"

家興： (Singing)"我拌餡兒來——"(Stop singing)你該怎麼辦？

家奇： 是啊，我該怎麼辦？

家興： 看，把皮兒放在左手，把一勺餡兒放到皮兒中間兒，用右手一擠，就好了！

家奇： 老婆，你真聰明，教得真好！

家興： 老公，你真能幹，學得真快！

家奇： 這哪兒是餃子啊？這不是狗耳朵嗎？

Lesson 10 春節

VOCABULARY

1	*春節	春节	Chūnjié	PN	Spring festival
2	*傳統	传统	chuántǒng	Adj.	traditional
3	*節日	节日	jiérì	N.	holiday
4	喜迎	喜迎	xǐ yíng	VP	to welcome
5	慶賀	庆贺	qìnghè	V.	to celebrate
6	新春	新春	xīnchūn	N.	the spring of a new year
7	日子	日子	rìzi	N.	day (formal)
8	*重視	重视	zhòngshì	V.	to pay special attention to (formal)
9	*不論	不论	búlùn	Adv.	no matter
10	*東亞	东亚	Dōng Yà	PN	East Asia
11	*系	系	xì	N.	department
12	開	开	kāi	V.	to hold
13	晚會	晚会	wǎnhuì	N.	party
14	*邀請	邀请	yāoqǐng	V.	to invite
15	所有	所有	suǒyǒu	Adj.	all
16	*參加	参加	cānjiā	V.	to take part in
17	*包	包	bāo	V.	to wrap
18	餃子	饺子	jiǎozi	N.	dumplings
19	包餃子	包饺子	bāo jiǎozi	VP	to make dumplings
20	*唱歌	唱歌	chàng gē	V.-O.	to sing
21	*跳舞	跳舞	tiào wǔ	V.-O.	to dance
22	快樂	快乐	kuàilè	Adj.	happy
23	*熱鬧	热闹	rènao	Adj.	lively and noisy
24	*表演	表演	biǎoyǎn	V.	to perform
25	*節目	节目	jiémù	N.	show, program
26	*犯愁	犯愁	fàn chóu	V.-O.	worried
27	*既然	既然	jìrán	Conj.	since, now that
28	左思右想	左思右想	zuǒsī-yòuxiǎng	IE	to think over and over
29	*終於	终于	zhōngyú	Adv.	finally
30	*根據	根据	gēnjù	Prep.	according to

31	* 陰曆	阴历	yīnlì	N.	lunar calendar
32	計算	计算	jìsuàn	V.	to calculate
33	* 農曆	农历	nónglì	N.	lunar calendar
34	* 陽曆	阳历	yánglì	N.	solar calendar
35	大約	大约	dàyuē	Adv.	approximately
36	* 左右	左右	zuǒyòu	N.	or so
37	* 非常	非常	fēicháng	Adv.	especially
38	重要	重要	zhòngyào	Adj.	important
39	瞧你	瞧你	qiáo nǐ	IE	Look at you!
40	* 首	首	shǒu	MW	*measure word for songs*
41	* 咱們	咱们	zánmen	Pron.	we, us (inclusive)
42	洋腔洋調	洋腔洋调	yángqiāng-yángdiào	IE	foreign accent
43	老外	老外	lǎowài	N.	foreigner
44	* 除夕	除夕	chúxī	N.	New Year's Eve
45	* 年夜飯	年夜饭	niányèfàn	N.	dinner on New Year's Eve
46	唄	呗	bei	Int.	duh
47	* 食品	食品	shípǐn	N.	food
48	一邊…一邊…	一边…一边…	yìbiān…yìbiān…		do A while doing B
49	小品	小品	xiǎopǐn	N.	a play
50	表演者	表演者	biǎoyǎnzhě	N.	performer
51	* 樹	树	shù	N.	tree
52	* 鳥	鸟	niǎo	N.	bird
53	成雙對	成双对	chéng shuāng duì	IE	to become a couple
54	* 老公	老公	lǎogōng	N.	hubby
55	* 老婆	老婆	lǎopo	N.	wife
56	親愛	亲爱	qīn'ài	Adj.	dear
57	知心愛人	知心爱人	zhīxīn àiren	NP	soul mate
58	愛人	爱人	àiren	N.	spouse
59	* 怕	怕	pà	V.	to be afraid
60	* 累壞	累坏	lèihuài	V.-C.	to be exhausted
61	和麵	和面	huó miàn	V.-O.	to make dough
62	擀皮兒	擀皮儿	gǎn pír	V.-O.	to make wrappers
63	拌餡兒	拌馅儿	bàn xiànr	V.-O.	to make fillings

Lesson 10 春節

64	怎麼辦	怎么办	zěnme bàn	IE	What shall I do?
65	*手	手	shǒu	N.	hand
66	*勺	勺	sháo	MW	spoon
67	*擠	挤	jǐ	V.	to squeeze
68	能幹	能干	nénggàn	Adj.	capable
69	*耳朵	耳朵	ěrduo	N.	ear

Supplementary Vocabulary:

1	草	草	cǎo	N.	grass
2	花兒	花儿	huār	N.	flower
3	頭髮	头发	tóufa	N.	hair
4	老北京雞肉卷	老北京鸡肉卷	lǎo Běijīng jīròu juǎn	NP	Old Beijing Chicken Roll
5	壽司	寿司	shòusī	N.	Sushi
6	肯德基	肯德基	Kěndéjī	PN	Kentucky Fried Chicken
7	停	停	tíng	V.	to stop
8	聞	闻	wén	V.	to smell
9	起飛	起飞	qǐfēi	V.	to take off
10	拍	拍	pāi	V.	to pat

GRAMMAR

1 不論……，S 都 VP：no matter..., S will VP

E.g.
a. 人們不論是在中國還是在外國，都會慶賀這個特別的日子。
  (No matter whether they are in China or abroad, people will celebrate this special day.)
b. 不論你會不會來，我都會等你的。
  (I will wait for you no matter whether you come or not.)
c. 不論你聽得進去聽不進去，你都得聽父母的話。
  (No matter whether you take your parents' advice or not, you have to listen to them.)

d. 不論你是願意還是不願意，你都得表演一個節目。
(You have to perform whether you are willing to or not.)

e. 我不論在哪兒，都會想念你的。
(No matter where I go, I will miss you.)

f. 不論男女老少，人們都喜歡音樂。
(People like music no matter whether they are male or female, old or young.)

2 S 準備 VP：sb. plans to do sth.

 a. 我準備下了課，就去吃飯。(I plan to go to eat right after class.)

b. 我的弟弟準備明年去中國學中文。
(My younger brother plans to go to China to learn Chinese next year.)

c. 你今年準不準備回家過春節了？
(Do you plan to go back home to celebrate the Spring Festival this year?)

d. 今天晚上，我的同屋不準備參加迎新晚會了。
(My roommate doesn't plan to take part in the party for the new students this evening.)

e. 你準備給我們表演一個什麼節目啊？
(What kind of show do you want to offer us?)

f. ——你們準備好了嗎？ (Are you ready?))
   ——我們早就準備好了。(Yes, we have been ready.)

g. 王老師說東亞系的中文老師準備開一個春節晚會。
(Professor Wang said that the Chinese teachers of the East Asian Languages and Cultures Department plan to hold a party for the Spring Festival.)

3 S 邀請 sb. VP：to invite sb. to do sth.

 a. 邀請所有學中文的學生參加。
(All the students who are learning Chinese are welcome to join us.)

b. 我想邀請你們全家來中國跟我們一起過年。
(I would like to invite your whole family to come to China to celebrate the New Year with us.)

c. 人家又沒有邀請我，我怎麼好意思去呢？
(I was not invited at all. I would feel embarrassed to go without invitation).

d. 她下個禮拜就要結婚 (jié hūn) 了，可是她連一個客人還沒邀請呢。
(She will get married next week. But she has not invited a single guest yet.)

Lesson 10 春節

4 V (一) V (Object)

In this lesson, we use a lot of expressions of "V (一)V". One thing we should mention is that when the verb is monosyllabic, then we just use "V (一)V". For instance, 包包餃子, 吃一吃, 喝一喝, 唱唱歌, 跳跳舞. But if the verb is disyllabic, like 休息, then we have to repeat the verb to indicate that the action is temporary, and won't last long：AB → ABAB. For instance, 休息休息, 準備準備, 慶賀慶賀, 邀請邀請, 復習復習, 介紹介紹, 認識認識.

這一課裡我們使用了很多"V(一)V"的表達。需要說明的是，當動詞是單音節的時候，我們用"V(一)V"的結構即可，例如：包包餃子、吃一吃、喝一喝、唱唱歌、跳跳舞。但是如果動詞是雙音節的時候，如"休息"，我們需要通過重疊動詞來表示動作是短暫的、不會持續很長時間，即 AB → ABAB。例如：休息休息、準備準備、慶賀慶賀、邀請邀請、復習復習、介紹介紹、認識認識。

> **E.g.**
> a. 明天要考試了，我們得好好準備準備，復習復習，還得好好兒休息休息。
>   (We are going to take the test tomorrow. We have to get well-prepared, fully review what we have learned, and also we should have a good rest.)
> b. 請你給我們兩個介紹介紹，讓我們兩個相互認識認識。
>   (Could you please introduce us two so that we could get to know each other a little bit?)
> c. 明天就是新年了，我們要好好兒慶賀慶賀。
>   (It will be the New Year tomorrow. We should really celebrate it.)
> d. ——我喜歡的女孩子不想參加我的生日晚會。
>   (The girl that I like doesn't want to come to my birthday party.)
>   ——那你得好好兒邀請邀請才行。
>   (Then you have to invite her again and again.)

NOTE: Verbs of V.-O. construction, e.g. 走路, 睡覺, 跑步, although they are disyllabic, can never follow this pattern.
注意：動賓結構中的動詞，如"走路、睡覺、跑步"，儘管它們是雙音節的，但也不能按雙音節動詞重疊的格式進行重疊。

To summarize, both adjectives and verbs can be reduplicated, but they have different intention. The reduplication of adjectives makes the sentence vivid, while the reduplication of verbs indicates that the action is temporary.
總結：形容詞和動詞都可以重疊，但是它們的目的不同。形容詞的重疊使得句子更爲生動，而動詞的重疊則表明這個動作是短暫的。
For monosyllabic adjectives and verbs, the reduplication follows the same rule: AA. For disyllabic adjectives, it should follow AABB. For disyllabic verbs, it should follow

ABAB. The V.-O. compound verbs can't follow this pattern; you can only reduplicate the "V" part.

單音節形容詞和動詞，其重疊都遵循 AA 的格式；雙音節的形容詞重疊，遵循 AABB 的格式；雙音節的動詞重疊，遵循 ABAB 的格式。動賓結構中的動詞，不能按雙音節動詞重疊的格式進行重疊，只能重疊其中的單音節動詞部分。

 S 左 V 右 V：... think it over and over

E.g. a. 他們左思右想，終於想出來了一個好主意。
(They finally have a good idea after thinking it over and over again.)
b. 我左思右想就是想不起來他是誰。
(I am thinking really hard, but I can't recall who he is.)
c. 我左思右想就是不明白她爲什麼不喜歡我。
(I think it over and over but I can't figure out the reason why she doesn't like me.)
d. 我左思右想終於決定跟他一塊兒去英國。
(After thinking hard, I decided to go to Britain with him.)

This structure is not productive. We have to learn them individually.
這個結構的拓展有限，我們需要分別單獨學習。

E.g. a. 她不喜歡我，我左請右請她就是不跟我跳舞。
(She doesn't like me. No matter how many times I invited her, she refused to dance with me.)
b. 我把書包丟了，我左找右找就是找不到。
(I lost my backpack. I looked everywhere, and I just couldn't find it.)
c. 他包的餃子太難看了，我左看右看就是看不出那些是餃子。
(The dumplings he made are just too ugly. I looked at them again and again and I just couldn't tell that they are actually dumplings.)

 再過 time，S 就 VP 了：in...sometime，S will VP

E.g. a. 再過幾天，就是春節了。
(In a few more days, it will be Spring Festival.)
b. 再過兩年，我就有錢了。(In a couple of years, I will become rich.)
c. 再過幾分鐘，飛機就要起飛了。(The plane will take off in a few minutes.)
d. 再過十分鐘，要是你還不來，我就走了。
(If you won't come in ten minutes, I will leave.)
e. 再過五分鐘就下課了。(The class will finish in five minutes.)

Lesson 10 春節

7) NP₁ 是根據 NP₂ VP 的：NP₁ is done according to NP₂

 a. 中國人的傳統節日都是根據陰曆計算的。
(Chinese traditional festivals are calculated according to the Lunar Calendar.)
b. 麥當勞(Màidāngláo)裡的漢堡包(hànbǎobāo)是根據中國人的口味做的。
(The hamburgers at McDonalds are prepared according to the Chinese people's taste.)
c. 這個字，我是根據老師教我的方法(fāngfǎ)寫的。怎麼能寫錯呢？
(As for this character, I wrote it according to the way my teacher taught me. How could it be written incorrectly?)
d. 這本小說是根據他的生活寫的。(This novel is written according to his life.)

8) S 怎麼 VP：how to do sth.

 a. 你會怎麼慶賀呢？ (How will you celebrate it?)
b. 我該怎麼辦呢？ (What should I do then?)
c. 這個字怎麼寫？ (How do you write this character?)

S 怎麼能不 VP 呢：how could you not do this?

 a. 怎麼能不參加呢？ (How could you not participate?)
b. 考試，你怎麼能不去呢？ (How could you not take the test?)
c. 我是你的老朋友，你怎麼能不認識我呢？
(I am your old friend, how could you not know me?)

9) Sentence, 不就 Aux.V. 了 / 就行了：sentence, then it will be...

 a. 你給大家唱首歌不就行了？
(You sing a song for us, and then it will be okay, right?)
b. 你把錢給他不就得(dé)了。(You just give him the money and that will be it.)
c. 你給我們說個笑話，就行了。(You tell us a joke, and that will be fine.)
d. 你把東西放在那兒就行了。(You just leave it there and it will be fine.)
e. 你把餃子放在碗裡就行了。
(You just put the dumplings into the bowl and it will be okay.)

S 再 V，也 VP：even A, still B

> E.g.　a. 咱們再練也是洋腔洋調的。
> 　　　(No matter how hard we practice, we will still sound like a foreigner.)
> 　　b. 別説了，你再説也沒用。
> 　　　(Stop it. No matter how hard you try to persuade me, it will still be useless.)
> 　　c. 別看了，你再看我也不給你。
> 　　　(Don't look at it any more. I won't give it to you anyway.)
> 　　d. 別想了，已經發生了，再想也已經是那樣兒了。
> 　　　(Don't think about it. It has already happened. It has already been like that no matter how hard you think about it.)

 S 一邊 A 一邊 B：S does A while doing B

> E.g.　a. 你一邊吃餃子一邊看什麼？
> 　　　(What do you watch while you are eating dumplings?)
> 　　b. 我一邊工作一邊學習。
> 　　　(I work and study at the same time.)
> 　　c. 我喜歡一邊聽音樂一邊看書。
> 　　　(I like reading while listening to music.)

NOTE: If the verbs are both monosyllabic, the pattern could be reducible to "邊...邊...".
注意：如果兩個動詞都是單音節的，這個句型可以簡化爲"邊……邊……"。

> E.g.　a. 我喜歡邊玩兒邊吃。(I like playing while eating.)
> 　　b. 我的狗邊叫邊咬 (yǎo)。(My dog bites while barking.)

 S 把 N 放到 (拿到 / 放在) somewhere (了)

Ba-construction is obligatory when somebody puts / moves something somewhere:
當物體被移動時，一定要用把字結構。

> E.g.　a. 你把我的書放在哪兒了？ (Where did you put my book?)
> 　　b. 我把書放在你的桌子上了。(I put the book on your table.)
> 　　c. 我把書拿到你的宿舍去了。(I have taken the books to your dormitory.)

When negated, 沒有 is used.
否定時，要使用"沒有"。

228

S 沒有把 sth. VP

E.g. a. 他沒有把桌子放在應該放的地方。
(He did not put the table in the place where he was supposed to put it.)
b. ——你是不是把酒放在你家了？ (Did you put wine at your place?)
——沒有，我沒把酒放在我家。(No, I didn't put wine at my place.)

13) A 成了 B 了：A became B

E.g. a. 你怎麼成了我家的貓了？ (How come you become my cat?)
b. 你的女朋友怎麼成了他的女朋友了？
(How come your girlfriend became his girlfriend?)

S 把 A V 成 B 了

E.g. a. 我把這個字寫成那個字了。(I wrote that character instead of this one.)
b. 對不起，我把你當成他了。(I am sorry that I mistook you for him.)
c. 我把"水餃"說成"睡覺"了。
(I intended to say "dumpling" but I said "to sleep" instead.)
d. 我把中國菜做成日本菜了。
(I intended to make Chinese food, but I made Japanese food instead.)

Summary:

When the verb is monosyllabic, then we just use V(一)V. But if the verb is disyllabic, like 休息, then we have to repeat the verb to indicate that the action is temporary, and won't last long：AB → ABAB.

For disyllabic verbs, the reduplication follows the pattern: ABAB. For disyllabic adjectives, it follows the pattern: AABB.

Ba-construction is obligatory when somebody puts/moves something somewhere: S 把 N 放到 / 拿到 / 放在 somewhere (了).

We use 沒有 to negate the Ba-construction.

走近中國──初級漢語教程
APPROACHING CHINA : ELEMENTARY CHINESE

Patterns:

- **不論……，S 都 VP** ‖ 人們不論是在中國還是在外國，都會慶賀這個特別的日子。
  (No matter whether they are in China or abroad, people will celebrate this special day.)

- **S 準備 VP** ‖ 我準備下了課，就去吃飯。(I plan to go to eat right after class.)

- **S 邀請 sb. VP** ‖ 我想邀請你們全家來中國跟我們一起過新年。
  (I would like to invite your whole family to come to China to celebrate the New Year with us.)

- **V（一）V（Object）** ‖ 明天就是新年了，我們要好好兒慶賀慶賀。
  (It will be the New Year tomorrow. We should really celebrate it.)

- **S 左 V 右 V** ‖ 他們左思右想，終於想出來了一個好主意。
  (They finally have a good idea after thinking it over and over again.)

- **再 過 time，S 就 VP 了** ‖ 再過兩年，我就有錢了。
  (In a couple of years, I will become rich.)

- **NP₁ 是根據 NP₂ VP 的** ‖ 中國人的傳統節日都是根據陰曆計算的。
  (Chinese traditional festivals are calculated according to the Lunar Calendar.)

- **S 怎麼 VP** ‖ 你會怎麼慶賀呢？ (How will you celebrate it?)

- **S 怎麼能不 VP 呢** ‖ 考試，你怎麼能不去呢？ (How could you not take the test?)

- **Sentence，不就 Aux. V. 了 / 就行了** ‖ 你把錢給他不就得了。
  (You just give him the money and that will be it.)
  你給我們說個笑話，就行了。
  (You tell us a joke, and that will be fine.)

- **S 再 V，也 VP** ‖ 咱們再練也是洋腔洋調的。
  (No matter how hard we practice, we will still sound like a foreigner.)

- **S 一邊 A 一邊 B** ‖ 我喜歡一邊聽音樂一邊看書。(I like reading while listening to music.)

- **S 把 N 放在 somewhere（了）** ‖ 你把我的書放在哪兒了？
  (Where did you put my book?)
  我把書放在你的桌子上了。
  (I put the book on your table.)

- **A 成了 B 了** ‖ 你怎麼成了我家的貓了？ (How come you become my cat?)

- **S 把 A V 成 B 了** ‖ 對不起，我把你當成他了。(I am sorry that I mistook you for him.)

Lesson 10 春節

IN CLASS ACTIVITIES

1 Answer the following questions according to the information given in the text:

① 春節是一個什麼樣的節日？

② 爲什麼說中國人很重視春節？

③ 王老師說東亞系的中文老師準備做什麼？

④ 大家準備在一起做什麼？怎麼過新年？

⑤ 家興跟家奇爲什麼犯愁？

⑥ 他們左思右想，終於怎麼了？

2 Please do role play according to the dialogues given below:

- A 你知道春節嗎？
- B 我當然知道啦。春節就是中國的新年。
- A 中國的新年是哪一天？
- B 中國的新年是根據陰曆計算的，所以每年過年的日子都不一樣。
- A 是嗎？聽起來挺有意思的。你怎麼知道的？
- B 我怎麼能不知道呢？你忘了我在中國住過三年呢。
- A 對，對，你看我忙得什麼都想不起來了。
- B 中國的孩子們最喜歡過年了。
- A 這又是爲什麼呢？
- B 這是因爲過年時，大人會給小孩子紅包。

A 紅包是什麼？他們爲什麼喜歡紅包？
B 紅包裡包的是錢，他們當然喜歡要紅包了。
A 哦，我真希望我也能去中國過年，拿紅包。
B 別做夢了，你又不是孩子。
A 呵呵，開個玩笑！
B 我也是。

上廁所 (cèsuǒ: WC)

A 對不起，請問洗手間 (xǐshǒujiān) 在哪兒？
B 廁所就在那兒。
A 我想去洗手間，不是廁所。
B 廁所就是洗手間，也叫衛生間 (wèishēngjiān)，也叫茅房 (máofáng)，也就是盥洗室 (guànxǐshì)。
A 謝謝。
……
C 喂 (wèi: hey)，請繳費 (jiǎo fèi: to pay)。
A 繳費是什麼？
C 繳費就是上廁所你得給錢。
A 哦，多少錢？
C 一人五毛 (wǔmáo: fifty cents)。給你手紙 (shǒuzhǐ: toilet paper)。

HOMEWORK

1 Please rewrite or complete the following sentences with the given structures:

① 感恩節是下個禮拜。（快 V 了）

➡ 感恩節快到了。

② 在外國的中國人跟在中國的中國人都要慶賀新年。(不論……, S 都 VP)

➡

Lesson 10 春節

③ 我打算過了年就出國。(S 準備 VP)

④ 我想來想去終於想出來了一個好主意。(S 左 V 右 V)

⑤ 她做了我喜歡吃的飯菜。(NP₁ 是根據 NP₂ VP 的)

⑥ 她說她不認識我。你說奇怪不奇怪？(S 怎麼能不 VP 呢？)

⑦ 你就算 (even if) 天天吃中國菜，說中國話，你還是美國人。(S 再 V，也 VP)

⑧ 除夕晚上中國人吃年夜飯的時候喜歡看電視。(S 一邊 A 一邊 B)

⑨ 你把我的字典拿到哪兒去了？(The Ba-construction)

2 Please fill in the following blanks with the words given, one for each blank:

表演　不論　參加　喜迎　傳統　根據　犯愁　重要

① 春節是中國的傳統節日，是人們 __喜迎__ 新年慶賀新春的日子。

② 一想到還要_____節目，他們就_____了。

③ 人們_____是在中國還是在外國，都會慶賀這個特別的日子。

④ 中國人的傳統節日都是_____陰曆計算的。陰曆也叫農曆。

⑤ 你打算_____這個晚會嗎？

⑥ 年夜飯有什麼_____食品？

⑦ 這個節日很_____嗎？

233

走近中國——初級漢語教程
APPROACHING CHINA : ELEMENTARY CHINESE

3 Translate the following sentences into Chinese:

① Spring Festival is an important Chinese traditional festival.

② No matter whether you are willing or not, you have to come to the party for new students.

③ My best friend likes making phone calls while watching TV.

④ How could I not remember your birthday?

⑤ How do you know that he is a foreigner? He sounds like a foreigner.

⑥ He seems to be a person who likes traditional food.

⑦ My Korean classmate will come to visit me in approximately a month or so.

⑧ I mistook him for his younger brother.

⑨ For me (對我來説：duì wǒ lái shuō), learning Chinese is the most important thing in the world.

⑩ I plan to put all my books into my backpack (書包：shūbāo).

Lesson 10 春節

4 Please use the following patterns to write a mini-essay on a special occasion. You have to use at least eight of the structures given:

S 就要 VP 了； S 準備 VP； S 邀請 sb. VP； Reduplication；

S 左 V 右 V； S V 出來 (Object)； S V 起 Object 來； 再過 time，就 VP 了；

NP₁ 是根據 NP₂ VP 的； S 怎麼能不 VP 呢？； S 一邊 A 一邊 B；

S 把 A V 成 B 了

5 Please read the following paragraph in Pinyin:

   Jīntiān shàng Zhōngwénkè de shíhou, lǎoshī ràng dàjiā fēnzǔ tán yi tán zìjǐ de àihào, ránhòu měi ge xiǎozǔ zài xiàng qítā tóngxué jièshào tóngbànr de yèyú àihào. Tóngxuémen liǎng ge rén yì zǔ, fēnchéngle qī zǔ. Dàjiā huò gè yǒu suǒ ài, huò zhìqù xiāngtóu, yuè shuō yuè rènào, qìfēn shífēn huóyuè. Jiāxīng gēn Jiāqí fēndàole yì zǔ. Jiāxīng shuō tā de àihào tài duō le, dōu bù zhīdào cóng nǎr shuōqǐ. Tā xiǎo de shíhou zuì xǐhuan tī zúqiú, hòulái yòu xǐhuanshàngle qí zìxíngchē, zài hòulái, tā yòu xǐhuanguo bàngqiú、lánqiú、wǎngqiú, xiànzài tā měi tiān dōu qù yóu yǒng. Jiāqí shuō tā zuì xǐhuan huà huàr, cóng xiǎo jiù xiǎng dāng yì míng huàjiā. Lìngwài, tā hái xǐhuan xià qí、tán jítā. Jiānglái, yàoshi yǒu jīhuì dehuà, tā hái xiǎng dào Zhōngguó qù xué shūfǎ. Dàjiā dōu shuō Jiāqí duōcái-duōyì, qín qí shū huà, yàngyàng jīngtōng.

CULTURAL NOTES

Chinese Spring Festival

Chinese New Year starts with the new moon on the first day of the new year and ends on the full moon 15 days later. The 15th day of the new year is called the Lantern Festival, which is celebrated at night with lantern displays and children carrying lanterns in a parade.

As introduced in earlier chapters, the Chinese calendar is based on a combination of lunar and solar movements. The lunar cycle is about 29.5 days. In order to "catch up" with the solar calendar, there is an extra month once every few years (seven years out of a 19-year cycle). This is the same as adding an extra day on leap year and why, according to the solar calendar, the Chinese New Year falls on a different date each year.

Everyone, young and old, rich and poor, looks forward to celebrating the noisiest, most joyous and longest festival of the year. In China, New Year's Day is a solemn occasion. It is used to be the time that every family performed religious rites at the family altar. It is the time for a family reunion.

Before the New Year's Eve, everyone tries to come back home from every corner of the country to join the entire family to celebrate the New Year. A big New Year dinner is served. Dumplings and fish are among the most popular food. Since the early 80's of last century, on New Year's Eve, Chinese people will watch the New Year's TV show after having a big dinner at home or at a restaurant.

The burning of long strings of firecrackers accompanies the New Year's Eve. Most adults and children do not touch their bed the whole night, busy with all kinds of activities welcoming the New Year.

At midnight following a nice family banquet on New Year's Eve, or early in the morning on New Year's Day, the young members of the family would bow and pay their respects to the parents and elders. In return, they will get "紅包" (hóngbāo) or "壓歲錢" (yāsuìqián). Because of the money in the "紅包", children are the ones who most like to celebrate the New Year.

In the morning on New Year's Day, people put on their new clothes and shoes. Men, with their wives, call on relatives and friends to wish them a "Happy and Prosperous New Year". The visitor is served tea (with sweet-meats in the South), melon seeds, both red and black, and fruits and delicacies such as puffed rice cakes, dumplings and deep-fried round doughnuts. In addition, liquor and tobacco are offered. Before leaving, the well-wisher present gifts of money wrapped in red paper to all the unmarried children of the family.

Starting from New Year's Day, people begin going out to visit friends and relatives, taking with them gifts such as fruits, wines, flowers, etc. The entire fortnight is a time for socializing and amusement. Common expressions heard at this time are, "過年好！新年快樂！(Happy New Year！)" and people in Canton will also say 恭喜發財！（Wish you make a fortune!）to congratulate the New Year.

On New Year's Day, the lights on the porch and in the parlor are not turned off but left on continuously. To retain good fortune and wealth in the home, the house is not swept for fear of sweeping out the good fortune. No knife is used, even to prepare meals. Quarrels are to be avoided. Words with bad connotations such as defeat, illness, surgical operations, coffin or death are not to be used. Dishes are handled carefully, for breaking a dish on New Year's Day indicate bad luck for the coming year.

The New Year celebration lasts for fifteen days, with various entertainment, including games of mahjong and dominos at home or at clubs. There are also animal shows featuring trained dogs and monkeys, theatrical plays staged by amateur and professional troupes, acrobatic performances, magic shows, puppet shows, storytelling and lion and dragon dances, especially in the countryside. Nowadays, traveling is a popular way to celebrate the New Year as well among younger generation.

LESSON 11 愛好

今天上中文課的時候，老師讓大家分組談一談自己的愛好，然後每個小組再向其他同學介紹同伴兒的業餘愛好。同學們兩個人一組，分成了七組。大家或各有所愛，或志趣相投，越說越熱鬧，氣氛十分活躍。家興跟家奇分到了一組。家興說他的愛好太多了，都不知道從哪兒說起。他小的時候最喜歡踢足球，後來又喜歡上了騎自行車，再後來，他又喜歡過棒球、籃球、網球，現在他每天都去游泳。家奇說他最喜歡畫畫兒，從小就想當一名畫家。另外，他還喜歡下棋、彈吉他。將來，要是有機會的話，他還想到中國去學書法。大家都說家奇多才多藝，琴棋書畫，樣樣精通。

1

老師：今天我們要互相談一談自己的愛好。

家興：我的愛好可多啦。

老師：太好了！大家兩個人一組，二、四、六、八、十、十二、十四，正好七個小組。

家興：家奇，咱們兩個一組，真巧。

家奇：老師，我們是自己說自己的愛好嗎？

老師：對。等一會兒每個小組的人要向其他同學介紹同伴兒的業餘愛好。

家興：聽說大家多才多藝，有不少人琴棋書畫，樣樣精通。

家奇：家興，你先說吧！

家興：我的愛好太多了，不知道從哪兒說起。

家奇：隨便，你想到哪兒就從哪兒說起。

家興：算了，還是從小說起吧。

家奇：好哇。你小的時候最喜歡什麼？

家興：我小的時候最喜歡踢足球，每天都要踢一會兒。

家奇：什麼足球？是美式足球嗎？

家興：不是美式足球。

家奇：我以爲美國人多半兒都喜歡玩兒美式足球呢。後來呢？

家興：後來，又喜歡上了騎自行車，再後來，我還喜歡過棒球、籃球、網球，現在我每天都去游泳。

2

家奇：我們兩個真是各有所愛。我最喜歡的是畫畫兒。

家興：怪不得，我一看見你就覺得你有一點兒奇怪。

家奇：爲什麼？

家興：我逗你玩兒呢。不過藝術家是有一點兒特別。對不起，請接著說。

家奇：從小我就想當一名畫家，對東方藝術特別有興趣。

家興：哦，這就是你爲什麼唸東亞藝術專業的原因了吧？

家奇：對。我就是因爲喜歡東方藝術，所以才主修東亞藝術專業。

家興：可這不是你的業餘愛好了。你還喜歡做什麼？

家奇：我還喜歡下棋、彈吉他。

家興：你會彈鋼琴嗎？

家奇：我小的時候學過鋼琴，可是後來不喜歡了。

家興："對牛彈琴"是什麼意思？

Lesson 11 愛好

家奇： 我現在不是正"對牛彈琴"嗎？
家興： 嘿嘿，我們只不過是有點兒志趣不相投。
家奇： 以後，要是有機會的話，我……

3

老師： 對不起，時間到了。下面請大家到前面來介紹一下自己同伴兒的愛好。
家興： 老師，讓我先說一說我的好朋友、好兄弟——李家奇同學的愛好吧！
老師： 好，家興，你先開始介紹吧！
家興： 我先問大家一個問題："李家奇的專業是什麼？"
同學： 東亞藝術。
家興： 對了。他從小就喜歡畫畫兒，想做一名畫家。
同學： 還有呢？
家興： 他也喜歡下棋。
同學： 什麼棋？
家興： 這我可沒有問，家奇？
家奇： 老師，GO 中文怎麼說？
老師： GO 就是圍棋。
家興： 對了，他還喜歡下圍棋。
同學： 我也喜歡下圍棋。
家興： 他還喜歡彈吉他。對不起，家奇，你說要是以後有機會的話，你還想做什麼？
家奇： 將來，要是有機會的話，我還想到中國去學書法。
老師： 好，謝謝家興。
家興： 不客氣。
老師： 請大家用我們學過的話說一說，家奇是一個怎麼樣的人？
大家： 多才多藝，琴棋書畫，樣樣精通。
家奇： 謝謝，不敢當，不敢當。

VOCABULARY

#					
1	愛好	爱好	àihào	N.	hobby
2	*讓	让	ràng	V.	to let
3	*組	组	zǔ	N.	group
4	*談	谈	tán	V.	to talk (about)
5	*向	向	xiàng	Prep.	to
6	其他	其他	qítā	Pron.	other
7	*同伴兒	同伴儿	tóngbànr	N.	teammate
8	*業餘	业余	yèyú	Adj.	sparetime, amateur
9	各有所愛	各有所爱	gè yǒu suǒ ài	IE	each have their own interests
10	志趣相投	志趣相投	zhìqù xiāngtóu	IE	to share the same interest
11	*氣氛	气氛	qìfēn	N.	atmosphere
12	十分	十分	shífēn	Adv.	very, extremely (formal)
13	*活躍	活跃	huóyuè	Adj.	active, lively
14	分到	分到	fēndào	V.-C.	to be assigned to
15	說起	说起	shuōqǐ	V.-C.	talking about
16	*踢	踢	tī	V.	to kick, to play (football)
17	*足球	足球	zúqiú	N.	football
18	喜歡上	喜欢上	xǐhuanshàng	V.-C.	to begin to like
19	*騎	骑	qí	V.	to ride
20	*自行車	自行车	zìxíngchē	N.	bicycle
21	*棒球	棒球	bàngqiú	N.	baseball
22	*籃球	篮球	lánqiú	N.	basketball
23	*網球	网球	wǎngqiú	N.	tennis
24	*游泳	游泳	yóu yǒng	V.-O.	to swim
25	*畫畫兒	画画儿	huà huàr	V.-O.	to draw/paint
26	當	当	dāng	V.	to become
27	名	名	míng	MW	*measure word indicating number of people*
28	畫家	画家	huàjiā	N.	painter
29	*另外	另外	lìngwài	Conj.	besides
30	下棋	下棋	xià qí	V.-O.	to play chess
31	*彈	弹	tán	V.	to play (musical instrument)

Lesson 11 愛好

32	吉他	吉他	jítā	N.	guitar
33	*將來	将来	jiānglái	TW	in the future
34	*書法	书法	shūfǎ	N.	calligraphy
35	*多才多藝	多才多艺	duōcái-duōyì	IE	versatile
36	琴	琴	qín	N.	general name for stringed instruments
37	*棋	棋	qí	N.	chess or any board game
38	*書	书	shū	N.	calligraphy
39	*畫	画	huà	N.	painting
40	樣樣精通	样样精通	yàng yàng jīngtōng	IE	to be good at everything
41	*精通	精通	jīngtōng	V.	to be proficient in
42	等	等	děng	V.	to wait
43	不少	不少	bùshǎo		a lot
44	*隨便	随便	suí biàn	V.-O.	Do as you please.
45	算了	算了	suànle	V.	Forget it.
46	好哇	好哇	hǎo wa	IE	Okay.
47	*美式	美式	Měishì	N.	American style
48	多半兒	多半儿	duōbànr	Num.	mostly, most of
49	怪不得	怪不得	guàibude	Adv.	no wonder
50	逗你玩兒	逗你玩儿	dòu nǐ wánr	IE	Just kidding.
51	藝術家	艺术家	yìshùjiā	N.	artist
52	*接著	接着	jiēzhe	V.	to continue
53	*專業	专业	zhuānyè	N.	major
54	*原因	原因	yuányīn	N.	reason
55	*東方	东方	Dōngfāng	PN	Eastern
56	*主修	主修	zhǔxiū	V.	to major in
57	*鋼琴	钢琴	gāngqín	N.	piano
58	對牛彈琴	对牛弹琴	duìniú-tánqín	IE	Playing music to cattle. It is useless to talk to sb. who doesn't understand you at all.
59	時間到了	时间到了	shíjiān dào le	IE	Time is up.
60	下面	下面	xiàmiàn	N.	next
61	前面	前面	qiánmiàn	PW	the front
62	*兄弟	兄弟	xiōngdi	N.	brothers
63	*開始	开始	kāishǐ	V.	to start

| 64 | *圍棋 | 围棋 | wéiqí | N. | Go (a Chinese board game) |
| 65 | *不敢當 | 不敢当 | bùgǎndāng | V. | I am flattered. |

■ Supplementary Vocabulary:

1	裙子	裙子	qúnzi	N.	skirt
2	房子	房子	fángzi	N.	house
3	白日夢	白日梦	báirìmèng	N.	daydream
4	意式建築	意式建筑	yìshì jiànzhù	NP	Italian style buildings
5	作家	作家	zuòjiā	N.	writer
6	書法家	书法家	shūfǎjiā	N.	calligrapher
7	歌唱家	歌唱家	gēchàngjiā	N.	singer
8	漢學家	汉学家	hànxuéjiā	N.	Sinologist
9	文學家	文学家	wénxuéjiā	N.	litterateur
10	一部手機	一部手机	yí bù shǒujī	NP	a cell phone
11	拉小提琴	拉小提琴	lā xiǎotíqín	VP	to play violin
12	打高爾夫球	打高尔夫球	dǎ gāo'ěrfūqiú	VP	to play golf
13	打保齡球	打保龄球	dǎ bǎolíngqiú	VP	to play bowling
14	打排球	打排球	dǎ páiqiú	VP	to play volleyball

GRAMMAR

1 A 讓 B VP：A ask B to do sth.

Compared with "A 叫 B VP", this structure is relatively a little bit more formal.
與"A 叫 B VP"相比，這一結構相對比較正式。

　a. 老師讓大家分組談一談自己的愛好。
　　(The teacher asked them to talk about their own hobbies in groups.)
　b. 老師讓每個小組向其他同學介紹同伴兒的業餘愛好。
　　(The teacher asked each group to introduce their teammate's hobbies to other students.)
　c. 我不想讓他來我家。(I don't want him to come to my house.)

Lesson 11 愛好

d. 過生日，你想讓你的父母給你買什麼？
(What do you want your parents to buy you for your birthday?)
e. 你不想讓我休息，是不是？ (You don't want me to take a break, right?)
f. 你想讓我說什麼呢？ (What do you want me to say?)
g. 要是你不讓我去，我就不幫你了。
(If you don't let me go, I won't help you any more.)

Other usage 其他用法

E.g. 對不起，請讓一下 / 讓一讓。
(Excuse me, please let me through.)

2 A 向 B 介紹 C：A introduces C to B

E.g. 每個小組向其他同學介紹同伴兒的業餘愛好。
(Each group will introduce their teammate's hobbies to other students.)

We can also reconstruct this structure by using the Ba-construction.
我們還可以用把字結構重組這個句子。

A 把 C 介紹給 B

E.g. 每個小組把同伴兒的愛好介紹給其他同學。
(Each group introduced their teammate's hobbies to other students.)

A 把 C 給 B 介紹了一下

E.g. 小王把他的女朋友給我們介紹了一下。
(Xiao Wang introduced his girl friend to us.)

3 S 或 (者) A 或 (者) B：either A or B

This structure is very useful in terms of describing actions taking place or coexisting at the same time.
這個結構主要用於描述同時發生的動作或同時存在的事物。

E.g. a. 大家或各有所愛，或志趣相投。
(They either have their own interests or they share the same ones.)
b. 放假的時候，同學們都出去了，或去南方，或去西部，玩兒得很開心。
(During the vacation, all the students left. They either went to the South, or to the West. They had a really good time.)

c. 過年的時候，非常熱鬧，人們或一起吃飯，或唱歌跳舞。
   (It is very lively during the New Year. People either eat together or sing and dance together.)
d. 他們多才多藝，或精通書法，或能歌善 (shàn) 舞。
   (They are really versatile. They are either really proficient in calligraphy or very good at singing and dancing.)
e. 那兒有很多外國人，他們或說意大利語，或說日語，或說韓語，或說法語。
   (There are a lot of foreigners over there. They are either speaking Italian, Japanese, Korean or French.)

4 四字格 (sìzìgé)：Four Character Expressions

In Chinese written language, there are some special patterns, words and expressions to be used. The four character expressions are among the most frequently used ones. As the name indicates, these expressions consist of four characters. Most of them are idiomatic expressions or proverbs. We have to learn them one by one. The ones we have learned are as follows:

在漢語書面語中，有一些特殊格式，四字格是其中之一。這一表達方式由四個字組成，大部分四字格是漢語成語或諺語，我們需要逐個學習。我們已經學過的四字格有：

沒精打采　多才多藝　琴棋書畫　樣樣精通　各有所愛　志趣相投
左思右想　一路平安　人見人愛　自言自語　一言爲定　對牛彈琴

a. 他沒精打采的，可能生病了。
   (He looks very exhausted and tired. Maybe he is sick.)
b. 哥大的學生大多都多才多藝。(Most of the students at CU are versatile.)
c. 他們兩個都喜歡打棒球，可以說他們志趣相投。
   (Both of them like playing baseball. You could say that they share the same interest.)
d. 我們兩個各有所愛：她喜歡網球，我喜歡棒球。
   (We each have our own interests. She likes tennis and I like baseball.)
e. 你自言自語地說什麼呢？ (What are you talking about to yourself?)
f. 你說你要把你的自行車給我？一言爲定。
   (You said you are going to give me your bicycle? Set in stone./It is a deal.)
g. 他的狗又聰明，又好看，人見人愛。
   (His dog is both smart and good-looking. Everybody likes him/her.)
h. 別跟他說了，你不是在對牛彈琴嗎？他聽不懂中文。
   (Don't talk to him any more. It's just like playing music to a cow. He doesn't understand Chinese.)

NOTE: Four character expressions don't take any objects even if they are predicates of the sentence.

注意：即便四字格是句子的謂語，其後也不能帶任何賓語。

 ☹ 我左思右想這件事。→ 這件事，我左思右想，可是沒想出來什麼。
(I think a lot about this matter. But I still have not figured out anything.)

☹ 我們志趣相投很多事情。→ 我們在很多事情上志趣相投。
(We share a lot in many aspects.)

5 從 sth. V 起：start doing from...

 a. 最後他說還是從小的時候說起吧。
(Finally he said that let him start from the time when he was little.)

b. 我還是從頭 (tóu) 做起吧。
(Let me start from the very beginning.)

c. 還是從我做起吧。(It is better to start from oneself.)

d. 我學來學去，每次都得從第一課學起。
(I have studied it for quite a while. But each time I have to start from Lesson one.)

e. 我從哪兒說起呢？(Where shall I start from?)

6 S……的時候 VP₁；後來，VP₂ 了；再後來，又 VP₃；現在，VP₄；將來 VP₅

This is another way to indicate sequence of actions or events. It is very useful when describing an experience.

這是表達動作或事件發生順序的另一種方式，常用於描述一種經歷。

 a. 我小的時候喜歡踢足球；後來，我愛上了棒球；再後來，我又喜歡上了籃球；現在，我特別愛玩兒網球；將來，我還準備學彈鋼琴。
(When I was little, I liked playing football. Later, I started to love baseball. Afterwards, I started to like basketball. Now I like playing tennis very much. In the future, I plan to learn how to play piano.)

b. 他剛開始的時候，是英文老師；後來，他學了法文；再後來，他又學了德文。現在，他英、法、德三種語言都說得很好；將來，他還準備學中文。
(At the very beginning, he was an English teacher. Later, he learned French. After that, he studied German. Now, as for the three languages of English, French, and German, he speaks all of them very well. In the future, he still plans to learn Chinese.)

7 S V 上 Object 了

S start to do...

a. 他喜歡上了騎自行車。(He started to like bicycle riding.)
b. 她愛上了中文。(She started to love Chinese.)
c. 他看上了他的好朋友的妹妹。
(He started to be interested in his good friend's younger sister.)

sb. has access to doing sth.; to be able to do sth.

a. 他們終於過上了好日子。(They finally started to live a good life.)
b. 我們住上了好房子 (fángzi)。(We started to live in good house.)
c. 我們終於吃上了真正的中國菜。(We are finally able to eat real Chinese food.)

8 要是A(的話), S 還想/就 B: if A, then S still want(s) to do...

This is the default structure of the conditional sentence "要是 A, S 就 VP." In this structure, 的話 can be dropped.
這是條件從句"要是 A, S 就 VP"的另一種形式，其中"的話"可省略。

a. 要是有機會的話，他還想到中國去學書法。
(If there is an opportunity, he still wants to go to China to learn calligraphy.)
b. 要是你喜歡的話，你就拿走吧。
(If you like it, then you take it.)
c. 要是你沒有錢的話，我就給你一點兒。
(If you don't have money, I can give you some.)
d. 要是我是你的話，我就去。
(If I were you, I would go.)
e. 要是你不想去，你就早點兒告訴我。
(If you don't want to go, then you should have told me earlier.)

9 S V 一會兒 (Object): S V for a little period of time

This structure indicates that an action lasts for a short while. It is different from "S V 一下", because the latter expresses the idea that an action will be completed instantly.
這個結構表示動作持續一小段時間，不同於"S V 一下，"後者表示動作立即完成。

a. 請等一會兒。(Please wait for a while.)
b. 他每天都要踢一會兒球。(He will play football for a while each day.)

246

Lesson 11 愛好

c. 在中國的時候，我每天都要看一會兒電視。
   (When I was in China, I would watch some TV each day.)

d. 週末我做了很多事情，看了一會兒電影，跟朋友聊了一會兒天，睡了一會兒覺，打了一會兒球，還彈了一會兒琴。
   (I did many things this weekend: I watched a movie for a while, then I chatted with my friend for some time, I slept for a while, played basketball for a while and also played piano for some time.)

e. 請等一下。(Give me a couple of minutes.)

f. 我只踢一下。(I will just shoot it.)

g. 請你把這本書看一下，看看你喜不喜歡。
   (Please take a look at this book to see if you like it or not.)

10 Compare 有不少人，有很多人，有人，沒有人，沒有多少人

有不少(的)人	有很多(的)人	有(的)人	沒有人	沒有多少人
quite a number of people	many people	some people	nobody	not so many people

 a. 我們班有不少人多才多藝。
   (There are quite a number of people in our class who are versatile.)

b. 有很多人沒有學上。(There are many people who can't afford to go to school.)

c. 有人喜歡吃酸的，有人喜歡吃辣的，可是沒有人喜歡吃難吃的。
   (Some people like eating sour stuff; some people like eating spicy food. But nobody likes eating things that are not delicious.)

d. 很多人都會說英語，可是沒有多少人會說韓語。
   (Many people can speak English, but not so many people can speak Korean.)

11 Suffix 式：…style

This suffix is very formal and productive. It is better to have a monosyllabic word before it than a disyllabic one.

後綴"式"很正式，能拓展出很多詞語。其前的詞素多是單音節的，雙音節的詞素較少。

美國	美式	日本	日式
英國	英式	韓國	韓式
意大利	意式/意大利式	中國	中式
西方	西式	東方	☹東式
男人	男式	女人	女式

NOTE: There is no such expression as 東式.
注意：沒有"東式"的表達。

a. 這是美式足球嗎？ (Is it the American football?)
b. 我的朋友喜歡西式餐館兒，不喜歡中式的。
　　(My friend likes Western-style restaurants, but not Chinese style.)
c. 你有女式眼鏡嗎？ (Do you have glasses for women?)
d. 我不喜歡老式桌子，我喜歡新式的。
　　(I don't like old-style tables. I like the new-style ones.)

12 Aspect marker 著 (zhe)

It is used to indicate something is in progress or something progresses. Usually, it goes with 正在 and 呢.
"著"表示動作正在進行的狀態，通常與"正在"和"呢"連用。

S + 正 / 在 / 正在 + V + 著 + O + 呢

a. 我正聽著呢。(I am listening.)
b. 外面正下著雨呢。(It is raining outside.)
c. 我正在吃著飯呢。(I am eating.)

Also it can be used to indicate something in existence.
"著"還可用於表示事物的存在。

PW + V + 著 + sth./sb.

a. 門口站著幾個人。(There are several people standing by the door.)
b. 學中文的學生個個手裡都拿著一本書。
　　(The students who are learning Chinese, each has a book in their hands.)
c. 床上睡著一個小男孩兒。(There lies a boy on the bed.)
d. 床下睡著一隻小狗。(There lies a small dog under the bed.)
e. 他的手裡拿著一瓶啤酒。(There is a bottle of beer in his hand.)

f. 他的手裡拿著什麼？ (What's in his hand?)
g. 桌子上放著什麼？ (What is on the table?)
h. 信裡寫著什麼？ (What is written in the letter?)

13 Suffix 家：X-er, X-ist

家 is a noun suffix meaning "-er" or "-ist" in English. It usually refers to the people who have been famous or have been recognized as a professional.

"家"爲名詞後綴，相當於英語中的 -er 或 -ist，常指很有名或精通某一專業的人。

E.g. 畫家　書法家　藝術家　作家　歌唱家　漢學家　文學家

Summary:

> In Chinese written language, there are some special patterns, words and expressions. The four character expressions are among the most frequently used ones. As the name indicates, these expressions consist of four characters. Most of them are idiomatic expressions or proverbs. We have to learn them one by one.

> Four character expressions don't take any objects even if they are the predicates of the sentence.

> "S V 一會兒" indicates that an action lasts for a short while. It is different from "S V 一下" because the latter expresses the idea that an action will be completed instantly.

> Suffix 式 is very formal and productive. It is better to have a monosyllabic word before it than a disyllabic one.

> Aspect marker 著 (zhe) is used to indicate something is in progression. Usually it goes with 正在 and 呢.

> Also 著 can be used to indicate something in existence.

> 家 is a noun suffix meaning "-er" or "-ist" in English. It usually refers to the people who have been famous or have been recognized as a professional.

Patterns:

- A 讓 B VP ‖ 老師讓大家分組談一談自己的愛好。
  (The teacher asked us to talk about our own hobbies in groups.)

- A 向 B 介紹 C ‖ 每個小組向其他同學介紹同伴兒的業餘愛好。
  (People in the same group will introduce their teammate's hobbies to other students.)

- A 把 C 介紹給 B ‖ 每個小組的人把同伴兒的愛好介紹給其他同學。
  (People in the same group will introduce their teammate's hobbies to other students.)

- A 把 C 給 B 介紹了一下 ‖ 小王把他的女朋友給我們介紹了一下。
  (Xiao Wang introduced his girlfriend to us.)

- S 或（者）A 或（者）B ‖ 大家或各有所愛，或志趣相投。
  (They either have their own interests or share the same ones.)

- 四字格 (sìzìgé)：Four Character Expressions ‖

  沒精打采　多才多藝　琴棋書畫　樣樣精通　各有所愛　志趣相投

  左思右想　一路平安　人見人愛　自言自語　一言爲定　對牛彈琴

- 從 sth. V 起 ‖ 最後他說還是從小的時候說起吧。
  (Finally he said let him start from the when he was little.)

- S……的時候 VP_1；後來，VP_2 了；再後來，又 VP_3；現在，VP_4；將來 VP_5 ‖
  我小的時候喜歡踢足球；後來，我愛上了棒球；再後來，我又喜歡上了籃球；現在，我特別愛玩兒網球；將來，我還準備學彈鋼琴。
  (When I was little, I liked playing football. Later, I started to love baseball. Afterwards, I started to like basketball. Now I like playing tennis very much. In the future, I plan to learn how to play piano.)

- S V 上 Object 了 ‖ 他喜歡上了騎自行車。(He started to like bicycle riding.)

- 要是 A（的話），S 還想 / 就 B ‖ 要是有機會的話，他還想到中國去學書法。
  (If there is an opportunity, he still wants to go to China to learn calligraphy.)

- S V 一會兒 ‖ 請等一會兒。(Please wait for a while.)

- Suffix 式 ‖ 這是美式足球嗎？ (Is it the American football?)

250

Lesson 11 愛好

- S + 正 / 在 / 正在 + V + 著 + O + 呢 ‖ 我正聽著呢。(I am listening.)
- PW + V + 著 + sth./sb. ‖ 門口站著幾個人。
  (There are several people standing by the door.)

IN CLASS ACTIVITIES

1 Answer the following questions according to the information given in the text:

① 今天上中文課的時候，老師讓大家做什麼？

② 老師叫每個組做什麼？

③ 爲什麼大家說家奇多才多藝？

④ 大家的愛好怎麼樣？

⑤ 同學們越說越怎麼樣？氣氛呢？

⑥ 家興說他小的時候喜歡做什麼？

⑦ 家奇說他將來準備做什麼？

2 Please do role play according to the dialogues given below:

- A 你有什麼業餘愛好？
- B 我的業餘愛好多極了，琴棋書畫，樣樣都愛。
- A 哦，你真是多才多藝。你會彈什麼琴？下什麼棋？
- B 我不會彈琴，也不會下棋。
- A 你又不會彈琴又不會下棋，那怎麼說你琴棋書畫樣樣都愛呢？
- B 樣樣都愛又不一定是樣樣都會。你喜歡什麼？
- A 我最喜歡踢足球。我也對籃球、棒球、網球，還有游泳很感興趣。
- B 我對這些都沒有什麼興趣，所以我們各有所愛。
- A 對，我們真是志趣不相投。
- B 昨天晚上的世界杯 (Shìjièbēi: World Cup) 你看了沒有？太有意思了！你聽懂了沒有？
- A 你說什麼？我什麼也沒聽見。
- B 嗐，我這不是對牛彈琴嗎？
- A 逗你玩兒呢，我也很喜歡看世界杯。
- B 看我說呢，我們還是志趣相投的嘛！
- A 呵呵，今天晚上我們一起去唱歌，怎麼樣？
- B 沒問題。

去銀行 (yínháng: bank)

- A 我想從 ATM 取 (qǔ: to withdraw) 一些 (yìxiē: some) 錢，怎麼取？
- B 你有 ATM 卡嗎？是哪家銀行的？
- A 有，是 CitiBank 的。
- B 哦，花旗 (Huāqí) 銀行的。那就是花旗銀行的自動取款機 (zìdòng qǔkuǎnjī: ATM)。
- A 謝謝。
- C 我想用美金 (měijīn: US dollar) 換人民幣 (rénmínbì: RMB), 請問匯率 (huìlǜ: rate) 是多少？
- B 一比六。您要換多少錢？
- C 五百美金。
- B 請您在這兒簽字 (qiān zì: to sign)。好，這是您的錢。請收好。
- C 謝謝。

Lesson 11 愛好

HOMEWORK

1 Please rewrite or complete the following sentences with the given structures:

① 感恩節是下個禮拜。(快 V 了)

➡ 感恩節快到了。

② 昨天,我弟弟請教了爸爸一個奇怪的問題。(A 向 B VP)

➡

③ 我認識那個多才多藝的人,可是我妹妹不認識他。(A 把 C 介紹給 B)

➡

④ 我想學彈吉他,不學中文了,可是我媽媽說不行。(A 讓 B VP)

➡

⑤ 他喜歡美國人說的英文。(Suffix 式)

➡

⑥ 週末,我有的時候去看電影,有的時候去參觀博物館。(S 或者 A 或者 B)

➡

⑦ 要是想學彈鋼琴,應該很小的時候就開始。(從 sth. V 起)

➡

⑧ 她開始喜歡他了。(S V 上 Object 了)

➡

⑨ 聽說你想學書法,我可以教你。(要是 A 的話,S 就 B)

➡

⑩ 請你先看一會兒書,好不好?(S 正 V 著呢)

➡

2 Please rewrite the following sentences with Four Character Expressions:

① 你爲什麽喜歡自己跟自己説話？

➡ 你爲什麽喜歡自言自語？

② 他覺得很不舒服，一點勁兒也沒有。

➡

③ 她真能幹，不論是彈琴、下棋、書法，還是畫畫兒，什麼都會做。

➡

④ 你喜歡踢足球，我喜歡游泳。

➡

⑤ 我們都喜歡書法，聽音樂。

➡

⑥ 我以爲我的話他聽得進去，其實他聽不進去。

➡

⑦ 他又會唱歌，又會跳舞。

➡

⑧ 誰都喜歡他。

➡

⑨ 我們説好了明天見。

➡

⑩ 他想來想去還是不知道我是誰。

➡

Lesson 11 愛好

3 Translate the following sentences into Chinese:

1. Some people like playing chess.

2. There are quite a number of people who like playing guitar, but not so many people who can play GO.

3. I would like to teach you, but where shall I start?

4. He plays piano for a while before he goes to bed each day.

5. My teammate is very versatile. He is very good at playing piano, chess, calligraphy, and painting.

6. What do you want us to buy you for your birthday?

7. I would like to introduce this famous artist to you.

8. Most of my classmates like learning foreign languages. They can speak either English, Chinese or Japanese.

9. I major in Eastern Art and Chinese painting.

4 Please use the following patterns to write a mini-essay about your hobby:

S……的時候 VP₁；後來，VP₂ 了；再後來，又 VP₃；現在，VP₄；將來 VP₅

S 對 sth. 有興趣；　　S V 上 Object 了；　　要是 A（的話），S 還想 / 就 B

5 Please read the following paragraph in Pinyin:

　　Zuìjìn Jiāxīng xīnqíng bù hǎo, kànqǐlái hěn jǔsàng, shàng kè de shíhou hěn shǎo shuō huà, yě bú ài kāi wánxiào le. Jiāqí wèn tā shì bu shì shēntǐ bú tài shūfu, tā shuō shēntǐ hái xíng. Jiāqí yòu wèn tā shì bu shì zuòyè tài duō, xuéxí fùdān tài zhòng. Tā shuō xuéxí máng shì hěn máng, kěshì hái néng duìfu. Zuìhòu, tā gàosù Jiāqí tā de nǔpéngyou gēn tā chuī le. Tā de nǔpéngyou shàng ge zhōumò dǎ diànhuà de shíhou tíchūlái fēn shǒu, shuō suīrán Jiāxīng de xìngqíng hěn hǎo, rén hěn cōngmíng, zhǎng de yě tǐng shuài, kěshì xiǎnglái–xiǎngqù, háishi juéde liǎng ge rén fēn shǒu hǎo. Tā shuō fēn shǒu zhǔyào yǒu liǎng ge yuányīn: yī shì liǎng ge rén lí de tài yuǎn, yì nián cái néng jiàn jǐ cì miàn; èr shì tā juéde Jiāxīng yǒu yìdiǎnr tài niánqīng, bǐ tā hái xiǎo jǐ suì, ér tā xiǎng zhǎo yí ge niánlíng dà yìdiǎnr de rén, gèng yǒu ānquángǎn. Suīrán Jiāxīng hěn zūnzhòng nǔpéngyou de xuǎnzé, kě xīnlǐ háishi tǐng nánguò de, hěn nán wánquán wàngjì guòqù. Tā xīwàng guò yí duàn shíjiān xīnqíng huì hǎo yìxiē, yǐhòu hái néng hé nǔpéngyou chéngwéi hǎo péngyou.

Lesson 11 愛好

Chinese Punctuation

In the documents of Classical Chinese, there was no punctuation. In Modern Chinese, punctuation marks are used. Some of Chinese language punctuation marks are similar to their equivalent Western ones only larger, in order to suit the characters that surround the mark.

When the text is written vertically, the quotation marks (引號 yǐnhào) —『 』and「 」— are used; but when the text is written horizontally both the above quotation marks and the English quotation marks— " " and ' ' —can be used.

In addition, there are book title marks, 《 "book title" 》, what in English is italicized or underlined; and chapter marks, 〈 "chapter title" 〉, what in English would be quotation marks.

A Caesura sign (頓號 dùnhào), nicknamed sesame dot, is the English equivalent of a serial comma. It is shaped like a teardrop with the narrow sharp end pointing top-left and round end pointing bottom-right: 、 (it may be depicted on your computer in another typeface font /).

A Partition sign is a dot at the centre of a character space: 間隔號 (jiàngéhào). One of its uses is to separate words in a foreign name, e.g. "Leonardo da Vinci" could be written in Chinese as "列奧那多·達·芬奇".

A Proper noun mark (專名號 zhuānmínghào), which exists as an underline beneath the noun, is occasionally used in Chinese. Some people might use it in teaching materials or some film movie subtitle/s. When the text runs vertically, the proper noun mark is written as a line to the left of the characters.

In Chinese, the ellipsis is written with six dots (……), not three.

Name of the punctuation	Punctuation	English Equivalent	Usage	Example
句號 jùhào (Period; full stop)	。	.	Used at the end of a narrative sentence	我會說中國話了。
逗號 dòuhào (comma)	，	,	To indicate pause in a sentence	我會說中文,也會寫中文。
頓號 dùnhào (caesura sign; serial comma)	、		Pause between words and phrases	我會說中文、英文、法文和德文。
分號 fēnhào (semicolon)	;	;	To indicate pause between sentences	我喜歡英文;他喜歡中文。
冒號 màohào (colon)	:	:	To introduce more information	他告訴我:他很喜歡中國菜。
問號 wènhào (question mark)	?	?	To appear at the end of a question	你不喜歡吃中國菜了?

（續表）

Name of the punctuation	Punctuation	English Equivalent	Usage	Example
感嘆號 gǎntànhào (exclamation mark)	！	!	To show strong feeling	太好了！
引號 yǐnhào (quotation marks)	" " ' ' 「 」 『 』	" "	To quote	他說："你應該好好學習。"
			To indicate certain titles or names	他是"三好"學生。
			To be ironic	他真是"多才多藝"，琴棋書畫什麼都不會。
括號 kuòhào (brackets)	（ ）	( )	To indicate explanation	我們都覺得他很能幹，多才多藝（琴棋書畫，樣樣精通）。
省略號 shěnglüèhào (ellipsis)	……	…	To indicate elision	他會說很多種語言：漢語、英語、法語、日語……
破折號 pòzhéhào (dash)	——	—	To explain as brackets do	我們都覺得他很能幹，多才多藝——琴棋書畫，樣樣精通。
			To indicate progress	學習——學習——再學習。
			To show transition	我有一隻狗——可是現在找不到了。
連接號 liánjiēhào	—	-	To indicate time period, places and numbers	1999—2000年 北京—紐約 100—200
書名號 shūmínghào (book title marks)	《 》	Italicization/ underlining	Book title	《走近中國》
	〈 〉	" "	Chapter title	〈點菜〉
間隔號 jiàngéhào (partition sign)	·		To separate words in a foreign name	列奧那多·達·芬奇
			To indicate separation between date and month	3·15　9·11

LESSON 12 失戀了

　　最近家興心情不好,看起來很沮喪,上課的時候很少說話,也不愛開玩笑了。家奇問他是不是身體不太舒服,他說身體還行。家奇又問他是不是作業太多,學習負擔太重。他說學習忙是很忙,可是還能對付。最後,他告訴家奇他的女朋友跟他吹了。他的女朋友上個週末打電話的時候提出來分手,說雖然家興的性情很好,人很聰明,長得也挺帥,可是想來想去還是覺得兩個人分手好。她說分手主要有兩個原因:一是兩個人離得太遠,一年才能見幾次面;二是她覺得家興有一點兒太年輕,比她還小幾歲,而她想找一個年齡大一點兒的人,更有安全感。雖然家興很尊重女朋友的選擇,可心裡還是挺難過的,很難完全忘記過去。他希望過一段時間心情會好一些,以後還能和女朋友成為好朋友。

1

家奇: 家興,好幾天沒看見你了,最近還好嗎?

家興: 還行吧!

家奇: 你好像變了一個人似的。上課很少說話,也不愛開玩笑了。是不是身體不太舒服?

走近中國——初級漢語教程
APPROACHING CHINA : ELEMENTARY CHINESE

家興： 身體還行。

家奇： 你看起來有點兒沮喪。是不是作業太多，學習負擔太重？

家興： 學習忙是很忙，可是還能對付。

家奇： 那到底是怎麼回事？

家興： 心情不太好。

家奇： 哦？

家興： 我的女朋友跟我吹了。

家奇： 什麼時候？

家興： 上個週末。

家奇： 你們吵架了？

家興： 沒有。那麼遠，怎麼有機會吵架呢？

家奇： 也許……

家興： 她打電話的時候提出來的。

家奇： 走吧，咱哥兒倆喝兩杯去。

2

家奇： 家興，你想喝什麼？我這兒有啤酒，也有紅酒。

家興： 給我來瓶啤酒吧！

家奇： 冰鎮的？

家興： 好，謝謝。

家奇： 不客氣。

家興： 家奇，再給我來一瓶。

家奇： 算了，別喝了。心裡不舒服，不能多喝，要不然容易醉。

家興： 家奇，她跟我分手就分手唄，還說什麼我性情不錯，人也很聰明，長得也挺帥，沒意思……

家奇： 嗯？

家興： 她說她想來想去，還是覺得分手好。

家奇： 爲什麼呢？

家興： 她說主要有兩個原因：一是我們離得太遠，一年才能見幾次面；二是她覺得我有一點兒太年輕。

260

Lesson 12 失戀了

家奇： 嗯？

家興： 我是比她還小幾歲，可她說什麼她想找一個年齡大一點兒的人，這樣才有安全感。

家奇： 是嗎？

家興： 算了，不說了。

3

家奇： 家興，喝杯茶，好不好？

家興： 好，謝謝了。

家奇： 不客氣。

家興： 我尊重她的選擇，可是心裡還是挺難過的。

家奇： 還是把她忘了吧！

家興： 完全忘記過去，恐怕很難。

家奇： 慢慢兒來吧，也許過一段時間就會好一些的。

家興： 也許我們以後還能成為好朋友。

家奇： 家興，說出來，心情好一點兒了吧？

家興： 好多了。不好意思，佔用了你不少時間。

家奇： 誰叫我們是好朋友呢？

家興： 下次，等你被甩的時候，儘管找我。

家奇： 多謝了，我還是等你找我吧。

VOCABULARY

1	失戀	失恋	shī liàn	V.-O.	to get dumped
2	心情	心情	xīnqíng	N.	mood
3	看起來	看起来	kànqǐlái	VP	It looks like…
4	沮喪	沮丧	jǔsàng	Adj.	depressed
5	*身體	身体	shēntǐ	N.	body, health
6	*作業	作业	zuòyè	N.	homework
7	*負擔	负担	fùdān	N.	burden
8	重	重	zhòng	Adj.	heavy

9	*對付	对付	duìfu	V.	to handle
10	吹了	吹了	chuīle	IE	to break up
11	上個	上个	shàng ge		last (week/month)
12	*週末	周末	zhōumò	TW	weekend
13	*提出來	提出来	tíchūlái	VP	to bring it up
14	*分手	分手	fēn shǒu	V.-O.	to break up
15	*性情	性情	xìngqíng	N.	temperament
16	想來想去	想来想去	xiǎnglái-xiǎngqù	VP	to think over and over
17	主要	主要	zhǔyào	Adj.	mainly
18	一是	一是	yī shì	Conj.	one thing is that…
19	二是	二是	èr shì	Conj.	another thing is that…
20	*年輕	年轻	niánqīng	Adj.	young
21	*而	而	ér	Conj.	but (formal)
22	*年齡	年龄	niánlíng	N.	age
23	大	大	dà	Adj.	old
24	*安全感	安全感	ānquángǎn	N.	the feeling of being safe
25	*尊重	尊重	zūnzhòng	V.	to respect
26	*選擇	选择	xuǎnzé	V.	to choose
27	*難過	难过	nánguò	Adj.	sad
28	*完全	完全	wánquán	Adv.	completely
29	*忘記	忘记	wàngjì	V.	to forget
30	過去	过去	guòqù	TW	the past
31	*一段	一段	yí duàn	Q.	a period of (time)
32	*一些	一些	yìxiē	Q.	some
33	*成爲	成为	chéngwéi	V.	to become
34	好幾	好几	hǎojǐ	Num.	several
35	還行吧	还行吧	hái xíng ba	IE	Not bad.
36	*變	变	biàn	V.	to change
37	*到底	到底	dàodǐ	Adv.	what on earth…, after all
38	*吵架	吵架	chǎo jià	V.-O.	to quarrel
39	咱哥兒倆	咱哥儿俩	zán gēr liǎ	IE	we two brothers
40	*啤酒	啤酒	píjiǔ	N.	beer
41	*紅酒	红酒	hóngjiǔ	N.	red wine

Lesson 12　失戀了

42	*瓶	瓶	píng	MW	bottle
43	冰鎮	冰镇	bīngzhèn	V.	cold/iced
44	別喝了	别喝了	bié hē le	IE	Don't drink any more.
45	*容易	容易	róngyì	Adj.	easy
46	*醉	醉	zuì	Adj.	drunk
47	*恐怕	恐怕	kǒngpà	Adv.	to be afraid that
48	慢慢兒來吧	慢慢儿来吧	mànmānr lái ba	IE	Take it easy.
49	說出來	说出来	shuōchūlái	VP	to speak out
50	*佔用	占用	zhànyòng	V.	to use
51	*被	被	bèi	Prep.	*used in passive structure*
52	甩	甩	shuǎi	V.	to be dumped
53	儘管找我	尽管找我	jǐnguǎn zhǎo wǒ	IE	Don't hesitate to talk to me.

■ Supplementary Vocabulary:

1	最好	最好	zuìhǎo	Adv.	had better
2	加菲貓	加菲猫	Jiāfēimāo	PN	Garfield
3	小偷	小偷	xiǎotōu	N.	thief
4	警察	警察	jǐngchá	N.	policeman
5	行李	行李	xíngli	N.	luggage
6	冰激淩	冰激淩	bīngjīlíng	N.	ice cream
7	健康	健康	jiànkāng	Adj.	healthy
8	傷透	伤透	shāngtòu	V.-C.	to be hurt badly
9	抓住	抓住	zhuāzhù	V.-C.	to catch
10	洗	洗	xǐ	V.	to wash

GRAMMAR

1 S 看起來：it seems that...；S appears to be...

 a. 他看起來很沮喪。(He seems to be very depressed.)
b. 雖然他已經六十多歲了，可是他看起來很年輕。
(Although he is already over sixty, he appears to be very young.)

c. 看起來你不太喜歡只是能說會道的人。
(It seems that you don't like people who are only good at talking.)

d. 看起來你還是不明白我對你的心。
(It seems that you still don't understand my feelings toward you.)

e. 看起來他不能再踢球了。
(It seems that he can't play football any more.)

f. 考試看起來很容易，可是做起來就很難了。
(As for the test, it is very easy at first glance, but it is very difficult to do it.)

g. 他的身體看起來很好，其實很差。
(He seems to be very healthy. But actually his health is poor.)

2 Sentence：一是……二是……：one thing is...; another thing is ...

a. 她說分手主要有兩個原因：一是他們離得太遠，一年才能見幾次面；二是她覺得家興有一點兒太年輕，比她還小幾歲。
(She said that there are mainly two reasons why she wanted to break up: one is that they are too far away from each other; another is that she felt Jiaxing is a little bit too young. He is even several years younger than she is.)

b. 我來中國有兩個原因：一是我想好好兒學學中文；二是我想在中國好好兒看看。
(There are two reasons for my coming to China: one is that I want to learn Chinese; another is that I want to travel in China.)

c. 他的女朋友喜歡他主要有兩個原因：一是他多才多藝；二是他很愛幫助人。
(His girlfriend likes him mainly for two things: one is that he is very versatile and another is that he loves helping others.)

d. 週末你最好不要去西安：一是時間不夠；二是太遠了。
(You had better not go to Xi'an. One reason is that there is not enough time. Another reason is that it is too far away.)

3 S V 來 V 去，……：S V again and again...

a. 她想來想去還是覺得他們最好分手。
(She thought it over and over again and decided that they had better break up.)

b. 我吃來吃去，還是吃不出來這是什麼。
(I had been eating it for a while but still had no idea what it was.)

c. 我學來學去就是學不會怎麼包餃子。
(I have been studying it over and over again but still don't know how to make dumplings.)

d. 我跟他說來說去，他還是不明白我在說什麼。
   (I explained it to him again and again, but he still didn't get the point.)
e. 我看來看去就是看不清楚。
   (I looked at it again and again but still couldn't see clearly.)
f. 我練來練去就是練不好書法。
   (I have been practicing over and over but I just can't do the calligraphy well.)

4 More examples on the Ba-construction

a. 還是把她忘了吧！ (Just forget her.)
b. 他把餃子都吃煩了。 (He is tired of eating dumplings.)
c. 我把學習看成世界上最重要的事情。
   (I consider studying the most important thing in the world.)
d. 男人把狗當成他們最好的朋友。 (Men take dogs as their best friends.)
e. 你把我當成什麼了？ (What do you treat me as?)
f. 我把考試當成喝涼水。
   (I treat tests just the same as drinking cold water. / Tests are nothing to me.)
g. 我把賬已經結了。 (I have already paid the bill.)
h. 昨天我把我的朋友送到了飛機場。
   (I saw my friend off all the way to the airport.)
i. 你把我的心傷透 (shāngtòu) 了。 (You hurt my feeling badly.)
j. 我考試得了一個A，把我高興壞了。
   (I got an A in the exam. I was extremely happy.)
k. 他把五個西紅柿吃了三個。 (He ate three tomatoes out of five.)

5 S 過一段時間 就／才 VP：S will be more... after a period of time

a. 他說也許過一段時間就會好一些的。
   (He said that he might feel a little bit better some time later.)
b. 我過一段時間就會去看你的。
   (I will visit you some time later.)
c. 我覺得你過一段時間就會習慣中國的生活的。
   (I think that you will be more used to Chinese life after some time.)
d. 北京過一段時間就會涼快一些的。
   (Beijing will get a bit cooler after a while.)
e. 我過一段時間才能去倫敦。
   (I can only go to London some time later.)

f. 我過一段時間才能把書還給你。
(I can only return the book to you some time later.)

g. 他過一段時間就會把中文學好了。
(He will master Chinese some time later.)

6 More about 了

We know that 了 can indicate completion of an action in addition to "change of a state". If 了 appears at the end of the sentence, it indicates change of a state.
我們知道"了"可以表示動作的完成和狀態發生改變。如果"了"在句末出現,它表示狀態的改變。

E.g. 我喜歡學中文了。(I like learning Chinese now.)

When it goes after a verb, before an object, then we refer to it as the particle 了, which indicates completion.
如果"了"出現在動詞後、賓語前,它表示動作的完成。

E.g. 我做了一天飯,現在很累。(I cooked for a day. I feel tired now.)

Sometimes it goes at the end of the sentence, but its function is hard to decide. It may indicate completion and change of a state at the same time.
有時"了"在句末出現,但它的功能很難確定。它可以同時表示動作的完成和狀態的改變。

E.g. ——你看書了沒有? (Did you read?)
——我看(書)了。(Yes, I did.)

If we want to say that somebody has been doing something for some time, then we will use two 了, in the structure as exemplified below:
如果我們想說某人做某事持續了一段時間了,那麼,在句子中要用兩個"了"。例如:

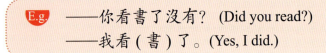

S V O V 了 duration 了; S V 了 duration O 了; O, S V 了 duration 了

E.g. 我看書看了一天了。/ 我看了一天書了。/ 書,我看了一天了。
(I have been reading for a day.)

With two 了 coexist in a sentence, it indicates that the action is still going on. If we want to express the idea that somebody hasn't done or didn't do something for some time, we will use the following structure:

Lesson 12　失戀了

兩個"了"在一個句子中同時出現，說明動作還在持續進行。如果我們想表達"某人還沒有做某事"或者"某人有一段時間沒有做某事了"的意思，要用如下結構：

S 多久 / 多長時間沒(有) VP 了
S time duration 沒(有) VP 了

E.g.
a. 你多久沒有吃北京烤鴨 (kǎoyā) 了？
(How long have you not had Peking Roast Duck?)
b. 好幾天沒看見你了。(I haven't seen you for several days.)
c. 我三年沒吃北京烤鴨了。(I haven't had it for three years.)
d. 我六年沒見過我最好的朋友了。(I haven't seen my best friend for six years.)
e. 我很久沒有看電影了。(I haven't seen a movie for a long time.)
f. 我很長時間沒跑步了。(I haven't jogged for a while.)

  S 到底 VP：what on earth ...

When 到底 is used as an adverb, it shows emphasis and，sometimes, with a tone of impatience.
當"到底"用作副詞時，它表示強調，有時帶有不耐煩的語氣。

E.g.
a. 那到底是怎麼回事？ (What on earth has happened?)
b. 你到底喜不喜歡我？(Do you like me or not?)
c. 你心裡到底是怎麼打算的？ (What do you actually plan to do?)
d. 你到底是會說中國話還是不會？ / 你到底會不會說中國話？
(Can you speak Chinese or can't you?)
e. 我們到底在哪兒呢？ (Where on earth are we?)

  而

As a conjunction, 而 connects two sentences to show transition. Unlike 但是 and 可是，it is very formal and used in written language.
"而"作爲一個連詞，它連接兩個句子來表示過渡。與"但是"和"可是"不同，它非常正式，常用於書面語中。

E.g.
a. 他比她還小幾歲，而她想找一個年齡大一點兒的人。
(He is several years younger than she is. But she wants somebody who is a little bit older.)
b. 他喜歡打籃球、棒球和網球，而我只喜歡踢足球。
(He likes playing basketball, baseball and tennis, but I only like playing football.)
c. 他哥哥又高又大，而他弟弟又瘦 (shòu) 又小。
(His elder brother is both tall and big, but his younger brother is both thin and small.)

267

d. 小王説三道四，而小張一言不發。
(Xiao Wang is talkative while Xiao Zhang is silent.)
e. 美國人大多喜歡美式足球，而中國人大多喜歡英式足球。
(Most Americans like football while most Chinese like soccer.)

9 恐怕 + sentence：I am afraid that…

Whether the subject is there or not, it is always interpreted as the first person singular.
不管有沒有主語，這個句型總要翻譯成第一人稱單數。

E.g.
a. 恐怕很難。(I am afraid that it is very difficult.)
b. 他恐怕不會來了。(I am afraid that he won't come.)
c. 中文恐怕很難學吧。(I am afraid that Chinese is very difficult to learn.)
d. 恐怕你再練也是洋腔洋調吧。
(I am afraid no matter how hard you practice, you will still have a foreign accent.)
e. 恐怕要下雨(xiàyǔ)了吧。(I am afraid that it is going to rain.)
f. 他恐怕有很多女朋友。(I am afraid he has many girlfriends.)

Never say:
不要説：

 我恐怕快要下雨了。(I am afraid that it is going to rain.)

10 Chinese passive structure：the Bei-construction

The Bei-construction is considered as the Chinese passive structure. In English, the English passive voice can be applied to virtually any verb：
被字結構可以説是漢語裡的被動語態。在英語中，英語的被動語態幾乎可以應用在任何動詞上。

E.g.
a. The man stole my cat. → The cat was stolen (by the man).
b. I wrote the book. → The book was written by me.

However, in Chinese, sentences that end up in the passive when translated into English may not have a passive construction in Chinese.
不過，那些可以翻譯成英語被動語態的句子，在漢語中可能並沒有被動形式。

E.g. 書，他拿走了。(The book was taken away by him.)

Some prepositions are also used in Chinese to show passiveness such as 叫，讓，給 and 被. Among which, 被 is the one that is most frequently used and the literal meaning of which is "to suffer". However, the Chinese passive structures are generally limited to the context in which the subject of the sentence has been affected by something unpleasant. (This is, of course, not necessarily always the case.) Depending on whether the noun phrase or doer is after 被 or not, the Bei-construction is classified into two types: the long passive and the short passive.

在漢語中，一些介詞也被用來表示被動，比如"叫""讓""給"和"被"。其中，"被"是最常用的，它的字面意思就是"被動"。漢語的被動語態通常受限於語境，句子的主語受到不愉快事物的影響（當然，也不總是這樣）。根據名詞短語或施事者是否在"被"之後，被字句可以分爲兩類：長被動和短被動。

The long passive uses the following structure:
長被動使用如下結構：

> **S 被 sb./sth. VP 了**

> **E.g.** 書被他拿走了。(The book was taken away by him.)

If there is no "doer" following the preposition 被, the structure is referred to as the short passive.
如果介詞"被"的後面沒有出現施事者，則結構爲短被動。

> **S 被 VP 了**

> **E.g.** 他被打了。(He was hit.)
> 他被甩了。(He was dumped.)

Summary:

> We know that 了 can indicate completeness of an action in addition to "change of a state". If 了 appears at the end of the sentence, it indicates change of a state.

> When 了 goes after a verb, before an object, then we refer to it as the particle 了, which indicates completeness.

> Sometimes 了 goes at the end of the sentence, but its function is hard to decide. It may indicate completeness and change of a state at the same time.

> If we want to say that somebody has been doing something for some time, then we will use two 了s in the structure as exemplified below:
> S V O V 了 duration 了; S V 了 duration O 了; O, S V 了 duration 了

> With two 了 coexist in a sentence, it indicates that the action is still going on.

If we want to express the idea that somebody hasn't done or didn't do something for some time, we will use the following structure:
S 多久 / 多長時間沒 (有) VP 了
S time duration 沒 (有) VP 了

In the structure "S 過一段時間 就 / 才 VP", when "才" is used, it means that the frequency of the action is not enough. While "就" indicates that something happened quite frequently.

When 到底 is used as an adverb, it shows emphasis and, sometimes, with a tone of impatience.

As a conjunction, 而 connects two sentences to show transition. Unlike 但是 and 可是, it is very formal and used in written language.

In the structure "恐怕 + sentence", whether the subject is there or not, it is always interpreted as the first person singular.

The Bei-construction is considered as the Chinese passive structure.

However, in Chinese, sentences that end up in the passive when translated into English do not have a passive construction in Chinese.

Depending on whether the noun phrase or doer is after 被 or not, the Bei-construction is classified into two types: the short passive and the long passive.

The long passive uses the following structure: S 被 sb./sth. VP 了.

If there is no "doer" following the preposition 被, the structure is referred to as the short passive: S 被 VP 了.

Patterns:

- S 看起來 ‖ 他看起來很沮喪。(He seems to be very depressed.)

- Sentence: 一是……二是…… ‖ 她說分手主要有兩個原因：一是他們離得太遠，一年才能見幾次面；二是她覺得家興有一點兒太年輕，比她還小幾歲。
  (She said that there are mainly two reasons: one is that they are too far away from each other; another is that she felt Jiaxing is a little bit too young. He is even several years younger than she is.)

Lesson 12 失戀了

- **S V 來 V 去, ……** ‖ 她想來想去還是覺得他們最好分手。
  (She thought it over and over again and decided that they had better break up.)

- **S 過一段時間就 / 才 VP** ‖ 他說也許過一段時間就會好一些的。
  (He said that he might feel a little bit better some time later.)

- **S V O V 了 duration 了; S V 了 duration O 了; O, S V 了 duration 了** ‖
  我看書看了一天了。/ 我看了一天書了。/ 書，我看了一天了。
  (I have been reading for a day.)

- **S 多久 / 多長時間沒 (有) VP 了** ‖ 你多久沒有吃北京烤鴨了？
  (How long have you not had peking Duck?)

- **S time duration 沒 (有) VP 了** ‖ 好幾天沒看見你了。
  (I haven't seen you for several days.)

- **S 到底 VP** ‖ 那到底是怎麼回事？ (What on earth has happened?)

- **而** ‖ 他比她還小幾歲，而她想找一個年齡大一點兒的人。
  (He is several years younger than she is. But she wants somebody who is a little bit older.)

- **恐怕 + sentence** ‖ 恐怕很難。(I am afraid that it is very difficult.)
  他恐怕不會來了。(I am afraid that he won't come.)

- **S 被 sb./sth. VP 了** ‖ 書被他拿走了。(The book was taken away by him.)

- **S 被 VP 了** ‖ 他被打了。(He was hit.)
  他被甩了。(He was dumped.)

IN CLASS ACTIVITIES

1 Answer the following questions according to the information given in the text:

① 最近家興怎麼了？

② 家興說他的身體和學習怎麼樣？

③ 家興到底怎麼了？

④ 家興的女朋友爲什麼要這麼做？

➡

⑤ 家興能把他的女朋友忘了嗎？爲什麼？

➡

⑥ 家興希望他們以後怎麼樣？

➡

⑦ 家奇說他將來準備做什麼？

➡

2 Please do role play according to the dialogues given below:

- Ⓐ 你覺得現在的女孩子是不是都太愛錢了？
- Ⓑ 你怎麼這樣問？
- Ⓐ 我的女朋友把我甩了，找了一個很有錢，比她大很多的男人。
- Ⓑ 別想太多了。女孩子大多覺得年齡大一些的男人會照顧人。
- Ⓐ 她還說什麼有安全感。我不明白錢就那麼重要？
- Ⓑ 我不覺得女孩子只喜歡錢。我沒有錢，可是我的女朋友很愛我。
- Ⓐ 我爲什麼沒有你那麼好的運氣呢？
- Ⓑ 不要太難過了，也許你還能找一個更愛你的呢？

在郵局 (yóujú: Post Office)

- Ⓐ 我想寄 (jì: to mail) 一封 (fēng: MW) 信 (xìn: letter) 到美國去，請問怎麼寄？
- Ⓑ 請您先把地址寫好，然後把郵票 (yóupiào: stamp) 貼 (tiē: to paste) 在信封 (xìnfēng: envelope) 上。
- Ⓐ 我還想寄一些書回去？請問得多長時間？
- Ⓑ 快件 (kuàijiàn: express mail) 大約一個禮拜左右。普通件 (pǔtōngjiàn: snail mail) 一個月左右。

Lesson 12 失戀了

A 哦，我寄普通件吧。有箱子 (xiāngzi: box) 嗎？
B 有。
A 一共多少錢？
B 八十五塊。
A 請問你們收 (shōu: to accept) 旅行支票 (lǚxíng zhīpiào: traveler's check) 嗎？
B 收。
A 太好了。
B 請您在這兒簽字 (qiān zì: to sign)。 這是收據 (shōujù: receipt)。

HOMEWORK

1 Please rewrite or complete the following sentences with the given structures:

① 感恩節是下個禮拜。（快 V 了）

➡ 感恩節快到了。

② 學習很忙，我很高興。 （S VP 是 VP，可是……）

➡

③ 我的同屋想去中國學中文是因爲他對中國很有興趣，還有他的女朋友是中國人。（Sentence: 一是……二是……）

➡

④ 我找我的書找了很長時間，可是還是沒有找到。（S V 來 V 去）

➡

⑤ 他不喜歡你，你忘了他吧。（the Ba-construction）

➡

⑥ 我剛來，還不太習慣大學生活，也許以後我會習慣的。（S 過一段時間就 / 才 VP）

➡

⑦ 你多久沒（有）彈琴了？（Please answer this question.）

➡ _____

⑧ 昨天你說你最喜歡騎自行車，今天又說不喜歡。（S 到底 VP）

➡ _____

⑨ 他的法國朋友喜歡唱歌。他的英國朋友喜歡彈吉他。（而）

➡ _____

⑩ 我想他沒有錢。（恐怕 + sentence）

➡ _____

2 Please rewrite the following sentences with Bei-construction:

① 他把我的足球踢壞了。 ➡ 足球被踢壞了。

② 有人拿走了你的錢包 (qiánbāo: wallet)。 ➡ _____

③ 飯吃完了。 ➡ _____

④ 我把飯吃完了。 ➡ _____

⑤ 他把書放到了桌子上。 ➡ _____

⑥ 他的女朋友跟他吹了。 ➡ _____

⑦ 誰打你了？ ➡ _____

⑧ 他買了所有的火車票。 ➡ _____

Lesson 12 失戀了

3 Translate the following sentences into Chinese:

① It seems that Chinese is very easy to learn.

_____

② There are two reasons why I like playing Go. One is that it is very interesting. The other reason is that I have a lot of friends who share the same interests.

_____

③ He likes drinking a lot. I told him again and again to quit it but he won't take my advice.

_____

④ I have been very busy recently. I can only go to a movie once a month.

_____

⑤ I think that you will be used to the college life after a while.

_____

⑥ I have been learning Chinese for almost a year.

_____

⑦ How long have you not been to the library? I haven't been to the library for a month.

_____

⑧ What on earth do you want to eat?

_____

⑨ I am afraid that he won't come.

_____

4 Please use the following patterns to write a mini-essay about your recent experience.

Sentence: 一是……二是……；　　　　S V 來 V 去；　　　　(S) 過一段時間就 VP；

S V O V 了 duration 了；　　S time duration 沒 (有)VP 了；

S 到底 VP ？　　　而；　　(S) 恐怕 + sentence；　　S 被 (sb./sth.) VP 了；

5 Please read the following paragraph in Pinyin:

Jiāqí xǐhuanshàngle yí ge nǚhái r. Zhè ge nǚhái r shì Zhōngguórén, yě shì xué Dōng Yà yìshù de, zhǎng de hěn piàoliang, gèzi bù gāo bù ǎi, nénggē-shànwǔ, xìnggé huópō. Xǐhuan tā de nánhái r tèbié duō. Jiāqí xǐhuan tā, yīnwèi tā búdàn cōngmíng nénggàn, érqiě xīndì shànliáng, duì rén tèbié yǒuhǎo, Jiāqí gēn tā zài yìqǐ de shíhou, gǎndào tèbié kuàilè, yuè gǎndào kuàilè jiù yuè xiǎng jiàndào tā. Jiāqí xiǎng zìjǐ kěnéng shì àishàng tā le, kěshì bù zhīdào tā yǒu méiyǒu nánpéngyou, yě bù zhīdào tā xǐ bu xǐhuan zìjǐ. Jiāxīng ràng Jiāqí qù yuē zhè ge nǚhái r kàn chǎng diànyǐng, wènwen nǚhái r de xiǎngfǎ. Jiāqí pà nǚhái r bú yuànyì, kě nǚhái r què zǎo jiù duì Jiāqí yǒu yìsi le. Tā juéde Jiāqí rén hěn zhēnchéng, yǒu zérèngǎn, yě yǒu yōumògǎn, xǐhuan bāng biérén de máng, zhèng shì tā yào zhǎo de báimǎ wángzǐ.

Lesson 12 失戀了

CULTURAL NOTES

Chinese Wedding

The contemporary Chinese wedding is a mixture of both traditional customs (please refer to http://www.chcp.org/wedding.html#intro for more information) and modern practices. It is a common practice that the bride wears both the Western wedding dress and Chinese clothing with the color red. On the wedding day, the groom will come to the bride's home to pick up his wife (-to-be) with a parade of famous and expensive cars. The brand name of the cars is an indication of how powerful or wealthy the newly married couples' families are, especially the groom's family. Usually, the groom's family is responsible for the wedding fees, apartment, and furniture. One of the traditions that remain is the character of double happiness.

Double Happiness

Each half of the symbol is the standard character for happiness, pronounced "xǐ" in Mandarin. Therefore, two 喜 together represent the wish for the two young newlyweds to have happiness together. The double happiness graph is a special Chinese character used for marital happiness. However, it's not used in regular Chinese writing or print.

LESSON 13 約會

家奇喜歡上了一個女孩兒。這個女孩兒是中國人，也是學東亞藝術的，長得很漂亮，個子不高不矮，能歌善舞，性格活潑。喜歡她的男孩兒特別多。家奇喜歡她，因為她不但聰明能幹，而且心地善良，對人特別友好。家奇跟她在一起的時候，感到特別快樂，越感到快樂就越想見到她。家奇想自己可能是愛上她了，可是不知道她有沒有男朋友，也不知道她喜不喜歡自己。家興讓家奇去約這個女孩兒看場電影，問問女孩兒的想法。家奇怕女孩兒不願意，可女孩兒卻早就對家奇有意思了。她覺得家奇人很真誠，有責任感，也有幽默感，喜歡幫別人的忙，正是她要找的白馬王子。

1

家興： 家奇，家奇，有什麼心事？

家奇： 沒什麼。

家興： 沒什麼？你一個人傻笑什麼？是不是愛上誰了？

家奇： 你怎麼知道？

家興： 我是過來人唄。她是誰？我認不認識？

Lesson 13　約會

家奇：她也是學東亞藝術的，是中國人，長得很漂亮，個子不高不矮，中等個兒。

家興：我也喜歡漂亮的女孩兒。

家奇：她還能歌善舞，性格活潑。

家興：跟你一樣，多才多藝。

家奇：比我能幹得多。

家興：你喜歡她是因為她又聰明又能幹，對不對？

家奇：我喜歡她不僅僅是因為她又聰明又能幹。

家興：哦？

家奇：主要是因為她心地善良，對人特別友好。

家興：太好了。我也喜歡心地善良的女孩兒。

家奇：每次看到有人需要幫助，她都會主動幫忙。

家興：跟我一樣。

家奇：比你熱心多了。喜歡她的男孩兒特別多。

家興：這並不奇怪，這樣子的女孩兒是很討人喜歡的。

2

家奇：可是不知道她有沒有男朋友，也不知道她喜不喜歡我。

家興：去問問她，就知道了。

家奇：嘿嘿，不太好意思。

家興：你不好意思？那我替你去問一下。

家奇：別，還是我自己去問吧。可是怎麼開口呢？

家興：你應該去請她看電影。要是她願意跟你去，就說明她對你有好感。

家奇：要是她不去呢？那多尷尬。

家興：如果你不問，你永遠也不會知道她的想法。單相思，可不是個滋味兒。

家奇：說得對，可是看什麼電影好呢？

家興：你們是學什麼的？她是哪國人？

家奇：看我，真笨！我請她看中國電影，她最喜歡張藝謀拍的片子。

家興：你不笨，你愛上她了吧？！

家奇： 我跟她在一起的時候，感到特別快樂。越快樂就越想見到她。
家興： 家奇，我看你的的確確是愛上她了。
家奇： 噓，小聲點兒，別讓人聽到了。

3

家奇： 小芳，你好！
小芳： 家奇，你好！
家奇： 你忙不忙？
小芳： 不太忙，你呢？
家奇： 我也是……嗯……
小芳： 你找我有事兒嗎？
家奇： 沒有什麼特別的事兒。聽說最近正在演一部張藝謀拍的電影……
小芳： 是呀，我正打算週末去看呢！
家奇： 真巧，我也打算週末去呢！你跟你的男朋友一起去嗎？
小芳： 我還沒有男朋友呢。
家奇： 太好了！！！
小芳： 家奇？
家奇： 對不起，我是說我們一起去看，行不行？
小芳： 好啊，那我請你看。
家奇： 不行，應該我請你，才行。
小芳： 爲什麼呢？
家奇： 因爲你心地善良，對人特別友好。
小芳： 家奇，你也是。
家奇： 你性格活潑、開朗大方，喜歡你的男孩子特別多。
小芳： 那你呢？
家奇： 我想我是愛上了你！
小芳： 家奇，我也很喜歡你。
家奇： 你也喜歡我？爲什麼？
小芳： 你人很真誠，有責任感，也有幽默感，喜歡幫別人的忙，正是我要找的白馬王子。

Lesson 13 約會

家奇： 我真有福氣！

小芳： 我才有福氣呢。

VOCABULARY

1	*女孩兒	女孩儿	nǚhái r	N.	girl
2	個子	个子	gèzi	N.	height
3	*矮	矮	ǎi	Adj.	short (height)
4	能歌善舞	能歌善舞	nénggē-shànwǔ	IE	good at singing and dancing
5	活潑	活泼	huópō	Adj.	lively
6	*男孩兒	男孩儿	nánhái r	N.	boy
7	*不但	不但	búdàn	Conj.	not only
8	*而且	而且	érqiě	Conj.	besides (formal)
9	不但…而且…	不但…而且…	búdàn…érqiě…		not only…, but also…
10	心地善良	心地善良	xīndì shànliáng	IE	good-hearted
11	友好	友好	yǒuhǎo	Adj.	friendly
12	感到	感到	gǎndào	V.	to feel (formal)
13	*場	场	chǎng	MW	*measure word for movies*
14	想法	想法	xiǎngfǎ	N.	idea
15	*卻	却	què	Adv.	but (formal)
16	*對…有意思	对…有意思	duì…yǒu yìsi	VP	to be interested in sb.
17	*真誠	真诚	zhēnchéng	Adj.	sincere
18	*責任感	责任感	zérèngǎn	N.	sense of responsibility
19	*幽默感	幽默感	yōumògǎn	N.	sense of humor
20	白馬王子	白马王子	báimǎ wángzǐ	NP	Prince Charming, Mr. Right
21	心事	心事	xīnshì	N.	sth. weighing on one's mind
22	傻	傻	shǎ	Adj.	silly
23	笑	笑	xiào	V.	to laugh
24	*傻笑	傻笑	shǎxiào	V.	to laugh in a silly way
25	過來人	过来人	guòláirén	N.	person who has had the experience
26	*中等個兒	中等个儿	zhōngděng gèr	NP	of the average height

27	*僅僅	仅仅	jǐnjǐn	Adv.	only (formal)
28	每次	每次	měi cì	NP	each time
29	有人	有人	yǒu rén	NP	somebody
30	*需要	需要	xūyào	V.	to need
31	*主動	主动	zhǔdòng	Adj.	active, to offer to do
32	*幫忙	帮忙	bāng máng	V.-O.	to help
33	熱心	热心	rèxīn	Adj.	warm-hearted, enthusiastic
34	*並（不/沒）	并（不/没）	bìng (bù/méi)	Adv.	*used to emphasize*
35	討人喜歡	讨人喜欢	tǎo rén xǐhuan	IE	lovable
36	*替	替	tì	Prep.	to do sth. in place of sb
37	開口	开口	kāi kǒu	V.-O.	to ask
38	說明	说明	shuōmíng	V.	to indicate
39	好感	好感	hǎogǎn	N.	good impression
40	*尷尬	尴尬	gāngà	Adj.	awkward, embarrassed
41	*如果	如果	rúguǒ	Conj.	*if (formal)*
42	*永遠	永远	yǒngyuǎn	Adv.	forever
43	單相思	单相思	dānxiāngsī	V.	unrequited love
44	不是個滋味兒	不是个滋味儿	bú shì ge zīwèir	IE	It is horrible. / It is a terrible feeling.
45	*滋味兒	滋味儿	zīwèir	N.	taste (of doing sth., metaphorical)
46	*笨	笨	bèn	Adj.	silly
47	張藝謀	张艺谋	Zhāng Yìmóu	PN	*name of a Chinese director*
48	*拍	拍	pāi	V.	to shoot (a movie)
49	*片子	片子	piānzi	N.	movie, film
50	噓	嘘	xū	Int.	*sound made to stop the noise*
51	小聲點兒	小声点儿	xiǎo shēng diǎnr	IE	Be quiet!
52	小芳	小芳	Xiǎofāng	PN	*a girl's name*
53	*部	部	bù	MW	*measure word for movies*
54	開朗大方	开朗大方	kāilǎng dàfang	IE	open and natural
55	*福氣	福气	fúqi	N.	a state of being lucky

Lesson 13 約會

Supplementary Vocabulary:

1	善	善	shàn	Adj.	kind, be good at (It can't be used alone.)
2	迪士尼	迪士尼	Díshìní	PN	Disney World
3	球迷	球迷	qiúmí	N.	fan of sports such as basketball, football…
4	石頭	石头	shítou	N.	stone
5	演員	演员	yǎnyuán	N.	actor, actress
6	郵票	邮票	yóupiào	N.	stamp
7	風景畫	风景画	fēngjǐnghuà	N.	scenery paintings
8	照片	照片	zhàopiàn	N.	picture
9	教室	教室	jiàoshì	N.	classroom
10	鷹	鹰	yīng	N.	eagle
11	瘋狂	疯狂	fēngkuáng	Adj.	crazy
12	服務	服务	fúwù	V.	to serve
13	歸來	归来	guīlái	V.	to return to an original place
14	演	演	yǎn	V.	to act

GRAMMAR

1. More about prepositions

So far, we have seen many structures with prepositions, which are listed below in the table:

到目前為止，我們見過很多介詞結構，如下列表：

	Meaning as verb	Meaning as preposition
給	to give	for (the benefit of)
用	to use	with (instrument), by means of
跟	to follow, to go along with	with (sb.), from (sb.)
為	to be	for the sake of, because of
替	to substitute for, to replace	on behalf of
在	to be located at	at / in (a place or time)
對	to treat, to match	to

（續表）

	Meaning as verb	Meaning as preposition
向	to favor sb.	to, towards
比	to compete	in comparison to
從	to follow	from

E.g. 給：我給你唱歌。(I will sing for you.)
你給我出去。(You go out for me.)
你給我記住。(You just remember it for me.)
別給我出難題了。(Don't give me any trouble.)
他給我買了一套茶具。(He bought a set of tea-ware for me.)

用：我用心學習。(I put all my heart into learning.)
你用什麼愛我？我用心愛你。(How do you love me? With my heart.)
在中國，我用筷子吃飯。(In China, I eat with chopsticks.)
我的朋友用中國法子給我泡茶。
(My friend steeped tea for me using the Chinese method.)
我妹妹用中文給她的朋友寫信。
(My younger sister wrote to her friend in Chinese.)

跟：別跟我來這一套了。(Don't play tricks on me.)
我跟他學意大利語。(I am learning Italian with / from him.)
前天家奇跟一個女孩子約會了。
(The day before yesterday, Jiaqi went on a date.)
昨天他還跟女朋友看電影去了，今天卻跟女朋友吹了。
(Yesterday, he went to see a movie with his girlfriend. Today, he broke up with his girlfriend.)

爲：我爲我的朋友高興。(I am happy for my friend.)
能爲你服務我很高興。(It is my pleasure to serve you.)
我的朋友爲我做了很多事情。(My friend has done a lot for me.)
他天天爲他的女朋友買花。(He buys flowers for his girlfriend everyday.)
我們爲新來的朋友開個晚會吧！(Let's have a party for our new friend!)

Lesson 13 約會

替： 那我替你去。(Then I will go instead of you.)
你能替我買票嗎？(Can you buy tickets for me?)
我不可能替你打人。(I can't hit people for you.)
請你替我問他好。(Please say hello to him for me.)
我願意替你做很多事，可是不能替你吃飯。
(I am willing to do many things for you, but I can't eat for you.)

在： 我在紐約住。(I live in New York.)
我弟弟在北京學中文。
(My younger brother is learning Chinese in Beijing.)
今天我妹妹不在家吃飯。(My sister won't eat at home today.)
我不喜歡在圖書館看書。(I don't like reading at a library.)
我在圖書館不喜歡看書，喜歡看報。
(I don't like reading books in the library, but I like reading newspaper there.)

對： 她對人特別友好。(She is very friendly to people.)
家奇早就對她有意思。(Jiaqi has been interested in her for a while.)
這就說明她對你有好感。
(This means that she has a good impression of you.)
同學們都對下圍棋有興趣。(Students are all interested in playing Go.)
你對你弟弟說什麼了？他看起來很沮喪。
(What did you say to your younger brother? He seems to be very depressed.)

向： 他向左游去。(He swims to the left side.)
她慢慢地向我走來。(She walks toward me slowly.)
他向我介紹了自己的生活。(He told me about himself.)
老師向我們介紹中國的傳統節日。
(The teacher explains Chinese traditional festivals to us.)
圖書館，怎麼走？向前走。
(How does one get to the library? Go straight ahead.)

比： 我比你跑得快。(I run faster than you do.)
他說中文比我說得好。(He speaks better Chinese than I do.)
我的心情比以前好多了。(I am in a better mood than before.)
中國的人口比美國的多得多。
(The population in China is much bigger than that of the U.S.)
我覺得紐約的地鐵比北京的地鐵方便 (fāngbiàn)。
(I think the subway in New York is more convenient than that of Beijing.)

從： 你是從哪兒來的？ (Where are you from?)
我是從西安來的。(I am from Xi'an.)
我想從電影院走到學校去。(I want to walk to school from the cinema.)
我從老師那兒學到了很多東西。(I learnt a lot from my teachers.)
我們從父母身上得到了很多愛。(We got tons of love from our parents.)

2 而且：besides

而且 as a conjunction connects two phrases or sentences to indicate something progressive. It is very often used together with 不但．

作爲一個連詞，"而且"連接兩個短語或句子，表示進一步。它經常和"不但"搭配使用。

S 不但 A，而且 B

E.g. a. 家奇很喜歡這個女孩兒，因爲她不但聰明能幹，而且心地善良。
(Jiaqi likes this girl because she is not only smart and capable, but also very kind-hearted.)
b. 我所喜歡的女孩兒不但開朗大方，而且能歌善舞。
(The type of girls that I like is not only open and natural but also good at singing and dancing.)
c. 紐約不但是世界的首都，而且也是世界文化(wénhuà)中心。
(New York is not only the capital of the world but also the center of words cultures.)
d. 春節不但是人們慶賀新春喜迎新年的日子，而且是人們走親訪友(zǒu qīn fǎng yǒu)的好時機。
(Spring Festival is not only the day to celebrate and welcome the New Year but also a good opportunity to visit friends and relatives.)

3 S 幫助 sb.；S 幫 sb. 的忙；S 給 sb. 幫（個）忙：

E.g. a. 他喜歡幫助別人。/他喜歡幫別人的忙。/他喜歡給人幫忙。
(He likes helping others.)
b. 他幫助過你嗎？/他幫過你的忙嗎？/他給你幫過忙嗎？
(Has he helped you?)
c. 喜歡幫助別人的人總是能得到別人的喜愛。
(Those who like helping others are always loved by others.)
d. 好朋友應該相互幫助。(Friends should help each other.)
e. 給別人幫忙也就是給自己幫忙。(Helping others is actually helping oneself.)

Lesson 13 約會

> f. 請你給我幫一個忙，好不好？ (Could you please do me a favor?)
>
> g. 她需要幫助，我們幫她一下吧。(She needs help. Let's give her a hand.)
>
> h. 大國應該幫助小國，大人應該幫助小孩。
> (Bigger countries should help small ones and adults should help children.)
>
> i. 他很熱心，總是在幫這個幫那個。
> (He is warm-hearted, always helping with this or that.)

NOTE: It is incorrect to say "我幫忙他" because 幫忙 is a V.-O. compound.
注意：不能說"我幫忙他"，因爲"幫忙"是一個動賓複合詞。

4 Num. + MW + NP

Number 數字	Measure word 量詞	Noun Phrase 名詞短語
一	部 / 場	電影
兩	名	畫家 / 藝術家 / 作家
三	瓶	酒 / 水 / 可樂
四	隻	貓 / 狗 / 鳥 / 手 / 眼睛
五	種	語言 / 話
六	張	票 / 床 / 桌子
七	本	書 / 字典
八	輛	自行車 / 汽車
九	家	飯館兒 / 超市 / 書店
十	口	人 / 飯
十一	位	老師 / 朋友 / 同學
十二	頓	飯
十三	把	椅子 / 叉子 / 刀子
十四	雙	筷子 / 手
十五	杯	茶 / 酒
十六	件 (jiàn)	衣服 (yīfu: clothes) / 事情
十七	間	教室 / 屋子
十八	所	學校 / 大學
十九	套	茶具

287

5 Verbal expression in series: Serial constructions

These structures usually involve two actions, often without any conjunctional devices. The second verb may follow the first verb directly, or the first verb may take an intervening object: 去上學 / 去學校上學. In Chinese this kind of structure is very common. It may be used to indicate purpose, wishes, or just to relate what has happened.

這個結構通常包含兩個沒有任何連詞標誌連接的動作。第二個動詞緊接著第一個動詞，第一個動詞可能會帶著賓語：去上學 / 去學校上學。在漢語中這種結構很常見。它可以表示目的、願望，或者僅僅表達已經發生的相關事情。

SVP_1+VP_2

a. 我去紐約參觀博物館。(I go to New York to visit museums.)
b. 他們到飛機場送朋友。(They went to the airport to see friends off.)
c. 我想到中國學中文。(I want to go to China to learn Chinese.)

6 S 自己 / 一個人 VP: sb. does sth. by/for oneself

a. 你自己去看吧。(You go and look for yourself.)
b. 還是我自己去問吧。(I might as well go and ask by myself.)
c. 我自己買的。(I bought it by myself.)
d. 你一個人笑什麼？(Why are you laughing by yourself?)
e. 我一個人住。(I live by myself.)
f. 她不願意一個人去國外。(She is not willing to go abroad by herself.)

7 才 used to show emphasis

"才……呢" is used to show emphasis only when there is a previous statement to deny or to show appreciation or to argue.

"才……呢" 表強調時，前面一般有一個表示否定、贊賞或者爭論的敘述。

S 才 VP 呢

a. ——我真有福氣。(I am so lucky.)
　——我才有福氣呢。(I am the real lucky one.)
b. ——你真笨！(You are silly!)
　——你才笨呢！(You are the silly one.)
c. ——你真聰明！(You are smart!)
　——你才聰明呢！(You are the smarter one.)

d.——我很喜歡吃中國菜。(I like eating Chinese food.)
——我才喜歡吃呢。(I am the one who likes it more.)

8 S 並不/沒 VP

並 precedes 不/沒 to emphasize the fact that something is not true or has not happened.

"並"放在"不/沒"前，強調某事不是事實或者沒發生過。

 a. 雖然我並不會打籃球，可是我是一個球迷 (qiúmí)。
(Although I can't play basketball, I am a fan of it.)
b. 我並沒去過中國。(I actually have not been to China.)

It is often used together with "S 以爲 A, 其實 B".
它通常與"S 以爲 A, 其實 B"連用。

S 以爲 VP, 其實並不/沒 VP

 a. 我以爲她很喜歡我，其實她並不喜歡我。
(I thought that she liked me, but actually she doesn't.)
b. 他以爲我多才多藝，其實並不是那麼一回事。
(He thought that I am versatile but actually it is not the case.)
c. 我以爲他把飯做好了，其實並沒有。
(I thought he had fixed the dinner, but he actually did not.)

9 Wh-word used as indefinites

Questions words such as 什麼, 誰, 哪兒, 怎麼, 幾, 多少 can also occur in sentences that are not questions (no question mark at the end!), in which case their meaning changes. These sentences are mostly negatives (i.e. containing 不/沒), and the meaning of the question words changes into the following:

"什麼, 誰, 哪兒, 怎麼, 幾, 多少"等疑問詞也能出現在沒有疑問的句子中（句尾沒有疑問標誌！）。在這種情況下它們的意思發生了變化。這些句子多是否定意義的（比如包含"不/沒"），疑問詞的意思轉換如下：

Structure	Meaning in English	Meaning in Chinese
不/沒……什麼	"nothing special", "nothing in particular", "not...anything"	"沒有什麼特別的", "沒有……什麼事物"
不/沒……誰	"nobody special", "nobody in particular", "not...anyone"	"沒有誰是特別的", "沒有……什麼人"

(續表)

Structure	Meaning in English	Meaning in Chinese
不/沒……哪兒	"nowhere special", "nowhere in particular", "not...anywhere"	"沒有什麼地方特別的", "沒有……什麼地方"
不/沒怎麼	"not particularly", "not that..."	"沒有什麼特別的", "不是那樣/那麼……"
沒幾……	"not that many"	"沒有那麼多"
沒多少……	"not that many"	"沒有那麼多"

E.g.
a. ——過生日你想要什麼?(What do you want for your birthday?)
　——我不想要什麼。(Nothing in particular.)
b. ——昨天你們買什麼了?(What did you buy yesterday?)
　——沒買什麼。(Nothing in particular.)
c. ——這幾個女孩子,你最喜歡誰?
　　(Who is your favourite among these few girls?)
　——我不喜歡誰。(Nobody in particular.)
d. ——去年你跟誰出國了?(Whom did you go abroad with last year?)
　——我沒跟誰呀。我自己去的。(I didn't go with anyone. I went by myself.)
e. ——過節你去哪兒了?(Where did you go during the holiday?)
　——我沒去哪兒。(I didn't go anywhere.)
f. ——你想怎麼做這個菜?(How do you want to fix the dish?)
　——我還沒怎麼想呢。(I have not thought about it particularly.)
g. 我不怎麼想去上課。(I don't want to go to class that much.)
h. 我沒幾個朋友。(I only have a few friends.)
i. 沒幾天就要放假了。(We are going to have a break in a few days.)
j. 沒有多少人會下圍棋。(Not so many people know how to play Go.)
k. 我誰都喜歡。(I like everyone.)
l. 我什麼飯都不會做。(I can not make any food.)

 S 約 + sb.+（一起）+ V + O：to ask sb. to do sth. together

E.g. a. 我想約她去看電影。(I want to ask her to go to see a movie together.)
　　 b. 我想約她一起吃飯。(I want to ask her to eat together.)

290

Lesson 13 約會

S 跟 sb. 約好 + (一起) + V + O: sb. will do sth. with sb. else

E.g. a. 我跟他約好下週一起吃午飯。(He and I will have lunch together next week.)
b. 他跟我約好一起到中國去學中文。
(He and I will go to China to study Chinese together.)

Summary:

而且 as a conjunction connects two phrases or sentences to indicate something progressive. It is very often used together with 不但.

Please note that it is incorrect to say "我幫忙他" because 幫忙 is a V.-O. compound.

Serial structures usually involve two actions, often without any conjunctional devices. The second verb may follow the first verb directly, or the first verb may take an intervening object: 去上學 / 去學校上學. In Chinese this kind of structure is very common. It may be used to indicate purpose, wishes, or just to relate what has happened.

"才……呢" is used to show emphasis only when there is previous statement to deny or to show appreciation or to argue.

並 precedes 不 / 沒 to emphasize the fact that something is not true or has not happened.

Questions words such as 什麼，誰，哪兒，怎麼，幾，多少 can also occur in sentences that are not questions (no question mark at the end!), in which case their meaning changes. These sentences are mostly negatives (i.e. containing 不 / 沒), and the meaning of the question words changes into the following:
不 / 沒……什麼："nothing special", "nothing in particular", "not... anything"
不 / 沒……誰： "nobody special", "nobody in particular", "not... anyone"
不 / 沒……哪兒："nowhere special", "nowhere in particular", "not... anywhere"
不 / 沒怎麼：   "not particularly", "not that..."
沒幾……：   "no particular number", "not that many"
沒多少……：   "no particular number", "not that many"

Patterns:

● 給 ‖ 我給你唱歌。(I will sing for you.)

● 用 ‖ 我用心學習。(I put all my heart into learning.)

● 跟 ‖ 別跟我來這一套了。(Don't play tricks on me.)

- 爲 ‖ 我爲我的朋友高興。(I am happy for my friend.)
- 替 ‖ 那我替你去。(Then I will go instead of you.)
- 在 ‖ 我在紐約住。(I live in New York.)
- 對 ‖ 她對人特別友好。(She is very friendly to people.)
- 向 ‖ 他向左游去。(He swims to the left side.)
- 比 ‖ 我比你跑得快。(I run faster than you do.)
- 從 ‖ 你是從哪兒來的？(Where are you from?)
- S 不但 A，而且 B ‖ 家奇很喜歡這個女孩兒,因爲她不但聰明能幹,而且心地善良。
 (Jiaqi likes this girl because she is not only smart and capable, but also very kind-hearted.)
- S 幫助 sb.；S 幫 sb. 的忙；S 給 sb. 幫（個）忙 ‖ 他喜歡幫助別人。/ 他喜歡幫別人的忙。/ 他喜歡給人幫忙。
 (He likes helping others.)
- S VP$_1$+VP$_2$ ‖ 我去紐約參觀博物館。(I go to New York to visit museums.)
- S 自己 / 一個人 VP ‖ 你自己去看吧。(You go and look for yourself.)
 你一個人笑什麼？(Why are you laughing by yourself?)
- S 才 VP 呢 ‖ ——我真有福氣。(I am so lucky.)
 ——我才有福氣呢。(I am the real lucky one.)
- S 並不 / 沒 VP ‖ 我並沒去過中國。(I actually have not been to China.)
- S 以爲 VP, 其實並不 / 沒 VP ‖ 我以爲她很喜歡我，其實她並不喜歡我。
 (I thought that she liked me, but actually she doesn't.)
- Wh-word used as indefinites ‖ ——過生日你想要什麼？
 (What do you want for your birthday?)
 ——我不想要什麼。(Nothing in particular.)
 我不怎麼想去上課。
 (I don't want to go to class that much.)
- S 約 + sb. +（一起）+ V + O ‖ 我想約她一起吃飯。(I want to ask her to eat together.)
- S 跟 sb. 約好 +（一起）+ V + O ‖ 我跟他約好下週一起吃午飯。
 (He and I will have lunch together next week.)

Lesson 13　約會

IN CLASS ACTIVITIES

1 Answer the following questions according to the information given in the text:

① 跟家奇約會的女孩兒是怎麽樣的一個人？

② 家奇爲什麽喜歡這個女孩兒？

③ 她覺得家奇是一個什麽樣的人？

④ 家奇跟她在一起的時候感覺怎麽樣？

⑤ 家奇不知道什麽？

⑥ 家興説他應該做什麽？

2 Please do role play according to the dialogues given below:

- A：你這兩天看起來挺高興的。
- B：是呀，我樂著呢！
- A：這麽高興，有什麽好事？
- B：我喜歡的女孩兒也喜歡上我了。
- A：真的嗎？是哪個女孩子啊？
- B：她性格開朗，善良漂亮，不高不矮，不胖 (pàng: over-weight) 不瘦 (shòu: skinny)。
- A：這麽好的女孩兒，能給我説説是誰嗎？
- B：不能告訴你。我和她天生一對。
- A：看你美的，不是自作多情吧？
- B：才不是呢，今天她還看了我一眼。

走近中國——初級漢語教程
APPROACHING CHINA : ELEMENTARY CHINESE

A 哦？只看了你一眼，你就不知道自己是誰了？
B 她的眼睛太美麗了，她笑起來更好看。
A 瞧你，我看你是愛上她了吧？
B 也許吧。

配 (pèi: to get) 眼鏡 (yǎnjìng: glasses)

A 我的眼鏡壞了，我想去修 (xiū: to fix) 一修。
B 你修什麼呀修。去眼鏡店再配一副 (fù: a pair of) 新的不就行了？
A 配新的不是太貴了嗎？
B 在中國配眼鏡要比在美國配便宜多了。再說驗光 (yàn guāng: optometry) 不要錢。
A 好，聽你的。
……
A 師傅，我想配一副眼鏡。
C 好，請你先選鏡架 (jìngjià: frames) 吧。
A 我就要這個吧。
C 好，我給你驗光。你想要什麼樣的鏡片 (jìngpiàn: lens)？
A 我要這個吧。一共多少錢？
C 一共四百二十塊。

HOMEWORK

1 Please rewrite or complete the following sentences with the given structures:

① 感恩節是下個禮拜。（快 V 了）

➡ 感恩節快到了。

② 我不舒服，不能去上課，請你告訴老師。（A 替 B……）

➡

③ 他跟人說話很友好。（A 對 B ……）

➡

Lesson 13 約會

④ 家奇喜歡小芳有兩個原因：一是她心地善良，二是她開朗大方。
（S 不但 A，而且 B）

⑤ 他一會兒替同學買書，一會兒為同學拿東西。（S 幫 sb. 的忙）

⑥ 我和我同學在一起。我們學中文。（A 跟 B 在一起 VP）

⑦ 現在我妹妹不跟我一起住了。（S 自己 / 一個人 VP）

⑧ 他以為我找到工作了，其實……（S 並不 / 沒 VP）

2 Please rewrite the following sentences using a Wh-word as an indefinite. (The Wh-words should appear in a negative structure. The meanings will be changed accordingly.)

① 我喜歡吃的東西很多。

② 他最近不太忙。

③ 過生日，他給我買了很多東西。

④ 我們喜歡書法，聽音樂。

⑤ 這兩個女孩子我都很喜歡。

⑥ 很多人都會畫畫兒。

⑦ 再過幾天就是春節了。

走近中國——初級漢語教程
APPROACHING CHINA : ELEMENTARY CHINESE

⑧ 我喜歡跟男朋友一起學習。 ➡ _____

⑨ 我不想喝茶。 ➡ _____

3 Translate the following sentences into Chinese:

① I thought that he would be willing to come, but actually he was not willing to come.
_____

② You are so handsome！ You are the one who is handsome. (才……呢)
_____

③ -He came back by himself. -Really? You go and see for yourself.
_____

④ We are buddies. We like being together, and we do a lot of things.
_____

⑤ We often play basketball together.
_____

⑥ I would like to introduce you to this famous artist.
_____

⑦ We want to go to London to visit museums there.
_____

⑧ We like him because he likes helping others.
_____

Lesson 13 約會

4 Please complete the following sentences with appropriate prepositions:

比　向　替　對　從　用　給　跟　爲

① 我可以幫你，可是我不能 ___替___ 你寫作業。

② 他_____我說："請你相信 (xiāngxìn: to believe) 我。"

③ 我_____他一起買了很多東西。

④ 我_____他做飯，他爲我泡茶。

⑤ 他_____我介紹了_____紐約來的朋友和家人。

⑥ 我_____他買了一本書。

⑦ 她_____中文說："我_____你高多了。"

5 Please write the appropriate measure words for the following phrases:

家　把　輛　名　套　部　杯　隻　件　雙　本　張　口　頓　種　所

一 ___部___ 電影　　兩_____茶具　　一_____藝術家　　三_____酒

一_____鳥　　　　兩_____事　　　一_____筷子　　　兩_____字典

一_____飯　　　　三_____人　　　兩_____超市　　　一_____車

一_____叉子　　　一_____語言　　兩_____學校　　　一_____床

6 Please read the following paragraph in Pinyin:

　　Xiǎofāng yào guò shēngrì le. Jiāqí xiǎng qù Zhōngguóchéng de Dà Zhōnghuá chāojí shìchǎng, gěi Xiǎofāng mǎi jǐ yàng tā zuì xǐhuan chī de Zhōngguó shípǐn, kěshì bù zhīdào zěnme qù. Jiāxīng juéde zhè hěn róngyì, ràng Jiāqí mǎi zhāng dìtú kàn jiù xíng le. Kěshì Jiāqí pà kànbudǒng, yīnwèi Zhōngguóchéng de jiēmíng hěn duō dōu shì yòng Zhōngwén xiě de. Jiāxīng jiù ràng Jiāqí xiān zuò dìtiě, dàole Zhōngguóchéng zài qù wènwèn biérén. Jiāqí zài dìtiě shàng pèngdào yí wèi hǎoxīnrén. Zhè ge rén cháng qù Dà Zhōnghuá chāojí shìchǎng. Tā gāosù Jiāqí chūle dìtiězhàn wǎng yòu guǎi, ránhòu yìzhí wǎng qián zǒu; dàole dìyī ge shízì lùkǒu wǎng zuǒ guǎi, zài wǎng qián zǒu jǐ bù, jiù huì kàndào hěn duō shāngdiàn. Dà Zhōnghuá chāojí shìcháng jiù zài mǎlù de duìmiàn. Jiāqí yìbiān zǒu yìbiān wèn, hěn kuài jiù zhǎodàole chāoshì. Chāoshì de dōngxi duō, rén yě duō, Jiāqí zhǎolái-zhǎoqù, jiùshì zhǎobudào xiǎng mǎi de dōngxi. Shǐ tā gǎndào qíguài de shì Zhōngguóchéng de hěn duō rén dōu bú huì shuō pǔtōnghuà. Ràng tā gǎndào gāoxìng de shì tā shuō de pǔtōnghuà bǐ Zhōngguóchéng de hěn duō rén dōu hǎo.

Chinese Concepts of Numbers

  Numbers play an important part in Chinese life. They are used everywhere. But they are not just numbers. In terms of language, numbers don't have to be accurate. It is always something that one should be able to interpret. For example, when somebody says "過兩天我們再說", it in no way means that it is just two days. Similarly, "給我買幾個杯子" also carries a specific meaning. Don't feel puzzled if you want to fix some Chinese food by following the directions of a real Chinese cook book.

  It is believed that "三 three" is a boundary line that people don't want to cross. Thus, if somebody does something inappropriate to offend somebody, this person might be forgiven for the first two times. But he would likely be punished if he did it again for the third time. Therefore, there is the expression: "一而再，可是不能再而三".

  Chinese people also believe some numbers will bring bad luck. "四" is always avoided for it sounds like "死". "七" is not considered a lucky number because it sounds like "去", which is an other way of saying "死". In contrast, "三", "六", "九" are lucky numbers. Business people especially believe this. If you do a little research, you may find many Chinese restaurants phone numbers containing those specific numbers and "八" in particular.

  Numbers are everywhere in the language. For example, "二百五（250）" means somebody who is rash. "三心二意" means somebody doesn't concentrate on one thing and, "三八" implies a woman who does not have good manners.

LESSON 14　中國城

　　小芳要過生日了。家奇想去中國城的大中華超級市場，給小芳買幾樣她最喜歡吃的中國食品，可是不知道怎麼去。家興覺得這很容易，讓家奇買張地圖看就行了。可是家奇怕看不懂，因爲中國城的街名很多都是用中文寫的。家興就讓家奇先坐地鐵，到了中國城再去問問別人。家奇在地鐵上碰到一位好心人。這個人常去大中華超級市場。她告訴家奇，出了地鐵站往右拐，然後一直往前走；到了第一個十字路口往左拐，再往前走幾步，就會看到很多商店。大中華超級市場就在馬路的對面。家奇一邊走一邊問，很快就找到了超市。超市的東西多，人也多，家奇找來找去就是找不到想買的東西。使他感到奇怪的是中國城的很多人都不會說普通話。讓他感到高興的是他說的普通話比中國城的很多人都好。

1

家奇：　家興，你去過中國城的大中華超級市場沒有？

家興：　大中華超級市場？我沒有去過。你去那兒做什麼？

家奇：　有事兒。

家興：　什麼事兒？讓小芳帶你去，不就行了？

家奇： 小芳要過生日了，我想去大中華給她買幾樣她最喜歡吃的中國食品。

家興： 這很容易，問問人就行了。

家奇： 可是我不想說英文。

家興： 買張地圖一看不就找到了？

家奇： 我看不懂。

家興： 你不會看地圖？上北下南，左西右東。

家奇： 不是我不會看，我想中國城的街名可能很多都是用中文寫的[1]。

家興： 對，我怎麼忘了？

家奇： 我以為你去過呢！

家興： 我只去過一次中國城。

家奇： 去中國城坐幾號地鐵？

家興： 這我知道。坐一號，在 Canal 下，就到中國城了。

家奇： 謝謝。

家興： 中國城很大，人很多，也很熱鬧。

家奇： 有人說到了中國城就跟到了中國一樣。

家興： 很多人都是這麼說的。你到了那兒，問問人就知道大中華超級市場在哪兒了。

家奇： 只好這樣了。

家興： 帶上手機，別把你走丟了。

家奇： 放心吧！把手機丟了有可能，把我丟了不可能。

家興： 這我相信。

2 （In the subway... ）

家奇： 對不起，這位女士，您是中國人吧？

女士： 是的。

家奇： 那您去過大中華超級市場嗎？

女士： 我常去。那兒的東西又多又便宜。

家奇： 那麻煩您告訴我怎麼到那兒，好嗎？

---

[1] It is not actually true that street names in China town are written in Chinese.

Lesson 14 中國城

女士： 好哇！出了地鐵站，往右轉。

家奇： 出了地鐵站，往右拐。然後呢？

女士： 然後一直往前走。

家奇： 然後一直往前走。

女士： 到了第一個十字路口往左轉。

家奇： 好，到了第一個十字路口往左拐。然後呢？

女士： 再往前走幾步，就會看到很多商店。

家奇： 嗯，好的。

女士： 大中華超級市場就是馬路對面中間那一家。不知道我說清楚了沒有？

家奇： 很清楚，謝謝你！

女士： 不客氣。

3

家興： 家奇，你找到大中華了沒有？

家奇： 找到了。我運氣很好，在地鐵上碰到一位好心人。

家興： 那就好。

家奇： 下了地鐵以後，我邊走邊問，很快就找到了超市。

家興： 不太難找吧？

家奇： 路是不太難找，可是給小芳買東西卻不太容易。

家興： 是不是你忘了要買的食品的名字？

家奇： 不是，是東西太多，我找來找去就是找不到。

家興： 你可以問人啊。

家奇： 是啊，我問了，使我感到奇怪的是，那兒的很多人都不會說普通話。

家興： 對，中國城有很多廣東人，他們說粵語。他們說話很難懂。那你就用英文問唄。

家奇： 他們聽不懂英文。其實，我要找的東西就在我的後邊。

家興： 是嗎？

家奇： 這次去中國城，讓我感到高興的是，我說的普通話比那兒的很多人都好。

家興: 家奇,那兒的東西很便宜吧?

家奇: 是啊,很便宜。比方說我三塊錢就買了兩磅葡萄。一條一斤多重的魚才五塊錢左右,而且條條都是活的。

家興: 聽說十幾塊錢就可以買一隻大龍蝦了。

家奇: 以後要是想吃海鮮的話,就到中國城去買。

VOCABULARY

1	*中華	中华	Zhōnghuá	N.	China
2	*超級	超级	chāojí	Adj.	super
3	*市場	市场	shìchǎng	N.	market
4	幾樣	几样	jǐ yàng	Q.	several kinds
5	*地圖	地图	dìtú	N.	map
6	*街名	街名	jiēmíng	N.	name of the street
7	碰	碰	pèng	V.	to run into
8	好心人	好心人	hǎoxīnrén	N.	good hearted person
9	*地鐵站	地铁站	dìtiězhàn	N.	subway station
10	*往	往	wǎng	Prep.	to, towards
11	*右	右	yòu	N.	right (side)
12	*拐	拐	guǎi	V.	to turn
13	*一直	一直	yìzhí	Adv.	straight
14	走	走	zǒu	V.	to walk
15	*十字	十字	shízì	N.	the cross
16	*路口	路口	lùkǒu	N.	intersection
17	*左	左	zuǒ	N.	left (side)
18	*馬路	马路	mǎlù	N.	road
19	*對面	对面	duìmiàn	N.	the opposite
20	*使	使	shǐ	V.	to make…feel
21	*普通話	普通话	pǔtōnghuà	PN	Mandarin
22	帶	带	dài	V.	to take
23	*北	北	běi	N.	(the) north
24	*南	南	nán	N.	(the) south

Lesson 14 中國城

25	西	西	xī	N.	(the) west
26	東	东	dōng	N.	(the) east
27 *	號	号	hào	N.	number
28	只好這樣了	只好这样了	zhǐhǎo zhèyàng le	IE	no other choices but this
29 *	帶上	带上	dàishàng	V.-C.	to bring sth. with
30 *	手機	手机	shǒujī	N.	cell phone
31 *	走丟	走丢	zǒudiū	V.-C.	to get lost
32	放心吧	放心吧	fàng xīn ba	IE	Don't worry!
33	相信	相信	xiāngxìn	V.	to believe
34 *	女士	女士	nǚshì	N.	lady
35 *	便宜	便宜	piányi	Adj.	cheap
36 *	轉	转	zhuǎn	V.	to turn
37	運氣	运气	yùnqi	N.	luck
38 *	廣東人	广东人	Guǎngdōngrén	PN	people from Guangdong Province, Cantonese
39	粵語	粤语	Yuèyǔ	N.	Cantonese (language)
40 *	後邊	后边	hòubian	N.	behind
41	比方說	比方说	bǐfang shuō	IE	for instance
42 *	塊	块	kuài	MW	measure word for money
43 *	磅	磅	bàng	MW	pound
44 *	葡萄	葡萄	pútao	N.	grape
45 *	條	条	tiáo	MW	measure word for things that are long or strip-like
46 *	斤	斤	jīn	MW	Catty (units of weight =500 grams=1.1 pounds)
47 *	活	活	huó	Adj.	alive
48 *	龍蝦	龙虾	lóngxiā	N.	lobster
49 *	海鮮	海鲜	hǎixiān	N.	sea food

Supplementary Vocabulary:

1	功夫	功夫	gōngfu	N.	kongfu
2	游泳衣	游泳衣	yóuyǒngyī	N.	swimming suit
3	商場	商场	shāngchǎng	N.	mall

| 4 | 書店 | 书店 | shūdiàn | N. | bookstore |
| 5 | 酒吧 | 酒吧 | jiǔbā | N. | bar |

GRAMMAR

1 Telling directions

(S) V 了……, 往 direction V, 然後……; 再 VP, 就 VP 了

E.g. a. 出了飛機場，往右拐，然後一直往前走，再過兩條街，就到了。
(After coming out of the airport, make a right turn. Then, go straight ahead. You will be there in two blocks.)

b. 下了汽車，往左轉，向東走五分鐘，右拐；再向前走五分鐘，就到了。
(After getting out of the bus, make a left turn. After walking about five minutes or so, turn right. Go ahead for another five minutes, then you will be there.)

c. 到了火車站，往西走，然後往左轉；到了十字路口再往前走幾步，就到了。
(Arriving at the railway station, walk to the west, then make a left turn. At the intersection, go ahead a bit more and you will be there.)

d. 她說出了地鐵站，往右拐，然後一直往前走；到了第一個十字路口往左拐，再往前走幾步，就會看到很多商店。大中華超級市場就在馬路的對面。
(She said that after leaving the subway, you should make a right turn. Then go straight ahead. At the first intersection, turn left. Go ahead a bit more, you will see many stores. The Grand China Supermarket is right on the opposite side of the street.)

2 Units of Chinese RMB

Chinese money is called 人民幣 (rénmínbì), or RMB in short, which means "The People's Currency". Chinese money has three basic units of currency: 元、角、分. These correspond to the American "dollar", "dime" and "cent". The difference is that, in Chinese, you always have to mention all three. So "¥3.69" is not "three dollar sixty-nine cents" but "three dollars, six dimes, nine cents".

中國貨幣叫做人民幣，或者簡稱RMB。RMB意思是"人民的貨幣"。中國貨幣有三種基本單位：元、角、分。它們類似於美元中的"美元""十美分""美分"。二者的不同在於漢語的貨幣表達中必須提及全部三種單位。比如"¥3.69"不是"三美元六十九美分"而是"三元六角九分"（三美元、六個十美分、九美分）。

Lesson 14 中國城

1 元 equals 10 角 , 1 角 equals 10 分. In daily speech, people also refer to the 元 as 塊 and 角 as 毛. The word 分 can often be left out.

1元等於10角，1角等於10分。在日常口語中，人們常把"元"說成"塊"，把"角"說成"毛"，而"分"常常被省略。

Informal Expressions			Formal Expressions		
塊	kuài	a dollar	元	yuán	a dollar
毛	máo	10 cents	角	jiǎo	10 cents
分	fēn	1 cent	分	fēn	1 cent

E.g.
一 (yì) 毛 / 角　　兩毛 / 角　　五毛 / 角
一 (yì) 塊 / 元　　兩塊 / 元　　五塊 / 元
十塊 / 元　　二十塊 / 元　　五十塊 / 元　　一百塊 / 元

Chinese currency is issued in the following denominations: one, two, five, ten, twenty, fifty and one hundred 元; one, two and five 角; and one, two and five 分. You may go to http://www.chinatoday.com/fin/mon to view the pictures of RMB.

中國發行了以下幾種面值的貨幣：1、2、5、10、20、50和100元；1、2、5角；和1、2、5分。你可以去http://www.chinatoday.com/fin/mon 這個網站看人民幣的式樣圖片。

Informal Way of Spelling Currency: 貨幣的非正式表達

Number+ Unit₁+ Number+ Unit₂+ Number	Number+ Unit₁/₂ + Number
¥ 2.25（兩塊兩毛五）	¥ 0.85（八毛五）
¥ 4.73（四塊七毛三）	¥ 99.90（九十九塊九）
¥ 37.41（三十七塊四毛一）	

Formal Way of Spelling Currency: 貨幣的正式表達

Number+ Unit₁+ Number + Unit₂+ Number+ Unit₃	Number+ Unit₁ + Number+Unit₂
¥ 64.79（六十四元七角九分）	¥ 0.75（七角五分）
¥ 177.43（一百七十七元四角三分）	¥ 10.50（十元五角）

Amount with "零"（líng）

If there is no figure for the intermediate unit, we have to use 零 as an intermediate. Also the last unit cannot be omitted.

如果數字沒有中間單位，我們必須使用"零"。這時，最後的那個單位不能省略。

> Number + Unit₁ + 零 (+ Unit₂) + Number + Unit₃
>
> ￥1.06（一塊零六分）
> ￥10.05（十塊零五分）
> ￥48.01（四十八塊零一分）
> ￥100.05（一百塊零五分）

NOTE: Spoken and written forms don't go together.
注意：口語和書面語形式不能混合使用。

> **E.g.** 五元八毛

3 Expressions of buying and selling

The most common way of asking for the price of something is: 多少錢？(How much?) Or, 幾塊錢？(How much?) if a small amount is expected.
問價格最常用的表達是"多少錢？"如果預計數額不大，也可以説"幾塊錢？"

If one is asking specifically how something is sold (i.e. how much per pound/catty etc.), we can say: 怎麼賣 (mài: to sell)？(How is it sold?) Or one can ask directly: 多少錢一斤？(How much per catty?)
如果要確切地問東西怎麼賣（比如：每磅/斤多少錢？），我們可以説："怎麼賣？"或者也可以直接問："多少錢一斤？"

Regarding the price of each individual item, we have to use the relevant measure words.
關於單個項目的價格，我們可以用相關量詞。

> NP 多少錢一磅/斤？；一磅/斤 NP 多少錢？；多少錢一磅/斤 NP？

> **E.g.** a. 葡萄多少錢一磅？(How much per pound for the grapes?)
> b. 一磅葡萄多少錢？(How much per pound for the grapes?)
> c. 多少錢一磅葡萄？(How much per pound for the grapes?)

Of course, Chinese also has words that correspond to the English "cost", as in "How much does this cost?". We can use 要, 賣 or 得 (děi). For instance:
當然，漢語中也有相當於英語"How much does this cost?"中"cost"的表達，我們用"要""賣"，或者"得 (děi)"。例如：

> **E.g.** a. 這瓶酒要十塊六毛八。(This bottle of wine costs ￥10.68.)

Lesson 14 中國城

> b. 那本字典賣九十二塊零五分。(That dictionary costs ￥92.05.)
> c. 這一頓飯得很多錢！(This meal costs a lot of money!)
> d. 一條魚只要五塊錢。(Each fish only costs five dollars.)
> e. 比方說三塊錢他就買了兩磅葡萄。
>   (For instance, he bought two pounds of grapes with only three dollars.)
> f. 我今天買了一條二十多塊錢的魚。
>   (I bought a fish at the price of more than 20 dollars today.)
> g. 我的魚一條就得二十多塊錢。(My fish costs more than 20 dollars each.)

4 使/讓 sb. (感到) Adj. 的 (事情) 是……：what makes sb. feel ... is that...

Both 使 and 讓 can be used in this structure. The only difference is that 使 is very formal while 讓 is colloquial.
"使"和"讓"都可以用在這個結構中。唯一的不同是"使"非常正式，而"讓"則偏於口語。

> a. 使他感到奇怪的是這兒的很多人都不會說普通話。
>   (What makes him feel strange is that many people here can't speak Mandarin.)
> b. 讓他感到高興的是他說的普通話比那兒的很多人都好。
>   (What makes him feel happy is that his Mandarin is better than many people there.)
> c. 讓我最高興的事情是我的中文說得很好。
>   (What pleases me the most is the fact that I speak Chinese very well.)
> d. 使我沮喪的是考試沒考好。
>   (What makes me feel depressed is that I did poorly in the test.)

5 (S) 讓/叫 sb. VP, 不就行/得了？：S let / ask sb. VP, and that will be fine.

> a. 讓/叫小芳帶你去, 不就行了？
>   (You ask Xiaofang to take you there, and that will be fine.)
> b. 你女朋友讓你做飯, 你做不就得了？
>   (If your girlfriend asked you to cook, then you just do it. That will be fine.)
> c. 他讓誰來, 誰來不就行了？
>   (If he asks somebody to come, then the person just comes. And that will be fine.)
> d. 要是你不想讓我去, 我不去, 不就行了？
>   (If you don't want me to go, then I won't go and that will be fine.)
> e. 讓他開車去, 不就行了。(Let him drive there, and that will be fine.)

6 去 PW 坐幾號地鐵 / 路公共汽車：which subway/bus to take to go to PW?

 a.——去中國城坐幾號地鐵？
　　　(Which subway should I take to go to China town?)
　　——去中國城坐一號地鐵就到了。
　　　(Take subway Number One and you can reach China town.)
b.——去哥大坐幾路公共汽車？(Which bus should I take to go to CU?)
　——去哥大坐 M4 或 M60 路公車就到了。
　　(You will reach CU by taking bus M4 or M60.)

去 PW 坐哪班飛機 / 趟火車： which flight / train to take to go to PW?

 a.——去加州坐哪班飛機好？(Which flight should I take to go to California?)
　　——去加州坐 136 次航班好一些。
　　　(It is better to take Flight 136 to go to California.)
b.——從北京到西安坐哪趟火車好？
　　(Which train should I take to go to Xi'an from Beijing?)
　——我覺得坐 T41 次好。(I think it is better to take T41.)

7 VP₁（很）有可能，VP₂ 不（太）可能：It is possible to VP₁, but not VP₂.

 a. 把手機丟了有可能，把我丟了不可能。
　　(It is possible that I will lose my cell phone but I will not get lost.)
b. 請你吃飯有可能，把我的錢給你不可能。
　　(It is possible that I will treat you to a meal but it is impossible to give you my money.)
c. 給你學習的機會很有可能，給你工作的機會不太可能。
　　(It is possible to give you the opportunity to study, but not the opportunity to work.)
d. 買東西有可能，賣東西不可能。
　　(It is possible to buy things but not to sell them.)
e. 一隻龍蝦五斤重有可能，五十斤重不可能。
　　(It is possible that a lobster weighs 5 catties, but not 50 catties.)
f. 他愛上她有可能，她愛上他不可能。
　　(It is possible for him to fall in love with her but not for her to fall in love with him.)

Lesson 14 中國城

8 NP MW MW 都 VP：each of the NP VP

In this structure, the reduplication of the measure word indicates that each noun phrase involved in the action must be plural. Please note that the position of the reduplicated measure word is fixed: it must go before the adverb 都.

在這個結構中，量詞的重疊表示和這個動作有關的名詞短語是複數。請注意重疊量詞的位置是固定的：它必須在副詞 "都" 的前面。

>
> a. 一條一斤多重的魚才五塊錢左右，而且魚條條都是活的。
>   (A fish over one catty only costs five dollars or so and each of them is alive.)
> b. 我們班的女同學個個都很漂亮，男生個個都很帥。
>   (Each of the girl students in our class is beautiful, and each of the boy students is handsome.)
> c. 我的朋友個個都多才多藝。(Each of my friends is versatile.)
> d. 他做的菜，個個都很好吃。(As for the dish he fixes, each is tasty.)
> e. 他賣的畫，張張都很貴。(As for the painting he sells, each is very expensive.)
> f. 她收養的狗，條條 / 隻隻都很可愛。
>   (As for the dogs she adopted, each is very cute.)

9 More about 多

多 with the literal meaning of "many" or "more" may also indicate approximate numbers. And the position of 多 depends on the actual number. If the numbers are in 10s (i.e. 10, 20, 30 etc.), or 100s, 多 comes after the number and before the measure word.

"多"，字面意義為 "many" 或者 "more"，可以用來表示概數。"多" 的位置取決於實際的數字。如果數字是幾十（比如：10, 20, 30 等）或者上百，"多" 位於數字後，量詞前。

> **Num. + 多 + MW + NP**

>
> a. 我有三十多塊錢。(I have 30 some *yuan*.)
> b. 他有十多個學生。(He has more than 10 students.)
> c. 我的朋友二十多歲。(My friend is more than 20 years old.)
> d. 這所大學有一百多個老師。(There are more than 100 teachers at the college.)

If the number is less than 10 (including 10), 多 follows the measure word.
如果數字少於 10（包括 10），"多" 跟在量詞後。

> **Num. + MW + 多 + NP**

>
> a. 我只有六塊多錢。[I only have more than six *yuan* (but less than *7 yuan*).]
> b. 一斤多重的魚只要十塊錢。(A fish over one catty only costs 10 dollars.)

c. 我在倫敦住了兩年多。
[I stayed in London for more than 2 years (but less than 3 years).]
d. 他十歲多了。(He is more than 10 years old. He is not yet 11.)
e. 他十多歲了。(He is more than 10 years old. He is between 11-19.)

Summary:

▶ Chinese has three basic units of money: 元，角，分.

▶ These correspond to the American "dollar" "dime" and "cent". The difference is that, in Chinese, you always have to mention all three. So "￥3.69" is not "three dollar sixty-nine cents" but "three dollars, six dimes, nine cents".

▶ 1 元 equals 10 角, 1 角 equals 10 分. In daily speech, people also refer to the 元 as 塊 and 角 as 毛. The word 分 can often be left out.

▶ If there is no figure for the intermediate unit, we have to use 零 as an intermediate. Also the last unit Cannot be omitted.

▶ Please note that spoken and written forms don't go together.

▶ The most common way of asking for the price of something is: 多少錢？(How much?) Or, 幾塊錢？(How much?) if a small amount is expected.

▶ If one is asking specifically how something is sold (i.e. how much per pound/catty etc.), we can say: 怎麼賣 (mài: to sell)？(How is it sold?) Or one can ask directly: 多少錢一斤？(How much per catty?)

▶ Of course, Chinese also has words that correspond to the English "cost" as in "how much does this cost?". We can use 要，賣 or 得 (děi).

▶ Both 使 and 讓 can be used in "使/讓 sb. (感到) Adj. 的 (事情) 是……". The only difference is that 使 is very formal while 讓 is colloquial.

▶ In the structure of "NP MW MW 都 VP", the reduplication of the measure word indicates that each noun phrase involved in the action must be plural. Please note that the position of the reduplicated measure word is fixed: it must go before the adverb 都.

▶ 多 with the literal meaning of "many" or "more" may also indicate approximate numbers.

▶ And the position of 多 depends on the actual number. If the numbers are in 10s (i.e. 10, 20, 30 etc.), or 100s, 多 comes after the number and before the measure word.

▶ If the number is less than 10 (including 10), 多 follows the measure word.

Lesson 14　中國城

- **Patterns:**

- **(S) V 了……, 往 direction V, 然後……; 再 VP, 就 VP 了**
  出了飛機場，往右拐，然後一直往前走，再過兩條街，就到了。
  (After coming out of the airport, make a right turn. Then, go straight ahead. You will be there after passing two blocks.)

- **NP 多少錢一磅/斤？/ 一磅/斤 NP 多少錢？/ 多少錢一磅/斤 NP？**
  葡萄多少錢一磅？ (How much per pound for the grapes?)
  一磅葡萄多少錢？ (How much per pound for the grapes?)
  多少錢一磅葡萄？ (How much per pound for the grapes?)

- **使/讓 sb.(感到)Adj. 的(事情)是……** ‖ 使他感到奇怪的是這兒的很多人都不會說普通話。
  (What makes him feel strange is that many people here can't speak Mandarin.)

- **(S) 讓/叫 sb. VP, 不就行/得了？** ‖ 讓/叫小芳帶你去，不就行了？
  (You ask Xiaofang to take you there, and that will be fine.)

- **去 PW 坐幾號……** ‖ 去中國城坐幾號地鐵？
  (Which subway should I take to go to China town?)

- **去 PW 坐哪班……** ‖ 去加州坐哪班飛機好？
  (Which flight should I take to go to California?)

- **VP_1 有可能，VP_2 不可能** ‖ 把手機丟了有可能，把我丟了不可能。
  (There is the possibility that I will lose my cell phone but I will not get lost.)

- **NP MW MW 都 VP** ‖ 一條一斤多重的魚才五塊錢左右，而且條條都是活的。
  (A fish over one catty only costs five dollars or so and each of them is alive.)

- **Num. + 多 + MW + NP** ‖ 我有三十多塊錢。(I have 30 some *yuan*.)

- **Num.+ MW+ 多 + NP** ‖ 我只有六塊多錢。
  [I only have more than six *yuan* (but less than 7 *yuan*).]

IN CLASS ACTIVITIES

1 Answer the following questions according to the information given in the text:

① 家奇爲什麽想去中國城的大中華超級市場？

② 小芳愛吃的東西容易找嗎？爲什麽？

③ 使家奇感到奇怪的是什麽？

④ 讓他感到高興的是什麽？

⑤ 爲什麽家奇覺得中國城的東西很便宜？

2 Please do role play according to the dialogues given below:

A 請問，這葡萄好吃嗎？酸不酸？
B 一點兒也不酸。不信，你嚐一個。
A 不錯，多少錢一斤？
B 十塊錢三斤。
A 太貴了，便宜一點兒！
B 够便宜了。
A 算了，我不買了。
B 好吧。你要是買十塊錢的，我就給你十塊錢四斤。
A 行，那我就買十塊錢的吧。
B 先生，還要什麽？
A 雞蛋多少錢一打 (yì dá: a dozen)？
B 一打五塊。
A 給我來一打吧。

Lesson 14 中國城

> A 賣龍蝦，賣大龍蝦了。
> B 怎麼賣？
> A 十塊錢一磅。瞧，個兒大，新鮮 (xīnxiān: fresh)。
> B 給我來一隻吧！
> A 兩磅，二十塊。
> B 給你五十。
> A 找您三十。
> B 謝謝。

HOMEWORK

1 Please rewrite or complete the following sentences with the given structures:

① 感恩節是下個禮拜。（快 V 了）

➡ 感恩節快到了。

② 我的弟弟昨天買了十五本書。（多）

➡

③ 他的妹妹是一九九六年二月生的。請問他妹妹多大了？（多）

➡

④ 我的朋友們都很和氣。（NP MW MW 都 VP）

➡

⑤ 也許他的哥哥會來。他是不會來的。[VP₁（很）有可能，VP₂ 不（太）可能。]

➡

⑥ 中國城怎麼走？（去 PW 坐幾號地鐵？）

➡

313

⑦ 他想去中國，我不想叫他去，他不高興。[(S) 讓 sb. VP, 不就行 / 得了？]

⟹ _____

⑧ 他要來看我，我很高興。[使 / 讓 sb. (感到) Adj. 的 (事情) 是……]

⟹ _____

2 Please write prices for the following items in Chinese:

① 西紅柿：￥1.50 / 斤

⟹ 西紅柿一斤一塊五

② 酸菜魚：￥18.00 / 個

⟹ _____

③ 吉他：￥388.00 / 把

⟹ _____

④ 豆腐：￥1.20 / 塊

⟹ _____

⑤ 雞蛋：￥2.98 / 斤

⟹ _____

⑥ 地圖：￥4.99 / 張

⟹ _____

⑦ 葡萄：￥5.08 / 磅

⟹ _____

⑧ 啤酒：￥10.00 / 瓶

⟹ _____

⑨ 字典：￥108.98 / 本

⟹ _____

Lesson 14 中國城

⑩ 龍蝦：￥10.98 / 隻

　→ _____

⑪ 筷子：￥3.00 / 雙

　→ _____

3 Translate the following sentences into Chinese:

① After coming out of the airport, turn right. Walk a couple of minutes ahead, and then make a left turn. And you will reach the subway station.

_____

_____

② What makes him really happy is that his girlfriend decides to visit him.

_____

③ If he wants to watch TV, then just let him do it and that will be fine.

_____

④ I don't know which bus I should take to go to the movie theater.

_____

⑤ There might be the possibility that he can play guitar, but not soccer.

_____

⑥ As for my friends, each of them are versatile.

_____

⑦ I have more than 20 dollars.

_____

⑧ He celebrated his birthday five months ago. He is over 80 now.

_____

4 Please read the following paragraph in Pinyin:

Shíjiān guò de zhēn kuài, Jiāxīng hé Jiāqí xué Zhōngwén yǐjīng xuéle yì nián le. Tāmen dōu juéde zìjǐ de shōuhuò hěn dà, biànhuà yě hěn dà. Zìcóng xuéle Zhōngwén yǐhòu, tāmen duì Dōngfāng wénhuà, yóuqí shì Zhōngguó wénhuà yǒule gèng shēn de liǎojiě. Xué Zhōngwén yě ràng tāmen yǒu jīhuì rènshíle hěn duō péngyou hé tóngxué. Tāmen hěn gǎnxiè xīnqín、nàixīn de Wáng lǎoshī, shì tā jiāohuìle tāmen Zhōngwén, ràng tāmen yuè xué yuè ài xué Zhōngwén. Jiāqí zuì xǐhuan xiě hànzì. Zài tā kànlái, měi yí ge zì dōu xiàng yì fú piàoliang de huàr. Jiāxīng zuì xǐhuan bèi kèwén. Yǐqián tā hěn shǎo bèi dōngxi, yě zuì pà bèi, xiànzài duì tā lái shuō, bèi kèwén bú zài shì wèntí le. Tāmen hái jìde gāng xué Zhōngwén de shíhou, sìshēng ràng tāmen tóu dà jí le. Xiànzài tāmen de shēngdiào hěn zhǔn, hěn duō Zhōngguórén dōu yǐwéi tāmen xuéle hěn duō nián Zhōngwén le. Tāmen juéde zhè yì nián shì tāmen zuì kuàilè de yì nián.

5 Please describe the directions from A to B with the following structures:

❶ 出了＿＿＿＿＿，往 ＿＿＿＿＿拐，然後＿＿＿＿＿；再＿＿＿＿＿，就到了。

Lesson 14 中國城

❷ 出了_____，向_____轉，然後走_____分鐘，_____拐，再向前走_____分鐘，就到了。

CULTURAL NOTES

Bargaining

　　Bargaining is a common practice in China. It is part of Chinese life. When buying from little stores or vendors, one has to bargain to get a good deal. And the vendors expect it as well. However, people don't bargain in big shopping malls and supermarkets. Sometimes, bargaining is more enjoyable than the purchase itself. And your bargaining skills often decide the price. Therefore, the same item may be sold at various prices. Perhaps that is why Chinese people often ask each other how much they spend on purchases for reference. What one usually does is:

First, you should check the price of an item in different shops to get a general idea about the price of the article that you are interested in. Then, you should offer half of the asking price and work from there. Also, it is important to try to find some flaws on the article as a excuse of depreciation. You can be stubborn and persistent when bargaining, but keep smiling. If the price is not what you have expected, walk away. You can always come back later. If the shopkeeper detains you, it may mean he is close to accepting your offer, and with a little more discussion he will accept the offer. Once the shopkeeper accepts your price, do not try to reduce the price further, that would be unfair. After all, the shopkeeper has agreed to the price you have proposed.

It is really enjoyable to buy at a satisfactory price. Make sure that the article you take is the one you want since there are some dishonest shopkeepers who will replace the purchased products with shoddy ones.

Dialects

Chinese dialects can be roughly classified into one of the seven large groups, i.e., Putonghua (Mandarin), Gan, Kejia (Hakka), Min, Wu, Xiang and Yue (Cantonese). Each language group contains a large number of dialects. These are the Chinese languages spoken mostly by the Han people, which represents about 92 percent of the total population. Tibetan, Mongolian and Miao, spoken by the minorities, are considered non-Chinese languages.

The dialects from the seven groups are very different. Although a Mandarin speaker in northern China may understand a little Cantonese, he/she usually can't speak it. Most non-Mandarin speakers, however, usually can speak some Mandarin with a strong accent. The reason for this is that Mandarin has been the official national language since 1913. Mandarin, or Putonghua, is mainly based on the Beijing dialect. Despite the large differences among Chinese dialects, there is one thing they all have in common -- they all share the same writing system based on the Chinese characters.

Since people from Guangdong Province were among the first immigrants to the United States, people in Chinatown mostly speak Cantonese. Also, due to the fact that they have been away from China for a long time, many of them can't speak Mandarin.

LESSON 15　快樂的一年級

　　時間過得真快，家興和家奇學中文已經學了一年了。他們都覺得自己的收獲很大，變化也很大。自從學了中文以後，他們對東方文化，尤其是中國文化有了更深的瞭解。學中文也讓他們有機會認識了很多朋友和同學。他們很感謝辛勤、耐心的王老師，是她教會了他們中文，讓他們越學越愛學中文。家奇最喜歡寫漢字。在他看來，每一個字都像一幅漂亮的畫兒。家興最喜歡背課文。以前他很少背東西，也最怕背，現在對他來說，背課文不再是問題了。他們還記得剛學中文的時候，四聲讓他們頭大極了。現在他們的聲調很準，很多中國人都以為他們學了很多年中文了。他們覺得這一年是他們最快樂的一年。

1

家興：　家奇，時間過得真快！
家奇：　是啊，時間過得太快了！我們學中文已經學了一年了。
家興：　回頭看看，我的進步太大了。
家奇：　是啊，收獲大，變化也很大。
家興：　說說你的變化？

家奇： 我覺得自己學了中文後，對東方文化，尤其是中國文化有了更深的瞭解。

家興： 我也是。學中文以前，我對中國文化所知甚少。

家奇： 比如，我以前不明白爲什麼中國人在吃飯上下那麼大的功夫，花那麼多的時間。

家興： 我也是現在才知道飲食在中國文化上的地位。

家奇： 中國文化太豐富了。

家興： 這跟中國歷史悠久有關。

家奇： 不學不知道，一學嚇一跳。

家興： 我覺得學中文還有一個好處，就是讓我們有機會認識了很多朋友和同學。

2

家奇： 我們幸運的是遇到了一位好老師。

家興： 是啊，王老師真是一個辛勤、耐心的好老師。

家奇： 我很感謝王老師。是她教會了我們中文，讓我們越學越愛學中文。

家興： 家奇，學中文，你最喜歡的是什麼？

家奇： 我最喜歡寫漢字。可是剛開始的時候每個漢字好像都一樣似的。

家興： 漢字，的確很難。

家奇： 可是，現在在我看來，每一個字都像一幅漂亮的畫兒，各有特點。

家興： 哦？有意思。

家奇： 你最喜歡什麼？

家興： 我最喜歡背課文了。

家奇： 背課文？

家興： 以前我很少背東西，也最怕背。

家奇： 我不喜歡背，每次背課文我都頭疼。

家興： 現在對我來說，背課文不再是問題了。

家奇： 我知道，我以爲你天生就會背呢。

家興： 我聽説中國學生個個都能背。

家奇： 是啊，他們從小學背到大學，功夫深著呢。

家興： 這就叫熟能生巧。

Lesson 15　快樂的一年級

3

家奇：學中文就得多聽，多說，多讀，多寫，多練。

家興：還有，多背。

家奇：記得剛學中文的時候，聲調多難啊。

家興：是啊，我的四聲總是有問題。

家奇：我的半三聲總唸不對。

家興：對了，我想起來了，你老把"騎馬"說成"氣馬"。

家奇：呵呵，還有"睡覺"跟"水餃"也分不清楚。

家興：你還記得有人把"王老師"叫作"忘老師"嗎？

家奇：呵呵，王老師說："別忘了，我不是忘老師，是王老師。"

家興：對，真有意思。

家奇：我們現在大不一樣了。

家興：瞧！我們現在聲調多準啊！

家奇：很多中國人都以為我們學了很多年中文了。

家興：真是多虧王老師一點兒一點兒地糾正我們。

家奇：她真有耐心！我們真有福氣！

家興：我覺得這一年是我最快樂的一年。

家奇：是啊，快樂的一年過得可真快啊！

VOCABULARY

1	*收獲	收获	shōuhuò	N.	gains, harvest
2	*變化	变化	biànhuà	N.	change
3	自從	自从	zìcóng	Prep.	ever since
4	文化	文化	wénhuà	N.	culture
5	*尤其	尤其	yóuqí	Adv.	especially
6	*深	深	shēn	Adj.	deep
7	*瞭解	了解	liǎojiě	V.	to understand
8	感謝	感谢	gǎnxiè	V.	to thank
9	*辛勤	辛勤	xīnqín	Adj.	hardworking
10	耐心	耐心	nàixīn	Adj.	patience

走近中國——初級漢語教程
APPROACHING CHINA : ELEMENTARY CHINESE

11	在…看來	在…看来	zài…kànlái		according to
12	*像	像	xiàng	V.	to look like, to resemble
13	*幅	幅	fú	MW	*measure word for pictures*
14	*背	背	bèi	V.	to memorize
15	課文	课文	kèwén	N.	text
16	不再	不再	bú zài		not any more
17	*剛	刚	gāng	Adv.	just
18	*頭大極了	头大极了	tóu dà jí le	IE	headache
19	回頭	回头	huí tóu	V.-O.	to look back
20	*進步	进步	jìnbù	V.	progress
21	*所知甚少	所知甚少	suǒ zhī shèn shǎo	IE	to know a little
22	比如	比如	bǐrú	V.	for example
23	*功夫	功夫	gōngfu	N.	time and energy spent
24	*花	花	huā	V.	to spend
25	*飲食	饮食	yǐnshí	N.	food and drinking
26	地位	地位	dìwèi	N.	position, status
27	*豐富	丰富	fēngfù	Adj.	rich, abundant
28	*歷史	历史	lìshǐ	N.	history
29	*悠久	悠久	yōujiǔ	Adj.	long
30	*有關	有关	yǒuguān	V.	be related to
31	*嚇一跳	吓一跳	xià yí tiào	VP	to be scared
32	*好處	好处	hǎochù	N.	good thing
33	*幸運	幸运	xìngyùn	Adj.	lucky
34	*遇到	遇到	yùdào	V.-C.	to encounter
35	*各有特點	各有特点	gè yǒu tèdiǎn	IE	All have their own characters.
36	*頭疼	头疼	tóuténg	Adj.	headache
37	天生	天生	tiānshēng	Adj.	born to be
38	*熟能生巧	熟能生巧	shú néng shēng qiǎo	IE	Practice makes perfect.
39	*騎馬	骑马	qí mǎ	V.-O.	to ride a horse
40	氣馬	气马	qì mǎ	VP	to anger a horse
41	水餃	水饺	shuǐjiǎo	N.	dumplings
42	分	分	fēn	V.	to tell from
43	叫作	叫作	jiàozuò	V.	to be called

Lesson 15 快樂的一年級

Supplementary Vocabulary:

1	人山人海	人山人海	rénshān–rénhǎi	IE	describing a very crowded situation
2	七上八下	七上八下	qīshàng–bāxià	IE	nervous
3	三心二意	三心二意	sānxīn–èryì	IE	not focused
4	一心一意	一心一意	yìxīn–yíyì	IE	focused, loyal
5	酸甜苦辣	酸甜苦辣	suān–tián–kǔ–là	IE	joys and sorrows, ups and downs of life
6	家常便飯	家常便饭	jiācháng–biànfàn	IE	commonly seen, not rare
7	十全十美	十全十美	shíquán–shíměi	IE	perfect
8	走馬觀花	走马观花	zǒumǎ–guānhuā	IE	to get a superficial understanding through quick and casual observation
9	五光十色	五光十色	wǔguāng–shísè	IE	colorful, multicolored

GRAMMAR

1 自從……(以後)，S 就……：after / ever since ... , then...

E.g. a. 自從學了中文以後，他就越來越愛吃中國菜了。
 (Ever since he learned Chinese, he likes eating Chinese food more and more.)
 b. 自從上了大學以後，他就更愛打籃球了。
 (Ever since he went to college, he likes playing basketball even more.)
 c. 自從學了中文以後，他們對東方文化，尤其是中國文化有了更深的瞭解。
 (Ever since they have learned Chinese, they have a better understanding about the Eastern culture, especially Chinese culture.)
 d. 自從我們分手以後，我再也沒見過她。
 (Ever since we separated, I have never seen her again.)
 e. 自從他有了孩子，他就更愛做飯了。
 (Ever since he had a child, he loves cooking even more.)
 f. 自從他來美國以後，他寫的書就更多了。
 (Ever since he came to the U.S., he writes more books.)

2 S 對 sth. 有了更深的瞭解：sb. has a better understanding about sth.

E.g. a. 自從學了英文，我對西方文化有了更深的瞭解。
 (I have a better understanding about the Western culture, ever since I learned English.)

b. 我到了紐約才對紐約藝術有了更深的瞭解。
(I have a better understanding of New York's art only after I had been there.)
c. 到了中國我才對中國的飲食文化有了更深的瞭解。
(Only after I went to China did I have a better understanding of Chinese eating culture.)
d. 自從到了法國，我才對法國人有了更深的瞭解。
(Only after I came to France did I have a better understanding of French people.)

3 在 sb. 看來：according to sb.

  a. 在他看來，每一個字都像一幅漂亮的畫兒。
(According to him, each character looks like a beautiful picture.)
b. 在我看來，學書法是最有意思的事情。
(According to me, learning calligraphy is the most enjoyable experience.)
c. 在我看來，聽音樂比打籃球更有意思。
(According to me, listening to music is more interesting than playing basketball.)

This structure is similar to the following srtucture:
這個結構與下面的結構很相似：

對 sb. 來說：according to sb.

  a. 對我來說，彈吉他比彈鋼琴容易多了。
(For me, playing guitar is much easier than playing piano.)
b. 對我來說，東方文化跟西方文化各有特點。
(For me, Eastern culture and Western culture all have their own characteristics.)
c. 對中國人來說，學習是最重要的事情。
(According to Chinese people, learning is the most important thing.)

4 不再 VP 了：no longer VP

This structure indicates change of a state.
這個結構表示一種狀態的改變。

a. 背課文不再是問題了。(Memorizing the text is no longer a problem.)
b. 我們不再是朋友了。(We are no longer friends.)
c. 我的朋友踢足球踢得很好，可是現在不再踢了。
(My friend plays soccer very well, but he doesn't play it any more.)
d. 現在，對他來說，學外文不再是一件頭疼的事了。
(Now, learning a foreign language is no longer a headache for him.)

Lesson 15 快樂的一年級

> e. 年齡大了，我不再像以前一樣，那麼喜歡買東西了。
> (Now that I am older, I don't like to buy as many things as I did before.)

5 Compare 怕 and 恐怕

"A 怕 B" means "A is afraid of B" while "恐怕 +sentence" means that "I am afraid that...".

"A 怕 B" 意思是 "A 害怕 B"；"恐怕 +sentence" 意思是我估計某事。

> **E.g.** a. 雖然老師很和氣，可是我還是有一點兒怕他。
> (Although the teacher is nice, I am still a little bit afraid of him.)
> b. 恐怕你不是怕他，你是尊敬他。
> (I am afraid that you are not afraid of him. You just respect him.)
> c. 我不怕天，不怕地，就怕考試。
> (I am afraid of nothing, except for the exam.)
> d. 我的朋友就要出國了，恐怕我沒有機會再跟老朋友一起下棋了。
> (My friend is going abroad. I am afraid that I will not have the opportunity to play chess with my old friend any more.)
> e. 恐怕你不愛吃中國菜吧？
> (I am afraid that you don't like eating Chinese food, right？)
> f. 恐怕他不是他們家的老大，是老小。
> (I am afraid that he is not the first child in their family. He is the youngest.)
> g. 誰怕誰呀！ (Who is afraid of whom?)

6 在……上： in the aspect of...; in terms of...

In this structure, the aspect that is concerned can be both something concrete, like an action, and something abstract.

在這個結構中，相關的方面可以是具體的，比如一個行爲動作，也可以是抽象的。

> **E.g.** a. 他們在吃飯上下了那麼大的功夫，花了那麼多的時間。
> (They spend so much time and energy on eating.)
> b. 我也是現在才知道飲食在中國文化上的地位。
> (I also didn't know until now how important a role eating plays in Chinese culture.)
> c. 我覺得他在學習上很用功。(I think he works really hard in terms of study.)
> d. 我的父母常常説：年輕人應該在學習上多下功夫，少玩點兒。
> (My parents always say that young people should spend more time studying and less time playing.)

e. 在聲調上，我不如你；可是在語法上，我比你好多了。
(In terms of tones, I am not as good as you are. But in terms of grammar, I am much better.)

7 A 跟 B 有關：A is related to B; A has sth. to do with B
A 跟 B 無關：A has nothing to do with B

E.g. a. 這跟中國歷史悠久有關。(This is related to the long history of Chinese.)
b. 我知道這件事跟他有關。(I know this has something to do with him.)
c. 他不開心跟他沒有找到工作有關。
(That he is not happy has something to do with the fact that he has not found a job yet.)
d. 我學中文跟我對中國文化有興趣有關。
(The reason that I am learning Chinese has something to do with my interest in Chinese culture.)
e. 他的中文學得很好跟他喜歡背課文有關。
(That his Chinese is very good has something to do with the fact that he likes memorizing the text.)
f. 他的球踢得很好跟他的哥哥有關。
(That he plays soccer really well has something to do with his elder brother.)
g. 這件事跟他無關。(This has nothing to do with him.)
h. 我的聲調好不好跟你無關。
(Whether my tone is good or not has nothing to do with you.)

8 有一個好處就是……：The good thing about this is that...

E.g. a. 學中文有一個好處就是你可以認識很多中國朋友。
(The good thing about learning Chinese is that you can have many Chinese friends.)
b. 看電視有一個好處就是你可以瞭解到世界各地發生的事情。
(The good thing about watching TV is that you can learn many things that are going on in the world.)
c. 在中國學中文有一個好處就是你得天天說中文。
(The good thing about learning Chinese is that you have to speak Chinese everyday.)
d. 跑步有一個好處就是越跑身體越好。
(The good thing about running is that the more you run, the healthier you will be.)
e. 下棋有一個好處就是你越下越聰明。
(The good thing about playing chess is that the more you play it, the smarter you will be.)

Lesson 15 快樂的一年級

9 大 as an adverb: greatly; totally

Please note that not all verbs can be modified by 大. The verbs that can be modified by the adverb 大 should be learned one by one.

請注意，並不是所有的動詞都可以用"大"來修飾。我們只能逐個學習可以被副詞"大"修飾的動詞。

 a. 我們現在大不一樣了。(We are totally different now.)
b. 我的聲調大有進步。(My tones have improved a lot.)
c. 學中文對找工作大有幫助。
   (Learning Chinese will be greatly helpful to find a job.)
d. 你的中文水平大有提高。(Your Chinese level has greatly improved.)
e. 他們的生活水平大有提高。(Their living standard has improved greatly.)
f. 他喜歡大說特說，他的弟弟喜歡大吃大喝。
   (He likes talking a lot, and his younger brother likes eating a lot.)

10 (Object)，S 分不清楚 (Object): S can't tell the difference between...

 a. 還有，"睡覺"跟"水餃"你也分不清楚。
   (Also, you can't tell the difference between 睡覺 and 水餃.)
b. 這兩個字我分不清楚。(I can't tell the difference between these two characters.)
c. 我分不清楚東西南北。(I can't tell directions.)
d. 他分不清楚好壞。(He can't tell what is good and what is bad.)
e. 他們是雙生兄弟，所以我分不清楚哪個是哥哥，哪個是弟弟。
   (They are twins. So I can't tell who is the older one and who is the younger one.)

Summary:

▶ "A 怕 B" means "A is afraid of B" while "恐怕 + sentence" means that "I am afraid that..."．

▶ In the structure "在……上"(in the aspect of ...; in terms of ...), the aspect that is concerned can be both something concrete, like an action, and also something abstract.

▶ Please note that not all verbs can be modified by 大. The verbs that can be modified by the adverb 大 should be learned one by one.

Patterns:

- 自從……(以後)，S 就…… ‖ 自從學了中文以後，他就越來越愛吃中國菜了。
  (Ever since he learned Chinese, he likes eating Chinese food more.)

- S 對 sth. 有了更深的瞭解 ‖ 自從學了英文，我對西方文化有了更深的瞭解。
  (I have a better understanding about the Western culture, ever since I learned English.)

- 在 sb. 看來 ‖ 在他看來，每一個字都像一幅漂亮的畫兒。
  (According to him, each character looks like a beautiful picture.)

- 對 sb. 來説 ‖ 對我來説，彈吉他比彈鋼琴容易多了。
  (For me, playing guitar is much easier than playing piano.)

- 不再 VP 了 ‖ 背課文不再是問題了。(Memorizing the text is no longer a problem.)

- Compare 怕 and 恐怕 ‖ 恐怕你不是怕他，你是尊敬他。
  (I am afraid that you are not afraid of him. You just respect him.)

- 在……上 ‖ 在吃飯上下那麼大的功夫，花那麼多的時間。
  (They spend so much time and energy on eating.)

- A 跟 B 有關 ‖ 這跟中國歷史悠久有關。(This is related to the long history of Chinese.)

- A 跟 B 無關 ‖ 這件事跟他無關。(This has nothing to do with him.)

- 有一個好處就是…… ‖ 學中文有一個好處就是你可以認識很多中國朋友。
  (The good thing about learning Chinese is that you can have many Chinese friends.)

- 大 as an adverb ‖ 我們現在大不一樣了。(We are totally different now.)

- (Object)，S 分不清楚 (Object) ‖ 還有，"睡覺"跟"水餃"你也分不清楚。
  (Also, you can't tell the difference between 睡覺 and 水餃.)

IN CLASS ACTIVITIES

1 Answer the following questions according to the information given in the text:

① 家興跟家奇學中文以後，覺得有什麼不同？

Lesson 15　快樂的一年級

❷ 爲什麼他們說很感謝王老師？

❸ 爲什麼家興說他最喜歡寫漢字？

❹ 家奇說他最喜歡做什麼？爲什麼？

❺ 他們剛學中文的時候，什麼讓他們頭大極了？

❻ 很多中國人都以爲什麼？

❼ 他們覺得這一年過得怎麼樣？

2 Please do role play according to the dialogues given below:

> **A** 我們學中文已經學了快一年了，你覺得你最大的收獲是什麼？
> **B** 最大的收獲就是我對中國文化有了更深的瞭解。
> **A** 我也是，比方說現在我對中國人的飲食習慣有了更深的瞭解。
> **B** 是啊，我以前總是覺得奇怪，爲什麼中國人吃飯的時候要說"再吃點兒，多吃點兒"。我說吃飽了，可是他們還是叫我多吃。
> **A** 這是因爲他們熱情好客。我的中國朋友們總是叫別人喝酒，好像別人不喝醉不行。
> **B** 這叫酒文化。中國人愛面子。面子對中國人來說，太重要了。
> **A** 真是有意思！還有，中國人收到禮物時，常常要等送禮的人走了以後，才把禮物打開。
> **B** 中國人喜歡紅色，覺得紅色能給人帶來好運氣。
> **A** 中國有一點我覺得不太好，中國學生的學習負擔太重了，尤其是中小學生。
> **B** 我聽老師說很多孩子週末也在學習。

> A 他們把學校的作業做完後，還要練習琴棋書畫，太累了。
> B 這叫望子成龍 (wàng zǐ chéng lóng: to hope one's children will have a bright future)。
> A 什麼叫望子成龍呢？
> B 望子成龍的意思就是父母希望自己的孩子將來能成為很重要，很有用的人。

留學 (liúxué: to study abroad)

> A 家興，最近忙什麼呢？
> B 還不是到中國留學的事兒。
> A 聽說你收到錄取通知 (lùqǔ tōngzhī: admission notice) 以後，就到處 (dàochù: everywhere) 打聽 (dǎting: to ask about) 出國應該做什麼準備。
> B 你怎麼什麼都知道啊？
> A 誰不知道啊？
> B 呵呵，我已經申請 (shēnqǐng: to apply) 好了護照 (hùzhào: passport) 和簽證 (qiānzhèng: visa)，上網訂好 (dìnghǎo: to reserve) 了機票。
> A 都準備好了吧？
> B 還差得遠呢！我還沒收拾 (shōushi: to pack) 好行李 (xíngli: luggage) 呢！
> A 還有一個多月，現在就收拾行李太早了吧？
> B 雖然是早了一點兒，可是我覺得早準備比晚收拾要強得多。
> A 說得好，我也該收拾了。

HOMEWORK

1 Please rewrite or complete the following sentences with the given structures:

① 感恩節是下個禮拜。（快 V 了）

➡ 感恩節快到了。

② 我去年開始學游泳。我的身體越來越好。[自從……(以後), S 就……]

➡

Lesson 15 快樂的一年級

③ 上個月，我有機會去中國。我更瞭解中國文化瞭。(S 對 sth. 有瞭更深的瞭解)
▶

④ 我覺得中國文化很有意思。(在 sb. 看來)
▶

⑤ 我覺得幫助別人就是幫助自己。(對 sb. 來說)
▶

⑥ 我以前覺得背課文很難。(不再 VP 了)
▶

⑦ 你學習比我好。(在……上)
▶

⑧ 我的中文水平提高了。我的語伴總是幫我。(A 跟 B 有 / 無關)
▶

⑨ 學中文可以認識很多人。(有一個好處就是……)
▶

⑩ 我的聲調跟以前很不一樣。(大 as an adverb)
▶

⑪ 我不知道誰是老師誰是學生。[(Object)，S 分不清楚 (Object)]
▶

331

2 Please fill in an appropriate word to complete the following sentences:

> 地位　感謝　怕　收獲　恐怕　尤其　豐富　耐心　背　變化

1. 我很喜歡王老師是因爲她很有 ___耐心___ 。
2. 我們覺得自己這一年的_____很大。
3. 已經很晚了，_____他不回來了。
4. 我喜歡是很喜歡學中文，可是我不喜歡_____課文。
5. 小張很喜歡吃中國菜，_____是餃子。
6. 我們都跟以前不一樣，他們兩個的_____最大。
7. 他很_____我父母對他的關心和照顧。
8. 中國文化太_____了。
9. 我也是現在才知道飲食在中國文化上的_____。
10. 我不_____你不學，就怕你不愛學。

3 Translate the following sentences into Chinese:

1. Ever since I went to college, I become more interested in dancing.

2. Ever since I took Chinese, I have a better understanding of Chinese culture.

3. According to my brother, learning math is a big headache.

4. I am afraid that he is no longer afraid of you.

5. Their break up has nothing to do with Xiao Zhang.

Lesson 15 快樂的一年級

⑥ The good thing about getting up early is that you will have more time.

⑦ The living standard (生活水準: shēnghuó shuǐzhǔn) of Chinese has been greatly improved.

⑧ My friend thinks that it is hard to tell the difference between 恐怕 and 怕.

⑨ I knew almost nothing about my girlfriend's family. (S 對 sth. 所知甚少)

4 Please use the following sentences to write a short essay about your experience of learning Chinese:

自從……(以後), S 就……;   S 對 sth. 有了更深的瞭解;   在 sb. 看來;

對 sb. 來説;   S 不再 VP 了;   在……上;   A 跟 B 有 / 無關;

有一個好處就是……;   (Object), S 分不清楚 (Object);

Yin and Yang

According to Chinese Culture, *Yin* and *Yang* represent the two opposite principles in nature. *Yin* stands for the feminine or negative nature of things. On the contrary, *Yang* symbolizes the masculine or positive side. *Yin* and *Yang* are considered to exist in pairs and are found everywhere such as the moon and the sun, dark and bright, female and male, cold and hot, passive and active, etc. They are considered, however, not static or just two separated things. The nature of *Yinyang* lies in the interchange and interplay of the two components such as the alternation of day and night.

The concept of *Yinyang* can be dated back to the Yin Dynasty (about 1400 BCE—1100 BCE) and the Western Zhou Dynasty (1100 BCE—771 BCE).

It is believed that the principles of *Yinyang* are an important part of *Huangdi Neijing* (Yellow Emperor's Classic of Medicine), the earliest Chinese medical book, written about 2,000 years ago. They still play an important part in traditional Chinese medicine and *Fengshui* today.

To sum up, although *Yin* and *Yang* are opposite in nature, they rely on each other, and they can't exist without each other. The balance of *Yin* and *Yang* is important. If *Yin* is stronger, *Yang* will be weaker, and vice versa. *Yin* and *Yang* can interchange under certain conditions so they are usually not *Yin* and *Yang* alone. That is to say, *Yin* can contain certain part of *Yang*. Also *Yang* can have some component of *Yin*.

詞語索引 VOCABULARY LIST
(拼音 – 繁體字 – 簡體字 – 詞性 – 英譯 – 出處)

A

Pinyin	Traditional	Simplified	POS	English	Lesson
ǎ	啊	啊	Int.	*to indicate a surprise*	4
à	啊	啊	Int.	*to indicate an agreement*	1
ǎi	*矮	矮	Adj.	short (height)	13
ài	愛	爱	V.	to love	3
àihào	愛好	爱好	N.	hobby	11
àiren	愛人	爱人	N.	spouse	10
ài	唉	唉	Int.	to sigh	6
ānquángǎn	*安全感	安全感	N.	the feeling of being safe	12
Àodàlìyà	澳大利亞	澳大利亚	PW	Australia	2

B

Pinyin	Traditional	Simplified	POS	English	Lesson
ba	*吧	吧	Pt.	*particle showing uncertainty*	1
bàba	*爸爸	爸爸	N.	dad	3
báimǎ wángzǐ	白馬王子	白马王子	NP	Prince Charming, Mr. Right	13
báisè	白色	白色	N.	white color	9
bān	*班	班	N.	class	2
bàn	半	半	Num.	half	6
bàn xiànr	拌餡兒	拌馅儿	V.-O.	to make fillings	10
bāng	幫	帮	V.	to help	6
bāng máng	*幫忙	帮忙	V.-O.	to help	13
bāngzhù	*幫助	帮助	V.	to help	6
bàngqiú	*棒球	棒球	N.	baseball	11
bàng	*磅	磅	MW	pound	14
bāo	*包	包	V.	to wrap	10
bāo jiǎozi	包餃子	包饺子	VP	to make dumplings	10
bǎobao	寶寶	宝宝	N.	baby	3
bǎobèi	寶貝	宝贝	N.	sweet heart	3
bào	報	报	N.	newspaper	3
bào míng	報名	报名	V.-O.	to register	6
bei	唄	呗	Int.	duh	10

335

běi	*北	北	N.	(the) north	14
Běijīng	北京	北京	PW	Beijing	1
bèi	*背	背	V.	to memorize	15
bèi	*被	被	Prep.	used in passive structure	12
běnlái	*本來	本来	Adv.	originally	4
bèn	*笨	笨	Adj.	silly	13
bǐ	*比	比	Prep.	compared with	8
bǐfang shuō	比方说	比方说	IE	for instance	14
bǐrú	比如	比如	V.	for example	15
biàn	*變	变	V.	to change	12
biànhuà	*變化	变化	N.	change	15
biǎoyǎn	*表演	表演	V.	to perform	10
biǎoyǎnzhě	表演者	表演者	N.	performer	10
bié hē le	别喝了	别喝了	IE	Don't drink any more.	12
bié jí	*别急	别急	IE	Don't worry.	9
bié luàn xiǎng le	别亂想了	别乱想了	IE	Don't think too much!	7
bié tí le	别提了	别提了	IE	Don't bring it up.	8
bìng (bù/méi)	*並(不/没)	并(不/没)	Adv.	used to emphasize	13
bīngzhèn	冰镇	冰镇	V.	cold/iced	12
bówùguǎn	博物館	博物馆	N.	museum	7
bù	*不	不	Adv.	not	1
búcuò	*不錯	不错	Adj.	not bad	4
búdàn	*不但	不但	Conj.	not only	13
búdàn…érqiě…	不但…而且…	不但…而且…		not only…,but also…	13
bùdéliǎo	不得了	不得了	Adj.	extremely	8
bùgǎndāng	*不敢當	不敢当	V.	I am flattered.	11
búguò	不過	不过	Conj.	but	7
bù hǎoyìsi	不好意思	不好意思	IE	to feel embarrassed	4
bú kèqi	不客氣	不客气	IE	You are welcome.	4
búlùn	*不論	不论	Adv.	no matter	10
bù shǎo	不少	不少		a lot	11

bú shì ge zīwèir	不是個滋味兒	不是个滋味儿	IE	It is horrible. / It is a terrible feeling.	13
bú yàojǐn	不要緊	不要紧	IE	It doesn't matter.	4
bú zài	不再	不再		not any more	15
bù	*步	步	N.	step	8
bù	*部	部	MW	*measure word for movies*	13
cái	*才	才	Adv.	not …until	8
cài	*菜	菜	N.	dish (of food)	3
càidān	菜單	菜单	N.	menu	5
càiyóu	菜油	菜油	N.	veggie oil	4
cānguān	參觀	参观	V.	to visit	7
cānjiā	*參加	参加	V.	to take part in	10
chāzi	叉子	叉子	N.	fork	4
chá	*茶	茶	N.	tea	4
chá lái le	茶來了	茶来了	IE	Here comes the tea!	4
chájù	茶具	茶具	N.	china, porcelain ware	4
chà	差	差	V.	to lack	4
chàyuǎnle	差遠了	差远了	IE	Not good at all.	6
cháng	*長	长	Adj.	long	7
cháng	*嚐	尝	V.	to taste	5
cháng yi cháng	嚐一嚐	尝一尝	VP	try (by tasting)	5
cháng (cháng)	常（常）	常（常）	Adv.	often	3
chǎng	*場	场	MW	*measure word for movies*	13
chàng gē	*唱歌	唱歌	V.-O.	to sing	10
chāojí	*超級	超级	Adj.	super	14
chāoshì	超市	超市	N.	supermarket	4
chǎo jià	*吵架	吵架	V.-O.	to quarrel	12
chǎo	炒	炒	V.	to stir fry	4
chéng shuāng duì	成雙對	成双对	IE	to become a couple	10
chéngwéi	*成爲	成为	V.	to become	12
chéngzhī	橙汁	橙汁	N.	orange juice	8
chī	吃	吃	V.	to eat	3

chū	出	出	V.	to go out	7
chū cuò	出錯	出错	V.-O.	to make mistakes	9
chūzūchē	*出租車	出租车	N.	taxi	7
chúxī	*除夕	除夕	N.	New Year's Eve	10
chuántǒng	*傳統	传统	Adj.	traditional	10
chuīle	吹了	吹了	IE	to break up	12
chūnjì	*春季	春季	N.	Spring	9
Chūnjié	*春節	春节	PN	Spring festival	10
cì	次	次	MW	time(s)	4
cōng	蔥	葱	N.	scallion	4
cōngmíng	聰明	聪明	Adj.	smart	3
cóng	從	从	Prep.	from	6
cónglái	從來	从来	Adv.	never	3

D

dǎ diànhuà	*打電話	打电话	VP	to call	8
dǎsuàn	*打算	打算	V.	to plan	4
dà	大	大	Adj.	old	12
dàjiā	*大家	大家	Pron.	everybody	2
dàxuéshēng	大學生	大学生	N.	college student	3
dàyuē	大約	大约	Adv.	approximately	10
dài	帶	带	V.	to take	14
dài shàng	*帶上	带上	V.-C.	to bring sth. with	14
dānxiāngsī	單相思	单相思	V.	unrequited love	13
dāng	當	当	V.	to become	11
dāngrán	*當然	当然	Adv.	of course	7
dào	*到	到	V.	to go to, to arrive	4
dàodǐ	*到底	到底	Adv.	what on earth…, after all	12
dào	倒	倒	Adv.	surprisingly	7
de	*的	的	Pt.	*particle indicating possessive*	2
de	*得	得	Pt.	*resultative marker*	5
Déguó	德國	德国	PW	German	2
děi	得	得	Aux. V.	have to	6
děng	等	等	V.	to wait	11

díquè	*的確	的确	Adv.	indeed	8
dìfang	*地方	地方	N.	place	1
dìtiě	*地鐵	地铁	N.	subway	7
dìtiězhàn	*地鐵站	地铁站	N.	subway station	14
dìtú	*地圖	地图	N.	map	14
dìwèi	地位	地位	N.	position, status	15
dìzhǐ	地址	地址	N.	address	6
dìdi	*弟弟	弟弟	N.	younger brother	2
dìyī	*第一	第一	Num.	the first	2
diǎn	*點	点	MW	o'clock	6
diǎn	點	点	V.	to order	5
diǎn tóu	*點頭	点头	V.-O.	to nod	5
diànshì	電視	电视	N.	T.V.	3
diànyǐngyuàn	*電影院	电影院	N.	cinema	7
dōng	東	东	N.	(the) east	14
Dōngfāng	*東方	东方	PN	Eastern	11
dōngxi	*東西	东西	N.	thing	4
Dōng Yà	*東亞	东亚	PN	East Asia	10
dōu	*都	都	Adv.	all	1
dòu nǐ wánr	逗你玩兒	逗你玩儿	IE	Just kidding.	11
duǎn	*短	短	Adj.	short (in length)	9
duànliàn	*鍛煉	锻炼	V.	to exercise	8
duì	對	对	Adj.	correct	1
duì bu duì	對不對	对不对	IE	correct or not	1
duìbuqǐ	對不起	对不起	IE	I am sorry.	4
duìfu	*對付	对付	V.	to handle	12
duìle	對了	对了	IE	by the way, in other news	4
duìmiàn	*對面	对面	N.	the opposite	14
duìniú–tánqín	對牛彈琴	对牛弹琴	IE	Playing music to cattle. It is useless to talk to sb. who doesn't understand you at all.	11
duì…yǒu yìsi	*對…有意思	对…有意思	VP	to be interested in sb.	13

pinyin	traditional	simplified	type	meaning	lesson
duō	*多	多	Adj.	many	1
duōbànr	多半兒	多半儿	Num.	mostly, most of	11
duōcái–duōyì	*多才多藝	多才多艺	IE	versatile	11
duō xiè le	多謝了	多谢了	IE	Thanks a lot!	4

E

pinyin	traditional	simplified	type	meaning	lesson
è	*餓	饿	Adj.	hungry	4
érzi	*兒子	儿子	N.	son	3
ér	*而	而	Conj.	but (formal)	12
érqiě	*而且	而且	Conj.	besides (formal)	13
ěrduo	*耳朵	耳朵	N.	ear	10
èr shì	二是	二是	Conj.	another thing is that…	12

F

pinyin	traditional	simplified	type	meaning	lesson
fāshēng	*發生	发生	V.	to happen	9
Fǎguó	法國	法国	PW	France	2
fǎzi	*法子	法子	N.	way	4
fàn chóu	*犯愁	犯愁	V.-O.	worried	10
fàn	*飯	饭	N.	food	3
fànguǎnr	*飯館兒	饭馆儿	N.	restaurant (informal way)	5
fàng xīn ba	放心吧	放心吧	IE	Don't worry!	14
fēijī	飛機	飞机	N.	airplane	7
(fēi)jīchǎng	*(飛)機場	(飞)机场	N.	airport	7
fēijīpiào	*飛機票	飞机票	N.	plane ticket	7
fēicháng	*非常	非常	Adv.	especially	10
fèihuà	*廢話	废话	N.	Nonsense.	9
fèi	費	费	N.	fee, expense	7
fēn	分	分	V.	to tell from	15
fēndào	分到	分到	V.-C.	to be assigned to	11
fēn shǒu	*分手	分手	V.-O.	to break up	12
fēnzhōng	分鐘	分钟	N.	minutes	4
fēngfù	*豐富	丰富	Adj.	rich, abundant	15
fēngjǐng	*風景	风景	N.	scenery	7
fúwùyuán	*服務員	服务员	N.	waiter, waitress	5
fú	*幅	幅	MW	*measure word for pictures*	15
fúqi	*福氣	福气	N.	a state of being lucky	13

fùqīn	*父親	父亲	N.	father	3
fùdān	*負擔	负担	N.	burden	12
fùjìn	*附近	附近	N.	vicinity, in the vicinity of	5
fùxí	*復習	复习	V.	to review	8
G gāi	*該	该	Aux. V.	should	6
gāngà	*尷尬	尴尬	Adj.	awkward, embarrassed	13
gǎnkuài	趕快	赶快	Adv.	hurry up	6
Gǎn'ēn Jié	感恩節	感恩节	PN	Thanksgiving Day	7
gǎndào	感到	感到	V.	to feel (formal)	13
gǎnxiè	感謝	感谢	V.	to thank	15
gǎnlǎnyóu	橄欖油	橄榄油	N.	olive oil	4
gǎn pír	擀皮兒	擀皮儿	V.-O.	to make wrappers	10
gàn	*幹	干	V.	to do	9
gāng	*剛	刚	Adv.	just	15
gāngcái	*剛才	刚才	TW	just now	9
gāngqín	*鋼琴	钢琴	N.	piano	11
gāo	*高	高	Adj.	high, tall	6
gāoxìng	高興	高兴	Adj.	happy	1
gēge	*哥哥	哥哥	N.	elder brother	2
gēmenr	哥們兒	哥们儿	N.	buddy	9
géwài	*格外	格外	Adv.	especially (formal expression)	9
gè	*個	个	MW	used before nouns without a special classifier of their own	1
gèzi	個子	个子	N.	height	13
gè yǒu suǒ ài	各有所愛	各有所爱	IE	each have their own interests	11
gè yǒu tèdiǎn	*各有特點	各有特点	IE	All have their own characters.	15
gěi	*給	给	Prep.	for	4
gēnjù	*根據	根据	Prep.	according to	10
gēn	*跟	跟	Prep.	with, from	3
gèng	*更	更	Adv.	even	4
gōngzuò	*工作	工作	N.	work	3
gōnggòng qìchē	*公共汽車	公共汽车	NP	bus	7

gōngfu	*功夫	功夫	N.	time and energy spent	15
gōngkè	*功課	功课	N.	homework	8
gǒu	狗	狗	N.	dog	3
gòu	*够	够	V.	enough	3
guǎi	*拐	拐	V.	to turn	14
guàibude	怪不得	怪不得	Adv.	No wonder	11
Guǎngdōngrén	*廣東人	广东人	N.	people from Guangdong Province, Cantonese	14
guìxìng	貴姓	贵姓	N.	honorable surname	2
guójiā	國家	国家	N.	country	7
guò	*過	过	V.	to pass	6
guò	過	过	V.	to celebrate	7
guòláirén	過來人	过来人	N.	person who has had the experience	13
guòqù	過去	过去	TW	the past	12
H hāhā	哈哈	哈哈	Int.	*sound of laughter*	2
hāi	咳	咳	Int.	*a sigh*	8
hái	還	还	Adv.	also	1
hái xíng ba	還行吧	还行吧	IE	Not bad.	12
háishi	*還是	还是	Conj.	or	4
hǎixiān	*海鮮	海鲜	N.	sea food	14
hài	嗐	嗐	Int.	sigh	7
Hánguó	韓國	韩国	PW	Korea	2
Hànyǔ	*漢語	汉语	N.	Chinese	6
hǎo	*好	好	Adj.	good	1
hǎochī	*好吃	好吃	Adj.	delicious	3
hǎochù	*好處	好处	N.	good thing	15
hǎogǎn	好感	好感	N.	good impression	13
hǎojǐ	好幾	好几	Num.	several	12
hǎoxiàng	*好像	好像	V.	it seems	8
hǎoxīnrén	好心人	好心人	N.	good hearted person	14
hǎo wa	好哇	好哇	IE	Okay.	11
hào	*號	号	N.	number	14

詞語索引

hē	呵	呵	Int.	to indicate a nice surprise	4
hēhē	呵呵	呵呵	Int.	a sound made in imitation of laughter	3
hē	*喝	喝	V.	to drink	4
hédelái	*合得來	合得来	Adj.	to get along well with	6
hé	*和	和	Conj.	and	1
héqi	和氣	和气	Adj.	gentle	2
hēihēi	嘿嘿	嘿嘿	Int.	laugh (something funny)	7
hěn	*很	很	Adv.	very	1
hóngchá	紅茶	红茶	N.	black tea (red tea in Chinese)	4
hóngjiǔ	*紅酒	红酒	N.	red wine	12
hòubian	*後邊	后边	N.	behind	14
hùxiāng	*互相	互相	Adv.	mutually	6
huā	*花	花	V.	to spend	15
huáyì	華裔	华裔	N.	overseas Chinese	2
huà	*畫	画	N.	painting	11
huà huàr	*畫畫兒	画画儿	V.-O.	to draw/paint	11
huàjiā	畫家	画家	N.	painter	11
huí jiā	*回家	回家	V.-O.	to return home	7
huí tóu	回頭	回头	V.-O.	to look back	15
huì	*會	会	V.	can	2
huó miàn	和麵	和面	V.-O.	to make dough	10
huó	*活	活	Adj.	alive	14
huópō	活潑	活泼	Adj.	lively	13
huóyuè	*活躍	活跃	Adj.	active, lively	11
huǒjī	*火雞	火鸡	N.	turkey	7
huǒbàn	夥伴	伙伴	N.	partner	6
huòzhě	*或者	或者	Conj.	or	7
J jīhuì	*機會	机会	N.	opportunity	6
jīdàn	雞蛋	鸡蛋	N.	chicken egg	4
jīdòng	激動	激动	Adj.	excited	7
jítā	吉他	吉他	N.	guitar	11

Pinyin	Traditional	Simplified	POS	English	Lesson
…jíle	…極了	…极了		extremely…	4
jíjí–mángmáng	急急忙忙	急急忙忙	IE	in a hurry	6
jǐ	*幾	几	Pron.	how many	3
jǐ yàng	幾樣	几样	Q.	several kinds	14
jǐ	*擠	挤	V.	to squeeze	10
jìsuàn	計算	计算	V.	to calculate	10
jì	記	记	V.	to remember	8
jìde	記得	记得	V.	to recall, to remember	9
jìzhù	記住	记住	V.-C.	to remember	8
jìrán	*既然	既然	Conj.	since, now that	10
jìmò	寂寞	寂寞	Adj.	lonely	7
Jiānádà	加拿大	加拿大	PW	Canada	2
Jiāzhōu	加州	加州	PW	California	1
jiā	*家	家	MW	*measure word for restaurant*	5
Jiāqí	家奇	家奇	PN	*Chinese name*	2
jiārén	家人	家人	N.	family	2
jiātíng	家庭	家庭	N.	family	3
Jiāxīng	家興	家兴	PN	*Chinese name*	2
jiàqī	*假期	假期	N.	vacation	9
jiàn miàn	*見面	见面	V.-O.	to meet	6
jiǎnyì	建議	建议	V.	to suggest	7
jiānglái	*將來	将来	TW	in the future	11
jiāohuàn	交換	交换	V.	exchange	6
jiāo	*教	教	V.	to teach	3
jiǎozi	餃子	饺子	N.	dumplings	10
jiào	*叫	叫	V.	to be named	1
jiàozuò	叫作	叫作	V.	to be called	15
jiēzhe	*接著	接着	V.	to continue	11
jiēmíng	*街名	街名	N.	name of the street	14
jiémù	*節目	节目	N.	show, program	10
jiérì	*節日	节日	N.	holiday	10
jiějie	*姐姐	姐姐	N.	elder sister	3

Pinyin	Traditional	Simplified	POS	English	Lesson
jièshào	介紹	介绍	V.	to introduce	3
jīn	*斤	斤	MW	Catty (units of weight =500 grams=1.1 pounds)	14
jīntiān	*今天	今天	TW	today	1
jǐnjǐn	*僅僅	仅仅	Adv.	only (formal)	13
jǐnguǎn zhǎo wǒ	儘管找我	尽管找我	IE	Don't hesitate to talk to me.	12
jǐnzhāng	*緊張	紧张	Adj.	nervous	6
jìn	*進	进	V.	to enter	4
jìnbù	*進步	进步	N.	progress	15
jìnr	勁兒	劲儿	N.	strength	8
jīngshen	*精神	精神	Adj.	vigorous	8
jīngtōng	*精通	精通	V.	to be proficient in	11
jiūzhèng	糾正	纠正	V.	to correct	6
jiǔ	*酒	酒	N.	drink (alcohol)	9
jiù	*就	就	Adv.	just, then	2
jǔsàng	沮喪	沮丧	Adj.	depressed	12
jùzi	*句子	句子	N.	sentence	9
juéde	*覺得	觉得	V.	to feel, to think	2
juédìng	決定	决定	V.	to decide	6
K kāfēi	*咖啡	咖啡	N.	coffee	4
kāi	開	开	V.	to hold	10
kāi fàn	開飯	开饭	V.-O.	start eating	4
kāi ge wánxiào	開個玩笑	开个玩笑	IE	Just kidding	7
kāi kǒu	開口	开口	V.-O.	to ask	13
kāi xué	開學	开学	V.-O.	school starts	9
kāilǎng dàfang	開朗大方	开朗大方	IE	open and natural	13
kāishǐ	*開始	开始	V.	to start	11
kàn	*看	看	V.	to read	3
kànjiàn	看見	看见	V.	to see	6
kànqǐlái	看起來	看起来	VP	It looks like…	12
kǎo shì	*考試	考试	V.-O.	to take an exam	8
kě	可	可	Adv.	*used to emphasize*	6

kě'ài	可愛	可爱	Adj.	being adorable	3
kělè	可樂	可乐	N.	coke	8
kěnéng	可能	可能	Aux. V.	maybe, perhaps	6
kěshì	*可是	可是	Conj.	but	1
kěyǐ	可以	可以	Aux.V.	may	3
kèqi	*客氣	客气	Adj.	polite	7
kè	課	课	N.	course, class, lesson	2
kèwén	課文	课文	N.	text	15
kěndìng	*肯定	肯定	Adv.	definitely, I am positive that	9
kǒngpà	*恐怕	恐怕	Adv.	to be afraid that	12
kǒu	*口	口	MW	measure word for population	3
kuài	*塊	块	MW	measure word for money	14
kuài	快	快	Adj.	quick	5
kuàicān	快餐	快餐	N.	fast food	8
kuàilè	快樂	快乐	Adj.	happy	10
kuàizi	筷子	筷子	N.	chopsticks	4
kùn	*睏	困	Adj.	sleepy	7

L

là	辣	辣	Adj.	spicy	5
lánqiú	*籃球	篮球	N.	basketball	11
Lǎo Sìchuān	*老四川	老四川	PN	old Sichuan (name of a restaurant)	5
lǎodà	老大	老大	N.	the first child	3
lǎogōng	*老公	老公	N.	hubby	10
lǎopo	*老婆	老婆	N.	wife	10
lǎoshī	*老師	老师	N.	teacher	2
lǎowài	老外	老外	N.	foreigner	10
lǎoxiǎo	老小	老小	N.	the youngest child	3
le	*了	了	Pt.	particle indicating a change of state	2
lèi	*累	累	Adj.	tired	3
lèihuài	*累壞	累坏	V.-C.	exhausted	10
lěng	*冷	冷	Adj.	cold	1
lí	*離	离	V.	to be ... away from	7

詞語索引

lǐbài	禮拜	礼拜	N.	week	6
lǐmào	禮貌	礼貌	Adj.	polite	6
Lǐ	李	李	PN	*surname*	2
lǐ	裡	里	N.	in, inside	3
lìshǐ	*歷史	历史	N.	history	15
lián	*連	连	Prep.	even	8
liànxí	練習	练习	V.	to practice	6
liǎng	*兩	两	Num.	two (when followed by a measure word)	3
liáo tiānr	聊天兒	聊天儿	V.-O.	to chat	7
liǎojiě	*瞭解	了解	V.	to understand	15
lìngwài	*另外	另外	Conj.	besides	11
liúxià	留下	留下	V.-C.	to leave	6
liúxuéshēng	留學生	留学生	N.	international student	1
liù	*六	六	Num.	six	3
lóngxiā	*龍蝦	龙虾	N.	lobster	14
lóuxià	樓下	楼下	PW	downstairs	4
lùkǒu	*路口	路口	N.	intersection	14
lǜchá	綠茶	绿茶	N.	green tea	4
lǜsè	*綠色	绿色	N.	green color	9
Lúndūn	倫敦	伦敦	PW	London	1
M ma	*嗎	吗	Pt.	*question particle*	1
māma	*媽媽	妈妈	N.	mom	3
má	*麻	麻	Adj.	spicy (numb)	5
máfan	*麻煩	麻烦	V.	to bother, to trouble	6
mápó dòufu	麻婆豆腐	麻婆豆腐	NP	*name of a Sichuan dish*	5
mǎlù	*馬路	马路	N.	road	14
mǎshàng	*馬上	马上	Adv.	right away	4
mǎi	*買	买	V.	to buy	4
mǎihǎo	*買好	买好	V.-C.	to have bought	7
màn	*慢	慢	Adj.	slow	5
mànmānr lái ba	慢慢兒來吧	慢慢儿来吧	IE	Take it easy.	12
máng	*忙	忙	Adj.	busy	3

māo	*貓	猫	N.	cat	9
máo	*毛	毛	N.	fur	9
méi	*沒	没	Adv.	not (to negate 有)	4
méijīng–dǎcǎi	沒精打采	没精打采	IE	to look tired and unhappy	8
méi yìsi	沒意思	没意思	IE	boring	7
Měiguó	*美國	美国	PW	America	1
Měishì	*美式	美式	N.	American style	11
měi	*每	每	Pron.	each	3
měi cì	每次	每次	NP	each time	13
mèimei	妹妹	妹妹	N.	young sister	3
mén	門	门	N.	gate, door	6
mèng	夢	梦	N.	dream	8
mèngjiàn	夢見	梦见	V.-C.	to dream of	8
mǐ	米	米	N.	rice	4
mǐfàn	*米飯	米饭	N.	cooked rice	4
Mìmì	覓覓	觅觅	PN	*name of the cat*	9
miāo	喵	喵	Onom.	*cry of a cat*	9
miào	*妙	妙	Adj.	Great!	9
míng	名	名	MW	*measure word indicating number of people*	11
míngzi	名字	名字	N.	name	1
míngbai	*明白	明白	V.	to be clear	3
mǔqīn	*母親	母亲	N.	mother (formal)	3

N

ná	*拿	拿	V.	to bring	7
náshǒucài	拿手菜	拿手菜	N.	(sb.'s) specialty	4
nǎ / něi	*哪	哪	Pron.	which	2
nǎr	哪兒	哪儿	Pron.	where	4
nǎli nǎli	哪裡哪裡	哪里哪里	IE	No, no.	6
nà / nèi	*那	那	Pron.	that	2
nà	*那	那	Conj.	in that case	4
nǎinai	*奶奶	奶奶	N.	grandmother	3
nàixīn	耐心	耐心	Adj.	patience	15

nánhái r	*男孩兒	男孩儿	N.	boy	13
nán	*南	南	N.	(the) south	14
nán	難	难	Adj.	hard, difficult	8
nán jì	*難記	难记	VP	difficult to remember	8
nánguò	*難過	难过	Adj.	sad	12
ne	*呢	呢	Pt.	*particle used for inquiry*	1
néng	*能	能	Aux.V.	can	3
nénggàn	能幹	能干	Adj.	capable	10
nénggē-shànwǔ	能歌善舞	能歌善舞	IE	good at singing and dancing	13
ǹg	嗯	嗯	Int.	*to show agreement*	4
nǐ	*你	你	Pron.	you	1
nǐ hǎo	你好	你好	IE	hello	1
nǐ yì yán wǒ yì yǔ	你一言我一語	你一言我一语	IE	eagerly to tell each other	9
nǐmen	*你們	你们	Pron.	you (plural)	2
niánlíng	*年齡	年龄	N.	age	12
niánqīng	*年輕	年轻	Adj.	young	12
niányèfàn	*年夜飯	年夜饭	N.	dinner on New Year's Eve	10
niàn	唸	念	V.	to attend school	8
niàn shū	*唸書	念书	V.-O.	to study	8
niǎo	*鳥	鸟	N.	bird	10
Niǔyuē	紐約	纽约	PW	New York	1
nónglì	*農曆	农历	N.	lunar calendar	10
nǚ	女	女	Adj.	female	6
nǚ de	女的	女的	NP	female	6
nǚ'ér	*女兒	女儿	N.	daughter	3
nǚhái r	*女孩兒	女孩儿	N.	girl	13
nǚpéngyou	女朋友	女朋友	N.	girlfriend	5
nǚshì	*女士	女士	N.	lady	14

O

ó	哦	哦	Int.	oh	7

P

pá	*爬	爬	V.	to climb	9
pà	*怕	怕	V.	to be afraid	10
pāi	*拍	拍	V.	to shoot (a movie)	13

pǎo	*跑	跑	V.	to run	8
pǎo bù	跑步	跑步	V.-O.	to jog	8
pào chá	*泡茶	泡茶	V.-O.	to steep tea	4
péngyou	*朋友	朋友	N.	friend	1
pèng	碰	碰	V.	to run into	14
píjiǔ	*啤酒	啤酒	N.	beer	12
piānzi	*片子	片子	N.	movie, film	13
piányi	*便宜	便宜	Adj.	cheap	14
piàoliang	漂亮	漂亮	Adj.	beautiful	2
píng	*瓶	瓶	MW	bottle	12
pútao	*葡萄	葡萄	N.	grape	14
pǔtōnghuà	*普通話	普通话	PN	Mandarin	14

Q

qíshí	*其實	其实	Adv.	actually	6
qítā	其他	其他	Pron.	other	10
qíguài	*奇怪	奇怪	Adj.	strange	2
qí	*騎	骑	V.	to ride	11
qí mǎ	*騎馬	骑马	V.-O.	to ride a horse	15
qí	*棋	棋	N.	chess or any board game	11
qǐ chuáng	*起床	起床	V.-O.	to get up	8
qǐlái	起來	起来	V.	to get up	8
qì mǎ	氣馬	气马	VP	to anger a horse	15
qìfēn	*氣氛	气氛	N.	atmosphere	11
qián	*前	前	TW	front, in front of	6
qiánmiàn	前面	前面	PW	the front	6
qián	錢	钱	N.	money	3
qiáng	*強	强	Adj.	strong, good	8
qiáo nǐ	瞧你	瞧你	IE	Look at you!	10
qīn'ài	親愛	亲爱	Adj.	dear	10
qīnrén	親人	亲人	N.	close relative	3
qín	琴	琴	N.	*general name for stringed instruments*	11
qīngchu	*清楚	清楚	Adj.	clear	9

詞語索引

qǐng gēn wǒ lái	請跟我來	请跟我来	IE	Please follow me.	5
qǐng màn yòng	請慢用	请慢用	IE	Please enjoy.	4
qǐng rén	請人	请人	VP	to hire sb.	3
qǐng shāo děng	請稍等	请稍等	IE	Please wait a minute!	4
qǐngwèn	請問	请问	V.	May I ask?	1
qǐng zhèbiān zuò	*請這邊坐	请这边坐	IE	Please be seated here.	5
qìnghè	慶賀	庆贺	V.	to celebrate	10
qù	*去	去	V.	to go	4
què	*卻	却	Adv.	but (formal)	

R

ránhòu	*然後	然后	Conj.	afterwards	6
ràng	*讓	让	V.	to let	11
rè	熱	热	Adj.	hot	1
rènao	*熱鬧	热闹	Adj.	lively and noisy	10
rèxīn	熱心	热心	Adj.	warm-hearted, enthusiastic	13
rén	*人	人	N.	person	1
rén jiàn rén ài	人見人愛	人见人爱	IE	to be loved by everybody	6
rènshi	*認識	认识	V.	to know sb.	1
Rìběn	日本	日本	PW	Japan	2
rìzi	日子	日子	N.	day (formal)	10
róngyì	*容易	容易	Adj.	easy	12
rúguǒ	*如果	如果	Conj.	if (formal)	13

S

sāi chē	塞車	塞车	V.-O.	traffic jam	7
shǎ	傻	傻	Adj.	silly	13
shǎxiào	*傻笑	傻笑	V.	to laugh in a silly way	13
shàng	上	上	V.	to go to	2
shàng	*上	上	N.	on, on top of…	9
shàng ge	上個	上个		last (week/month)	12
Shànghǎi	上海	上海	PW	Shanghai	1
shàng kè	*上課	上课	V.-O.	to go to class	2
sháo	*勺	勺	MW	spoon	10
shǎo	*少	少	Adj.	few, less	6
shéi / shuí	*誰	谁	Pron.	who	3

351

pinyin	traditional	simplified	POS	English	lesson
shēntǐ	*身體	身体	N.	body, health	12
shēn	*深	深	Adj.	deep	15
shénme	*什麼	什么	Pron.	what, what kind of	1
shēng bìng	生病	生病	V.-O.	to get sick	8
shēngyi	生意	生意	N.	business	3
shēngdiào	聲調	声调	N.	tones	6
Shèngdàn Jié	聖誕節	圣诞节	PN	Christmas	9
shī liàn	失戀	失恋	V.-O.	to get dumped	12
shífēn	十分	十分	Adv.	very, extremely (formal)	11
shízì	*十字	十字	N.	the cross	14
shíjiān	*時間	时间	N.	time	6
shíjiān dàole	時間到了	时间到了	IE	Time is up.	11
shípǐn	*食品	食品	N.	food	10
shǐ	*使	使	V.	to make...feel	14
shìjiè	*世界	世界	N.	world	9
shìchǎng	*市場	市场	N.	market	14
shìde	*似的	似的	Pt.	It seems that...	8
shì	*事	事	N.	matter, thing	4
shìqing	事情	事情	N.	things	3
shì	*是	是	V.	to be	1
shōudào	收到	收到	V.-C.	to receive	6
shōuhuò	*收穫	收获	N.	gains, harvest	15
shōuyǎng	*收養	收养	V.	to adopt (a pet)	9
shǒu	*手	手	N.	hand	10
shǒujī	*手機	手机	N.	cell phone	14
shǒu	*首	首	MW	*measure word for songs*	10
shū	書	书	N.	book	7
shū	書	书	N.	calligraphy	11
shūfǎ	*書法	书法	N.	calligraphy	11
shūfu	舒服	舒服	Adj.	comfortable	1
shūcài	*蔬菜	蔬菜	N.	vegetables	8
shú néng shēng qiǎo	*熟能生巧	熟能生巧	IE	Practice makes perfect.	15

shù	*樹	树	N.	tree	10
shuǎi	甩	甩	V.	to be dumped	12
shuài	*帥	帅	Adj.	cool, handsome	6
shuāng	雙	双	MW	pair	4
shuǐguǒ	*水果	水果	N.	fruits	8
shuǐjiǎo	水餃	水饺	N.	dumplings	15
shuǐpíng	水平	水平	N.	level	6
shuì jiào	*睡覺	睡觉	V.-O.	to sleep	7
shuō	說	说	V.	to speak, to say	3
shuōbúdìng	說不定	说不定	Adv.	perhaps	7
shuōchūlái	說出來	说出来	VP	to speak out	12
shuōdào	說到	说到	V.-C.	to talk about	9
shuō de yě shì	說的也是	说的也是	IE	I agree.	6
shuō huà	*說話	说话	V.-O.	to speak, to talk	3
shuōmíng	說明	说明	V.	to indicate	13
shuōqǐ	說起	说起	V.-C.	talking about	11
sǐ	*死	死	Adj.	extremely	8
Sìchuāncài	四川菜	四川菜	N.	Sichuan dish / food	5
sìshēng	四聲	四声	N.	four tones	6
sùshè	宿舍	宿舍	N.	dormitory	4
suāncàiyú	*酸菜魚	酸菜鱼	N.	fish with pickled vegetable	5
suānlàtāng	*酸辣湯	酸辣汤	N.	hot and sour soup	5
suàn	算	算	V.	to count	6
suànle	算了	算了	V.	Forget it.	11
suīrán	*雖然	虽然	Conj.	although	3
suí biàn	*隨便	随便	V.-O.	Do as you please.	11
suì	歲	岁	N.	age	9
sūnzi	孫子	孙子	N.	grandson	3
suǒ zhī shèn shǎo	*所知甚少	所知甚少	IE	to know a little	15
suǒyǐ	*所以	所以	Conj.	therefore	2
suǒyǒu	所有	所有	Adj.	all	10

T

tā	*他	他	Pron.	he, him	1

tā	*她	她	Pron.	she, her	2
tā	它	它	Pron.	it	9
tài	*太	太	Adv.	too	1
tán	*談	谈	V.	to talk (about)	11
tán	*彈	弹	V.	to play (musical instrument)	11
tǎo rén xǐhuan	討人喜歡	讨人喜欢	IE	lovable	13
tào	套	套	MW	a set of	4
tèbié	特別	特别	Adv.	especially	3
tī	*踢	踢	V.	to kick, to play (football)	11
tíchūlái	*提出來	提出来	VP	to bring it up	12
tígāo	提高	提高	V.	to improve	6
tì	*替	替	Prep.	to do sth. in place of sb.	13
tiān	天	天	MW	day	2
tiānqì	天氣	天气	N.	weather	1
tiānshēng	天生	天生	Adj.	born to be	15
tiān tiān	天天	天天	NP	everyday	9
tiáo	*條	条	MW	measure word for things that are long or strip-like	14
tiào	*跳	跳	V.	to jump	9
tiào wǔ	*跳舞	跳舞	V.-O.	to dance	10
tīng	聽	听	V.	to listen to	5
tīngdǒng	聽懂	听懂	V.-C.	to understand	9
tīngshuō	*聽説	听说	V.	to hear sth. from others	5
tǐng	*挺	挺	Adv.	quite	7
tóngbànr	*同伴兒	同伴儿	N.	teammate	11
tóngwū	*同屋	同屋	N.	room mate	7
tóngxué	同學	同学	N.	classmate	1
tóu dà jí le	*頭大極了	头大极了	IE	headache	15
tóuténg	*頭疼	头疼	Adj.	headache	15
Tǔ'ěrqí	土耳其	土耳其	PW	Turkey	2
túshūguǎn	圖書館	图书馆	N.	library	6
W wàiguó	外國	外国	N.	foreign country	1

詞語索引

wán	完	完	V.	(finish) up	5
wán	完	完	V.	to run out	8
wánquán	*完全	完全	Adv.	completely	12
wánr de kāixīn	玩兒得開心	玩儿得开心	IE	Have a good time!	7
wánwanr	玩玩兒	玩玩儿	VP	to have some fun	7
wǎn	*晚	晚	Adj.	late	6
wǎnhuì	晚會	晚会	N.	party	10
wǎnshang	晚上	晚上	TW	evening	3
Wáng	*王	王	PN	*surname*	1
wǎng qiú	*網球	网球	N.	tennis	11
wǎng	*往	往	Prep.	to, towards	14
wàng le	*忘了	忘了	VP	to forget	9
wàngjì	*忘記	忘记	V.	to forget	12
wéiqí	*圍棋	围棋	N.	Go (a Chinese board game)	11
wèi	為	为	Prep.	for	6
wèi shénme	為什麼	为什么	IE	why	3
wèi	*位	位	MW	*measure word for people (polite form)*	5
wèidào	*味道	味道	N.	taste	5
wénhuà	文化	文化	N.	culture	15
Wényīng	文英	文英	PN	*Chinese name*	2
wèn	問	问	V.	to ask	3
wèntí	*問題	问题	N.	question	3
wǒ	*我	我	Pron.	I, Me	1
wǒmen	我們	我们	Pron.	we, us	2
wǔ	*五	五	Num.	five	3
wǔfàn	*午飯	午饭	N.	lunch	4
wùhuì	*誤會	误会	V.	to misunderstand	9
X xī	西	西	N.	(the) west	14
xīhóngshì	西紅柿	西红柿	N.	tomato	4
xīwàng	*希望	希望	V./N.	to hope; hope	9
xíguàn	習慣	习惯	V.	to be used to doing sth.	4

xǐ yíng	喜迎	喜迎	VP	to welcome	10
xǐhuan	*喜歡	喜欢	V.	to like	1
xǐhuanshàng	喜歡上	喜欢上	V.-C.	to begin to like	11
xì	*系	系	N.	department	10
xià qí	下棋	下棋	V.-O.	to play chess	11
xiàcì	*下次	下次	TW	next time	4
xiàmiàn	下面	下面	N.	next	11
xià yí tiào	*嚇一跳	吓一跳	VP	to be scared	15
xiān	*先	先	Adv.	first	3
xiànzài	*現在	现在	TW	now	4
xiāngxìn	相信	相信	V.	to believe	14
xiāng	香	香	Adj.	delicious	4
xiǎng	*想	想	Aux. V.	would like to, to miss, to think	2
xiǎngfǎ	想法	想法	N.	idea	13
xiǎnglái-xiǎngqù	想來想去	想来想去	VP	to think over and over	12
xiàng	*向	向	Prep.	to	11
xiànglái	*向來	向来	Adv.	all along	8
xiàng	*像	像	V.	to look like, to resemble	15
xiǎo	*小	小	Adj.	young	1
Xiǎofāng	小芳	小芳	PN	*a girl's name*	13
xiǎokàn wǒ le	小看我了	小看我了	IE	I am not that silly.	4
xiǎopǐn	小品	小品	N.	a play	10
xiǎo shēng diǎnr	小聲點兒	小声点儿	IE	Be quiet!	13
xiǎoshí	小時	小时	N.	hour	6
Xiǎoxiǎo	小小	小小	PN	*a name*	1
xiào	笑	笑	V.	to laugh	13
xiě	*寫	写	V.	to write	8
xièxie	*謝謝	谢谢	V.	Thank you.	2
xīndì shànliáng	心地善良	心地善良	IE	good hearted	13
xīnqíng	心情	心情	N.	mood	12
xīnshì	心事	心事	N.	sth. weighing on one's mind	13
xīnkǔ	辛苦	辛苦	Adj.	laborious	3

xīnqín	*辛勤	辛勤	Adj.	hardworking		15
xīn	新	新	Adj.	new		1
xīnchūn	新春	新春	N.	the Spring of a new year		10
xìn	*信	信	N.	letter		6
xīngfèn	*興奮	兴奋	Adj.	excited		2
xīngqī	*星期	星期	N.	week		6
xīngqīwǔ	星期五	星期五	TW	Friday		6
xíng	*行	行	V.	(to indicate agreement) ok, fine		4
xìng	*姓	姓	V.	to be surnamed		1
xìngfú	幸福	幸福	Adj.	happy		3
xìngkuī	*幸虧	幸亏	Adv.	luckily		7
xìngyùn	*幸運	幸运	Adj.	lucky		15
xìnggé	*性格	性格	N.	personality		6
xìngqíng	*性情	性情	N.	temperament		12
xìngqù	*興趣	兴趣	N.	interest		6
xiōngdi	*兄弟	兄弟	N.	brothers		11
xiūxi	*休息	休息	V.	to rest		8
xūyào	*需要	需要	V.	to need		13
xū	噓	嘘	Int.	*sound made to stop the noise*		13
xuǎnzé	*選擇	选择	V.	to choose		12
xuéqī	*學期	学期	N.	semester		9
xuésheng	*學生	学生	N.	student		1
xuéxiào	*學校	学校	N.	school		5
Y yánjiūshēng	研究生	研究生	N.	graduate student		3
yǎnjing	*眼睛	眼睛	N.	eyes		9
yánglì	*陽曆	阳历	N.	solar calendar		10
yángqiāng-yángdiào	洋腔洋調	洋腔洋调	IE	foreign accent		10
yàng yàng jīngtōng	樣樣精通	样样精通	IE	to be good at everything		11
yāoqiú	*要求	要求	N.	requirement		6
yāoqǐng	*邀請	邀请	V.	to invite		10
yào	*要	要	V.	need		2
yào	要	要	Aux.V	will		3

Pinyin	Traditional	Simplified	POS	English	Lesson
yàobùrán	要不然	要不然	Conj.	otherwise	7
yàobúshì	要不是	要不是	Conj.	if it were not for	7
yàoshi	要是	要是	Conj.	if	6
yéye	*爺爺	爷爷	N.	grandfather	3
yěxǔ	*也許	也许	Adv.	perhaps	7
yèyú	*業餘	业余	Adj.	spare time, amateur	11
yī	*一	一	Num.	one	1
yī...jiù...	一…就…	一…就…		as soon as…, then…	5
yìbiān…yìbiān…	一邊…一邊…	一边…一边…		do A while doing B	10
(yì) diǎnr	（一）點兒	（一）点儿	Q.	a little bit of, some	4
yídìng	一定	一定	Adv.	definitely	3
yí duàn	*一段	一段	Q.	a period of (time)	12
yígòng	*一共	一共	Adv.	altogether	3
yíhuìr	一會兒	一会儿	Q.	in a while	4
yí lù píng'ān	一路平安	一路平安	IE	Have a safe trip!	7
yìqǐ	一起	一起	N.	together	3
yī shì	一是	一是	Conj.	one thing is that…	12
yì tiān dào wǎn	一天到晚	一天到晚	IE	from morning till night	8
yíxià	*一下	一下	Q.	a little bit	3
yìxiē	*一些	一些	Q.	some	12
yì yán wéi dìng	*一言爲定	一言为定	IE	Okay. / It is a deal./set in stone	5
yíyàng	*一樣	一样	Adj.	same	2
yìzhí	*一直	一直	Adv.	straight	14
yīshēng	醫生	医生	N.	doctor	3
yǐjīng	*已經	已经	Adv.	already	7
(yǐ)hòu	*（以）後	（以）后	TW	later	4
yǐwéi	以爲	以为	V.	to think wrongly	7
yìshùjiā	藝術家	艺术家	N.	artist	11
Yìdàlì	意大利	意大利	PW	Italy	2
yìsi	*意思	意思	N.	meaning	9
yīnwèi	*因爲	因为	Conj.	because	2
yīnlì	*陰曆	阴历	N.	lunar calendar	10

yīnyuè	*音樂	音乐	N.	music	3
yǐnshí	*飲食	饮食	N.	food and drinking	15
yīnggāi	*應該	应该	Aux. V.	should	7
Yīngguó	英國	英国	PW	Britain	1
Yīng–Hàn	英漢	英汉	NP	English-Chinese	7
Yīngyǔ	*英語	英语	N.	English	6
yǒngyuǎn	*永遠	永远	Adv.	forever	13
yòng	*用	用	V.	to use	4
yōumògǎn	*幽默感	幽默感	N.	sense of humor	13
yōujiǔ	*悠久	悠久	Adj.	long	15
yóuqí	*尤其	尤其	Adv.	especially	15
yóujiàn	郵件	邮件	N.	e-mail	6
yóuxíng	遊行	游行	V.	parade	7
yóu yǒng	*游泳	游泳	V.-O.	to swim	11
yǒuhǎo	友好	友好	Adj.	friendly	13
yǒu	*有	有	V.	to have	1
yǒudiǎnr	有點兒	有点儿	Adv.	a little bit	6
yǒuguān	*有關	有关	V.	be related to	15
yǒu liǎng xiàzi	有兩下子	有两下子	IE	to be really sth.	4
yǒumíng	有名	有名	Adj.	famous	5
yǒu qián	有錢	有钱	VP	to be rich	3
yǒu rén	有人	有人	NP	somebody	13
yòu	*又	又	Adv.	furthermore	3
yòu...yòu...	又…又…	又…又…		both... and...	5
yòu	*右	右	N.	right (side)	14
yúshì	於是	于是	Conj.	herefore	6
yǔbàn	*語伴	语伴	N.	language exchange partner	6
yǔyán	語言	语言	N.	language	6
yùdào	*遇到	遇到	V.-C.	to encounter	15
yuánlái	原來	原来	Adv.	originally	5
yuányīn	*原因	原因	N.	reason	11
yuǎn	遠	远	Adj.	far	7

yuànyì	*願意	愿意	Aux. V.	to be willing		6
yuēhǎo	約好	约好	V.-C.	to make an appointment		6
yuēhuì	*約會	约会	N./V.	dating; to date		6
yuè	*越	越	Adv.	more		5
yuè...yuè...	越⋯越⋯	越⋯越⋯		the more..., the more...		5
Yuèyǔ	粵語	粤语	N.	Cantonese (language)		14
yùnqi	運氣	运气	N.	luck		14
Z zài	*在	在	Prep.	to be at		3
zài...kànlái	在⋯看來	在⋯看来		according to		15
zàijiàn	再見	再见	V.	goodbye		1
zàishuō	*再說	再说	Conj.	besides		5
zán gēr liǎ	咱哥兒倆	咱哥儿俩	IE	we two brothers		12
zánmen	*咱們	咱们	Pron.	we, us (inclusive)		10
zérèngǎn	*責任感	责任感	N.	sense of responsibility		13
zěnme	怎麼	怎么	Pron.	how come		7
zěnme bàn	怎麼辦	怎么办	IE	What shall I do?		10
zěnme gǎo de	怎麼搞的	怎么搞的	IE	What's wrong?		8
zěnme huíshì	怎麼回事	怎么回事	IE	What has happened?		8
zěnmeyàng	怎麼樣	怎么样	Pron.	how about...		4
zhànyòng	*佔用	占用	V.	to use		12
Zhāng	張	张	PN	*surname*		1
Zhāng Yìmóu	張藝謀	张艺谋	PN	*name of a Chinese director*		13
zhǎng	*長	长	V.	to grow (appearance)		6
zhǎo	*找	找	V.	to look for		6
zhàogù	照顧	照顾	V.	to take care of		3
zhè; zhèi	這	这	Pron.	this		3
zhème	這麼	这么	Pron.	so		4
zhème qiǎo	這麼巧	这么巧	IE	What a coincidence!		9
zhèyàng	這樣	这样	Pron.	in this way		12
zhēn	*真	真	Adv.	truly		1
zhēnchéng	*真誠	真诚	Adj.	sincere		13
zhēn yào mìng	真要命	真要命	IE	It is killing me.		8

zhènghǎo	正好	正好	Adv.	to be about	6
zhī	*隻	只	MW	measure word for animals	9
zhīdào	*知道	知道	V.	to know (a fact)	1
zhīxīn	知心	知心	Adj.	to know what one is thinking about	9
zhīxīn àiren	知心愛人	知心爱人	NP	soul mate	10
zhīxīn péngyou	知心朋友	知心朋友	NP	one's best friend	9
zhǐ	*只	只	Adv.	only	3
zhǐhǎo zhèyàng le	只好這樣了	只好这样了	IE	no other choices but this	14
zhìqù xiāngtóu	志趣相投	志趣相投	IE	to share the same interest	11
zhōngcān	*中餐	中餐	N.	Chinese food (formal expression)	5
zhōngcānguǎnr	中餐館兒	中餐馆儿	N.	Chinese restaurant	5
zhōngděng gèr	*中等個兒	中等个儿	NP	of the average height	13
Zhōngguó	*中國	中国	PW	China	1
Zhōngguóchéng	中國城	中国城	N.	China town	4
Zhōnghuá	*中華	中华	N.	China	14
Zhōngwén	*中文	中文	N.	Chinese langauge	1
zhōngwǔ	中午	中午	TW	noon	4
zhōngshí	*忠實	忠实	Adj.	loyal	9
zhōngyú	*終於	终于	Adv.	finally	10
zhǒng	*種	种	MW	kind	6
zhòng	重	重	Adj.	heavy	12
zhòngshì	*重視	重视	V.	pay special attention to (formal)	10
zhòngyào	重要	重要	Adj.	important	10
zhōumò	*週末	周末	TW	weekend	12
zhǔdòng	*主動	主动	Adj.	active, to offer to do	13
zhǔxiū	*主修	主修	V.	to major in	11
zhǔyào	主要	主要	Adj.	mainly	12
zhǔyi	*主意	主意	N.	idea	4
zhùyìdào	*注意到	注意到	V.-C.	to notice	9
zhù	*祝	祝	V.	to wish	8

zhù nǐ hǎo yùn	祝你好運	祝你好运	IE	Good luck!	7
zhuānyè	*專業	专业	N.	major	11
zhuǎn	*轉	转	V.	to turn	14
zhǔnbèi	*準備	准备	V.	to plan	7
zhǔnshí	*準時	准时	Adv.	on time	4
zīwèir	*滋味兒	滋味儿	N.	taste (of doing sth., metaphorical)	13
zìcóng	自從	自从	Prep.	ever since	15
zìjǐ	*自己	自己	Pron.	self	3
zìxíngchē	*自行車	自行车	N.	bicycle	11
zìzài	*自在	自在	Adj.	comfortable, at ease	7
zìdiǎn	*字典	字典	N.	dictionary	7
zǒngshì	總是	总是	Adv.	always	6
zǒngsuàn	*總算	总算	Adv.	finally	6
zǒu	走	走	V.	to walk	14
zǒudiū	*走丟	走丢	V.-C.	to get lost	14
zúqiú	*足球	足球	N.	football	11
zǔ	*組	组	N.	group	11
zuìhòu	最後	最后	Adv.	finally	5
zuìjìn	*最近	最近	N.	recently	8
zuì	*醉	醉	Adj.	drunk	12
zūnzhòng	*尊重	尊重	V.	to respect	12
zuǒ	*左	左	N.	left (side)	14
zuǒsī–yòuxiǎng	左思右想	左思右想	IE	to think over and over	10
zuǒyòu	*左右	左右	N.	or so	10
zuòyè	*作業	作业	N.	homework	12
zuò	*坐	坐	V.	to sit	4
zuò	*做	做	V.	to make, to do	3

補充詞語

A ǎi	矮	矮	Adj.	short (in height)	8
àiqíng diànyǐng	愛情電影	爱情电影	NP	romance movie	6

B	bǎ	把	把	MW	*measure word for things with handles*	4
	bái	白	白	Adj.	white	8
	báilǐng	白領	白领	N.	white collar	6
	báirìmèng	白日夢	白日梦	N.	daydream	11
	bāozi	包子	包子	N.	steam bread with fillings	5
	běi	北	北	N.	north	9
	Běijīng Dàxué	北京大學	北京大学	PN	Peking University	4
	Běijīng kǎoyā	北京烤鴨	北京烤鸭	NP	Peking Roast Duck	4
	běn	本	本	MW	*measure word for books*	2
	běnzi	本子	本子	N.	notebook	2
	bǐ	筆	笔	N.	pen, writing tools	2
	bì yè	畢業	毕业	V.-O.	to graduate	6
	bīngjīlíng	冰激淩	冰激凌	N.	ice cream	12
C	cài	菜	菜	N.	dish (cooked), vegetable	2
	cǎo	草	草	N.	grass	10
	cǎoméi	草莓	草莓	N.	strawberry	5
	Chángchéng	長城	长城	PN	Great Wall	4
	chàng gē	唱歌	唱歌	V.-O.	to sing	3
	chāorén	超人	超人	N.	superman	8
	chídào	遲到	迟到	V.	be late	8
	chǒngwù	寵物	宠物	N.	pet	9
	chōu yān	抽菸	抽烟	V.-O.	to smoke	8
	chūntiān	春天	春天	N.	spring	1
	chūzūchē	出租車	出租车	N.	taxi	6
D	dǎ bǎolíngqiú	打保齡球	打保龄球	VP	to play bowling	11
	dǎ gāo ěrfūqiú	打高爾夫球	打高尔夫球	VP	to play golf	11
	dǎ lánqiú	打籃球	打篮球	VP	to play basketball	3
	dǎ páiqiú	打排球	打排球	VP	to play volleyball	11
	dǎ wǎngqiú	打網球	打网球	VP	to play tennis	3
	dàngāo	蛋糕	蛋糕	N.	cake	5

	de	地	地	Pt.	*to indicate the way that an action is carried out*	6
	de	的	的	Pt.	*to indicate possessive*	1
	děng	等	等	V.	*to wait*	3
	diǎn	點	点	MW	*o' clock*	4
	diànhuà	電話	电话	N.	*telephone*	4
	diànnǎo	電腦	电脑	N.	*computer (colloquial)*	4
	diànyǐngyuàn	電影院	电影院	N.	*movie theater*	4
	Díshìní	迪士尼	迪士尼	PN	*Disney World*	13
	dōng	東	东	N.	*east*	9
	dōngtiān	冬天	冬天	N.	*winter*	1
	dòngzuò diànyǐng	動作電影	动作电影	NP	*action movie*	6
	dòufu	豆腐	豆腐	N.	*tofu*	5
	duìhuà	對話	对话	N.	*dialogue*	1
	dùn	頓	顿	MW	*measure word for meals*	4
E	Éwén	俄文	俄文	N.	*Russian (language)*	3
F	fángzi	房子	房子	N.	*house*	11
	fēnzhōng	分鐘	分钟	TW	*minute*	3
	fēng	風	风	N.	*wind*	8
	fēngjǐnghuà	風景畫	风景画	N.	*scenery paintings*	13
	fēngkuáng	瘋狂	疯狂	Adj.	*crazy*	13
	fúwù	服務	服务	V.	*to serve*	13
G	gàosù	告訴	告诉	V.	*to tell*	6
	gēchàngjiā	歌唱家	歌唱家	N.	*singer*	11
	Gēlúnbǐyà Dàxué	哥倫比亞大學	哥伦比亚大学	PN	*Columbia University*	4
	gōngfu	功夫	功夫	N.	*kongfu*	14
	gōngjīn	公斤	公斤	MW	*kilogram*	8
	gōngrén	工人	工人	N.	*worker*	6
	gōngsī	公司	公司	N.	*company*	6
	Gùgōng	故宮	故宫	PN	*Forbidden City*	4
	guǎngchǎng	廣場	广场	N.	*square*	6
	Guǎngzhōu	廣州	广州	PW	*Guangzhou*	5

	guàng jiē	逛街	逛街	V.-O.	to stroll along the street, to go window shopping	6
	guīlái	歸來	归来	V.	to return to an original place	13
	guìxìng	貴姓	贵姓	N.	honorable surname	1
	Guóqìng Jié	國慶節	国庆节	PN	National Day	7
	guǒzhī	果汁	果汁	N.	fruit juice	4
H	Hāfó Dàxué	哈佛大學	哈佛大学	PN	Harvard University	4
	hànxuéjiā	漢學家	汉学家	N.	Sinologist	11
	hǎokàn	好看	好看	Adj.	good-looking	2
	hē jiǔ	喝酒	喝酒	V.-O.	to drink	3
	hēi	黑	黑	Adj.	black	8
	huār	花兒	花儿	N.	flower	10
	huǒguō	火鍋	火锅	N.	hot pot	5
J	jīchì	雞翅	鸡翅	N.	chicken wings	7
	jìsuànjī	計算機	计算机	N.	computer (formal)	4
	jiācháng-biànfàn	家常便飯	家常便饭	IE	commonly seen, not rare	15
	Jiāfēimāo	加菲貓	加菲猫	PN	Garfield	12
	jiàn	件	件	MW	*measure word for clothes*	2
	jiànkāng	健康	健康	Adj.	healthy	12
	jiǎozi	餃子	饺子	N.	dumplings	5
	jiàoshì	教室	教室	N.	classroom	13
	jié hūn	結婚	结婚	V.-O.	to get married	8
	jié zhàng	結賬	结账	V.-O.	Check, please.	5
	jǐngchá	警察	警察	N.	policeman	12
	jīngjì	經濟	经济	N.	economy, economics	4
	jiǔbā	酒吧	酒吧	N.	bar	14
	júzi	橘子	橘子	N.	tangerine	5
	juédìng	決定	决定	V.	to decide	4
K	kāfēitīng	咖啡廳	咖啡厅	N.	cafe	7
	kàn diànyǐng	看電影	看电影	VP	to see a movie	3
	kēhuàn diànyǐng	科幻電影	科幻电影	NP	science fiction movie	6
	kěkǒu-kělè	可口可樂	可口可乐	N.	coca cola	5

	Kěndéjī	肯德基	肯德基	PN	Kentucky Fried Chicken	10
	kǒngbù diànyǐng	恐怖電影	恐怖电影	NP	horror movie	6
	kū	哭	哭	V.	to cry	8
	kuài	快	快	Adv.	quickly	4
L	lā xiǎotíqín	拉小提琴	拉小提琴	VP	to play violin	11
	lǎo Běijīng jīròu juǎn	老北京雞肉卷	老北京鸡肉卷	NP	Old Beijing Chicken Roll	10
	lǎohǔ	老虎	老虎	N.	tiger	8
	lìshǐ	歷史	历史	N.	history	4
	liǎn	臉	脸	N.	face	9
	mǎi dān	買單	买单	V.-O.	Check, please.	5
M	mài bào	賣報	卖报	V.-O.	to sell newspaper	6
	mántou	饅頭	馒头	N.	steam bread	5
	māo	貓	猫	N.	cat	4
	máobǐ	毛筆	毛笔	N.	brush (pen)	4
	miàntiáo	麵條兒	面条儿	N.	noodles	5
N	nán	南	南	N.	south	9
	nián	年	年	TW	year	3
	nín	您	您	Pron.	you (polite form of 你)	1
	níngméng	檸檬	柠檬	N.	lemon	6
	niúnǎi	牛奶	牛奶	N.	milk	4
	nóngmín	農民	农民	N.	peasant	6
P	pāi	拍	拍	V.	to pat	10
	pàng	胖	胖	Adj.	over-weight	8
	pángbiān	旁邊	旁边	PW	side	4
	píjiǔ	啤酒	啤酒	N.	beer	8
	píng	瓶	瓶	MW	bottle	2
	píngguǒ	蘋果	苹果	N.	apple	5
	pútao	葡萄	葡萄	N.	grape	5
Q	qīshàng-bāxià	七上八下	七上八下	IE	nervous	15
	qǐfēi	起飛	起飞	V.	to take off	10
	Qīnghuá Dàxué	清華大學	清华大学	PN	Tsinghua University	4
	qiūtiān	秋天	秋天	N.	autumn, fall	1

詞語索引

qiúmí	球迷	球迷	N.	fan of sports such as basketball, football…	13
qúnzi	裙子	裙子	N.	skirt	11
rénshān-rénhǎi	人山人海	人山人海	IE	*describing a very crowded situation*	15
sānxīn-èryì	三心二意	三心二意	IE	*not focused*	15
shān	山	山	N.	mountain	7
shàn	善	善	Adj.	kind, be good at (It can't be used alone.)	13
shāngtòu	傷透	伤透	V.-C.	to be hurt badly	12
shāngchǎng	商場	商场	N.	mall	14
shāngdiàn	商店	商店	N.	store	4
shànglóu	上樓	上楼	V.-O.	to go upstairs	9
shàng wǎng	上網	上网	V.-O.	to surf on the internet	6
shēntǐ	身體	身体	N.	health	7
shénme shíhou	什麼時候	什么时候	NP	when, at what time	5
shēngrì	生日	生日	N.	birthday	4
Shèngdàn Jié	聖誕節	圣诞节	PN	Christmas Day	7
Shèngdàn Lǎorén	聖誕老人	圣诞老人	NP	Santa Claus	7
shèngdànshù	聖誕樹	圣诞树	N.	Christmas tree	7
shíquán-shíměi	十全十美	十全十美	IE	perfect	15
shítou	石頭	石头	N.	stone	13
Shídài Guǎngchǎng	時代廣場	时代广场	NP	Times Square	7
shíhou	時候	时候	N.	time	5
shíjiān	時間	时间	N.	time	4
shòusī	壽司	寿司	N.	Sushi	10
shòu	瘦	瘦	Adj.	skinny	8
shū	書	书	N.	book(s)	2
shūdiàn	書店	书店	N.	bookstore	14
shūfǎjiā	書法家	书法家	N.	calligrapher	11
shuā yá	刷牙	刷牙	V.-O.	to brush teeth	8
shuǐ	水	水	N.	water	2
shuǐguǒ	水果	水果	N.	fruit	5

	shuì jiào	睡覺	睡觉	V.-O.	to sleep	3
	shuō huà	说話	说话	V.-O.	to speak, to talk	2
	sījī	司機	司机	N.	driver	7
	sì	四	四	Num.	four	4
	suān	酸	酸	Adj.	sour	5
	suān-tián-kǔ-là	酸甜苦辣	酸甜苦辣	IE	joys and sorrows, ups and downs of life	15
T	tái	台	台	MW	*measure word for equipment*	4
	tán	談	谈	V.	to talk	3
	tèsècài	特色菜	特色菜	N.	specialty in a restaurant	5
	tī zúqiú	踢足球	踢足球	VP	to play football	3
	Tiān ānmén	天安門	天安门	PN	Tian'anmen (Square)	4
	tián	甜	甜	Adj.	sweet	6
	tiào wǔ	跳舞	跳舞	V.-O.	to dance	3
	tīng	聽	听	V.	to listen to	5
	tīng yīnyuè	聽音樂	听音乐	VP	to listen to music	3
	tíng	停	停	V.	to stop	10
	tóufa	頭髮	头发	N.	hair	10
	túshūguǎn	圖書館	图书馆	N.	library	4
W	wèi	位	位	MW	*used to show respect for people*	1
	wénxuéjiā	文學家	文学家	N.	litterateur	11
	wén	聞	闻	V.	to smell	10
	wūzi	屋子	屋子	N.	room	4
	wǔguāng-shísè	五光十色	五光十色	IE	colorful, multicolored	15
X	xī	西	西	N.	west	9
	Xī'ān	西安	西安	PW	Xian city	5
	Xībānyáwén	西班牙文	西班牙文	N.	Spanish (language)	3
	xīguā	西瓜	西瓜	N.	watermelon	5
	xǐ	洗	洗	V.	to wash	12
	xiàtiān	夏天	夏天	N.	summer	1
	xiāngjiāo	香蕉	香蕉	N.	banana	5
	xiǎoshí	小時	小时	TW	hour (formal)	3

詞語索引

	xiǎotōu	小偷	小偷	N.	thief	12
	xiě xìn	寫信	写信	V.-O.	to write a letter	4
	xīngqī	星期	星期	TW	week	3
	xīngxing	星星	星星	N.	star	9
	xíngli	行李	行李	N.	luggage	12
	xiūxi	休息	休息	V.	to rest	3
	xuě	雪	雪	N.	snow	8
Y	yǎn	演	演	V.	to act	13
	yǎnyuán	演員	演员	N.	actor, actress	13
	yǎng	養	养	V.	to raise, to bring up	9
	yí bù shǒujī	一部手機	一部手机	NP	a cell phone	11
	yì shuāng xié	一雙鞋	一双鞋	NP	a pair of shoes	9
	yì tiáo shé	一條蛇	一条蛇	NP	a snake	9
	yìxīn-yíyì	一心一意	一心一意	IE	focused, loyal	15
	yīfu	衣服	衣服	N.	clothes, clothing	2
	yǐzi	椅子	椅子	N.	chair	4
	yìshì jiànzhù	意式建築	意式建筑	NP	Italian style buildings	11
	yīng	鷹	鹰	N.	eagle	13
	yóu	油	油	N.	oil	4
	yóu yǒng	游泳	游泳	V.-O.	to swim	3
	yóuyǒngyī	游泳衣	游泳衣	N.	swimming suit	14
	yóupiào	郵票	邮票	N.	stamp	13
	yuè	月	月	TW	month	3
	yuèbing	月餅	月饼	N.	moon cake	7
	yuèliang	月亮	月亮	N.	the moon	9
Z	zájì	雜技	杂技	N.	acrobatics	5
	zhāng	張	张	MW	*measure word for things those are flat*	4
	zhàopiàn	照片	照片	N.	picture	13
	zhào xiàng	照相	照相	V.-O.	to take pictures	8
	zhéxué	哲學	哲学	N.	philosophy	4

zhī	枝	枝	MW	measure word for stick-like objects	2
zhòng	重	重	Adj.	heavy	8
zhōngjiān	中間	中间	PW	middle	4
Zhōngqiū Jié	中秋節	中秋节	PN	Mid-autumn Festival	7
zhōngtóu	鐘頭	钟头	TW	hour (colloquial)	3
zhù	住	住	V.	to live (at a place)	3
zhuāzhù	抓住	抓住	V.-C.	to catch	12
zhuǎngào	轉告	转告	V.	to pass a message to sb.	8
zìyán-zìyǔ	自言自語	自言自语	IE	to talk to oneself	6
zǒu lù	走路	走路	V.-O.	to walk	3
zǒumǎ-guānhuā	走馬觀花	走马观花	IE	to get a superficial understanding through quick and casual obser-vation	15
zuǐ	嘴	嘴	N.	mouth	9
zuì	最	最	Adv.	the most	5
zuìhǎo	最好	最好	Adv.	had better	12
zuòjiā	作家	作家	N.	writer	11
zuò fēijī	坐飛機	坐飞机	VP	to take an airplane	6
zuòhǎo	做好	做好	V.-C.	to finish cooking	4